England
and
Another Shore

England
and
Another Shore

—— A Life ——

To Karen A udy Wilson

By

Audrey Wilson

iUniverse, Inc.
Bloomington

England and Another Shore
A Life

iUniverse books may be ordered through booksellers or by contacting:

iUniverse
1663 Liberty Drive
Bloomington, IN 47403
www.iuniverse.com
1-800-Authors (1-800-288-4677)

ISBN: 978-1-4620-3647-9 (sc)
ISBN: 978-1-4620-3648-6 (ebk)

Printed in the United States of America

iUniverse rev. date: 11/23/2011

Acknowledgements

For Mark the instigator, my family, those who shared my life, and for St. John's Choir and their Director, Betsy Calhoun, who gave me music at the close.

A special thanks to Bill Cummings. It is only through his kindness and computer skills that these pages ever reached the publisher.

To Dr. Bonnie Braendlin and Dr. Jeanne Ruppert who took so much trouble to correct and proof read, I am very grateful.

Chapter 1

First memories.

"Look!" said Nanny, "All the street lights of London have come on at once. That's electricity for you!" She went on to explain that there used to be gas lamps which a lamplighter had to light one by one with a ladder and torch. We were walking home through Hyde Park in the winter dusk. That is my first memory and I was two years old. It is perhaps enhanced by the fact that a few years later I was to read "The Lamplighter" by R. L. Stephenson which recalled the incident and gave me my first experience of memory.

At that time we lived in an elegant house in Mayfair where the living room did not have paper on the walls but brocade, silken soft to touch and I think gold, very different from the scratchy touch of the nursery wall paper. I remember Nanny saying it was disgraceful that the children were on the fifth floor and no fire escape, which gave me my lasting fear of fire. I used to touch the wall and if it appeared hard all was well, but if soft, oh dear. There was a balloon seller at the gate before you crossed Park Lane and sometimes Nanny would buy us one and she did that night. I learned all the nursery rhymes by heart by the time I was two, just by hearing them read to me, and used to be shown off reciting them, until I did that once in a hotel and Mummy was embarrassed and so was I.

Our life in Mayfair didn't last long as my father lost all his money in one of his frequent reversals of fortune and we moved to the country somewhere. My sister grew too fond of her pacifier and Mummy was told to get rid of it, so one evening she seized it from Bettina's mouth and with a dramatic flourish threw it out of the window. Bettina set up a heartrending wail and I rushed out to the garden, found it easily, waited till Mummy had said her goodnight and then popped it back into Bettina's mouth, soil and all. It wasn't found till next morning and there was great consternation. Nanny denied knowing anything and it was not thought that I would have had the savvy to go out in the dark. I think Bettina kept it a bit longer but she remembered it was I who brought it back. However, at four she didn't show much gratitude when she threw a soda siphon at me. It didn't hit me but both parents said, "Why did you do such a thing to your sister?" Bettina replied, "She disobeyed me." I remember laughing and so did Mummy and Daddy for Bettina was a gentle soul and we were very devoted to one another.

I remember one day asking Nanny on seeing a lovely picture of a mother and child, "Who is this?" "Oh", said Nanny, "you will have to ask your mother about that."

"Why can't you tell me?" I asked. "It is God; you will have to ask your mother." Sometime later I saw another lovely mother and child with flowers all around. It was full of meadow flowers and I thought it most beautiful. "Who is that?" I asked Mummy. "Oh, that is the baby Jesus." "And the beautiful lady?" "She is Mary but we Protestants have thrown out Mary." I was astounded. How could there be a baby without a Mother? I was determined I wouldn't throw out Mary. The bathroom had a linoleum wall of squares but at the end there was a larger square and I said to myself, "That is my square which is a bit off but I have included Mary." I became religious through the painting. I asked for it for Christmas. Mummy said if I liked she would take me to church but we could leave as soon as I was tired. We went to St. Mary's Finchley church, which I learned afterwards was one of the St. Mary churches which were built on the hills around London in the 15th century; Harrow, Finchley, Highgate, Hampstead. We sat down beside a window with a beautiful Madonna and child in the blue splintered glass of the 15th century and I was fascinated. Mummy kept saying, "We can go any time you are tired, darling." I wasn't tired, I loved that window and the music but I think Mummy became tired for she kept on asking me, but we stayed through the whole service.

(Aside)

It was clever of you to think of scattered memoirs for St. Augustine was right: when you knock on the door of memory

3

dozens of doors open beyond, memory on memory, and they have a certain spell which eases the tension of swinging from door to door. They don't come chronologically, for we had already arrived at Finchley and I remember an incident before we left Park Street which I had completely forgotten. I had heard from Nanny that we would be leaving that house as Daddy had lost all his money, and I went down one morning from the nursery on the fifth floor to where he was dressing to go to wherever he went, and there was some money on the table between him and Mummy. I said, "Daddy, if you give me a penny each day, I will be rich when I grow up." He said airily "Kid, when you are eighteen you'll be worth thousands of pounds." I don't know if Mummy was suffering from her first experience of Daddy's frequent reversals of fortune, but she said tartly, "She would do better to take your penny each day," and I somehow knew she had a point but I liked the sound of thousands of pounds and I didn't like carrying heavy pennies around, so left it. On the subject of money and carrying it around, I remember dropping a farthing through a grating in the street because one couldn't get anything with it. I didn't know then that two farthings made a halfpenny and with that you could get a little bun which you could hold between thumb and finger, a shiny bun with currants in, and simply delicious. Farthings were connected with the haberdashery, the only place they were still used, I think, where you could get a reel of cotton (spool of thread) for tuppence three farthings (2 pennies 2d, three farthings). However, farthings were soon abolished together with halfpenny (ha'penny) buns which became penny buns, bigger, but not so nice a shape.

Before I return to Finchley, a brief description of my parents. A more disparate pair would be hard to find as will be shown.

Chapter 2

My mother's early life.

My mother was born in the last decade of the nineteenth century in Nottingham, near Sherwood Forest, where Stilton cheese is made. She was the last of fourteen children and her mother died when she was fourteen. She remembered going shopping with her mother and then going to the market where my grandmother had a glass of champagne for sixpence! When she died my mother was taken in by a singing teacher, Mme Moulds, who taught her how to sing and gave her dancing lessons, and at fifteen my mother obtained a part in the pantomime at Nottingham. She was a great success and offered a part in London. I should explain pantomime if I can; each Christmas there were various pantomimes under the titles of "Puss in Boots," "Cinderella" or "Dick Whittington" et al. which followed more or less the old stories together with topical dialogue, songs and dances, with the peculiarity of the principal boy being played by a girl and the old crone being played by a man. It was a family affair and children were taken to their first stage experience and usually understood not one word of what was going on. It was very popular until WWII and for all I know is still continuing in the provinces somewhere and perhaps even in London.

Mme. Moulds entrusted Mrs. Bishop, a dear friend of hers in London, to look after my mother. My mother was always looked after; she was little, she was pretty, she could sing and dance, and she had apparently a wonderful time in London. She joined "The Will of the Wisps" and afterward "the Arcadians" as a musical comedy actress. I grew up with her songs but she explained to me that most of those I liked best belonged to the lead singer; she was the soubrette and did a song and dance. I know she sang "Toyland, Joyland" and she did have a lovely voice, but whether or not she sang "Vilia, O vilia, the witch of the wood" on the stage I don't know. She could have, it remained the definitive version for me. She also sang "Come, come, I love you only" from "The Chocolate Soldier" but my favorites were a rather Victorian sort of ballad, "There is a garden splendid, there blooms a rose . . . ." and a hymn, "It was the eve of Christmas, the snow lay deep and white / I sat beside my window and looked into the night/ I heard the church bells ringing. I saw the bright stars shine/ and childhood came again to me with all its dreams divine/ . . . . (and then soaring up) and then the gates rolled backward, I stood where angels trod/ it was the star of Bethlehem that led me back to God." I can still see the night nursery in darkness and hear her in the day nursery in the light singing; it was one of my first highs. She didn't seem very interested in God otherwise; she never went to church until my sister and I took her in our teens. She wasn't interested in death or what happened afterwards. My sister was devoted to her and terrified of dying before her mother. "We don't all come together and we don't all go together," said my mother, one of the most sensible things I ever heard her say.

She did sing us some of her own songs which were pretty dreadful; my sister used to go out of the room when she started on them but I could never forget "Maudie" which made me laugh. "They know me as Maudie of Margate/ and I stroll every night on the pier/and the fellows all say/ as I'm wending my way /'Oh isn't our Maudie a dear?/ They say I am quite the attraction/ and all of the natives declare/ though folks come for a day/ quite a month they will stay/ for Maudie of Margate is here!" It was so atrocious I could never forget it. She was a very good dancer and could do a high kick and put on a top hat and deliver "Alexander's Ragtime Band" as well as I have ever heard it and she did that until she was 60 and absolutely overwhelmed my husband who had never seen anything like her. She made him do the Charleston with her and that was a high evening. He said the first time he came to dinner she wore a long green velvet gown with fur on it and gave him wine which he had never had before! He was very attached to her.

I have galloped beyond myself. My mother has just arrived in London, aged fifteen. She met Moyna Bandman in "The Will of the Wisps" very soon, who became a staunch friend, devoted to Mummy. Moyna married the Director of the Bandman Opera Company and soon enrolled Mummy in it too and under its auspices swept her off to the Far East while still in her teens. The Bandman Opera Company toured the outposts of the British Empire wherever Britishers could be found, Singapore, Hong Kong, Calcutta, Ceylon (Sri Lanka), and was apparently a roaring success. Mummy said she had a wonderful time and everybody was so good to her. They did go to Peking too which was not part of the British Empire but I suppose there was an English colony there. I asked her to tell me about these places, especially Peking." Peking? Oh that is where we did "The Sylvan Princess" was all I could get out of her. I thought it was brave of her to go off to the Far East, but apparently she didn't have a qualm and didn't see much of it. The Bandman Opera Company was very well known and applauded wherever they went and I suppose for the many Britishers out east, a touch of home. It still seems strange that she had the nerve but Moyna, who became a lifelong friend, always looked after her. My father couldn't stand Moyna. She was certainly an actress, but my mother never seemed one until she sang or danced.

Chapter 3

Aside.

Before I start on my father's early life, to match my mother's, which could be Chapter 4, I want to ask a question and a favor. Do we have to stick with chronology? I think dispensing with it is one of the few benefits of deconstruction. Could we not include the present with the past? You write "no personal letters" but could I not write to you as audience, including "*Lesefrüchte*" as they occur? I don't want to wait for Keith to be born and grow up to the Yorick he is, I don't want to wait until you appear on the scene. Could we not include "spots of time" throughout my life? This idea came to me through that wonderful book you recommended, *A Year in the Life of Shakespeare.* (Shapiro) Best thing on *Hamlet* I have ever read. I'm sure I knew Shakespeare invented Soliloquies starting with Brutus "Between the acting of a dreadful thing . . . ." and "It must be by his death," and I knew he read Montaigne but didn't realize till Shapiro that Shakespeare shaped the essay into a soliloquy, not only to express his inner self by turning inwards but by turning it outwards to the audience. Shapiro says the audience had never looked into another's mind and they reveled in it. Was it Shapiro that turned you to Montaigne and "Sliced Strawberries" which influenced me quite a bit? I'm writing these memoirs at your behest. Keith may enjoy having them read aloud, he sticks to the oral tradition, and perhaps Jennifer might be interested but I can't think of anyone else. I would do better to write them as to you, and would like to include those times we had in Europe, with or without D, that cappuccino in the mist and then Soglio and the Alsace wine route etc. They could be written as Asides or in the general text. I favor Asides and then go back to early youth. What do you think?

I must copy out what Shapiro wrote on Shakespeare: "hendiadys," literally one by means of two, a single idea conveyed through a pairing of nouns linked by "and," i.e. "sound and fury," "the book and volume of my brain" . . . . the words bleed into each other. "Volume," of course, is another word for "book" but also means "space." The destabilizing effect of how these words play off each other is slightly and temporarily unnerving." 287, Harper, 2005

In this way I could keep my *Lesefrüchte* and also the communication which has been a most intellectual stimulus over the years.

Chapter 4

My father's early life.

My father was born at Blackheath, London. It still had the huge heath where the young Richard II had faced and placated the rebels. It was surrounded by 18th century houses like an old print, and adjoining was Greenwich Park with its ancient Spanish chestnuts, the Observatory and its Date Line, Meridian 0 separating the east and west of the world. Down below facing the river was Wren's Royal Naval College.

My father was born of a German father and a Portuguese mother. This was a great shock to me when I first heard it for I grew up loving England and all the poets who extolled her and didn't relish hearing of my mixed heritage. However, I was assured my father was English because he was born in England. He certainly seemed English; he was a keen golfer, a crack shot and rode to hounds. I was fond of my grandfather who had a grey beard and piercing blue eyes. He and I were the only ones of my immediate family who had blue eyes. My mother, sister, father and his three sisters, and my two cousins who mattered all had brown eyes, so I was drawn to my grandfather for this reason. He once held a large shell to my ear and told me I could hear the sea in it, which I did and always remembered. He also gave me my Ur Christmas tree, fragrant with filigree ornaments and live burning candles. My father said it was dangerous but I loved it and I was glad to read of it later in *Buddenbrooks*.

I did not like my grandmother who was dark and surly and had a strange story. Her maiden name was Colombo and she claimed to be the sole surviving descendant of Christopher Columbus and she produced a heavy gold signet ring with his coat of arms, a bird with a twig in its mouth above a chevron and underneath the motto "*Dum spiro spero*" (While I live I hope). Apparently Columbus was so long finding land that his crew mutinied (I did read of this later in history) so Columbus, a la Noah, sent off a bird which returned with a branch so he was saved. She gave the ring to my father who passed it to me as his eldest child and I gave it to my son John who had it appraised and it was apparently made at the end of the 18th century. I had always hoped it belonged to Columbus. The truth of this story did not seem to matter to anybody, they accepted it and my cousins and sister and I were all given in our teens little silver signet rings with the crest on them. Mine vanished down the plug while I was washing dishes, and the same fate happened to my sister's. I don't know if my cousin still has hers. I felt someone should have gone to the Herald's Office about this, but I don't know that anyone did. Aunt Dora, my favorite aunt, accepted it so we all did. Maybe she did go.

My father went to school in England but as he wanted to study engineering and there was no School of Engineering at Oxford or Cambridge at the beginning of the 20th century, he went to Leipzig. He spoke German well, and it was from him I first learned the charming Viennese *Gruss, Servas!* He then joined the Indian Army as a cavalry officer in the Cossapore Artillery and according to him led the last cavalry charge in India. We had a photo of him in cavalry uniform and he had a cavalry sword which I kept in my bedroom as a child. Apparently he did other things as well which included his engineering skills, perhaps in connection with the railroad in India. When India was discussed he always said they were better off than China, thanks to the Civil Service and the railroad given by the British. "They would never have got to their precious Ganges without the British railway," I remember him saying. He also sold American cars to maharajahs. There was a story, vouched for by my mother, that he once leapt on a ship leaving Calcutta for New York without any luggage, in order to get ahead of a rival to be the first to sell a Hupmobile (supposedly an American car) to a maharajah. Apparently he became quite wealthy doing this sort of thing but had a lot of ups and downs in his fortunes.

He saw my mother on the stage in Calcutta and fell violently in love with her, deluging her with poems. I learned of this when I offered my first poem to my mother at the age of ten. "Oh no, "she said with horror, "no more poetry, I had enough with your father!" I was astounded to hear that my father wrote poems and wanted to see them. "I don't know where they got to," said my mother. I only saw one of my father's poems later on, and didn't think much of it.

He courted her for some time and had many rivals including a faithful swain called Billy who wrote her for years after her marriage and even sent me a christening cup. Many was the time I heard her say, "I'd have done better to marry Billy," and I couldn't help agreeing with her. My father was constantly unfaithful; my mother usually found out and told us all about it at a young age. This definitely prejudiced my sister and me against marriage. However, they stayed together and had some good times. They both loved dancing and theatre, and divorce was not an option before WWII. They were married in Colombo, Ceylon, (Sri Lanka) in 1915 and stayed for a while in India. I think my mother enjoyed being a mem-sahib and having servants wait on her hand and foot. She picked up some Indian phrases; "Coochbewanee" was one of them. She could never give a very adequate description of it, but I learned later it meant "illogical."

In 1917 my father decided that the age of cavalry charges was over and that he could serve England better as an engineer in the RFC. (forerunner of the RAF) so they came back to England. He was born Harry Frederick Robert Speyer. In order to join the RFC he had to change his name by deed poll to Robertson. This was an even greater shock to me than when I found out that my grandfather was German, and my grandmother Portuguese. My cousin was about ten when she asked me why my father's surname was different from Grandpa's. I had no idea and was stunned when Daddy explained. "Royalty were doing it, kid, changing Saxe-Coburg to Windsor, I was in good company." I was horrified and kept very quiet about it and never told anyone and kept assuring myself that my father was English because he was born in England. However later I couldn't help realizing that "Audrey Speyer" would have been a more elegant name than the unmetrical "Audrey Robertson" but I quickly repressed this thought.

My cousin, who as a child knew my father, told my son that although he was very witty and intelligent, you couldn't believe a word he said. I think this is a fair statement. She had heard my father misleading earnest horticulturists in the garden at Manor Farm. When they announced a plant as "coryopsis" he would say, "Oh no, you are wrong there, it is "coryanthus" and he said it with such aplomb that he got away with it. With a smattering of Latin he would make up astounding names. We as children knew what he was doing but visitors did not. He made people laugh, as when once as host he had handed the Stilton cheese around the table and it was returned to him with very little left. "So none of you like the rind," he said. Another time he asked a woman guest when carving chicken if she wanted breast or dark meat, and when she answered "a little of the chest" he handed her "Two slices of the bosom." My mother related these tales to us with some pride.

I don't know where my parents lived when they returned from India. My memories start with Park Street but they include a lot of changing houses, including one at the river at Maidenhead or Henley, where they had a boat named

"Audrey." This was the first time I saw my name in print and I was impressed. I remember there was a garden. When asked to recall a memory of my childhood my mother could only recall one, and it happened there. I do not remember it except as she told it. I was three and there was another little girl of three there, named Lelia. I've never heard that name since. According to my mother I wanted Lelia to come and play in the garden, and she was reluctant. The story went like this: A: "Come into the garden, Lelia." L: "Naw, naw." A: "Oh please do come into the garden, Lelia." L: "Naw, naw." A: "GO into the garden, Lelia" and I gave her a push so she went flying. My mother loved that story and would laugh heartily while telling it. It became a family phrase to persuade someone to do something they were reluctant to do.

One of the places we lived in after leaving Park Street was a flat in Kensington Gardens, and I remember two incidents from there. My mother took me to bowl my hoop in the gardens. This was unusual for Nanny usually did so. A woman stopped us and said, "What a charming little girl! How old is she?" "Four," said my mother, "I always think four is a delightful age." I bridled. My mother did not usually compliment me, and now I was both "charming" and "delightful." I bowled my hoop with élan towards the Peter Pan statue. The other incident involves a clock and my father. I think Nanny was trying to teach me to tell the time and I knew the figure "four" because it was my age. I like to think it was 4 p.m. when my father came, opened the clock and turned it to 3p.m. I set out a loud wail and can still remember the horror I felt, I don't know why, but it seemed to me terrible to tamper with time. "You shouldn't do that," I told him, "It is wrong!" "Good heavens, kid, you're crazy, "said my father, "it is Daylight Saving Time. We have to put the clocks back." I continued to wail, and as I didn't often cry, I still remember it.

Before we went to Finchley, we lived in several places, including a short stay in Hampstead where I retrieved my sister's pacifier from the garden and Grandpa came and gave us an Easter Egg Hunt. I am starting to realize that if there is to be any structure in these memoirs, it must be built around three gardens. The first was Finchley, the next Manor Farm in Sussex where my aunt and uncle lived, and lastly, the garden here in Tallahassee.

Chapter 5

Finchley. The First Garden.

It was still the country at Finchley when we went to live there but roads were being paved every day and the smell of tar recalls those day. The house was set in a large garden, about an acre, with a front lawn and at the back was another lawn with a vegetable garden and an apple orchard. On either side was woodland and to the left a path ran through the wood with bluebells just starting to appear. Every day there were more and more and they surged over the banks like waves until they became a sea under the light green leaves of beeches, so light they were almost gold. Nobody has ever written adequately about them. A.E. Housman perhaps did it best: "And like a skylit water stood/ bluebells in the azur'd wood." "Azure" gives something of the dazzle.

"Why didn't you call me 'Bluebell'?" I asked my father. "Because it is a metal polish," he replied. I saw the justice of that remark. I knew the tin that was used to polish the guard round the electric fire in the nursery. How unjust though, what a terrible world where people could so tarnish a word that should have been kept sacred! I later learned they were wild hyacinths, and their scent was in the air. I spent hours in that wood.

The apple orchard was also a delight; the flowers, tight red buds, were surrounded by white petals that blossomed into small clouds. My fifth birthday party was held there and we played hide and seek through the light and shadow. Moyna, who had spirited my mother off to the Far East, was there, with her three children, Millicent and the twins Pat and Sally, whom we always called Pally and Sat. Aline, another actress friend who was French and who had married a Frenchman, was there with her little boy, Ian, who called his mother " *'tite Maman cherie,*" which I found a bit much. We didn't get on well as children, but later in the war we became good friends and read "Four Quartets" aloud to each other. My friend Ray said it was all nonsense that one could only be happy with one man; she could think of at least five she could have been happy with had things been different. I think Ian comes into that category for me. On my visits home I always met him in the National Gallery. Aline also brought her nephew Colin, whose name I liked. There was a beautiful little girl called June whose mother was an artist, and who did a painting in my autograph album of the Pied Piper whose eyes always haunted me. I felt I could have followed him. Uncle Jack, who was my godfather, was home on leave from Shanghai where he was a wine merchant. He gave me a locket with a ladybird, which I loved for years and then lost.

In Finchley, on one of those long summer evenings when children were put to bed so early, I heard someone on Gravel Hill outside whistling a long melancholy tune. It was haunting in the dusk, mournful in the same way the trains were at night, and in the morning I tried to hum to my mother the tune. "Oh yes," said my mother cheerfully and proceeded to sing molto allegro, "Way down upon the Suwannee River." "Oh no," I said horrified, "it didn't have words and it was sad and slow." "Oh well," said my mother, "you can sing it any way you like." I was thankful that whoever it was had whistled it slowly.

Nanny with her high buttoned black boots left. My father wished us to learn French. I wanted to go to school like June, but my father had this anachronistic idea that we should be taught at home with a French governess.

Chapter 6

Finchley, Mlle Gehrig.

Children have to put up with everything. There was no idea of protest; my father's word was law. Mlle Gehrig arrived from the French part of Switzerland. She was as grey as her name, but she taught me how to read and it was in this way: I learned from a book called *Told in* a *Garden* with pictures on one page and very few words on the other. Mlle would read one page and I would repeat and remember it and then I would say it over and over to myself looking at the words until they began to unravel. There was no question of phonics. I remember being very aggrieved one day when she scolded me for spelling "elephant" as "elepant" in dictation. "I could have understood it," she said, "if you had spelt it with an 'f'." I realized there was another letter after 'p' which I had forgotten, but why an 'f'? "Because 'f 'sounds like 'ph'," she explained. I was astounded. "Are there many letters that sound like others?" She said that there were many and that I would come across them in time. That was my introduction to phonics. I realized there were hurdles on the road to reading that had to be remembered.

Told in a *Garden* must have been given me by my Aunt Dora who gave me all the good books of my childhood and youth. I know she gave me my first taste of literature, *A Child's Garden* of *Verses for Children* by Robert Louis Stevenson. Mlle Gehrig showed me how I could learn a poem by heart and recite it. She chose "My Little Shadow." I don't think it would have been my choice as I liked some of the other poems much better, but I still remember it. "I have a little shadow that goes in and out with me/ and what can be the use of him is more than I can see/ He is very very like me from my heels up to my head/And I see him jump before me when I jump into my bed/ One morning very early before the sun was up/ I rose and saw the shining dew in every buttercup/ but my lazy little shadow like an arrant sleepyhead/ Had stayed at home behind me and was fast asleep in bed." Mlle didn't know what "arrant" meant, and nor did my mother, and father was off in Poland or Austria laying down tramlines or telephones which was the sort of thing he did, so it was not till I found it years later in Shakespeare that I found it meant "thorough." I was proud to recite, but I think my mother was afraid it would go to my head as I had recited all the nursery rhymes at two in a hotel and embarrassed her, so I learned no more by heart. It was years before I understood the last stanza and that it used poetic license in describing the shadow as being fast asleep in bed.

Among the other poems by RLS I liked better was "The Lamplighter," which described a man going round with a lantern to light each gas lamp. It was my first experience of memory for I remembered Nanny at Hyde Park telling us of the lamplighter who came before electricity. RLS as a boy was often ill and had to stay in bed and wrote of "the pleasant land of counterpane" where he marshaled his soldiers. Another poem told of his Nanny at night holding him by the window to see all the other lighted windows in town where perhaps nannies were holding other sick little boys.

My favorite was about him, apparently better, kneeling in a wood by a stream, making boats out of leaves with a stick in them to send away "for other little children to bring my boats to shore." I thought he was rather optimistic, for how did he know that other children would be there to recognize his leaves as boats? I think it was the first time I recognized in poetry a sense in the words beyond the words, of loneliness.

Once I started to read there was no stopping me and I spent hours with a book in the laburnum tree. At one time it had long golden tassels which were fascinating; they did not last but it was still pleasant up there. I think someone at the birthday party had shown me how to climb or do children just learn by themselves?

Chapter 7

Finchley. The Cars.

The same year we went to Finchley we went to the seaside in the summer. I think it was Sidmouth in Devon for the hedges were high with buttercups beyond. Uncle Jack came with us for he was still on leave and he brought a car and let Daddy drive. Bettina and I were in the back. Suddenly my father saw something in a field he wanted to look at and they opened a gate and drove through the buttercups and got out leaving us in the car. They only went a few yards when the car suddenly started to move, and we started to yell. The car went faster but Daddy soon caught up, wrenched open the door, got in and pulled the brake and we stopped. My heart was racing and I still remember it. My sister does not but she was only three and a half. I told her about it often enough. Everything was peaceful and normal and suddenly all was chaos.

That was one incident. Another was when Mummy and I were paddling in shallow water and I heard the foghorns out to sea and I asked what they were. When I was told I said: "They are beautiful." "But sad." said my mother. "All sad things are beautiful," I replied. I saw from my mother's face I had said something wrong. "I don't know what to make of you," she said. I remember her astonished stare and how she loved paddling.

It was at Sidmouth that Daddy put a live lobster in the bath. My son insists I put this story in, he thinks it is funny, I think it is disgraceful. Bettina and I were always bathed together, she by the taps and I at the comfortable end. Years later I walked in on her in her bath and found she still sat against the taps. I still remember the lobster and screaming. Mummy screamed too and Daddy soon removed it, but it might have ~~bitten~~ "pinched" something with its horrible black claws.

When we went back to Finchley Daddy bought a car, a small one with a covered part for the driver and a passenger, Mummy, who had Bettina on her lap but there was no room for me. I had to sit in the dickey seat at the back. I was lifted in and slid under a waterproof cover on to a little seat. I had to have my raincoat and hood on for it often rained and there I was in the wind and rain in complete isolation. Of course it did not always rain but it was always windy. There was no seat belt and I was afraid I would be blown away. My parents did not seem worried but my sister looked back at me anxiously over Mummy's shoulder. I never felt more isolated and complained bitterly and so did my sister.

I do not suppose it was our complaints but rather that my father's fortunes took a sudden reversal as they had a way of doing. This time it was on the upgrade for the small car vanished, a big car arrived, called a De Dion Bouton,

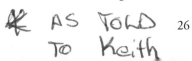
AS TOLD TO Keith

26

and it was big enough for all of us. A chauffeur, Thomas, came with it. He drove my father to Golders Green station in the morning and fetched him in the evening and my sister's life was changed. She spent ages in the garage or outside watching Thomas as he took care of the car, asking him questions. He would open the bonnet (hood) for her and explain about the inside. When he drove my mother around, Bettina would sit in the front asking questions about the various knobs and when my father drove she did the same. "If she had the height, she could drive the car," said my father with pride. He was delighted with her interest. As I learned to read, she learned about cars and she adored Thomas. He was a kind young man and rather tickled and amazed that a small girl would take such an interest. I never forgot my scare with the car at Sidmouth. "If I knew then what I know now," said Bettina at four years old, "I could have stopped the car." I didn't think she could have done, for how could she have flown over the seat to get to the brake or have had the strength to pull it, but I kept quiet, for I saw she was in an enchanted land.

Chapter 8

Finchley. Christmas.

I remember the Christmas we drove to Grandpa's in the car. Daddy had said the day before that it would take two hours to drive from north west London to south east London, Blackheath. As we started I said: "Just think, in two hours we will be there!" I recalled last year and the live candles. "And in six hours it will all be over till next year," said my father. At first I was rather dampened but consoled myself that that was just his way. It was on this occasion he said that anticipation was the best part of life. Later I remembered the phrase. At five years old I proved him wrong. The actual candles on the tree burning away were finer than I had imagined, and the balloons and the presents; it was the year Grandpa gave me a wooden jewel box. The jewel box was magnificent, far too large for a five year old who only had one ladybird necklace, but I loved it and kept it all my life. It had a shelf with compartments and underneath an area where afterwards I placed letters and precious papers. I kept my Matriculation papers there and if I had not had such a box I doubt I would have saved them, so it played a crucial part in my later life. Aunt Dora said my grandfather bought all the presents for his grandchildren himself.

I remember my cousin Donald on that occasion; he also had received something splendid and was excited about it. My cousin Rita recalls that my sister and I were dressed in dreadful yellow woolen dresses that we wore every Christmas for three years until we grew out of them. I remember the return journey, holding my heavy jewel box happily on my lap.

Chapter 9

Finchley, Mlle Gehrig.

Lessons with Mlle Gehrig were not very interesting. She did tell us about hell and that Adam and Eve were there. I was worried about them and actually wondered for a while if there were anything I could do to get them out, and decided that I wasn't up to it and would have to leave it to God. She introduced new ideas of religion into my irreligious family. She told me I should tell my mother that we should not have lessons on Good Friday because it was the day Christ had died. My mother was flummoxed. "Well then, all right, this year you needn't have lessons but it is the last year you don't have lessons on Good Friday." I was astounded at her lack of logic; my mother was as "couchbewanee" as her favorite Indian word.

Mlle Gehrig tried to teach us manners. There was Fuller's chocolate cake which we especially enjoyed. The icing was not usual; it tasted like a slice of chocolate softened, and I liked to save it to the end. Mlle had told me before that this was not polite and on this occasion she said: "Well, you have the choice. Either I finish the story and you leave the chocolate or you don't get the end of the story." She thought she had me on a toast for I was a sucker for her stories, William Tell etc. I thought she could probably be prevailed upon to finish the story later or I could make up the end. "I'll have the chocolate," I said. "*Qu'elle est bête*," she muttered and I had to agree with her. There was not much love between us. I can't remember that she read to us after I learned to read. I read to my sister for years; she was fond of Beatrix Potter and tales about horses. I read *Black Beauty* to her several times, and we both enjoyed ourselves.

(Aside)

(Isn't this getting too much for you? I feel as though Montaigne has gone to my head and I'm like the Sorcerer's Apprentice and can't stop it! You must tell me the truth. I can't feel you can be interested in all these details of so long ago. I think there are more in the earlier years. As I reflect in bed at night there seem fewer memories from when I was eleven and twelve, but that may be because I haven't concentrated on those years yet. Things keep bobbing up that had long been forgotten. Please restrain when necessary.)

Mlle Gehrig taught us to crayon and paint, which I enjoyed, and to cut out and paste, which I didn't. Children's paint books in those days had firm outlines which one was supposed to keep inside. "I want my rose bigger," I said. "It is messy if you go over the lines," said Mlle. I did do one freehand painting. My Aunt Dora had given me *The Enchanted Forest* which somehow became lost in our many moves to my sorrow for it was enchanted. There were black and white illustrations and one I copied in black paint. An elf was dancing over a moonlit pool with pines around and through them was the sky. I probably would always have cared for the sky between the trees, but it was enhanced by this illustration. I kept the sketch in Grandpa's jewel box for many years and often enjoyed looking at it. In the end I gave it to someone who loved the woods as much as I did.

Mlle was a great walker and that was fine as long as it was in the woods around Finchley, but she occasionally wanted to walk along the long road to Golders Green and back, which must have been at least four miles and that was far for a five year old. I envied my sister in the stroller. The only comfort was an art gallery half way which I enjoyed, but I grew very tired. I found myself wondering whether Father Christmas was registering my hateful thoughts about Mlle against next Christmas, but before then I had been enlightened by my younger sister. "How did you find out?" I asked. "Because I saw Daddy come in and take the stockings and return with them filled." "Why didn't you tell me?" I asked. "I didn't want to spoil it for you," she said. I didn't miss him, Christmas to me was Grandpa's and the candlelit tree, but I did wonder if other children learned that Father Christmas were not true, what about the Christ Child? I knew it was not the same thing, but I wasn't sure if they did. It was years before I found someone to share this concern. My own children insisted on Santa Claus.

My eldest son put an orange out for him for years and I remember him running in after watching television. "He has been sighted at 30,000 feet over Seattle!" Children seem to need Santa.

I grew closer to my mother at Finchley for that was where she came in and sang to us in bed at night. I have already mentioned her songs. I loved her when she sang the beautiful ones. My parents also came in to see us before they went to the theatre or dancing. First of all came a scent of flowers and then my mother. I remember a peach velvet dress, soft to touch. My father also looked splendid in a black and white dinner jacket. He entered our lives more at this time for he took us to get an ice cream cone every Saturday night. Once he jumped out at me from behind a bush on the way home and I had hysterics. He also took us to see a fire which terrified me and enhanced my fear of fire. He was always unexpected. I had my introduction to classical music through him for he had a record of Caruso singing "*M'appari tutt' amor.*" I was in the garden and heard it through the window. I can still hear it. It was not like my mother's songs or the tunes she had on the gramophone. I remember two of hers, "I'm tickled to death, I'm single" and "When the sun goes down, and the stars peek through." That latter was a pretty tune, but quite different from Caruso. I asked my father what language he was singing and he said it was in Italian and I wondered why we were not learning that instead of French.

My parents went to the South of France one winter and sent us an amazing present. A brown box arrived which opened with the most heavenly scent. In it were two wicker baskets of tangerines and on the top sprays of yellow mimosa. I can never eat a tangerine without the echo of that scent.

When I was five my mother sent me on my first errand alone. It was to the florist's in Ballards Lane on our side of the road to get a bunch of violets. I was proud and contented that it should be for flowers. Strangely enough, forty years later when I returned to Finchley to visit a friend that florist was still there. Our house had gone and the garden and woods; a Roman Catholic church stood in its place. Gravel Hill and St. Mary's Church, which I think I only visited that once, were all that remained, a veil of transparent past over the crowded streets. I looked for the ice cream shop where we had gone each Saturday but it had vanished together with the toy shop which was the scene of one of my first adventures.

It had been on the other side of Ballards Lane which I was forbidden to cross alone, but once with Daddy I saw in it a wooden yellow duck on wheels that I thought my sister would like for her birthday and determined to get it as a surprise. We had sixpence a week pocket money and I had saved up eight sixpences which I thought should be enough.

As soon as my sister was out of the stroller she started dragging a wooden horse and cart everywhere she went, up and down kerbs, up and down steps. Dobbin and his cart were heavy and I can recall her anxious face when occasionally they became stuck. I thought a duck would be easier. I don't know how I managed to slip out alone and cross the street but I did and the duck was still there. I entered and asked for it handing out my eight sixpences and saw immediately it was not enough. It was a dreadful moment, but the two girls conferred and then one said, "Let her have it." I was grateful and hid it carefully until the birthday. I don't think it ever took the place of Dobbin.

Another store I remember going to with my mother was the fishmonger's. I didn't like the poor dead fish or the smell but the fishmonger was a cheery man and he asked me one day if I knew the name of some strange little things to which he pointed; they were shrimps. I didn't but felt he and my mother expected something. "Whales," I suggested. The fishmonger never forgot it and would wave at me each time I passed, mouthing the word. I was embarrassed.

We were not to stay very long at Finchley. I think I saw the bluebells return twice. We learned of this when I complained that the prints in the billiard room were hideous, they were golf cartoons. "Never mind, kid," said my father, "we won't be here long, I've only rented it for a couple of years and then we will go to the country and you will learn to ride." "Will there be a garden?" I asked. "There will be the downs and the sea," was the reply. We knew the downs from motor rides: the green hills along the southeast coast which explode into the white cliffs at Dover and Beachy Head. "Won't that be very far from your office?" asked my practical sister. My father looked a bit apologetic. "Well, yes, that is why your mother and I will stay in a flat in town in the week to be near my office and the theatre and dancing your mother likes, and we will come down each weekend and go riding with you." My mother added: "And your father will join the East Sussex Foxhounds which he has always wanted to do." My father looked very happy and I realized this was his dream, but how could he afford two houses and what about us? We set up a wail, "All alone all week with Mlle!" "Oh, she will be leaving and we will get somebody young and beautiful to play with you on the sands." "What about Thomas and the rabbits?" asked my sister. "Oh they will have to go. I will keep the car down in the country and drive myself," said Daddy, "and your mother might learn." Bettina drooped but revived on learning she would ride a real horse.

I haven't mentioned the rabbits, they didn't mean much to me. Beatrix Potter's Peter Rabbit seemed much more attractive than my own. My sister looked after mine, but every child we knew at that time had one, and the worst thing you could say of anyone was "May his rabbits die!" We kept that as a family imprecation. My father liked the rabbits and on Sunday afternoon we had them out on the lawn. They were comatose through being kept in hutches without much exercise and my sister and I used to prod them with celery or carrots. "Let the rabbits be!" proclaimed my father one Sunday and this was such an odd use of the verb "to be" that we both remembered it and used it for the rest of our lives as a synonym for "Let well alone."

Another memory of Finchley. My mother was distressed that I did not seem interested in dolls and to please her I remember trying to fake an interest and knelt down to wrap the doll in a blanket in its crib. I was stung by a wasp in the knee as I did so. I am sure a psychologist would say that is the reason I did not like dolls but I know I did not care for them before that. What amazes me is that I had quite forgotten about that wasp until I thought about dolls and would have said I had never been stung. Memory is astounding.

The most indelible memory I have of Finchley after the bluebells was Mlle Gehrig's round enamel tin. She kept reels of cotton (spools of thread) in it and it portrayed Castle Chillon, Lac Lemon and the mountains beyond. I had never seen a castle or a lake or mountains and was enthralled and stared at it for hours. It became clearer in my mind's eye than the bluebells for I only saw them a brief while each year and I gazed at the tin each day. Years later at school when I studied Byron and read "The Prisoner of Chillon" with its splendid last line, "I learned to love despair," against my will the tin appeared and I could not get rid of it. Even when I went to Leysin with M. and D. and we visited Chillon it still was there, a round enamel tin. It did not vanish until one evening we had supper at Evian on the French side of the lake, and saw Chillon, dark against the water, with purple mountains behind and beyond Les Dents du Midi, glitter and snow in the sunset. Above them the tremendous sky broke open, crushed gold and rose petals, and the tin vanished.

Chapter 10

On to Sussex.

We said farewell to Mlle Gehrig without a tear, whereas there had been tears for Nanny. Mlle Titchikoff arrived, young, blonde and bouncy, completely different. She was a White Russian. I never quite knew what that was, my mother was not very clear about it, and Mlle herself said she was so young when she left she could not remember much except porcelain eggs made by Faberge. I do not think we learned anything with her, I cannot remember a lesson. She helped my mother with the move from Finchley. They made lists of things, the condition they were in when we arrived and when we left. Bettina and I liked our mother's phrase: "It's only wear and tear and I don't think she can grumble." I don't know why we liked it, we used to chant it. I thought the cushions in the morning room might have shown unusual wear and tear. Daddy liked to have pillow fights with them which only he enjoyed.

I cannot remember the move although it must have been momentous. Nothing of the day arises in the memory no matter how hard I search. I recall I was surprised at where we were going to live. It was in a boarding house on the front in Eastbourne. A road with pavements on each side in red brick divided us from wide lawns, excellent for flying kites, and the sea. To the left was a Martello tower erected in the time of the Napoleonic wars for fear of invasion. We had meals downstairs with other people and it seemed odd to see strangers passing on the stairs. My parents had a bedroom and sitting room on first floor where we were supposed to have lessons during the week. My sister and I and the governess had two small rooms at the top of the house, on the fifth floor. No fire escape. My old fear of fire arose. It was amazing how soft wallpaper could feel to an anxious child who felt that softness presaged fire. I told my mother of my fear but she pooh-poohed it saying that there would be no fire. My sister was not afraid of fire and kept telling me to stop pushing the wall. She was, however, afraid of the dark so we had to have the door open a crack.

The boarding house was run by a friendly woman called Mrs.Biddle, who had a Chow with a black mouth. One night he came up to our floor and pushed open our door. I sat up in bed and screamed and he leapt up and bit my hand, drawing blood. Thank goodness it was the weekend and my parents were there and took me to the doctor. The bite was not deep and in those days there was no question of rabies shots, but there was an uneasy truce between the chow and me. Mrs. Biddle liked children and did not mind us coming down to her sitting room where there were lots of books and an edition of "Little Folks," published before WWI, which fascinated me with the pictures of clothes. I first learned of the war between the Cavaliers and Roundheads in a story and wanted to know more. Mrs. Biddle told me to ask Mlle Titchikoff, but Mlle T. was hardly ever there. She and Mrs. Biddle's daughter became friends at first sight and were always going off, arm in arm, to play tennis or something. I do not remember a lesson with her and felt this was not right but did not want to get her into trouble with my parents. However, one day Bettina and I were alone on the red bricked pavement outside, and I was attacked from behind by a snarling dog. My intrepid sister grabbed it by its collar and held on till the worried owner arrived. The dog did not bite me although it was snapping. I was afraid it would turn round and bite Bettina. After the experience with the Chow I was the worse for wear and tumbled down into Mrs. Biddle's room in tears. I think Mrs. Biddle must have told my parents that Mlle T. was not exactly a governess who took good care of her charges for she left suddenly. All I learned from her was more on hell.

We did have one experience with her which was unforgettable. It was during the week when the parents were away. We were having supper in our dressing gowns in the sitting room and there was a knock on the door. One of the other boarders, a nice man whose name I never knew, said Mlle should puts coats on us and bring us down to the front door to see an unprecedented occurrence in England, the Northern Lights or the Aurora Borealis. Mlle was very excited for she had seen it in Russia but it was hardly ever seen in England for we were too far south. I have never forgotten it, flashing green and blue lightning with no thunder. It was splendid over the sea and when I read of it in Stifter's *Bergkristall* years later I remembered it exactly as he described it.

Chapter 11

Riding.

My father introduced a groom to us who would first take us out singly and then together. My father was off to the Continent but when he came back he would take us out. All went well. As the eldest, Jimmy took me out first on Sammy, a gentle little pony, and I learned to walk and trot. I liked the second for you had to learn to "post," rise in your stirrups according to the horse's rhythm. Jimmy taught us a rhyme: "Keep your head and heart well up, your hands and your feet well down; your knees keep close to the horse's side and your elbows close to your own."

When we reached the Downs, he let us canter and then gallop a little but we never went further than Beachy Head. After a week he decided he could take us out together and I had to switch to a bigger mare, Sybil. Most horses have beautiful faces but Sybil did not. She had an ugly grey hanging jaw and a mouth of iron. My father recognized it at once and asked if Jimmy did not have a better mount for me but he did not; those were the only two rental horses he had. Most people had their own mounts and stabled them with him. We were not up to that so I had to put up with Sybil. I have always hated the name. The first time Daddy took us out we went far beyond Beachy Head and a wide expanse of downs and sea stretched before us. On our right was the Weald of Kent where the earth changed from white chalk to rich loam and there were fields of rich gold barley, light gold wheat and the silver green of oats. Here and there was a field of dark soil, lying fallow. I always loved the colored fields, the first of England seen from a plane.

"We are coming to the five mile gallop, "said my father. Whether it was the sound of the name she knew or the sight of it, Sybil was off in a flash. I heard my father shouting but had no hope in hell of stopping her; all I could do was to cling on. I gripped with my knees but could not keep my elbows to my side. They were stretched out way ahead of me by the head of the horse which had suddenly become huge and far away. At first there was terror and then speed. I have never known such speed, except several years later in skiing, when I again was out of control, but then there was glory. I was one with the downs and sky and the fields of barley rushing by me, and the sea far below, the white cliffs and Eastbourne with its pier stretched out small far away, terror, speed and glory. Sybil stopped when she felt like it, and I awaited my father. "Well, you held on," he said grudgingly; "I shall have to keep a hand on her rein when we reach that place so she knows she can't do that again, and he did and she learned she could not take off, but it was an experience I have not forgotten. Sybil and I never grew fond of each other as Sammy and Bettina did. She threw me once going downhill where on the downs you have to zigzag. She had her own way of doing that, not mine, and she just pitched me over head, mercifully not into a gorse bush. I was bruised but knew I must get back at once, for Daddy impressed that on us. "If you fall off your horse, get on again." "What if your bones are broken?" "They won't be," he said.

Chapter 12

Miss Risdon and Sussex.

The next governess was Miss Risdon, a born teacher and the only reason I was not completely illiterate when I finally went to school. I still remember what she taught me. She realized I loved poetry and introduced me to "The Lady of Shalott" which I learned by heart when I was eight years old. She encouraged me to say it aloud. I used to declaim to my sister in bed at night until she asked me to do just the horses part. "By the margin willow veiled/ Slide the heavy barges trailed/ By slow horses and unhailed/the shallop flitteth silken sailed,/ Skimming down to Camelot." Bettina thought it was sad, and indeed it was. That poem haunted me for years.

Miss Risdon discovered that my sister, at six years old, could not read because she had always listened to me. She taught Bettina to read, although my sister never really took to it. She read *Black Beauty* herself, but I had already read it to her twice. She did however learn Sir Walter Scott's poem "Lochinvar." It had a galloping rhythm and we used to chant it to ourselves in bed at night. Miss Risdon also taught us the rudiments of mathematics so that I was not completely disgraced when I eventually went to school. Mlle Gehrig had taught us addition and subtraction but Miss Risdon taught us Long Division and I was quite interested to learn that you could really take away a number by withdrawing one from the line above. I found that quite magical. She made learning fascinating, and one of the things she taught was that flowers came in families; roses and pears and apples all belonged to the family Rosacae; beans and peas and sweet peas from the family Leguminacae. She took us to the downs and showed and named the various flowers: cowslips, scarlet pimpernel which only bloomed if it were not going to rain; valerian, one of the few flowers that could bloom near the sea because it could stand the salt; campion, thrift, which if remember, came from the leguminacae family. I asked about bluebells but learned they had to grow under the shade of beech trees, far from the salt sea, but there were harebells, also blue but growing singly, and paler. I could not learn enough.

My father left his car during the week at Eastbourne. The idea was that Mummy would learn to drive. The only memory I have of her driving is when she stalled trying to reverse, and Bettina showed her how to start the car.

Miss Risdon could drive and it was she who drove us around the little Sussex villages, Alfriston, Jevington and Wilmington. At Wilmington there was a huge figure carved in the chalk in the downs behind. Nobody knew how old it was; some said prehistoric but why the turf had not grown back remained a mystery. In each little village there was a cross with names on it and Miss Risdon told us these were memorials to the young men who had died in WWI. There were so many of them; some had their ages written too and they were very young, many under twenty. In Eastbourne there was a larger memorial and underneath the words: "Age shall not wear them, nor the years condemn/In the going down of the sun and in the morning/ we will remember them." I think Miss Risdon lost her fiancé in the war. She told us the songs they sang, and they were all very sad. "There's a long, long trail a-winding into the lands of my dreams, where nightingales are singing, and a white moon beams." "Keep the home fires burning." "If you were the only girl in the world, and I were the only boy."

There were beautiful old churches in the villages and gardens filled with flowers. I still see those villages in the curves of the downs. They seemed so small to have lost so many. I became haunted by WWI. On Saturday Daddy took us to a small theatre on the pier at Eastbourne, "Freddy's Follies" where they still sang those sad songs.

We were introduced to older history by Miss Risdon. There was the Roman road which still existed across the downs above Wilmington which had also been used by pilgrims going to Canterbury. Along that road were some ruins of Roman villas with wonderful mosaics of the seasons. I remember winter vividly—a sardonic looking Roman holding an empty twig and scowling, and one could just see how he loathed the long wet English winters. The Romans built well, their straight paved roads were still there.

She also drove us to Battle, near Hastings, where the Normans defeated the Saxons in 1066. It was a flat plain with a Roman fort, nothing much to see, but she showed us pictures of the Bayeux Tapestry embroidered by Norman ladies to celebrate their victory. The Saxons were on foot and the Normans on horseback which did not seem fair. There was also a detail of Edward the Confessor, King of England, handing the crown to Harold but apparently Harold had become shipwrecked off the coast of Normandy and had had to swear loyalty to William, and on those grounds William invaded, but the oath of loyalty was to him as Duke of Normandy. Harold had just defeated the Danes in the North and had to march all across England before the fight. We saw how he was pierced by an arrow in the eye and killed. Miss Risdon told us that every year on the anniversary of that battle (I forget which day it was) there was in the obituary column of *The Times* a tribute to "Harold, last Saxon king of England, who died fighting for his country." Nobody knew who had put it in, some said Winston Churchill. However, apparently it was in the end not such a bad thing, for the English language was enriched by the Norman French. When in the field animals retained their Saxon names, cow or pig, but on the table they became French, beef or pork. Many of the villages we knew had been entered in William's Domesday Book.

On the way back from Hastings we passed Pevensey Bay at dusk. Strange little lights were jumping about all over the marshy bay. Miss Risdon told us they were called "Will-o-the–Wisps" by the country people and "*ignis fatii*" (foolish fire) by the Romans who had first named them. There were small fires caused by gas from organic matter in the marsh and in the daytime you couldn't see them. They only became visible when it grew dark. Mummy was with us and was intrigued by the name "Will-o-the Wisps" for that was the name of her first musical show. She had no idea of its origin and was fascinated. Years later, during WWII, I remembered the "foolish fires" and wondered how the RAF coped with them. England was all blacked out with no lights, and yet these little fires could not be extinguished and must have been a clear landmark to the Germans that this was Pevensey Bay. I never found anybody who knew the answer, but worked out for myself eventually that during the Battle of Britain in 1940 most of the dog fights over the southeast coast were in the daytime. I remember seeing the RAF Spitfires coping with the Messerschmidtts with their Iron Crosses clearly identified from where we stood in the fields of Sussex watching, so that the fires at dusk did not matter. Later in the war however the fires must have been visible to the U-boats in the Channel and would have been an aid.

My mother started coming down to visit us during the week. I expect it was dull for her with Daddy away all day in the office or on the Continent. She announced that one of us could sleep with her "for a treat." As the eldest I went first but it was no treat to me. My mother's tummy went in and out at a different rhythm to mine and her legs got in my way. I asked in the morning if I could have some other "treat." Mummy laughed, she had a good sense of humor, and from then on Bettina slept with her. I wondered how parents could sleep together. I never forgot how uncomfortable it was to have a tummy next to you going at a different rhythm.

My mother and Miss Risdon started playing tennis together. I was amazed how young they looked in their short white dresses. During this time Mummy shocked us by having her hair "shingled." I liked her soft brown hair with a little bun at the back. With her short hair and short dress she hardly seemed a mother, particularly when she danced the Charleston and sang "Tea for two, and two for tea." My sister was awed and said "You could make a lot of money with that song." Mummy laughed, "Someone already has, "she said. I forget which one of us asked if Daddy danced the Charleston, we could not imagine it. No, he didn't.

I think one of the reasons Mummy started coming down to see us during the week was that Moyna Bandman with her three girls had moved to Eastbourne. She was in between husbands. She was the one who had spirited my mother off to the Far East in the Bandman Opera Company. She had been in Egypt with her last husband and had brought back some astounding Egyptian hangings. I suppose that was my first aesthetic experience. I was enchanted with these dancing girls in profile and strange boats. Miss Risdon told us that the originals were very old, older than the Romans. I thought the Romans were the oldest there were, but Miss R unrolled ages before them. She started taking us to church and told us that Abraham, Jakob, Isaac and Joseph were older than the Egyptians or at least as old. The world grew larger for me.

Chapter 13

Sussex.

I was introduced to the centuries-old Church of England liturgy with its psalms, responses and hymns and luckily there was a pleasant old clergyman, the Rev. Hanks, who had a special service for children and gave us pictures to illustrate texts. I remember the lilies of the field (learned later they should have been anemones) "that toil not neither do they spin but Solomon in all his glory was not arrayed like one of these. If God so clothed the grass of the field which is here today and gone tomorrow, how much more will he care for you, o ye of little faith." I liked that and the picture that went with it of tall lilies in an otherwise very English looking field. My sister years later went back to see the Rev. Hanks when he was retired and said he was a very foolish old man and she thought she had learned most of her religion from me. I remember telling her something he said in a sermon about "Weary me not with vain repetitions as the heathen do" which was a great comfort to her for she had spent hours on her knees praying for everybody she had ever met. I told her it was only necessary to pray for family and friends. I was not so keen on the knees as she was. I liked watching the sunset from my bed, golden behind the downs. I think Mummy had taught us one prayer, a rather frightening one: "Jesus tender, shepherd hear me, bless thy little lamb tonight; In the darkness be Thou near me, keep me safe till morning light." What was so frightening about the darkness that one had to be saved from? I dropped that prayer together with a similar: "Now I lay me down to sleep, pray thee Lord my soul to keep, and should I die before I wake, I pray thee Lord my soul to take." I thought it was too early to think of dying and so made up my own prayers. I liked the chanting of the psalms and the responses and it did not seem to matter that I did not understand them. "O God who art the author of peace and lover of concord, in knowledge of whom standeth our eternal life, whose service is perfect freedom . . . ." I never understood that even as an adult, but enjoyed hearing it, and it was a joy to hear it years later in the Episcopal church in America.

The Bandman children had a governess, Miss Brazier, but they also went to school, and I would have been very jealous if I had not had Miss Risdon to teach me. I was friends with Millicent and Sally all my life but Pat, aged seven, told me my first dirty joke and I still remember how it horrified me. With my wretched memory of course I could not forget it all these years. I wonder if I could exorcise it now, "Scotty, Scotty Highlander, marching off to war/ the wind blew up his petticoats and showed his long cigar/ the cigar was long and hairy, he showed it to the queen/

the queen gave him sixpence to have it painted green." I can still remember the bedroom where she told me, and my revulsion. I thought I was going to be sick, to throw up. Eventually I was able to tell my sister, and she took it much more lightly and told me to forget it, but of course I couldn't. But she did comfort me in that I realized I was peculiar in taking it so seriously. I grew up to enjoy a risqué story as well as anyone but I never liked Pat any more.

Miss Brazier had an interesting story to tell. She had been governess earlier in her life to the Royal Family, in particular to Prince John, the youngest son of George V, who had something wrong with him and died young. It was the first time I had heard of the Royal Family and was very interested. Miss Brazier said John was a sweet child, and she could not tell us what was wrong with him. She said he was devoted to his parents which I don't think the other children were.

The governesses became friends and took their two families for many picnics on the downs and further inland where we saw the Weald of Kent with all its coloured fields stretched out before us. A lifetime later my sister touched me by asking me if remembered lying in a field, on a hill, just the two of us, looking down on the Weald. Apparently I had told her to remember it always; around us poppies, buttercups and daisies with down below fields of dark gold barley, pale gold wheat and silver green oats. "You told me to remember it always, just as it was, and I have," she said. I was astounded for I had forgotten the incident until she recalled it and then I remembered it. My sister often amazed me, with her perspicacity. She understood me although I was so different from her. She loved and respected me, and I was not sure that my parents did either. I think I would have been far more warped by my childhood if I had not been so sure of my sister's love, understanding and admiration.

I do remember another incident from that time. I was lying on a hill, looking down on the Weald and saw a steam train draw up and stop at a station. Later it started and I saw the puff of dark smoke and seconds after heard the well known hoot, but why wasn't the hoot at the same time as the puff of smoke? I saw that happen several times and was always amazed. It was a shame I did not ask my father about it; he could have explained the different speeds of light and sound. He would have been pleased that I had noticed it. Also it worried me that at the swimming pool legs through water appeared at different angles from what they actually were.

Miss Risdon took us to the swimming pool, a green strangely smelling place, where we were taught swimming, and then she took us into the sea. It was cold but exhilarating, and I learned to swim quite well and with her beside me swam from the pier to the base of Beachy Head, quite a long way.

I feel reluctant to tell this story for I have never met anyone who climbed Beachy Head or would believe that my father took my sister and me up a steeply cut path in the chalk (I was eight, she was six and a half). I went first, then Bettina and he at the rear to catch us if we fell. He had seen this path from the beach and thought it was could be managed. It was slippery, the chalk did not hold our plimsolls (tennis shoes) well, but we made it, and lay on the turf at the top looking down at the steepness below that we had conquered. I have never told this story for I thought no one would believe it. My mother was certainly furious with Daddy when we came home to tell the tale, and I felt it was not a very good thing for a father to have done so kept quiet about it.

Chapter 14

Books, the Beach and Visitors.

I found a book on Mrs. Biddle's shelves that I liked and asked if I could borrow it. It was *Little Women* by L.M. Alcott. I was enchanted with the four sisters and the father away at war. Miss Risdon tried to explain that it was far away and long ago and I never really understood about the war, but it did not seem to enter into things much. I went into another world: by day I lived in Eastbourne, had lessons, rode at weekends, but in the evening when I went to bed I entered into the world of the March sisters and sometimes it seemed just as real. I told Miss Risdon about it. She said I was a true reader but that she wished I could play with other children. And it happened.

Eastbourne had a shingle beach with breakwaters to hold back the stones, and they also kept off the wind. As soon as the tide went out we would go to the beach and find a breakwater near the band. There was a bandstand with a smart brass band; they played the WWI songs, waltzes, the Blue Danube and the Skaters Waltz especially, lots of

Gilbert and Sullivan and some old English airs "Do you ken John Peel with his coat so gay,/do you ken John Peel at the break of day/With a view Halloo he is far far away / with the fox and the hounds in the morning." Miss R told us this was a hunting song which Daddy would know and Bettina liked it very much. Soon the sand appeared and a group of children to play ball. There was more than one ball going in different directions. It was fun to watch. Soon the ball appeared near me on its way out to sea and I caught it quite expeditiously and returned it. I was asked to join in and so a golden age began.

I never knew their names, we didn't speak much. Occasionally "Oh good shot" "Bad luck" or "Well done!" was the limit of conversation. We made no arrangements to meet again, but every day when the tide turned we were there and we played for hours, throwing, running after and catching the balls in endless afternoon. The balls were often lost out to sea or became sodden in pools and had to be replaced so it was a good thing to bring along a ball. Miss R kept me supplied with tennis balls. I remember hearing snatches of music from the band for the wind blew it around and it was part of the sky and the sea and throwing the ball and the especial pleasure of catching a high ball. Rilke in *Kindheit* (Childhood) writes "*die Bälle, die glorreiche Kurven / und ein Kind, ach ein vergehendes, unter den fallenden Ball*," which J.B. Leishman and Stephen Spender translated as ". . . the balls, their glorious curving / and a child, passing, passing, under the falling ball." I thought that was a felicitous translation, better than "a child vanishing under the falling ball" for they did not vanish, they kept reappearing.

My sister did not play, she did not like catching the ball as much as I did, but she did like a game the children taught us to play before there was enough sand to throw and catch. It was Hopscotch. You drew eight squares in the sand, four up, four down and threw a stone into the first square. Then you had to hop over that square with the stone, on to the next, and hop around the whole square without stepping on any line. Then you threw a stone into the second square, and so on around the block. If you didn't get the stone in the correct square you were out, and also if you stepped on a line, so you had to keep your wits about you.

My aunt and cousin Rita came to visit us. Rita was horrified that I played ball with children whose names I did not know, and did not want anything to do with them. I thought she was quite ridiculous but I was also a little relieved because I was not sure she would be able to catch well enough. She was never strong, and often fainted. I envied her this weakness and thought it was most dramatic and wished I could but I never managed it. She told me later that she envied me. We both hated driving in the car with my grandfather and father for they both smoked Havana cigars, and that made us feel very sick. Once I actually had to get out of the car to throw up on the road and since then was allowed to sit in the front with the chauffer away from the smoke. I could understand how she envied me, and felt sorry for her.

When she came down to the sea to visit us we went to play on another beach and she did like hopscotch, the only game I remember her playing. She brought a book with her, *Anne of Green Gables* by L.M. Montgomery, and I picked it up and could not put it down. I asked if I could be excused from tea in order to read a little more before I had to give it back. "I'll get a copy for you tomorrow, dear," said my aunt. I stared. How could she? It wasn't my birthday or Christmas and I did not think that Eastbourne would hold such a treasure but it did, and in time my aunt gave me nearly all the Anne books except for one I found. Again I went into a golden land. Anne was actually far more like me than Jo March, and when I found out she loved "The Lady of Shalott" I was hers forever. I determined to name my daughter "Anne." Miss Risdon had read it and said Mark Twain had remarked that it was the best child's book he had read. Again it was far away in Nova Scotia and long ago, in the last century, but it was the first time I had met a writer who expressed my love of landscape and I think it was that which impressed me most. I read the book many times, even as an adult; it became a part of my life. My aunt enjoyed it too and from then on we shared books together, discussing them. Rita was very good at crosswords and she, my aunt and I did them together for years, and eventually Bettina joined in.

Grandpa also came to visit us and stayed at the Grand Hotel. Granny had died and he was lonely. He stayed a long time and when Mummy and Daddy were in town he invited Bettina and me to lunch with him alone. Miss

Risdon brought us and fetched us but did not stay. We were rather abashed facing him alone. He asked us to order what we liked and I always ordered cold ham and tongue until he suggested I should try something else. "I don't eat what I don't know, "I remember saying to him and he replied "My dear child, you are going to have a dull life." I realized the justice of this remark and asked my father for something else to order. He suggested "*sole bonne femme*" which was filleted sole cooked with mushrooms and was absolutely delicious, so from then on I always ordered that. Grandpa sometimes visited us in our boarding house over the weekend when my parents were there. I remember him sitting in an armchair saying "I am done up," a phrase I had never heard before. He also twiddled his thumbs, which fascinated my sister, who sat on the floor cross—legged and copied him until he stopped her saying "Forwards, forwards, never twiddle your thumbs backward or you will be sat on all your life." My sister obediently followed him, and certainly she was never sat on. I remember there was a photo of King Edward VII in the boarding house who resembled my grandfather, except Grandpa was slimmer and more elegant.

On my ninth birthday I remember Grandpa had his godson to lunch with us, whose birthday was on the same day as mine. His name was Cyril and he was 2l, an age apart, but years later we became fast friends. He was a sort of second cousin, the nephew of the uncle who had married my Aunt Min. He was the most handsome and the shyest man I had ever met, and I felt sorry for him having his twenty-first birthday with an old godfather and two children. We had nothing to say to each other then, but years later we remembered meeting.

Aline, one of my mother's actress friends, who was French, came down with her son Ian. I liked her very much (she told wonderful stories), but I cannot remember Ian very much at that time, though we became good friends in later life.

The most interesting person I remember was Uncle Alban, a naval captain who had married Ivy, another actress friend of my mother's. He brought us kites and one for himself and taught us how to fly them on the lawns opposite the boarding house. He said the grass was flatter than on the beach and we could run without being scared of tripping over stones. We were both fascinated by kites. Uncle Alban was also a bell-ringer and persuaded my mother to introduce him to our vicar. In England church bells do not play tunes but each bell has a mathematical number which the ringers have to follow. Usually there were four to six bell-ringers in a church and the bells were rung by hand, following charts, with the strange names of Grandsire Trebles, Double Bobs, etc. If there were four bells the charts would run, perhaps, 1, 2, 3, 4, and then 2, 3, 4, 1, followed by 3, 4, 2, 1 or any variation of numbers. The vicar was delighted to have another bell-ringer, and Uncle Alban said he would always be welcome wherever he went, for bell-ringers were dying out.

The bells were a great part of our life in Eastbourne, dominated by the Town Hall bell, which rang the Westminster chimes at every quarter and struck the hour. Grownups complained that they were kept awake at night by the bells, but I liked to wake hearing the quarter and then usually was asleep before I knew which hour it preceded. The Town hall bell dominated the hour; it rang first and deepest, but then it was followed by two or three church chimes. A lifetime later I made a French friend who told me that what she missed in America were "*les cloches et les fleurs sauvages*" (the bells and the wild flowers), and I understood what she meant. On Sunday when two or three churches rang the chimes, there was quite a jangle. In memory I liked best hearing a village church playing the chimes alone for morning and evensong, but as a child I enjoyed the tintinnabulation. When the war came, church bells were forbidden; they were to be the sign of invasion, so they remain a part of childhood along with the horses' hoofs, clip-clop in the morning, signifying the arrival of the milk.

Chapter 15

The Hunt Breakfast.

Visitors came and went over the years we were in Sussex, but during our first year there we had a great treat: we were invited to a Hunt Breakfast. One of the reasons we came to live in Sussex was so that Daddy could ride to hounds with the East Sussex Foxhounds. He had gone off several times with the groom in the horse van for the hunts were far inland, but this time the Hunt met near at hand and we were invited to this special occasion. It was held in one of the great manor houses in Sussex looking over the downs, which were wonderful for hunting as there were no farmers' fields to avoid.

The courtyard was full of beautiful horses neighing, bridles jangling, hounds baying, and horns blowing now and then. Very smart men and women were on horseback in black suits and white stocks round their necks. A few important men were in "pink," which was really red, but so called in hunting parlance. Footmen were handing round drinks and hot chocolate on silver trays. I felt we had stepped into a pageant of long ago. Many of the women were riding side saddle, very elegant. My mother used to ride that way but she gave up riding soon after we came to Sussex. Years later she told me she had had a miscarriage in London, and did not enjoy riding any more. I asked her then why women used to ride side saddle and she said it was because people thought if girls rode astride it would destroy their maidenheads.

My sister was entranced at seeing all the horses at the Hunt Breakfast. "Will I ever be able to go hunting with you?" she asked my father. "As soon as you can jump a ditch," he said "but as you would probably be the youngest, you might have to be blooded; that is, you would have to have the blood of the dead fox smeared on your forehead, and you would be given the brush (tail) to keep." Bettina felt she could manage. I shuddered. He knew better than to ask me. When I was six years old he had taken me shooting with him in the woods. (Hunting in England is reserved for hunting the fox; shooting is for birds.) At first I had enjoyed it; I loved the woods and was a good walker, but then a pheasant flew over, a beautiful bird with bronze and blue feathers, and Daddy shot it and it fell right in front of us. He picked it up and handed it to me. "You can carry it if you like," he said. I was appalled. "Carry it yourself," I said, "and I'm never coming out shooting with you again." "Have it your own way, kid," he replied. I did not belong to this hunting/shooting family into which I was born, but did enjoy the Hunt Breakfast for its beauty, excitement, and especially the horns.

After a while a few huntsmen set off with the hounds to find the trail of the fox and when they did they sounded the horns and called out "View Halloo" just as in the old song, "Do ye ken John Peel." People streamed out of the courtyard on their shining horses on to the downs and away down the hill, jumping over the stream and up the next hill and away on a frosty morning with the horns still blowing. I had never seen anything so exciting.

We started jumping lessons on our rides. There an area on the downs for this purpose with hedges and small and taller fences. Bettina excelled and at seven she was riding in gymkhanas, jumping and winning prizes. We were all very proud of her. I learned to jump and once I was off Sybil quite enjoyed it, but I never wished to emulate my sister. She rode once to hounds, and obtained the brush, of which she was very proud.

Chapter 16

Miss Risdon, memories.

When the tide was at its lowest the sea left a shining glass mirror on the sand, and in it clouds were reflected, the white fluffy clouds of afternoon, cumulus clouds. I pointed them out to Miss Risdon and said they made me think of sailboats. "Stately Spanish galleons, "she said. I did not know what those were and she promised to show me pictures in a book. They were tremendous ships, with huge sails, the Spanish Armada, and long ago they had threatened England with invasion.

I had already heard of so many invasions. First the Romans with Julius Caesar announcing "I came, I saw, I conquered." I had seen the ruins of the Roman villas along the Roman road to Canterbury. I knew that they had defeated the Britons and driven them west to Cornwall and Wales. Then there were the Angles and Saxons, who had left their names in Sussex villages. "Hurst" was Saxon for "wood" and Ticehurst and Wadhurst were familiar. Then there were the Vikings or Danes who had attacked the northeast coast and left their mark in towns ending with "by" like Grimsby and Whitby.

Then there had been another kind of invasion, Christianity. Apparently the Angles were fair haired and blue eyed and some had been captured by the Romans and sent to Rome as slaves in the sixth century. Pope Gregory had seen them and said they were "angels not Angles" and should be told of Christianity, so he sent St. Augustine to Canterbury to convert the Anglo-Saxons. "How did he do that?" I asked. Apparently the Venerable Bede in the 7th century had written the first history of England and had told this story. A bird had flown into the hall and out again, and the Saxon chief had said that our life was like that. "We come we know not whence, and we go we know not whither, and if you can tell us anything more about what comes before and after, we will listen." So they listened to the Gospel stories and as in those days everybody believed what their chief believed, it was not hard to convert England to Christianity. I liked that story especially about the bird and that it had been remembered for centuries.

How did the Spanish Armada invade and when? I was told they never did invade. The great Spanish galleons were attacked by smaller English ships that set them alight and then there was a great storm and many of the Spanish ships were wrecked on the coasts of Cornwall. Not all of the sailors were drowned, some were washed up on shore and stayed and married there. "Some people say that is why the Cornish people are so dark, "said Miss Risdon," but most of them were of Celtic origin, the Britons who had been pushed west by the Romans, so they were dark anyway."

I was fascinated by the idea of people being washed up on shores not their own and staying there and starting a new life. "It was not only enemies," said Miss Risdon, "but fishermen who carried stories from one place to another." She was interested in this. She got out the map of Europe and showed me how the stories of Arthur and his knights had first started in Wales in the sixth century in the oral tradition. Arthur then moved to Cornwall where he had a castle, Tintagel. She showed me how close the coast of Cornwall was to Brittany in France, where some of the early Britons had been pushed by the Romans. Fishing boats were often stranded on both coasts and the fishermen exchanged tales and the Arthur tales spread through France more quickly than they did in England so that in the twelfth century a French poet first made them famous, and it was not till the fifteenth century that an English poet, Malory, wrote them down. Since then they had trickled down through the English poets, right up to Tennyson, who wrote "The Idylls of the King "and "Morte d'Arthur."

I pricked up my ears at the name of Tennyson, remembering "The Lady of Shalott." "Couldn't we read this?" She hesitated, "I could tell you some of the tales of 'Idylls of the King'; I have 'Morte d'Arthur' here with me but might be a bit hard for you to read." "It would not be too difficult. You read ahead some lines, and then I follow you, and if I don't know any word, you can tell me. It will be English and history too." I had enjoyed the stories of the invasions and knowing many places where they landed. It was also interesting to see on the map of Sussex and Kent many of the villages in William the Conqueror's Domesday book, but I did not find the Norman kings very interesting. Miss Risdon would not agree. We had to continue with the Norman dynasty, but we would read "Morte d'Arthur" aloud. Much of what I have read since I have forgotten, but the dying Arthur and Sir Belvedere remain.

Arthur was dying alone without any of his knights except Sir Belvedere, and Arthur's one wish was that his magic sword, Excalibur, should be thrown into a certain lake. This was the sword he had seized from a tree as a youth when no one else could free it. Arthur impresses on his one remaining knight the importance of returning Excalibur so he can die in peace. Sir Belvedere starts off towards the lake but he is enraptured by the magic sword and its jewels and reflects that nothing will be known of Arthur if Excalibur is lost, so he hides it, and returns with some prevarication. Arthur sees through it and sternly commands his knight to fulfill his dying request. Sir Belvedere reaches the lake this time, brandishes the sword to throw it, but the sun shining on the jewels dazzles him, and again he hides it and returns to Arthur who is now at death's door and reproaches his knight. At last Sir Belvedere rushes to the lake, closes his eyes against the flash of the jewels, and flings the sword into the water. An arm comes up to take it, "clothed in white samite, mystic, wonderful." I assumed "white samite" was some suitable material and only queried "mystic." Sir Belvedere returns to Arthur and tells him how the sword was received, and this was what Arthur was awaiting so he could die in peace. He says to Belvedere "If you should never see my face again, pray for my soul. / More things are wrought by prayer than this world dreams of . . ." and dies.

It took quite a while to read aloud with Miss Risdon going first and explaining any words I did not know and I then following. Bettina enjoyed it for the poem was full of horses and swords which she liked, and Tennyson has a chanting rhythm. She grew to enjoy hearing poetry read aloud although she never read much, only horse stories.

We were both very grateful to Miss Risdon for introducing us to a gymnasium class held by the Bandman's school. In the winter it was too wet and windy to walk on the downs and she thought we needed more exercise as well as the companionship of other children. I do not know how she managed this; my parents of course paid but they would never have thought of it themselves. It was not held at the school but after hours in a gymnasium in the old part of Eastbourne. At 4 pm in winter it was already dusk and I remember climbing the dark cobbled streets, with here and there a lighted window behind which a man sat working on a saddle. The bells from the Town Hall sounded much louder than down by the sea. It was like walking into another age but the gymnasium itself was very modern.

Its greatest attraction was called the Giant Stride. It had a huge pole right up to the roof and at the top there were eight rope ladders attached to a swivel so they did not get entangled in each other. Children stood holding a rope ladder at some distance from the pole, holding on with two hands to a rung of the rope ladder above their heads and with the right foot on the bottom rung, the other foot poised to hit the ground. At the sound of "One" they hit the ground with the left foot to push off and swung into the air. At "Two" they descended to hit the ground again to ascend even higher, and so it went on getting higher and higher until the smaller children could no longer reach the ground, but just clung on to the rope ladder getting the most magnificent flight. I never saw anything like it again in any gym and it was the nearest thing to flying. Everybody loved it and I don't remember any accidents.

We also learned to vault the horse, an immense stuffed creature twice as big as we were, with handles on top. You ran up a plank, jumped, caught the handles and swung yourself over. I could never believe I had done it. Climbing rope was easy. Bettina was especially good at it. She had spent so much time gripping the horse with her knees, it was nothing to her to shin up a rope, and though one of the smallest she was often at the top first. It was an exhilarating hour and no gym class I had at school later ever equaled it. We were very impressed with Miss Risdon for getting us into it.

She also made it possible for us to see Queen Alexandra, the widow of Edward VII and the mother of George V who was then king. It was an unexpected visit to open a fete for charity and there was to be a fair. My parents had stayed in London for the weekend so we had no pocket money left, but Miss Risdon advanced us some so we could partake in the sideshows. We had no idea what a fair was, much less a queen. She was tall, slim, elegant, dressed in grey silk and with a beautiful, sad face and gray hair piled up on top. She had been a Danish princess before she was married and she looked as royalty should.

The fair did not amount to much. There were gifts displayed on tables and one bought rings and endeavored by throwing them to trap the gift desired. There was half a large nut; much bigger than a walnut, carved with a most exquisite face. I desired that nut more than anything I had ever wanted. I spent all my pocket money on rings trying to land on it, Bettina gallantly spent all her money and tried too; then Miss Risdon had a try but in vain. She said "Well, if you had succeeded in getting it, it would have got broken or lost, sooner or later. As it is, you will always remember it" and I have.

The most tangible memory is a book of pressed wild flowers we gathered on the downs. It is at the bottom of Grandpa's jewel box. Miss Risdon wanted us to paint the flowers before we pressed them, for the colors always faded. This proved difficult. Cowslips were strong enough to bring home in jars but harebells and scarlet pimpernels just wilted, so we took raincoats to sit on and water and paint boxes up to the flowers and endeavored to get the colors right. Here Bettina, as so often in her life, struck out on a different path. She did not want to paint flowers, she wanted to draw horses, and she proved very good at it. She did not need any to copy, she had them in her mind's eye, beautiful, noble, sad faces, and she wanted to do them in pencil. Miss Risdon offered her brown crayon, but she would have none of that.

Not only on the downs but at home when I was painting flowers or berries she would sit for hours drawing the faces, manes and necks of horses. Daddy was so proud of them he took one sketch to his office.

Miss Risdon introduced me to berries, to the pointed scarlet hips of the wild rose and to the dark round haws of the hawthorn; they were easy to carry home and paint. She read to us from Kipling's "Puck of Pook's Hill" where he extols the three great trees of England as "the oak, the ash and the thorn." She told us the thorn was the hawthorn. I was surprised for it was a scrubby little tree beside the towering oak and the graceful ash with its shivering leaves, silver green. She explained the hawthorn was the main ingredient in the hedgerows, the boundaries of the fields that separated pale wheat, dark gold barley, fierce yellow mustard, the ploughed field lying fallow, the stubble field and the ashen green of oats. They were planted centuries ago and were the backbone of England, weathering the wind, rain, snow and drought, sheltering the delicate flowers of Queen Anne's lace and wild roses; for two weeks in May they bloomed in glory. That is why they have two names, Hawthorn and May. I did not remember seeing them bloom. "We will have to go to the downs to paint them," she said; "they are considered unlucky to have in the house, and your mother is superstitious." So we went to the downs and saw them in bloom, rich white petals with thick yellow stamens, rosacae. They had a heady scent and from the distance there was a glint of gold in the snow, the stamens.

I saw them once more as a child and then did not see them bloom again until the last time I saw England. I did not know then it was to be the last time, but looked them into my mind's eye. I was in a bus with M's students coming down to London from a matinee of *Hamlet* at Stratford. It was late afternoon and the light was long over the multi-colored fields surrounded by foaming snowdrifts. I remembered A.E Housman who wrote what I thought of as the exile's song although it was not called that, but I recalled it each May. He wrote of the broom, the yellow broom that starts blossoming with the hawthorn but lasts much longer. He thought of his Shropshire hills, but the gorse on the South Downs I had known is much the same as the broom.

"'Tis time I think by Wenlock Edge/ the golden bloom should blow/the hawthorn sprinkled up and down/ should charge the land with snow/time will not wait the loiterer's time/ who keeps so long away/so others wear the broom and climb/ the hedgerows heaped with May./O tarnish late on Wenlock Edge,/ gold that I never see/Lie long high snowdrifts in the hedge/ that will not shower on me." I remembered Miss Risdon and her reverence for hawthorn. I did not know it was the last time I would see England, but I had a sense of farewell.

Chapter 17

Domestic Tragedy.

I find it hard to forgive my father, I still do. He decided he wanted his children to grow up speaking French so he instructed my mother to dismiss Miss Risdon and to engage a French governess. My mother cried, but to no avail; my father ruled the roost. Years later I read somewhere that when one recalled the past, one remembered only the threads of gold and the darkness was shrouded. It must be so for I have few memories of this time; Miss Risdon kissed me goodbye and left me her Palgrave's *Golden Treasury of English Verse* and *Morte d'Arthur* and she was gone.

Ironically a French governess could not be found and a stupid elderly woman arrived who kept announcing her name as "Miss Cowe, domestic cow with an E." We none of us could stand her and we learned nothing. I had started fractions and decimals but was only given baby sums of long division. It is hard for me to remember what I actually said to my father and what I imagined saying. I was afraid of him; he could get angry, hunching his shoulders like a bear, shouting, banging the table and throwing bits of toast around. We all feared his rages.

I think I remember bringing up the fact that I was not learning anything in arithmetic or anything and wanted to go to school. It was pointed out to me that it cost a lot to have a governess who was needed to look after us when my parents were in London, and we could not afford to go to school as well. I asked why we had to live separated and not like other families; I said I had learned nothing since Miss Risdon left. All Miss Cowe taught us was a stupid game of "How many eggs in my basket?" You picked up five bits of gravel from the promenade, and chose how many you would keep in your right hand, and asked the person next to you. If they guessed right you handed over your stones. If wrong they gave you how much they were in error.

Miss Cowe did not stay long and a young country woman arrived, Miss Le Pla, and she was my salvation. She told my mother she had been employed as a nursery governess and she could not teach me anything. "What that child reads at nine is beyond me (Morte d'Arthur!); I never had a head for poetry. She should go to school and be taught by teachers from the university, because she could be a scholar." My mother was flummoxed and did not know what to do, but luckily her actress friend, Aline, was there and she suggested that Miss Le Pla talk to my father. "He will pay more attention to her," she said. I listened behind the door when she accosted my father with the same speech. He was impressed for she was really doing herself out of a job. He told her he hoped she would stay a few months until he expected to move the family to London. He would consider what she said about school; this was the first I had heard of it.

Later that weekend my parents told us of the projected move. Daddy was looking for a house where he could entertain his foreign clients and where we could all be together. Miss Le Pla would stay with us till then, when they would endeavour to find a French governess for us, for he was determined we should learn French. "Shall we go to school?" Daddy said he was considering it but we would still need a governess to take and fetch us. It was never thought possible that Mummy might do that; children were accompanied to school by nannies, governesses or maids—a different world! "What about riding?" Bettina let out a wail. "I have looked into that," replied my father, "and it is possible for us to ride at Richmond at the weekend. They have good stables there, and I have seen the horses, but that is expensive too." He looked at us. "I would rather go to school than ride," I said. Utter hush. "We will see what can be done," said my father, and it was left at that.

Bettina was not happy at leaving the downs but she was consoled by the fact that she would have a dog, which she had long wanted. I would miss the downs too, especially sunset seen from our bedroom window, gold over green hills, but they were closely connected in my mind with Miss Risdon and I did not want to think of her. Daddy had always told us when we had to go to the dentist or face something unpleasant "throw your mind and think of something else" and I did. Instead of thinking of her I imagined what it would be like at school. I simply could not face the bleakness of missing her; I learned it was a mistake to care for anybody very much and I tried to shut her out of my mind.

I cannot recall that Miss Le Pla taught us anything before we left Eastbourne except how to ride bicycles; that was fun. I do remember Mummy taking me to church one day and they sang the words "Lo, He abhors not the Virgin's womb." I asked her what they meant and she said I was too young to know. I said if I were old enough to sing the words I should know what they meant. "I'll ask Daddy," I said. "Oh no, no," said Mummy, "Don't do that." "Miss Risdon would have told me," I said. "She always explained words I didn't understand." Mummy grew upset, "You are a difficult child, I hope you do go to school."

The long bleak winter drew to an end and in the spring we went to Hampstead; I cannot remember the move. Again it was a rented house but this time my parents furnished it. It was large, three floors, and I was very disappointed in the garden. It was just a square lawn that did not get much sun, and there were no flowers. There was, however, one unexpected solace. A blackbird came every evening at twilight, sat in the same tree and sang most beautifully. Bettina and I both were fascinated and I remember us sitting at the top of the steps leading from the living room to the garden, listening.

Chapter 18

Hampstead in the Twenties.

Although radio had been discovered in 1924, I think, it was not till the very end of the decade that people had radios. The houses were still silent and entertainment and trade was in the streets. The criers called out their wares as they had done for centuries. The gypsy woman who sold lavender outside used the same chant as in my nursery rhyme book although the price had gone up. In the book it was "Who'll buy my lavender, sixteen branches, sir, for one penny!" It was now for "sixpenny." We were always sent out for lavender; little girls had to make bags to store in drawers, wardrobes and cupboards. I think the stalks themselves were strewn between the sheets in the linen closet for it always smelled very sweet there.

Then there was the muffin man. "Listen to the muffin man, tinkle, tinkle, hear his bell. Muffins and crumpets to sell, toasted and hot, toasted and hot." He rode on a large tricycle with what must have been some sort of oven in front. Crumpets, sold by the muffin man, were served hot and buttered and were a great treat. He was very popular for toasters had not yet been invented and it was hard, hot and uncomfortable to toast a piece of bread in front of an electric or open fire. It usually fell off the fork or became burnt. Toast was put in the oven by cook and served cold in toast racks. Toasters were one of the best inventions of my times.

Then there was a strange assortment of street criers. The rag and bone man pushed a barrow and wailed out, "Rags and bones, any old rags, any old rags." Cook always brought him down her old rags. I asked what he used them for and she said "to make paper." She had no bones for him because of the dog. Then another crier called out "Any old iron, any old iron" and I could never find out if we or anybody gave him anything. "Pots and pans to mend" was the tinker's cry, but I think he mended other things too.

Cook used to like to go down and talk to anyone who came around. She was a Scot and very fond of the bagpipes. She would rush out if she heard a piper coming. "Don't they stir your blood?" she said. The further away they were the better I liked them. "Royalty 'as them piping round their dinner table," she told me. I was not sure how she knew this but later I learned at Balmoral they did have a piper playing outside during dinner. Bettina and I preferred the organ grinder. We were not allowed to touch his monkey for he was supposed to have fleas. He had a sad little face and his master had a sad selection of melodies. Mummy would not let us go out with pennies if he played "The Last Rose of Summer" for on the stage this was supposed to be unlucky. I told the man this and he obliged with the

Londonderry Air or "Danny Boy." Mummy liked this and would sing all the verses. The saddest verse always amused us, "Or come ye back when I am dead, as dead I well may be." We thought that a bit much.

The ice cart came down our road but did not stop at our house for we had a refrigerator, albeit a very small one, with a tiny freezer at the top which just had room for ice cube trays. If these were not taken out every day they became wedged in ice and hard to remove, but Daddy needed ice cubes for his Scotch each night so usually this was no problem. Uncooked meat, fish and eggs were kept in the refrigerator, also butter till sliced in quarters and placed in a covered silver plate in the larder, a small room apart from the kitchen built on the cold north side of the house. Once cooked, the "joint" of beef was placed there under a wire sieve. It was served hot with Yorkshire pudding on Sunday, cold on Sunday night with pickles and chutney and the most dreadful apology for a salad—a wilted lettuce leaf, a slice of tomato, a slice of hard boiled egg with a dab of mayonnaise. It was often said that the best thing learned from America was how to make a salad. The menu for Monday and Tuesday was unchanging; hash (stew) on Monday, minced meat on Tuesday, served with mashed potato on top as Shepherd's Pie. After that it could vary: Daddy liked pheasant, partridge or grouse in season and these unplucked birds would hang in the larder until "high." Cook had to pluck them. Cheese stayed in the larder under small sieves.

There were a great many sieves in the kitchen in those days; they were used for rinsing and sieving fruit—gooseberries, raspberries, and blackberries—which were mixed with custard and cream, placed in the refrigerator to chill and called "fool." When there were parties we children were used to help pod peas and top and tail beans and sieves were used to separate them. I remember sitting on the steps leading down to the garden, podding peas and listening to the blackbird.

We were also called upon to help in Mummy's delicious lobster dish, learned from Granny. It was a lot of work and only used for parties. It called for hen lobsters; roe was mixed with chopped hard boiled eggs, homemade mayonnaise, parsley and the flesh of the little clawlets which we children had to pick out. It took hours to get the flesh out with picks and we could eat one out of every four; the rest was mixed in with the roe, egg and mayonnaise, and placed beside the cooked lobster in the shell. Bettina and I watched the dinner parties from the top of the stairs. There were usually eight people, for two tables of Bridge. There was no longer a table cloth but beautiful chiffon place mats on the polished table with two wine glasses at each place, a finger bowl for fruit and linen napkins cocked up at each place. First came the lobster with champagne, than an entrée with red wine. After that came dessert, then grapes, which had to be cut with special silver scissors and eaten with fingers, afterwards rinsed in finger bowls. The ladies then arose and left the men to cheese and port, which had to be passed to the left.

The postman came twice a day, parked his Mail van and walked the length of the street, opening and shutting each gate carefully, and placing the mail in the letter box in each front door. He did not pick up letters; these had to be posted in the round red pillar boxes at nearly every other corner. To post a small parcel one went to the Post Office, usually part of a tobacconist's store where this could be done and stamps could be bought. To send a large package or to move household goods to another place one asked for a Carter Paterson placard to place in the window. Of all the itinerant vans that roamed the streets of London, Carter Paterson vans lasted the longest. The job of their drivers was to patrol the streets, look out for their placard and then ring the doorbell and make arrangements. After the advent of the telephone this might have seemed a very antediluvian way of doing things, but before WWII many people did not have the telephone as was obvious by the growth of public telephone boxes, which sprung up, round and red as the pillar boxes. One had to wait in the rain a long time to get to the phone, and then produce the exact change so as not to be cut off after three minutes for a local call. It was well nigh impossible to make a "trunk" (long distance) call from a public telephone. The operator did not know how much it cost to phone Sussex, and while she found out, more pennies had to be dropped into the insatiable maw of the telephone.

We had our first telephone at Hampstead. It was an up-right with a human operator. Mummy sang us a topical telephone ditty which she had learned from a Musical: "Kitty, kitty, isn't it a pity/ In the city/ you work so hard/ with your

1, 2, 3, 4, 5, 6,/ 7, 8, 9 Gerrard,/ with your lips so close to the telephone/ when they might be close to mine." It was a catchy tune. My mother was scared of the telephone. She held it six inches away from her and shouted and she did not appear to realize that she could close the conversation. I had to use drastic methods to break her of this. One Monday morning the milkman came to be paid for the week, and she was on the phone. He was waiting at the door; we told her of this and she realized the urgency of the occasion but raised her shoulders to us to indicate the impossibility of breaking the telephone conversation. At last I leant down and pulled the plug from the wall and held it up saying "How now, brown cow?" She laughed, and she learned from this how she could stop a telephone conversation. My aunt had an amusing story to tell: they moved to a small village where the operator knew everyone. She called a local friend and was told: "You can't get Mrs. Benson now; she is in the grocery store and after that she will go the Post Office. It will be half an hour before she is home."

In the ten years we lived in that house in Fawley Road we never met our neighbors. The only time we saw them was when they came out for the Choc Ice cart. There was no ice cream shop near us, as in Finchley, and the only place to get ice cream was at a restaurant or exclusive tea shop, so the man who sold Choc Ices was very popular. These were slabs of vanilla ice cream coated in chocolate and wrapped in silver paper, easy to stack in his small refrigerator. You unwrapped the top and hastily bit a piece before the part in your hand melted; they were hard to eat but delicious.

Bettina received her promised dog as soon as we arrived in Hampstead. He was a Cairn terrier, very intelligent and sweet. My sister fed and exercised him and he obeyed her, he tolerated me, he did not like my father and he adored my mother and liked nothing better than to sit in her lap, which he did for hours.

Miss Le Pla unwittingly did us another great favor; she introduced us to three little girls who lived in the next street. They were out exercising their dog with a nanny, and we were doing the same with our Nicky. One of the children ran over and said to Miss Le Pla, "Do you come from Beaconsfield for our Nanny thinks she knows you?" It turned out they were acquainted so of course they introduced us all and we became friends. Dulcie was the eldest at thirteen, then Daphne (always called "Jimmie" for she looked like a boy), who was already ten, a little older than I and Audrey who was Bettina's age of eight. Audrey and I had never met anybody of the same name, and we did not like it. Jimmie and Bettina became lifelong friends although in the end my sister grew a little tired of her for she would keep sentimentalizing over "the old days" and my sister was not sentimental. At that time, however, they became fast friends for both were devoted to dogs. Jimmie had already decided to be a vet when she grew up. Dulcie was a student, always reading, and it might have been thought we would have become friends, but there is a vast difference between thirteen and nine and somehow we never bridged it although she did help me regarding the Public Library.

They lived in the next street and had the great advantage that a huge cricket field was at the bottom of their garden, and we could play there all through the week. I cannot remember that we were supervised except by Dulcie. There were iron railings near the Pavilion and we taught the Edwards to vault them as we had done with the horse in the gymnasium at Eastbourne. It was harder to vault from the grass than from a plank but I suppose we had sufficient bounce; they were all impressed and could not rest till they had done it. We four younger children then used the railings to play ships, cowboys and Indians and whatever children did play before television while Dulcie read in the long grass. I asked her where she obtained her books and she told me of the Public Library and that one could obtain a ticket there and get it signed by a parent.

I had seen the Library when Mummy took us shopping on the Finchley Road. I did not enjoy shopping. I hated the butcher's shop and would never go inside, but the fish were open to the street, and I thought they looked as if they had died in agony. The only writer I found who was sympathetic to fish was Hermann Hesse in *Narziss und Goldmund* and I never forgot the passage. It seemed strange no one else cared. I think that my mother went and picked out the meat and fish she wanted and that it was delivered by van in the afternoon. She certainly never schlepped it.

When we passed the Public Library I asked if I could go in and get a ticket for her to sign. "Your father will have to sign it," she said. "You know he makes all the decisions." He refused to sign it; he did not want dirty books coming into the house, spreading infection. I was crushed and Bettina felt for me. She already had her dog and went riding in Richmond Park at the weekends. I did not ride; I had opted for school but had to wait till September. A long empty summer stretched ahead. Bettina had a suggestion: "I can sign his signature, I've seen him do it often enough, it is nothing but a squiggle." Neither of us had the slightest compunction, so she signed the card but now how was I to get there? Mummy would not take me against Daddy's orders, but Dulcie told us that one could walk to the top of the cricket field where there was a gate on to Finchley Road, just opposite an island to the Public Library. There were no safety crossings in those days, just islands which were a help for the traffic went different ways on either side. One only had to concentrate on one side and watch for a break in the buses. There were many buses and they barreled down Finchley Road not stopping for you; it was up to you to avoid them. Standing on an island one had a chance.

It was a long walk through the cricket field. I had never crossed Finchley Road alone. Clutching my signed card I made it, entered the Library and was led to the children's section but then was bewildered, knowing nothing of the cataloguing system. I found Kipling's "Puck of Pook's Hill" which Miss Risdon had read to us and a horse book with pictures for Bettina, but what I really wanted was a book on Keats. There was a Keats poem in the book she left me which I liked. I had to ask someone and was directed to the Adult section where I found a small book and returned to the Children's section, where I had seen a young librarian stamping books to be taken out (only three were allowed at a time). He was a nice young man, he stamped them for me and then said, "You have a Catholic taste." "Oh no," I distinctly remember replying, "I am a Protestant." He then explained to me that "Catholic" could mean "universal" or "all-embracing." "I would like to read everything," I said, "but don't know where to start." "I can help you," he said, "I will let you take the Keats today although you really need an adult ticket for that. Do you think your mother will sign an adult card for you?" I was sure Bettina would (in for a penny, in for a pound). Of course she did and the young man led me well.

At first he introduced me to *Treasure Island* and *Kidnapped* by R. L. Stevenson, an old friend now grown up. Of all the books I read in school I have forgotten the names of most, but those I read that summer I remember. I had to hide them in my room and read them either there or in the cricket field. Miss Le Pla and Mummy never said anything; perhaps they thought Dulcie had lent them to me. I read *David Copperfield* and *Oliver Twist* but Dickens was never one of my favorites, too much pathos and not enough poetry. Walter Scott's *Ivanhoe* was heavy going and heavy to carry, but I liked the history in it, and told the librarian. He then gave me Thackeray, *Henry Esmond,* which I think was about the 1745 rebellion, and a D.K. Broster, *The Gleam in the North,* which made me a lasting Jacobite. I was led to Thackeray's *Vanity Fair* which I thought taught me about life. I could never have imagined anyone as manipulative as Becky Sharp. I was impressed that George, who loved

Amelia so long, after marriage was more attached to their daughter. I thought of Daddy who seemed more devoted to Bettina than to Mummy. I liked the description of the ball the night before Waterloo and the confusion of the battle and was completely transported to another world.

I asked the librarian for a book on WWI and he gave me Ernest Raymond *Tell England*. It was the story of two boys who went to school together and one was killed, and it was set in Sussex in places I knew. I renewed it so many times the librarian suggested I ask for it as a Christmas present, which I did and it became my favorite since *Anne of Green Gables*. He also suggested that I ask for *Poems of Today* as a gift. These included the war poets—Brooke, Owen, Sassoon, Edward Thomas, Walter de la Mare, Yeats and many others—and made a lasting impression.

What I liked best about our new house was the Duo-Art electric piano. It played rolls of music chosen mostly by my father. Bettina and I were both enthralled by "Light Cavalry Overture" which we thought was by Suppe, but later it was von Suppe and he was from Vienna. It was riding programmed into music: trotting, cantering, galloping and then a funeral march. Daddy played it nearly every evening after dinner and listening upstairs we rode our pillows to the music. His "Poet and Peasant Overture" generally followed and then "Raymond Overture" by Thomas. My father's taste was eclectic; there was no Bach, Beethoven or Mozart but Liszt's Second Hungarian Rhapsody, some Chopin, the melody from Thais transcribed for piano and another transcription, Schubert's song "*Litanei*" (Litany for

All Souls). The rolls were easy to install and I often played the Schubert for myself during the day. Mummy had some current tunes of the day: "Who stole my heart away?" and "What'll I do when you are far away?," but Bettina and I did not care for those.

Mummy's old singing teacher, Mme Moulds, visited us from Nottingham and brought me the most wonderful book, *Little Songs of Long Ago*, with simple music on one side of the page and on the other illustrations by Willabeek Le Mair in pastel shades of blues, lilac, green, white and rose. It first came out in 1913 so was already old but, it was still in print in the 70's. It gave me my lasting love of pastels. Both music and illustrations were enclosed in ovals. The songs included "A little Nut Tree" and "I saw three ships," and I desperately longed to play them. Mme Moulds told Mummy she should take us to the Dalcroze Music studio in Wigmore Street and she did. We went on the 13 bus. We learned singing by sol-fa and the treble and bass clef of the piano. We also learned to dance; it was a wonderful experience but it didn't last long. With my mother's help I managed to pick out some of the tunes in *Little Songs* but I wanted to learn to play the piano. Mummy played Victorian ballads such as "Three green bonnets." We could not stand them. Why couldn't I learn the piano? Well, it was hard to find a teacher who would come to the house, and Mummy couldn't drive in London. Eventually one was found but she could only come late in the day and that was fatal. She was there when Daddy came home and wanted his cigar and whisky and soda; he didn't want scales. I could understand it and did not like the teacher much. She rapped my knuckles with a ruler if my hands were not in the right position, but I felt damaged when Daddy said it was clear I had no talent. In view of my lasting love of classical music I do not think that was true. She left just when I was beginning to appreciate Chaminade, "Sunset at Sea."

Although there was a great deal of traffic on the Finchley Road, there was practically none around us. This was because there were no garages beside the houses. The neighborhood had been built in Victorian times as the red pillar box at the corner witnessed, with its VR sign. I read somewhere that the first cars had been built with the engine in front because the horse had always been in front, and it was not till the VW that they realized the engine could also be in the back. I think the same sort of thinking must have been the reason that in the twenties no cars were parked outside their houses. Horses had always been stabled and cars were just as valuable and even more expensive than horses, so of course they should be protected from the weather. Nowadays the roads of neighborhoods such as we lived in are stacked with vehicles parked outside, but our car was "stabled" ten minutes walk away in West End Lane in a garage converted from stables. In charge during the daytime was always a young red haired boy named Ronnie, who Daddy said was the best mechanic he had ever met. Bettina was delighted to find someone again to show her about cars, and I remember him lifting the bonnet and explaining what was within to my earnest sister while Daddy paid the weekly bill.

A pleasant Sunday tradition started. In the late afternoon Daddy took us to the Leicester Square cinema in London where the latest American films were showing. An organist, Sandy Macpherson, arose on an enormous organ and gave a short recital first, and then played appropriate music. My film memories start with the Talkies, Gary Cooper in *Beau Geste*, a story of three brothers, one of whom joined the Foreign Legion and was later given a Viking's funeral. I afterwards read the book by P.C. Wren and enjoyed both greatly. The film I remember most starred a little girl, Deanna Durbin, who sang beautifully in *One Hundred Men and a Girl* with Stowkovski conducting. She sang "*Il mio bambino caro*" and "*Su le libre*" and I was enchanted.

Usually we went home afterwards to cold beef and salad but on birthdays and special occasions Daddy took us to the Troc or Trocadero Restaurant downtown where a dance band played and he and Mummy danced. Here I had the Ur "*sole bonne femme*" in all its mushroom glory.

Before she left us Miss Le Pla took us down to her home in Beaconsfield for the day. She introduced us to the birthplace of William Penn who was born there and afterwards went on to found the Society of Friends, Quakers, in the great state of Pennsylvania which was named after him. She showed us the small meeting house where the Quakers had first met; no stained glass windows, no pulpit, just white walls and chairs in circles. She told us they had no preacher but anybody who wished could speak. I think she was a Quaker herself. I had the feeling that they were very good people and always remembered that plain white meeting house.

We were sorry to see Miss Le Pla go but a French governess was at last found who would take us back and forth to school and teach us French on the way and in the evenings. Her name was Mme Mirre and she was a horrible woman. Most governesses who fetched children from school were content to chatter outside but she didn't like to be kept waiting and would explode into furious French and embarrass us. She had inexplicable rages, one at my birthday party, which ruined the day. I hated her.

Chapter 19

School.

At last the long awaited day arrived. We had already bought our uniforms weeks before: White shirts, navy blue serge tunics for winter, alpaca for summer, blazers with Threave House on one pocket, a navy coat, raincoat and hat. We did not like hats; Bettina was reluctant to put hers on and hated the elastic under the chin. So did I but was prepared to put up with it. Mummy said the uniforms cost a great deal of money and I felt slightly guilty.

The English school system is different from the American. A child starts at six years old and ends or did in my day at seventeen and not all people the same age are in the same class. They are divided into Forms: First and Second Form; Lower and Upper Third; Lower, Middle and Upper Fourth and Fifth; then the Sixth Form. I was placed in the Upper Third and Bettina in the Second, both still in Lower School. We started with a hymn and roll call and then went to our various classrooms where we stayed all day and the teachers changed. The desks were of heavy wood with lids under which books were kept and there was a place at the top for your pencil box and an ink pot and pen. Fountain pens had not yet arrived. I remember with distaste the scratchy nibs which often made blots. The lids were covered with the initials of past students to which one added one's own with a penknife. I made a note to bring one and some blotting paper. We had been told to bring a pencil box. In the classroom roll was called again and I found myself next to a red-haired sprite with a huge grin and one tooth over the top of her bottom lip. Her name was Honor and the first thing she said was "Can you play netball?" I said I couldn't, and she then asked, "Well, then, can you throw a ball high up and catch it while running?" I thought back to the days on the beach and said I could throw and catch a tennis ball. I wasn't sure about the running but realized I had often had to run to catch a high ball. She seemed pleased. "Let's have lunch together and I'll show you a quick way out so we can get the netball first and then we will try throwing and catching while running in the garden." She explained that she was the shooter of the netball team but needed an attacking center to get the ball to her and nobody could catch or throw or run. I wasn't sure I would come up to expectations and had rather an anxious morning.

I expected I would be behind in arithmetic and indeed I was. They were well into fractions and decimals and I had only started and then done nothing with them for months. The teacher was kind and said she would give me some homework to help me catch up and meanwhile I should sit by Margot and do what she did, so I swapped desks for that class, but returned next to Honor for History which went well and so did Geography. English was after lunch. At noon a bell rang and Honor grabbed my hand and raced with me to the dining room where she found seats by the door. As soon as lunch was over, she seized my hand again and pulled me down a passage through the kitchen that led outside to a garden with swings and netball posts and a large lawn. She picked up a netball and casually shot it through the hoop. "Now we will try running, and throwing the ball high over the others." "The others?" I asked blankly. "The other team, silly, they will all be taller than us." It was harder to throw a netball high than a tennis ball but I eventually got the knack and catching it was much easier, even while running. Honor was pleased. "You'll do, I'll tell the coach on Wednesday to try you out for Attacking Center." "But will he listen to you?" I asked, "after all I have never played the game." "He'll listen, he likes me," said Honor, "all you have to do is to keep your eyes on me, run the way I do, catch the ball and return it to me."

A bell rang again and we had to go in for afternoon classes. I cast my eyes longingly at the swings. Honor was contrite. "Did you want to swing? I'm sorry." "I've never been on a swing," I said. She was horrorstruck. "Well, tomorrow we'll get out quickly from lunch and grab a couple of swings, and I'll show you how to do it. There's nothing to it."

We went in to English and it was *Hiawatha* by Longfellow. We were handed out books and the teacher wrote the first few lines on the blackboard. "Now we will first learn these lines by heart and then parse and analyse them." I had not the faintest idea what "parse and analyse" meant, so felt I had better get them by heart as quickly as possible, which was not hard, for they had a catchy kind of rhythm. "The first one to know them by heart, put up your hand and be prepared to say them to the class," said the teacher. It did not take me very long and I looked around and everyone was still studying hard, so felt I had better do something I could do, for I realized that I would not be much use in the second part of the assignment. I put up my hand. "Stand up," said the teacher. I was glad Miss Risdon had taught me to stand straight and to speak clearly, thinking of the words, when I recited poetry. The words sounded much better than they read, and I realized Longfellow must have been trying to capture an Indian chant. "By the shores of Gitchee Gummee,/ by the shining big sea water/Stood the wigwam of Nokomis/ daughter of the moon, Nokomis./ Bright before it beat the water/ beat the clear and sunny water/Beat the shining Big Sea Water."

I received a round of applause and the teacher said "I think that deserves a star." Our names were written up on the wall and above them were rows of golden stars. She put a star by my name and my cup flowed over. I had never had such an honor. I soon came down to earth because then we were asked to write down all the parts of speech we knew. Nouns and verbs came to mind, but apparently there were adjectives that modified nouns; adverbs that modified verbs, pronouns, prepositions, conjunctions and articles, etc. I wrote them down and determined to learn them. Then the question came: "At first reading, what part of speech does not seem to be used in these lines?" Margot put up her hand. "Adverbs," she said. "It would seem so," said the teacher, "for how does an adverb usually end?" Margot again replied "With an 'ly.'" "Nevertheless," said Miss Henderson (I suddenly remember her name)," there is an adverb, 'Bright', because it modifies 'beat.'" We also learned that there was alliteration in the repetition of the letter "b." I was tremendously impressed with all this new knowledge. After class Honor thumped me on the back, "I almost liked poetry when you read it, I never have before."

It was an eventful day in my life and that is why I remember it so clearly. That night I went to sleep with the parts of speech jumbled in my mind together with the fear of not being able to catch and return the ball and also the longing for the swing.

I was made Attacking Center and did get a swing next day but could never get enough time on it; we were limited to five minutes. Honor invited me to spend the night; she had a swing in her garden. She taught me how to swing high, even to stand up and swing. She had two elder brothers, one of whom went to Westminster School where they still wore the top hats, and an elder sister. Her father was a clergyman and her mother had red hair. They were all very kind. Honor took me to a roller skater rink which was another new experience. I do not think I had any lessons, just clung on to the rail and Honor's hand until I had the courage to let go. She came to spend the night with me and loved listening to the Duo-Art piano, especially when the evenings drew in and we listened in the firelight. She did not care for poetry as I did, especially not if it were sad, and she never read a book. She did read *Tell England* with me, each of us taking a page in turn. She said afterwards it was the only book she ever read but she never forgot it.

Honor and I were not alike, but she taught me laughter and I realized how good it was to laugh and to make others do so. I was never as funny as she was, she was a born mimic. I moved up to the next form before she did but we still had lunch together, Singing, and also Art with Mr. Kell. He taught us how to make clouds by dropping a little water from the brush on to the page and then introducing purple or rose. I was enchanted and put clouds into every painting and thought of being an artist. The singing teacher told us we would always remember "*Dum spiritus meus*" from Bach's Mass in B Minor after we had forgotten all our other songs and I accordingly did, but also "The Wraggle Taggle Gypsies" and "Early one morning."

I recall so clearly the first day of school but then it seems the days turned to weeks, months, even years, and I do not remember anything special about them. I made friends with the girls in the next form. They were a year older than I and far more sophisticated. Ruth, two Annes, and Isabel, more intellectual than Honor, even though they called themselves the "Pins" and made me a "safety pin." When Honor arrived she joined me in their circle and they were glad to have her and made a special category of pin for her. Honor was what the French I think call an "*Allumeuse*". She lit people up.

I suppose it was inevitable that I should learn the facts of life from an older girl. I was horrified and rushed home to my mother to accuse her of not telling me herself, if indeed it were true, that you had to go to bed with a man to get a baby. "I thought you were too young," said Mummy. "Well, now that I have found out by myself, have you anything to add?" My mother was flummoxed and then, with her genius for the unexpected, said "Never lie down with a man in a boat!" I gasped, "Was that how I was conceived?" "Oh Audrey you are a dreadful girl. No, no." "Well, then it must have been Bettina," I returned, "or you wouldn't have thought of it. I'm going to tell Bettina myself and not let her hear it from strangers" and rushed off. My sister already knew. "How" I gasped. "From the dogs," she said. "Horses too." Life was too much. "Why didn't you tell me?" "Because I knew it would upset you," said Bettina. "Doesn't it upset you?" I asked. "I don't intend to have a baby," said my sister, "you don't have to." I reeled. I wanted to have children and to bring them up myself, not with nurses or governesses, but I didn't like the sound of the process. My Austrian friend, Hanni, years later told me she had first heard all this from others but her mother had comforted her by saying that it was the mystery of love which she would one day find out.

Honor invited me to spend a weekend with her family at the seaside at Pagham. Their cottage was made of two Southern Railway carriages which had been abandoned and Mr. Strong paid nothing for them. He and his sons with some help removed them to near the beach, placed the wheels halfway up in the earth and concreted them in. They were the kind of carriage that had six separate compartments with seats facing each other and a corridor outside with a toilet at each end. They were connected with water and electricity for there were beach bungalows nearby. They removed the seats and luggage rack, took away the partitions between two compartments and joined two together to make three bedrooms out of one carriage, and a kitchen dining space, living room and a bedroom for Honor's parents from the other carriage. The two brothers shared a bedroom, and Honor and her sister each had one. She was away. I think there were double bunks in Honor's room. I thought it was the neatest thing I had ever seen. I cannot remember if they had a bathroom. They only went there in the summer when they swam in the sea every day and the toilets were hooked up to a septic tank. It seemed quite fantastic at the time to be living in a railway carriage but they had fixed it up very nicely with curtains, and one looked right out at the sea. To enter one used one of the two steps still attached to the railway carriages; the others had been removed. From the outside it looked just like railway carriages but inside it was painted white all over.

Pagham had a lovely beach but was not built up at all, just a few beach cottages and an abandoned harbour further back which had been built by the Romans. Over the centuries the tide had receded as it often does in England and now the harbour was a deserted place, haunted by ghost ships of the past. There was a small village nearby with a few shops, very different from the seaside at Eastbourne with its pompous promenade and Victorian pier. I loved the place and have never forgotten it. The nearest seaside town was

Bognor which had been renamed Bognor Regis, for King George V had stayed there to recuperate after an illness.

We swam twice a day and we all played cricket on the sand, even Mrs. Strong. Brian, Honor's brother who went to Westminster School, told me that I could bowl and catch a ball pretty well for a girl. We walked for miles on the sand but always came home by the harbour and I remember wishing I could paint it with clouds above, but no one had a camera so was not able to remember it well enough.

I told Honor of my recent discovery of the facts of life and she was sympathetic. Her mother had told her but she didn't think I knew and so had never mentioned it. She said her older sister was already interested in boys and had told Honor it might not be so bad. We stayed up late at night talking in our double bunks. I had already decided I would like to write but was also interested in art. Honor said she wanted to have a good time, but did want babies in the end. It was a wonderful weekend.

Thanks to Bettina, Mme Mirre left. It was the Depression and Daddy kept complaining of financial losses. Bettina said she had a schoolfriend, who lived in a flat opposite the island crossing to Heath Drive where our school was, and her nanny had promised to wait for us each morning and afternoon, so we no longer needed Mme Mirre to take us to school and back. We had both done quite well in French but more due to the charming Mlle Maryat who taught at school than to Mme Mirre. Daddy agreed she could leave and so we entered five years of the happiest carefree times of our lives when we came closer to our parents.

Chapter 20

My Parents

When we started to learn to play tennis at school, my father became interested and bought us the most astonishing gadget for the back lawn called Kumbak Tennis. It was two bamboo poles secured into heavy round bases which were placed eight feet apart. Between the two poles was a heavy band of rubber with a smaller string of rubber in the middle attached securely to a tennis ball. It was for one or two players. The first player threw the tennis ball into the air to serve and the second player had to hit it as it returned. One played in turn and it really simulated a game of tennis. Daddy enjoyed playing too, and I remember it particularly because it was the first time he and I ever enjoyed something together. I don't count riding for although I enjoyed it I never felt that I lived up to his expectations as a rider, for I couldn't always control my horse. This game was different; I sometimes beat him. He suggested that we go to a real court and play a family doubles tennis, so Mummy and I played against Daddy and Bettina. It was the first time we wore shorts, white, and we felt very chic.

Daddy also enjoyed golf and took us with him to walk around the course. For this we had to drive out into the country, past Finchley and our old house, which I didn't like to look at for it was now a church surrounded by a car park and the garden was gone. A straight road for miles, originally one of the Roman roads out of London, ran straight from Baker Street to Tally Ho Corner, where it became country and the Hadley Woods Golf Course. Daddy played with friends and afterwards we all had tea, and I remember particularly the sultana tea cake, which was very good. One of his friends said to him at tea one day: "Harry, you play very well for a one-eyed man." "Sharpens the focus," returned my father. Walking home from the garage, I asked him what the friend meant. "Oh, I've only got one eye, didn't you know?" said my father and tapped the glass eye. I fell off the pavement in horror. "Can I tap it?" asked my intrepid sister, and she did. I felt I was going to throw up. "How did you lose it?" continued Bettina. "In a tiger hunt," said my father. Later my aunt, his sister, told me that it was one of his wild tales. The truth was far more pathetic. He lost it as a boy while being caned. He turned suddenly and the cane caught his eye. The horror overwhelmed me. How dreadful it must have been, the pain and losing one's eye! I never asked if he ever took it out, I could not bear the thought, but it did change my attitude to my father. I could not feel so bitter about Miss Risdon and not being allowed to learn the piano when I considered what he must have suffered as a boy. I had always disliked it when he made up lies about the names of flowers to confuse people, but I felt the tiger hunt was rather a gallant lie, very like him.

Another way in which my father was unusual is that he was very interested in the occult. He had worked with Conan Doyle and Sir Oliver Lodge in making ESP and occult experiments. He used to say he could tell what we were thinking if we concentrated and put our hands in his and looked at him. I did not feel that it was really so difficult to tell what your ten year old daughter was thinking when you knew she disliked the whole thing. I was always religious and felt it wrong to try and contact spirits without the benefit of religion. I felt there were evil spirits as well as good, and only God could protect you from the evil. I tried to find a church when we went to Hampstead that would have the service with the psalms and liturgy I knew, but the only church near us was Presbyterian and I did not care for the music. Eventually I found a church and persuaded my mother and sister to come but not my father. He said he was a Master Mason, and they did good works and that was enough for him.

Soon after we went to school and Mme Mirre left we caught the measles. We had to be in a darkened room and I could not read and Mummy really turned up trumps. She read to us for hours from *Dr. Doolittle* which we all three enjoyed very much. I think she would have been happier if she had been able to look after us herself for years. It was my father's idea to have a governess. She appeared to me in a new light for she was certainly devoted. Day after day she read and sang to us.

My fondest memory of her is connected with her songs. When still in the first year of school I found an American book in the library about a saintly child called Elsie Dinsmore. It took place during the Civil War. A man called George (have never liked the name since) poured boiling oil into someone's eyes. I had a *crise de nerves* and screamed and screamed and would not stop. The doctor was called (in those days they made house calls) and gave me a sedative and told my mother not to leave me. She sat by my bed and sang and sang and when her memory lagged I prompted her till we even got down to love among the chickens. "He was a Dorking, proudly stalking, only a bantam she, but she was proud and cried out aloud, cockadoodle–ack a doodle doo." As long as I had her voice to cling on to I did not have to think of the horror I had read. My father also helped me. I was in bed clinging on to my mother's hand while she sang, and Daddy said: "Throw your mind, kid, think of the downs." That really registered. It was possible by an act of will to throw one's mind. He had told us about this before and I had used it when Miss Risdon left. It had not occurred to me on this occasion but I profited by his advice and learned to do it. I also asked for the Duo-Art piano to be played and to hear "Light Cavalry." My stomach still cringes at this memory. It occurs to me that perhaps it was because I had so lately learned of my father losing his eye that I was so sensitive to torture to the eyes.

Chapter 21

Upper School.

Here I was fortunate enough to have two brilliant teachers, one for English and one for History. Miss Barter introduced us to Shakespeare by leading us through two plays a term, starting with *Midsummer Night's Dream*. We each had the play which we read aloud, with Miss Barter reading the best parts; but we read along with her and so were introduced into the magic of iambic pentameter, wielded by Shakespeare. When we came to *Henry* V she took us to Westminster Abbey to see the flags of Agincourt in the Henry VII chapel. They were ghosts of flags. The material had worn so thin since 1415 that they were transparent veils with faded colors, but they were the flags of Agincourt. I was enthralled by history since then. After the war I wanted to show two American friends the flags but they were no longer there. I think they were taken down when the war started and they must have crumbled into dust. Even the oldest guide knew nothing of them, but I had seen and remembered them.

An ice skating rink was built on the Finchley Road between Hampstead and Golders Green, and an ice skating craze hit the school. Every Saturday morning Honor and I with three other friends would meet at the top of the road at 9:30 am and catch the 13 bus. It was only a tuppenny ride (two pennies). We clattered up to the top of the bus and the conductor who had grown to know us did not bother to climb up and get our fares. He had a kind of game with us. There was yet no stop for the rink but the driver was kind enough to slow down and we would throw ourselves off the bus and the conductor would grab two or three of us to get our pennies while the others he let go. Years later I told Howard about this and he was aghast. His Puritan hackles rose. "You cheated the bus system.! How many months or years did you do this? You should reckon up how much you owe the London Transport and send them a check!" I then realized that perhaps I was lacking in a sense of guilt. I had none about encouraging Bettina to forge my father's name to get me a ticket for the library and none about jumping off the bus. It was a game we had with the conductor as far as I was concerned.

When we arrived at the skating rink it was like entering another world. There was a band that played "The Skater's Waltz" and Strauss waltzes. We were given skates and boots for Christmas, and we all had a few lessons. The other girls were given dancing lessons but Mummy said there wasn't enough money for that. Years later she said that was her one regret, that she had not let me take dancing lessons on ice. "So much money went on other things; you should have had lessons," she said. I was rather touched at this but at the time did not mind. Honor did not progress to dancing class either but we both could do backward V 8s, as they were called, and we looped around the rink holding hands and doing those together and had a wonderful time.

One morning there was a special skating exhibition and to our surprise it was Marion, the head girl at our school, who performed. Apparently she was Junior Ice Skating champion of England and had been coached by Sonja Henie. She must have been seventeen, going on eighteen, for it was her last term and there were rumours that she was engaged. We knew her from afar. She had fair blond hair to her shoulders and was dressed in a shining white dress that seemed to have wings to it. She swooped and swirled and plunged and seemed to me like a gull. I had never seen anything so beautiful.

To my surprise I met her crossing the hall at school the following Monday. It was the prerogative of the head girl to ring the bell for lunch recess but she could delegate it. I had never spoken to her but was so enthralled by her performance just blurted out "You were so beautiful on Saturday, you seemed to fly like a gull." She smiled and then said, "I say, would you like to ring the bell at twelve o'clock for me? I'm in third floor class at this time and it is a pain having to come down. Are you in class here at this time?" I gasped at the honor. Generally only sixth form girls rang the bell and I was only lower fourth but she could delegate whom she wished. "I'm sure you could do it and you would never forget." "Could I watch you do it once," I asked, "to be sure to get it right." She took the bell from its little ledge and rang it three times. "Yes, I could do that," I said. "Well then, we'll go and tell your teacher," and we did. After that we sometimes met at lunch or recess and she thanked me for being so reliable at ringing the bell and saving her coming down three flights of stairs to do so. Others envied me. I still see the bell on its little ledge and remember the power and responsibility I felt as I swung it to and fro.

At Sports Day at the end of term Honor won the high jump for her age group, jumping five feet when she herself was five feet tall. Marion came to congratulate her and I was standing by. She told me that from now on the sixth form class would be on the ground floor at twelve o'clock so the next head girl could ring it without any trouble; she thanked me again and said she was giving up exhibition skating as she was now out of the Junior class and that she was going to be married next year. I did not expect to see her ever again but to my surprise I did.

I had a friend called Jean who was at boarding school but during the holidays I took my bike to where she lived as it was nicer biking there. One day we were on the pavement near Jean's home when I saw someone gardening in a house near hers and it was Marion. I was so surprised I fell off the bike and Jean who was behind me did too. Marion looked up and saw us both. She knew Jean as a neighbour and she invited us both in for lemonade and biscuits. She introduced us to her mother who was working on a shining white dress. I asked her if it were her wedding dress and she said no, it was for the Chelsea Arts Ball. It was white satin with chiffon over it. I remembered the lovely dress Marion wore when she did that exhibition skating and thought she was like a gull and asked her mother if she had made that. She was pleased and said she had and then she showed us photos of Marion skating in dresses she had made, all stunning. "If you come by next week," said her mother, "this dress will be finished and Marion can model it for you." I will be back in boarding school next week," said Jean. "Would you like to come, Audrey," said Marion, "come to tea and then I will put it on for we have to go early to the ball," so I accepted, feeling a bit abashed.

I came next week at the appointed day and after tea she went up to change, and then appeared at the top of the staircase. She was in a shining white sheath with floating chiffon, she had violets on her shoulder, Parma violets, for the scent descended the stairs with her. I had never seen anything so beautiful. I stood entranced and then the violets were in my face and she kissed me. I still remember what I felt then. "If all the rest of my life is misery, at least I have known what it is to be perfectly happy."

I never went back. I think I hurt her feelings for she phoned once or twice but I made some excuse. I spent much time wondering why I never returned. I think firstly I was overwhelmed by the feeling I had, and afraid, remembering Miss Risdon. Also, I felt had seen something so beautiful and I wanted to remember her like that, descending the stairs all in white.

Soon after that I became friendlier with Isabel who had three brothers who played cricket and who allowed me to play with them as I threw quite well for a girl, they said. Alan Cobham's Flying Circus came to town and took people up to loop the loop in an open bi-plane. Isabel and I dressed in her brother's clothes for we did not think they would take twelve year old girls without parents but they accepted us as boys. I asked how we would stay in as there were no seat belts. "Centrifugal force," the pilot said. I did not think much of that as my cap flew off when we turned upside down.

This was the time of "dares" and, truth to tell, I instigated many of them. I cannot understand now why I was so crazy but suppose it was because the first ten years of my life had been so isolated and sheltered, and now freedom went to my head. It was I who suggested to Isabel that we climb through the trapdoor on to our roof and from there we could jump over the narrow passage that divided us from the next house, the tradesmen's entrance, on to the next roof and back again and descend by drainpipe. I do not know why my mother was never aware of what we were doing or why neighbours did not see us and tell her. We never met the neighbours and there were no children on our street. I suppose most of the men were away at work and the women were not watching the rooftops. It is amazing that we did not kill ourselves for the houses were three stories high.

Chapter 22

Junior Oxford Exam and a row with my father.

This craze lasted several months but then we were faced with another challenge, a scholastic one. Isabel and I, the two Annes, Margot and another girl, were summoned one day to the study of the Headmistress and told we had been chosen to enter the Junior Oxford Examination, administered by the University of London, in order to prepare us for Matriculation, which we would take four years later in order to enter a University. It was entirely up to us to choose whether we wished to do so or not, but if we did we would do honour to the school. It would involve one term of very hard work. We would follow the same curriculum as others in the class but would be given extra work after school and in the Easter holidays. On the appointed day we would go down to the University of London and take the printed examination there. We would be examined in English History from the Wars of the Roses till the end of the Tudors; in English the texts would be *The Tempest* and Keats's *The Eve of St. Agnes;* in Math it would be Arithmetic,

Geometry and Algebra; and in French grammar, vocabulary and something by Daudet. I do not think Isabel wanted to do it, and only five of us signed up.

It was hard work, complicated by the fact that Miss Barter, the brilliant English teacher, resigned on account of ill health and a new teacher came, fresh from the University, Miss Varn. She was a good teacher but could not replace Miss Barter to my mind, but I was helped greatly by the young librarian in the Public Library, who introduced me to Keats's Letters. This experience was an eye opener not only to Shakespeare but to life. "The world is a vale of soul-making"; "the essence of great art is its intensity, examine *King Lear* and you will see it throughout"; the famous paragraph on Negative Capability. I cannot recall it by heart but he said something to the effect that we should not be concerned with busying ourselves like the bee, but rather be open like a flower to receive in Passive Capability. When he went into a room "not myself comes back to myself but the personalities of everybody there invade me. If I go outside it is no different, I see a sparrow and pick about the gravel." He had imagined the mountains but when he actually saw them "the space, the tone . . . my imagination surpassed was at rest . . . . yet I was worldly enough to imagine a fleet of ships sailing across the lake." His imagination never was at rest. He had a genius for picking out the best lines of Shakespeare, "the tender horns of cockled snails." I was so glad to be studying Shakespeare and Keats.

As the exam neared I grew very nervous about History. The Wars of the Roses till the end of the Tudors was a long time and there were so many dates to remember. I said at dinner one night I was glad that I was at least sure of the date of the battle of Agincourt, 1415. "Oh no, kid, you are wrong there," said my father. "It was 1514." Sheer rage overwhelmed me. I knew my father's game of confusing people over the names of flowers or dates, when he knew nothing about them at all, but that he would try it with me now just infuriated me. All that I had suffered from my father, the loss of Miss Risdon, his refusal to let me learn the piano, and now this attempt to confuse me over dates, went to my head. I stood up, realizing that I was hunching my shoulders as he did when he went into a rage. I was also chagrined that my vocabulary to express my anger was so childish. I remember I said, "I know perfectly well that the date of Agincourt was 1415. How dare you try to confuse me with your stupid games when so much is at stake! [that was how I thought in those days] I think you are a beastly, beastly man!" By this time my sister had run around the table and stood by my side with the carving knife. This touched me very much for I knew she was devoted to my father, far more than I was, but the fact that when push came to shove she would stand by me, was a great help. He rose to his feet, hunching his shoulders and glared at us both. He had never laid a hand on either of us but who knew now what would happen? Nobody had ever stood up to him. Usually in a rage he would bang on the table and shout and throw toast about. What would he do now? He threw down his napkin and left the room. Mummy burst into tears.

The next night he stayed at his club and the following night we met at dinner as though nothing had happened.

I think he was sorry, for a week before the exam he and Bettina drove Mummy and me down to a lovely old guest house in Sussex. It was near the Roman villa with the mosaic of the morose looking Roman with an empty twig, representing winter. They fetched us a few days later. This was so that I would have complete quiet and rest to study. It was already the Easter holidays. It had a beautiful garden and there was a huge white lilac bush tumbling over the wall filling the air with scent. At night it looked like a waterfall. "O holy and immortal white, forever falling through the night, forever to remain." We had our meals there. I do not know what Mummy did; she was not a country person. I do remember that there was a young man there studying for his Entrance exam to Oxford in History. He was interested that I was doing the Junior Oxford Exam; he had done it four years earlier and he asked me if I would like to climb up to Chanctonbury Ring to see the dawn. I was delighted. I would not have known the way myself but knew there was a fantastic view over Sussex from the top. When I told him I was studying the Wars of the Roses to the Tudors, he said that there would be an essay either on Henry V or Elizabeth and if I wanted to concentrate on Elizabeth he could help me by telling me all he knew. It would also be a good thing for him to say it aloud. He told me about her speech to the troops at Tilbury before the Spanish Armada. I have forgotten most of it but I remember she said "I may have the body of a woman, but I have the heart of a king." He also told me that when Elizabeth was eighteen she was imprisoned in the Tower and given a night to write down her belief on Transubstantiation. She wrote "His were the words that spake it/He took the bread and brake it/ and what His words do make it/ I do believe and take it." The Catholics could do nothing against her for that.

We started at about 4 am and walked through the dawn chorus. I knew it started with the blackbirds but did not know the names of the innumerable birds that followed and hoped my new friend might. He seemed so erudite but he did not. I must call him Jack for I cannot remember his name. He did not even recognize the larks when they started whirling around us, singing higher and ever higher until they vanished from sight but not sound. It must have been a late Easter and an early spring, for the hawthorns were white with blossom and their dew and scent brushed on our jackets as we climbed the chalk path up the downs until they vanished, together with the gorse, and there was only the high down ahead crowned with beeches at the top, Chanctonbury Ring. Jack said they had been planted to commemorate the battle of Waterloo 1815. I wondered how beeches could grow in the chalk for no other trees did and he said they must have taken good soil up there. I had never seen a sunrise and luckily there were a few clouds in the sky for the sun to gild when it rose with all Sussex beneath it. Young wheat was pricking green through the fields but mostly they were still dark from the plough. I seemed to remember Miss Risdon telling us that barley and oats were planted later. The woods were not yet leafy and looked like blue bruises over the hills but the leaves on the beeches were coming out, more like green flames than leaves.

I told Jack some of the Shakespeare I knew from *Henry V* and he said that I should quote all I could remember for it would impress the examiners. He left a day before we did and the landlady asked if I would like to sleep out in the caravan where he had been sleeping. It had a Dutch door which opened half way up so one could see out, and I liked the idea of seeing the stars from bed. It was in a field of buttercups. The sky was much darker than the London sky and the stars much bigger and brighter and I enjoyed the night. In the morning, however, I had the fright of my life. I was awoken by a terrific sound and a huge white face like an ogre's looked through the Dutch door. It was a cow. I screamed and it vanished but left me with a lasting fear of cows which Bettina could never understand. She could just wave her arms and they lumbered off. I expect they sensed my fear for they never moved for me.

At last the first day of the two-day exam arrived. It was not held at the University of London, but at the Merchant Taylor's school in the city, which was one of the oldest of the public schools. Browning and Lamb had attended there and other famous writers. We were greeted by the Registrar in the most beautiful room. It was paneled with a fireplace and bookcases on either side. I decided then and there that if ever I could have the room I wanted, it would be just like that. The first exam was History and the essay was on Elizabeth, so I was well prepared and very grateful to Jack. That afternoon we had French and the next morning Math, and the last exam was English. We had studied *The Tempest* and Keats's *St.Agnes' Eve*. To our horror the texts were

Coriolanus and Tennyson's *Morte d'Arthur*. We looked at each other aghast. One of the Anne's who was tall and very grown up arose and went up to one of the two examiners and explained our situation. We were led out to the Registrar, picking up Miss Varn on the way. She was seated outside, waiting for us. She was horrified, thinking she would be blamed. The Registrar was kind. He explained the texts we had studied were for the previous year. Evidently Miss Barter had been given them and when Miss Varn took over she had not checked.

The Registrar said that if we had passed our previous exams we would not fail the Junior Oxford but be passed in History, French and Math "unless one of you young ladies would like to attempt the English examination." I looked at it. I had read *Coriolanus* to myself as I had read all the Shakespeare plays, except *Titus Andronicus* which was too bloodthirsty. I remembered Shakespeare had taken it from Plutarch, together with a famous classic comparison of the body politic with the human body. I recalled only one line of poetry in it, to his wife, "My gracious silence, hail!" It was three years since Miss Risdon had left but I still remembered *Morte d'Arthur* and could quote from it better than I can now. "I have not studied these texts in school, but have read them, and I would like to attempt it," I said. "In which case," said the Registrar, "I will write a note explaining your situation, and you will attach it to your examination." He addressed Miss Varn, "I suggest you take the other young ladies to the Temple Gardens." They filed out and the examiner took me back. I thought I had better face the worst first and turned to the *Coriolanus* questions. I could answer some of the short answer questions but the essay was beyond me and I did not attempt it. *Morte d'Arthur* was a relief; I felt quite happy about it, even the essay. With time left on my hands I started on an essay I would like to have been given on Shakespeare's influence on Keats, quoting from *The Tempest, St. Agnes' Eve* and Keats's Letters. I ended up quite enjoying myself and told Miss Varn, who was very upset, that I would much rather have spent the time on the texts we did than on the correct ones. We had to wait three weeks for the results.

My birthday came before the results and my father had planned a tremendous treat, perhaps as an "*amende honorable*." He had tickets for *White Horse Inn*, our first evening performance. He had seen it in Austria as *Weissl Roessl* and loved the music and now we were to hear the English version. As it happened, we had yet another treat that day. My father and sister rode every weekend at Richmond, and some of the old mail coaches driven by horses were kept down there, and now they were to be renovated and sold to Bertram Mills' Circus. Perhaps the Royal Family took some as they still used horse drawn carriages for funerals. Before the sale three of the coaches were to make a four-in-hand farewell trip from Richmond to Boxhill in Surrey on May 4th and my father had purchased tickets for us on the ll a.m. coach Mummy said it was too much excitement for one day and it was one of the most exciting days of my life.

The coachmen were dressed in 18th-century costumes, and there were postilions with post horns at the back of the coach. At each village people turned out to greet us and the postilions blew their horns. Afterwards when I read Eichendorff and heard Schubert I remembered that ride. It was a fine day, the windows were open, and it was as if I heard Schubert and Eichendorff whom I did not yet know. At lunch Daddy let me taste his White Lady cocktail which had Cointreau in it, enchanted orange juice. In the evening we heard *White Horse Inn* with music by Benatsky. Later I read Alma Werfel who said he was nicknamed "Benutzky" as he used other people's music. (*Nutzen* is "to use" in German.) There were certainly Austrian folk tunes in his music, and perhaps Schubert. The backdrops were the Austrian Alps and Wolfgangsee. I was enchanted.

After that even the results were an anticlimax although it was the highpoint of my scholastic career. I passed in English, with Honours in History, and was given a special prize.

Chapter 23

Manor Farm—the second garden.

Although I was very happy at school, Manor Farm made an even more profound and lasting impression on me. About a year after I started school my uncle and aunt purchased a 16th-century Elizabethan manor house with farm and woods attached. My uncle was a very wealthy man for his father started a munition works at Greenwich by the river in WWI, and between the wars it made tractors and industrial machines of all kinds. We were definitely the poor relations and this disturbed the rest of my family but it did not worry me, because I was so fond of my aunt, and she was always at her best with me. Some people called her strong-minded or even domineering but she was never like that with me. I think it was because we both loved books. She had a good mind and should have gone to the university but in her day very few girls did, including Virginia Woolf. My aunt was "finished off," as they used to say, in Germany and then she married.

Manor Farm was in East Sussex, near Brightling, which was probably as high as Chanctonbury Ring and had a magnificent view. She invited my family down for the weekend but Daddy and Bettina did not want to go because they rode at Richmond then, and Mummy would not go without them. My aunt had the chauffeur drive across London to pick me up and we went down alone for the first time. My cousins were already at boarding school. I was glad to go and see Sussex again, and we passed several small villages with old Gothic churches that were probably in the Domesday Book of William the Conqueror that I remembered from Miss Risdon. Three miles past Robertsbridge we turned to the left down a small country road, which my aunt explained went through their property and was open to all because it was an ancient Right of Way, to Socken'ersh Manor and the village of Burwash where Rudyard Kipling lived. My uncle was not pleased about this but there was nothing he could do about it. If enough people used it during a year it became a Right of Way, by an old law.

We drew up by a wrought iron gate which led to a paved courtyard in front of the house, and to the right was a stone wall bounding a flower bed filled with pink tulips and forget-me-nots. In the middle was a fountain with a little Italian *putto* playing in it and beyond that a grass tennis court and further off a bank of daffodils in bloom. I stopped my aunt from entering the house. "Couldn't we see the garden first?" She agreed and led me round the house to a large stone terrace from which one could see for miles. Below was a lawn which had obviously been mown and rolled for centuries for it was like green velvet, an Elizabethan bowling lawn. It was a steep drop from the terrace with a stone wall; clumps of purple aubretia and yellow allysum fell from holes in the wall. To the right was an unmown bank filled with white narcissus and ahead were more lawns falling away to a stream and then a cherry orchard arose in full bloom with primroses beneath. From the terrace one could see Sussex stretching for miles with its woods and fields. "You would like to go into the orchard," suggested my aunt. "Oh yes." The terrace ended and we went past the Oast House. These oast houses were frequent in Kent and Sussex and had been used to cure the hops for beer. The houses were round, made of old red brick with a coned white roof vented in the top to let in the air but not the rain, and the hops were laid on the floor in rows until they were ripe for distilling. It was one man's job to do nothing but go around the oast houses and decide on the day. This was no longer done and most had been converted for living purposes.

We turned right after the Oast House, past what would be the herbaceous border in the summer but now the blue spikes of lupins and delphiniums were still in bud and the front border was bright with yellow snapdragons. To the left was the sunken rose garden, another Elizabethan feature, with a high brick wall at the back and low brick walls on either side from which clumps of alyssum and verbena fell. There was a sundial in the middle surrounded with formal triangles of pruned rosebeds, bordered with pansies. At the end was an old, no longer used well, covered with honeysuckle and with a view over the orchard, fields and woods.

We went into the orchard, climbing a little until we reached the woods with a five-barred gate. My aunt unlatched it and we went into the beech woods and there I saw them, under the light green leaves, waves and waves of bluebells, seas of them. I had not seen them since Finchley, and then only a little path but now they went on forever. I burst into tears. My aunt hugged me and said, "I knew you would love it as much as I do, probably more than the others, except perhaps Donald." "I've never felt like this before," I gasped, "I feel I belong here." "And so you do, darling," said my aunt, "you shall have your own room here, the same as the others and you shall come down every weekend." "That won't be possible," I wailed, "Daddy and Bettina will always want to ride at Richmond and Mummy won't leave them." My aunt considered. She knew her brother. "Well then," she said, "until you are old enough to come by train yourself, I will send the chauffeur for you and you will drive down with us," and so I did. It became my first real home since Finchley, and far more beautiful. We had always lived in rented houses. I never felt I belonged anywhere till Manor Farm and when I think of England, that is what I remember.

Keats said one will have in heaven what one loved most on earth "repeated in a finer tone." C.S. Lewis said heaven would include the England he knew in his youth. Rilke said one built one's own death by what one cherished most in life. My heaven will include the Austrian Alps, the Salzkammergut, North Carolina in the fall and the garden around me now, but the first foretaste of heaven was the garden, the woods and the view from Manor Farm.

I became close to my cousin, Donald, at Manor Farm. When we first went there, he was too young to shoot and I do not think he ever cared for it very much but he had to conform. He loved photographing the birds, in their nests. He showed me the walks through the woods, the way to the lake through the bluebell woods, the way to Sockn'ersh Manor and Burwash. My cousin, Rita, did not care for the woods as much as we did. She did not like to get her shoes muddy, and of course it often rained. I did not mind it; we walked for miles through the rain and it was so wonderful when the sun came out. When Donald started shooting he said he was often scared I would get shot, but I kept away from the shots. Donald taught me how to row on the lake in a dinghy, and although I never mastered sailing, enjoyed it when he put up the sail. We had a wonderful time.

My aunt always invited lots of friends at the weekend. She told me she felt so fortunate to have found such a wonderful place, she had to introduce as many people as possible to it. There were always at least twelve, sixteen or twenty there at the weekend to make tables for bridge. Donald and I did not care to play; we preferred table tennis in the Oast House, where we played for hours. He taught me how to play and at first he beat me all the time but gradually I learned from him to serve from way beyond the back line with a spin, and I beat him enough times for it to be interesting.

This Oast house had been modernized by previous owners with a garage beneath and a bedroom and bath at one end. The rest of the round room contained a ping pong table, a gramophone and Donald's records. He liked Paul Robeson and Harry Lauder, a Scottish singer very well known at the time with so heavy a brogue his words could hardly be understood as English. "Just a wee deoch un doris, a wee yin that's a'/ a wee deoch un doris afore ye ging awa'." He also sang "Loch Lomond" in a way I always remember. Later I taught Donald to dance to the records of Fred Astaire whom we both liked very much.

We took time out to go and hear the owls which Donald liked very much. He knew each kind of owl. I did not care for them so much for one thing I inherited from my mother was her superstition; she believed owls presaged death. I often thought of that, and I believe I told Donald. I much preferred the nightingales which I had heard the month before when he was still at boarding school. The place to hear the nightingales was by the stream in the orchard or by the lake. They liked to sing by water. Jefferson is supposed to have said that the mocking birds were America's nightingales, but only the nightingales have that ventriloquist quality on the long plangent note that comes at the end of the warbling. It is the most haunting sound.

Many interesting people came to stay for the weekend, including the Astronomer Royal and his wife, who lived at the Observatory at Greenwich. He brought down a small telescope which he installed on the terrace and showed and named for us the constellations A few years later his wife offered to present Rita and me at Court, which she could do as she had been presented. I would have liked the pomp and ceremony, but when she was young Rita was very shy and retiring and refused; she was sorry later.

Canon Raven who was the Chaplain at St. Johns College, Cambridge, was often there and offered to confirm us both. He could not instruct us as he was only there for the weekend but he suggested the vicar at Brightling could. Rita accepted but I felt the vicar preached the most ridiculous sermons I had ever heard. I needed to know the answers to some questions, such as the Fall of Man, and refused because I had already read C.S. Lewis "The Problem of Pain" and wanted answers. My mother was not very helpful. "Well you needn't bother," she said, "it's not that important." On the contrary, I felt it was very important. Donald was confirmed at Rugby and he did not think much of the vicar at Brightling either. I did enjoy the liturgy and the music at the 14th-century church, though, and we went there every Sunday. We walked along the road to church, which must have been two miles or more, but on the way back we ran down through the fields and reached home far sooner.

The Vicar of the church at Blackheath, his wife and son were down one weekend. They were not the usual hunting/ shooting /fishing sort. His wife played the piano and the son sang the Shakespeare songs written by a contemporary of Shakespeare, Arne. I was blown away; I had never heard these musical settings and wondered why anyone ever sang anything else.

Anthony was my age, fourteen, but his voice had not yet broken. He and I and Rita and Donald played doubles tennis, and I remember one evening afterwards, strolling through the garden, watching the sunset with him, and it was glorious and then it faded and he said: "Ichabod, the glory has departed." I was astounded. "What is that line?" He said "It comes from the Bible; my father has often said it." "It is poetry." And then he said, "Do you like poetry?" "Yes, do you?" And then we were reciting to each other, and somehow holding hands while we did. It was amazing to find someone of one's own age who loved poetry.

During that summer we met many weekends, and he introduced me to Bach. At that time the BBC had no classical music station. I had heard Mozart's "*Exultate, jubilate*" and had bought that record but had not heard any Bach. Anthony played Bach to me on his mouth organ. I do not know what it was, perhaps the Air on the G String. I was determined to learn more of Bach so went to the awe-inspiring His Master's Voice on Oxford Street. It was more like a museum than a store. I approached someone whom I recognized later as Captain Peacock. I was fourteen and rather small for my age. He inclined towards me, "How can I help you, Madam?" I had never been called "madam" before. "I like Bach, but don't know what." He motioned to an underling, "Are you free?" A Mr. Humphries glided up. "Can you help this young lady?" Mr. Humphries obliged and came up with the Fifth Brandenburg Concerto which was a wonderful choice. Bettina enjoyed it too and we listened to it on the steps leading down to our miserable garden where the blackbird sang.

I could not wait to tell Anthony that I had found some Bach on my own but when I went down to Manor Farm at the weekend Donald met me with a long face. "I am afraid I have some bad news," he said, "Anthony will not be coming here again; his father wrote a letter to the paper which my father considers Bolshie, and he doesn't want them here anymore." I was dumbfounded. "I am so sorry, I know you liked each other, but now you will just have to put up with me." I clutched at his sleeve. "Oh it's not a question of putting up with you; table tennis is better with two but it was so good to have someone to talk to who liked poetry." I suppose I could have asked Donald to find out Anthony's address. He did not know mine and at that time there were only telephone directories for districts, not for the whole of London, but I was too shy and so was he. He told me he had never cared for any girl as much as he did for me. He wanted to kiss me and I knew it and I wanted it too, but we were both fourteen in another age so Ichabod is what remains and the Bach Fifth Brandenburg Concerto.

Chapter 24

Change.

After the Junior Oxford I cannot remember anything particular happening at school. The years passed until the dreadful day when we were summoned to assembly and told that Threave House would be closing at the end of the term as the headmistress had religious mania. We did not know her very well. She taught us Scripture once a week, of which I remember nothing; she was the only woman who ever told me not to sit with my legs crossed. I was so amazed at this I asked my mother about it, and she said to forget it.

We were all appalled at the news and what it would mean to us. I was only fourteen and looked forward to many more years at school. Honor was already fifteen and the Annes and Ruth were sixteen. The last three decided that they were ready to be "finished off" in Switzerland. At that time it was not usual in England, as in America, for girls to go to the university. Of all those I grew up with only Dulcie Edwards went to Reading University. Instead they were sent abroad to "finishing" schools usually in Switzerland or

France to learn French. For Honor this was not possible as her people were not well off on a clergyman's salary. She had already met Peter whom she was later to marry; he was a policeman which we thought very funny because her sister had married a white Russian, Prince Imeritinsky, and was therefore known as Princess. Peter had been to public school and was hoping to get into Scotland Yard, but every applicant had to do a year on the "beat" as a Bobby patrolling the streets of London. Honor decided she was going to The Cordon Bleu to learn catering. "You are going to be a cook?" I was horrified. "Not a cook, a caterer, where I can earn lots of money and help Peter." Honor always amazed me. She had met Peter and he was very nice, but that she had already decided to get engaged when she was eighteen and married soon after, was just beyond me. "I'm not a brain," she said, "and I love to cook. The teachers all want you to go on to the university so you have to continue school to get London Matriculation, but why should I?" Life was falling apart.

Bettina and I went to Jean's boarding school for two terms which was not a success. I have never seen my sister so miserable. She missed the dogs and riding and she loathed communal life. I realized I was not cut out for it either, I particularly disliked hairwashing. I had washed my own hair for years, it was curly and short and dried quickly with a towel. At school Matron came from room to room and washed each girl's head in the basin and then we had to dry each other's hair. There were no hair dryers in the thirties. I found other people's wet hair repellent. Most of them had long hair, and when wet it was lank, dank and damp and took forever to rub dry.

I enjoyed the garden, which had lovely flowers, and tennis. I cannot remember learning anything at that school except my introduction to Virgil. I had studied Latin for four years and hated Caesar's horrid wars but the fourth book of the *Aeneid*, Dido's book, overwhelmed me with its poetry. The teacher was uninspiring, a short elderly woman who became embarrassed when someone asked what Dido and Aeneas were doing in the cave. It was Virgil who spoke: his empathy with Dido when she says, upon Aeneas announcing his leaving, "If I only had a child of yours, a little Aeneas playing by my chair, then I would not feel so utterly bereft." I could not believe a Roman, a man, had written those lines, and then his melancholy throughout, "*lachrymae rerum*" (the tears of things). The window was open, wallflowers were blooming outside and their dark velvet colors and scent seemed to melt into the words. Years later I wrote a poem about it.

WALLFLOWERS IN ENGLAND

Virgilian velvet
lies within these flowers.
Imperial red and Dido's gold,
maroon the death of kings
with lavender for rue,
the faded rose of columbine
and chestnut glossy brown,

the yellow of the sun,
all drowsy in a honeyed haze.

And after boring years in school
of Caesar's Gallic wars
On May the third began
the glorious *Aeneid.*

A window was ajar
and from the flowered wall
Rolled wave on fragrant wave,
Which Virgil adumbrated
Until the velvet petals were
transmuted into Latin.

After two terms at boarding school we were both back home going to school at St. Margaret's in Hampstead. Bettina was very impressed by Honor's decision to quit school study at fifteen and learn cooking. She wanted to do the same in a year or so and she could at St. Margaret's which had a Domestic Science branch. It was in the old part of Hampstead and we had a long climb up Frognal (corruption of Frog Lane), past the 15th—century St. Mary's Church (which was never open so I could never find out if it was similar to my first church at Finchley.) We went past Heath Street with its 18th-century houses, which I liked.

I do not remember learning anything at that school but I made another lifelong friend, Kay. Bettina left school earlier than I did and Kay and another friend and I used to go and have tea in one of the cafes in the High Street. It was the autumn term, and dusk fell early and there was something mysterious in Heath Street and the little alley ways that looked so old and the graveyard by the church. When the lights came on we were still out in the dark, exploring different places to have tea, and it was fascinating.

Kay was born and bred a Londoner and at fifteen she knew all the bus and tube routes and she introduced me to Saturday matinees in the West End and the Old Vic. I saw John Gielgud in *Hamlet* seven times when I was fifteen. Kay came with me the first time, but I was so enthralled I had to go back and hear it again and again. I felt I was hearing Shakespeare as his contemporaries did, but without knowing any criticism I did not know, as they did, that the Ghost coming from below the stage was evil. They knew this from the Mystery plays which were acted out in wagons; was below, earth was the wagon and a ladder stood for heaven. I thought the Ghost was good for Hamlet loved him. Apart from this error I think had a wonderful introduction to the play. Ever after I heard it with Gielgud's voice.

After it closed at the Haymarket Kay led me to the Old Vic by tube, with changes, which I would never have managed myself. We heard *Romeo and Juliet* with one week Gielgud as Romeo and Olivier as Mercutio, and the next week they changed roles; then Olivier in *Richard III* and Shylock in *The Merchant of Venice* with Gielgud as Antonio; Gielgud as Lear which was so impressive and terrible I could not bear to see it again but I saw him many times as Prospero in *The Tempest*. I did not care for Olivier as *Othello* for he played it blackface and I do not think Shakespeare meant it that way, but he was very good in *Henry V* with Ralph Richardson as the Chorus. After *Hamlet* I liked best Gielgud in *Richard II* which I saw many times. "O! that I were as great/ as is my grief, or lesser than my name/or that I could forget what once I was/and not remember what I must be now . . ."

Kay also introduced me to ballet. Pavlova was doing her dance of the Dying Swan at the Golders Green Hippodrome, quite near us. Her parents took her for an evening performance but Mummy wasn't interested and Daddy was on the continent. Kay said there was a Saturday matinee and I should go, so I did on my own and came under another spell, most suitable for a Humanities major—music, visual beauty and movement, everything except words, and it was a surprise that I could get the same kind of high without words. I wanted to see more ballet but Kay said the Sadler's Wells ballet was only done at night and I would have to persuade my mother to take me for we did not yet go out at night alone. In the end I persuaded Mummy; I told her she would love it as she had been a dancer, so she agreed to go although she did not like the tube. She became as devoted to it as I was and we saw many memorable performances with Margot Fonteyn and Robert Helpman. The first was *Les Sylphides* and I was fascinated with Margot Fonteyn and her exquisite dancing, particularly her arms, which were so graceful and delicate they looked as if they should have held wings. We saw her in all the Tchaikowsky ballets, *Coppelia, Spectre de la Rose* which I believe had first been choreographed by Diaghalev for Nijinsky. It had music by Weber and I remember it especially. Frederick Ashton was the choreographer for the Sadler Wells Ballet at that time and he was a genius. He designed new ballets never seen before and I recall the *Dante Sonata* with music by Liszt. The dancers were all in white casting black shadows behind them, unforgettable. Then there was *The Wanderer's Sonata* by Schubert but I think Liszt orchestrated it. It was originally a song about the wanderer from the mountains who can never find rest anywhere and it ends "*Dort wo Du nicht bist, das ist das Glück*" (there, where you are not, there is happiness). Perhaps Schubert orchestrated it. Robert Helpman danced it against a mountain backdrop with scrim between him and the audience, suggesting clouds. I would like to think it was Schubert's orchestration for it was so good, but Ashton was very keen on Liszt.

I enjoyed going with my mother. She insisted on taking a taxi home. I thought this was extravagant for she had paid for our tickets and they were expensive. "After all the money your father has spent, "she said, "we can take a taxi home."

I did not stay long at St. Margaret's for my father discovered they did not give London Matriculation, the entry to the university, but School Certificate. He must have found this out himself for I do not remember making enquiries. In fact, I was so enthralled with the theatre and ballet, I recall little of my studies at that school. He announced one day that he had ascertained that I could not matriculate if I stayed at St. Margaret's so next term I was to go to the London Polytechnic, downtown near Oxford

Circus. I was not pleased to lose my friends and our teas but I soon found out I received a far better education at the Poly; it was the first co-educational school I had attended and the teachers were excellent. There was a young man who taught English who was the best teacher I had in school. We studied Milton's *Paradise Lost* for Matric, and he pointed out the debt to Virgil, not only for his epic similes but for his cadences. We did the earlier Milton too and I discovered there was someone in the 17th-century besides Shakespeare. The teacher read aloud first and then asked if anyone would like to try. A boy in my class whom I afterwards saw on TV said he would like to, and two others and I did. Milton was wonderful read aloud. Perhaps because of his blindness and love of music he concentrated on the sound.

The next term this young teacher taught Virgil, the sixth book of the *Aeneid.* My Latin was rusty as it was not given at St. Margaret's and I was not taking it for Matric, but I could not resist it, and fell under Virgil's spell again. I loved the Elysian fields. I asked the teacher why, after having a vision of the future glory of Rome, Aeneas had left the underworld by the gate for false dreams. He said many had asked that question and a modern classicist, Bowra, had suggested that people had concentrated too much on pious Aeneas, the stoic, and not on Virgil, the poet. He told me Virgil had been forced by the Emperor Augustus to write an epic for Rome to stand for what Homer had done for Greece and if he had refused it would have meant exile, perhaps death. He said it was told that Virgil had tried to destroy his work but had been prevented. I could not find the Bowra source, which he recommended, but years later I remembered what he had said.

The Shakespeare text we studied for Matric was *The Tempest,* the same we had falsely been given for Junior Oxford so that was easy for me, and *Paradise Lost* was the other. One student asked the teacher about *Paradise Regained* and he said: "No one ever reads it, there is only one great line in it, 'Thou shalt not tempt the Lord, thy God,' He said, and stood." I also took History, French, and Math and was allowed to take Botany instead of Biology as I could never imagine cutting up a frog.

I had time my last term for another elective and took this same teacher's Plato's *Republic* and that really blew my mind. I was so excited about the Ideal Forms and the Allegory of the Cave that I attempted to explain it to the family over the dinner table. I shall never forget how my father laughed at my attempts. Mummy never got it but I think Bettina did, years later, after I gave her *Jonathan Seagull.* I also took typing and shorthand at the Polytechnic and those came in very useful later. I certainly worked hard that year and did not go down to the farm except for the holidays, but took off for matinees on Saturdays with Kay.

Chapter 25

Bettina and Manor Farm.

I was therefore at home the weekend Bettina dropped her bombshell. Daddy had continued driving the family on Sundays to the cinema at Leicester Square where they showed the latest American films. Bettina said she had a surprise for his birthday to be delivered just before he went for the car, which was still "stabled" in the garage about ten minutes walk away. Mummy, Daddy and I were in the living room when suddenly Daddy said: "that is our car horn hooting outside." We all rushed to the front door and there was Bettina alone in the car which she had driven from the garage! We all gaped, how was this possible? One could at that time get one's driver's license at fifteen and she had turned fifteen two months ago, but how could she have learned to drive and got her license without anyone knowing? It turned out that Ronnie, the red-haired boy at the garage, had taught her to drive on his half-day off which was on Wednesday afternoons. Bettina had gone straight to the garage from school and as she came home at different times on various afternoons Mummy did not worry. Ronnie had not taken time off from work, and she had put petrol in the car with her pocket money. She could reverse, double park, drive in traffic, although Ronnie had not taken her downtown thinking that Daddy would like to do that first, but she had been in traffic as bad at Finchley Road and Swiss Cottage. He had taken her to get her license and she had had no trouble at all. I was impressed because some time ago I had gone to Robertsbridge with Donald and Mr. Piggott, who had taught him to drive, and Donald failed the test the first time. Everyone knew that London tests were harder than those given in the country. Daddy was tickled pink. "I must give that young man something." "Oh no," said Bettina, "he did it as a friend. You can thank him. He's at the garage now."

The red-haired boy had grown up since I last saw him and his hair did not stick up on end anymore. He was relieved that Daddy was pleased. Ronnie said that Bettina was perfectly capable of driving downtown as she had been used to heavy traffic on the Finchley Road, but he felt my father would want to be with her the first time. She drove down to Leicester Square and parked in the big garage near the cinema but Daddy drove back as it was dark and Bettina had not yet driven with lights. She soon did.

She had started taking cooking lessons at St. Margaret's at fourteen, and regaled us with delicious dishes when Cook was out. She spoilt me horribly by making me the most exquisite sandwiches when I went to matinees. We had to be there about two hours beforehand and queue up for the gallery at half a crown (2s.6d). The sandwiches were of thin brown bread and better without crusts, tongue, watercress and mustard. They added to the anticipation and I can still taste them.

She also learned something very useful at cooking school; how to change electric plugs. The electric system in England before the war was chaotic. We had always had two prong plugs but when the useful gadgets like electric toasters and kettles came in they had to have three prongs, and it took an engineer to change the plugs and we had had to wait for Daddy. The electric toaster was a delight. Before that one stood in front of a gas, electric or coal fire holding the toast which often fell off before done and one's shins became roasted.

Bettina had a special relationship with our black Labrador, Win. She exercised her on the heath each day with her friend Jimmy and her dog. As they went to different schools, they met at the Whitestone Pond. One day when Bettina was at the pond Win became anxious. She was on a leash, kept pulling it, looking at Bettina as if trying to tell her something. Jimmy was late which was unusual. At last Bettina decided to let Win have her way and show where she wanted to go. She led Bettina to the Vale of Health where they seldom went and to the pond, which had frozen over. A crowd was gathered there. Apparently a dog had fallen in and a young boy had gone in after the dog and was now being pulled out and an ambulance was called. "That is not a boy," Bettina told the crowd, "it is a girl with short hair and my friend." She gave the ambulance the telephone number of Jimmy's parents and took her dog back home.

It was fortunate she was there to give the information and take care of the dog. Jimmy soon recovered.

Bettina did not like Manor Farm; she thought it was haunted. When my uncle first bought the farm they had a couple of horses. It was no country for riding; too many woods and the fields all sown with barley, oats or wheat, not open like the downs. She and I did ride down the open-to-all road that ran through Uncle's property to Sockn'ersh and Burwash village. Each time we did so the horses shied at a certain point in the hedge, coming and going they shied at the same place. Bettina was very interested, dismounted and looked all around to see what had spooked them but could find nothing. We asked Mr. Piggott, the gardener, about it. He had noticed it too but merely said in his rolling Sussex dialect, "Summat bad must have happened there. Stands to reason in four hundred years." Bettina did not like it and never wanted to go to the farm again.

When my aunt found out Bettina could drive she asked her as a favor to come down for a few days in the holidays, and take her over to Hastings to a meeting, so Mr. Piggott would not have to leave the garden. Bettina had to oblige but she insisted on bringing Win with her who was a house dog and slept in a basket in Bettina's room. Bettina and Auntie Dora were having dinner on trays by the fireplace in the dining room the first night, and a few minutes before they switched on the 9 p.m. news Win arose from her place at Bettina's feet, growling. She went the whole length of the large paneled room to the far right corner and stood there, haunches up, growling. Bettina called her back, and she was a very well trained dog and always obeyed, but not this time. She stood facing the corner, hair on end, growling. When Bettina switched on the news she stopped. The next night, at the very same time, a few minutes before the 9 pm news, she did the same thing. Bettina was scared stiff; she felt Win saw something bad. The third night it happened Bettina told Auntie Dora she had to take Win and go home. She had already driven to Hastings so Auntie Dora had to agree.

After the incident with Jimmy and the pond we all felt Win had some kind of second sight, and Daddy said Bettina need not go down to the farm again if she did not want to. He was very interested in the occult and took the incident quite seriously.

It did not worry me, I loved the oak linenfold panelled dining room. I always sat at the side of the table looking out into the garden. Donald sat near or next to me and if the celery became stuck at the top of the table, which it often did, he would get up and fetch it. We both loved celery; I always think of him when I eat it. I had a special feel for that dining room for I was allowed to do the flower arrangement on the long refectory table.

I became very friendly with Mr. Piggott who taught me a lot about gardening, when and how to prune and fertilize roses, when to change annuals and how to stamp them in firmly, "heel and toe." He also showed me how to cut flowers, particularly sweet peas, down to the next leaflet. The sweet peas grew in the vegetable garden, not among other flowers, because they needed a deep trough of manure to do well. I had been cutting them for some time and bringing them in for Auntie to fix but she was late one afternoon, and the bowl was already there, so I started to arrange them. Sweet peas come in pale pink, dark rose, lilac, purple and white and most people put them in haphazardly and they are pretty like that. I thought I would clump them in shades so that they would reflect more in the dark oak table. Mrs. Piggott, the cook, was thrilled and said to my aunt that I should always do them, as I did them best, my first compliment.

Chapter 26

Matriculation and Germany.

I do not remember this exam as well as the Junior Oxford but I went to the University of London to take it and the printed exams were on University paper. I found them very impressive and kept them, together with my certificate of Matriculation, in the bottom drawer of Grandpa's jewel box. It was well I did so for they came in useful later. I sometimes think that if I had not had that box I would not have had anywhere to keep them and would not have bothered. It struck me later that this was one of the coincidences that Jung would have called a "synchronicity."

My father seemed proud and insisted on accompanying me to the University of London to apply for the autumn term, but we had an unpleasant surprise. One could not enter the University until eighteen, and I was only just seventeen. What was I to do now? My aunt stepped into the breach. My cousin Rita had left school a year before at sixteen, and spent several months in a "finishing" school in Switzerland where she had learned French, and had become less shy and retiring. My aunt suggested that she send Rita and me for several months to a family in Germany to learn that language. She had several connections in Berlin, Munich and other places in Germany, and so did my father. I was thrilled at the idea; I had never been abroad and the idea of learning a new language appealed to me.

My aunt knew of a Graf and Gräfin (Count and Countess), who had lost their castle and their money in the Depression and who now used their flat in Berlin to house foreign students who wished to learn German. My aunt said she had several friends as well in Berlin who would take us to concerts and operas as well as to museums and palaces. We would not go to school but an excellent teacher would come in every day to teach us grammar and vocabulary and no English would be spoken. Auntie Dora thought we would learn enough in three months or so to go on to Munich and the Bavarian Alps and so it was arranged. All the family came to Victoria Station to see us off, and my aunt came with us to Berlin and left us at the Rehbinders.

It was a beautiful flat. My room was small, painted pale green with high ceilings and curving rococo decorations and looked on to a courtyard with a little fountain; it smelt of apples. Rita and I were told not to talk to each other in English but to try as soon as possible to use what little German we learned daily. There was an American boy there, George, who had been in Germany some time and he helped us out, and another boy. We were all very serious about learning the language.

We had a very good teacher, Ada von Menshausen. She soon found out I liked poetry and she gave me Rilke's *Neue Gedichte* and translated one for me: "*Die Blätter fallen, fallen wie von weit*" (the leaves are falling, falling from afar) and encouraged me to look up vocabulary so that I could understand the poems. I fell under Rilke's spell. Rita was better on Grammar. The Germans do not only have a different gender for each noun but the adjectival endings are different according to whether the noun is masculine, feminine or neuter. There is a lot of memory work involved. I think my love of words helped me study. I liked to learn the different ways of expressing sensations but I was never clear on the genders and tried to speak quickly, or in the plural, where the adjectival endings were the same. I did not find the verbs as hard to remember as in French; quite a few were similar to English verbs. I remember studying very hard, writing out vocabulary, which was a pleasure, but the adjectival endings and noun genders were a pain.

The Graf and Gräfin were like ghosts from another age; they did not seem quite real. The Graf was a thin old man who with great ceremony lit his samovar for tea in the drawing room every afternoon. We were expected to be there and to make conversation, but not about politics. It was already Hitler's Germany and we gathered neither of them liked him. The Gräfin came from Vienna I think. She was usually dressed in a long skirt used for riding side-saddle and she spoke often of the Lipizzaner horses. She was very elegant but somehow far away.

The household was really run by the cook, Frau Rupp, who cooked excellent meals and took a fancy to Rita and me. She gave us hard boiled eggs on creamed spinach very often because we liked it; the boys were not so keen. I never tasted sauerkraut there but Hungarian goulash and Wiener Schnitzel were often on the menu. Frau Rupp took us to the open air market to buy the vegetables. I had not seen one before; the climate in England is not suitable. I was delighted with the colors of the vegetables and all the flowers. A young man came up to me and offered me a bunch of primroses; when I tried to pay he shook his head and handed me the flowers.

Friends of my aunt invited us to the opera. It was Wagner's *Reingold*. I had hoped for Mozart as I had already queued for the gallery to hear Ezio Pinza in *Don Giovanni*. *Reingold* was incredibly long and there was a two—hour interval in the middle when the Germans went to eat in the restaurant, which seemed part of the opera. The smell of beer and sauerkraut is always connected with that opera for me. I asked our teacher if we could not hear a Mozart opera and she took us to *Zauberflöte*. I know some people think the Lady of the Night is too shrill, but this one was delightful with a fairy voice, thin as silk. I was delighted with her and rather upset that she turned out to be evil. Of course I liked the bass choruses of "*Isis und Osiris*" and "*In diesen heiligen Hallen.*" In fact, *Zauberflöte* remained my favorite opera for life.

We were also taken to hear Furtwängler conduct Beethoven's "Pastoral Symphony." The music for "After the Storm" has remained in my mind always. Rita said that Hitler was at that performance but I do not remember him there. We did see him at a torchlight procession for Thor and Woden, and that really scared me. It seemed so barbaric. George, the American boy, had heard him speak and said he was a raving lunatic, so we never wanted to hear him and he was not mentioned at the Rehbinders.

A Jewish friend of my father's took us out to dinner and he was the first to tell us of what Hitler was doing to the Jews. We were of course horrified and rather scared. Daddy's friend was leaving Germany shortly and already had his passport and plans made, so we were glad about that. We tried to talk to our teacher, Ada, about the situation but she said it would be good if we knew as little as possible.

We visited the museums but I do not remember them as clearly as those we saw in Munich later. I do remember one great Rembrandt in the Kaiser Friedrich Museum. We were taken to Potsdamm which I enjoyed for its 18th-century elegance, and to Charlottenburg Schloss where we heard a Haydn Trio play in contemporary dress, and that has stayed with me. We were invited to a ball at the British Embassy and were accompanied by George and the other boy. I wore a dress of my mother's, blue taffeta with a few chiffon flowers on the skirt, and felt very elegant; it was my first ball.

What else remains of Berlin? The Tiergarten; we lived near there and Rita and I walked there a lot. I recall stepping off a pavement and having the strongest case of "déjà vu" that I had ever had. I suppose all young people experience it at some time or other and I certainly had but never so strongly. I was sure I had been there before in another life. Perhaps one of my ancestors had.

While I was in Berlin my family moved from the house we had rented in Hampstead for ten years to the first house they had owned, a smaller place in Hendon. We had often passed Hendon on the Great North Way with its impressive sign: "To the North." I was sorry to miss the excitement; my mother and sister assured me they would wait for my return to plan the garden. I had the first and only letter I had ever had from my father and I could not read it. His writing was illegible as I had often heard Mummy say. I kept it in the bottom drawer of Grandpa's jewel box as his only letter and years later after correcting hundreds of student papers and using a magnifying glass, I deciphered it. In it he laid out a plan for the garden which was just what I would have wanted, with apple and cherry trees in the background. He also said he would await my return.

After a few months in Berlin we moved to Munich, to a student house run by one of the Gräfin's friends. Here the atmosphere was much more casual. There were several English students, and we were left more on our own and there was no teacher. We knew German quite well by this time; I had even started dreaming in German. A young man from Oxford, Michael, fell in love with me, and I had my first kiss on a helter-skelter. It was not as exciting as I had imagined but quite pleasant. I was getting worried that at seventeen I had not yet been kissed. He had asthma and had been told he might die before he was twenty five. I thought this quite romantic. He had a friend, David, who obligingly fell for Rita and we did quite a lot together, but I chiefly remember dancing with Michael and he always asked for an English tune popular at the time, "When I grow too old to dream, I'll have you to remember." I enjoyed this and also visiting the art museums in Munich with him. He was reading English at Oxford so we had quite a lot in common. In *Die alte Pinakothek* in Munich he introduced me to Greek art and that really made an impression. I had not seen any before, had not visited the British Museum. Munich was supposed to be Hitler's city but I felt his presence far less there than in Berlin. Although Rita and I never developed a taste for beer the boys took us to the beer halls where one could get wine, and there was a very cheerful atmosphere. We heard another Mozart opera, *Die Entführung aus dem Serail,* at the rococo theatre built by Cuvillier and saw the most beautiful palace, the Amalienburg.

After about a month in Munich we moved on to Schliersee in the Bavarian Alps. The mountains did not catch my heart as the Salzkammergut did years later. The first impression was foreboding; it was a grey day when we arrived, but I soon learned to love and watch for the *Alpenglühen*, the rose light that lit the peaks at sunset, and then turned to lilac and silver. Michael and David came with us and we stayed with a very pleasant woman in a chalet a little way up the mountain, looking down on the lake.

One evening we were standing there watching the *Alpenglühen*; dusk fell and the fireflies came. I had never seen fireflies before; we had glow-worms in England in the honeysuckle around the old well at the end of the sunken rose garden, but the fireflies were more entrancing. Lights were coming up around the lake and suddenly a voice started singing, a beautiful voice. "Schubert" someone suggested but nobody knew the song, and I was haunted by it for years. Eventually I heard it again, recognized it and learned the name. "*Der Jungling an der Quelle*" (The Youth at the Spring). Years later I wrote a poem of the memory.

SCHUBERT

Child in the mountains at night,
fireflies were piercing the fields
sprinkling the scent of the hay
grasses occasionally lit.

Someone was singing there down by the lake,
lamps were reflected in drops,
music was seizing the dark.

"Schubert" suggested a voice,
No one remembered the song,
always remaining unknown,
sweeter than anything else.
Later it came back again
now with a name,

Schubert "The Youth at the Spring."
Friends called their daughter "Louisa"
also because of the song;

then it was shortened to "Lou"
ending the spell held so long.

We used to go down and dance in a garden café by the lake where they served a wonderful drink, "Bowle:" It was made of white wine and champagne with strawberries drowned in it the night before. It was heady and full of bubbles. Rita and I used to see if we could walk a straight line along the bedroom carpet when we came home to make sure we had not drunk too much.

We climbed the Rotwand, my first mountain, and I was glad that Michael's asthma made him go slower than David, but it did not seem to bother him much. We had a great month there and made excursions to Innsbruck with its golden roof and to Oberammergau where we saw the costumes for the Passion Play, which was not given that year. Michael asked me to visit him at Oxford when we returned and I said I would love to if my parents allowed it. "Tell them I will get you a room at The Mitre," he said. It was a happy time. He and David left to return to England and Rita and I went on to visit Rothenburg and Nuremberg on the way back to Berlin and home.

Rothenburg was a medieval town, filled with what I liked best in Germany, the beautiful flowering window boxes. I had never seen them in England. They were often filled with geraniums, an English flower. They also sometimes had flowers of many colors new to me called *fliessendes wasser* (flowing water) which appeared after the war in England and America as "Impatience." I had seen the window boxes in Berlin and Munich but never in such splendor as in Rothenburg where they lit up the old half-timbered houses and brought them to life.

Nuremburg was a grimmer medieval town and we did not like it from the first. And there we had a dreadful experience. We were walking along a street and suddenly quite near to us a soldier started attacking a man for no apparent reason. I screamed and Rita turned to a passer-by and asked what was happening. "It is an SS officer beating up a Jew. Don't you see his yellow star?" We stared at each other in horror and Rita said: "Let's go to the post office and ring up Mother and tell her we want to come home at once." We did this and Auntie said we should return to the Rehbinders immediately and she would send the tickets home to Berlin that day. Did we think we could return alone? We both felt adult enough to do that and could not wait to do so. I had never seen any violence before this, not even in American films, for there was still a censor.

The Graf and Gräfin seemed more ghost-like than ever. I am not sure if they recognized us although it had been only two months since we left. Frau Rupp did, however, and hugged us both and cooked us hard-boiled eggs with creamed spinach. Our teacher, Ada, came round to see us and she and Rita exchanged addresses; they corresponded till the war or even afterwards. Our return is rather vague but I do remember seeing for the first time the white cliffs of Dover from a ship and knowing they symbolized home.

The family met us at Victoria with Bettina driving a splendid new car Daddy had given her for her sixteenth birthday, a Lincoln Mercury. I had never seen her look so happy; she looked small in the driver's seat. It was the family car but always known as Bettina's, for she drove it the most. Rita went down to the farm with her family and I returned with mine to Hendon, our new home. It was on a hill, looking over London, and from my window I saw the familiar chimney pots. The garden was waiting for me although some roses had been planted and were blooming.

Daddy was very proud and pleased at how well I spoke German, and we often talked together in that language. He felt there would soon be a war between England and Germany and said he had invested a great deal of money in the Bristol Oil Wharves. If there were a war he would become very rich and if not, more and more people were going to buy cars and would need oil. He was the most interested in all I had to tell of Germany and he said something I remember, "Of course, if they split the atom, that will be the end of the world as we know it." I asked him to explain and from him first learned of the atom, neutrons, protons etc. I was fascinated and wished later I had told him of the phenomenon I had noticed as a child, sitting high up on the Downs and looking over the Weald. From afar I had seen a steam train draw up at a station and seen the puff of smoke which always ensued. The sound of the hoot had come some seconds later although I knew it had sounded at the same time. This had always intrigued me and I wished I had asked Daddy about it. He would have been glad to explain. We became closer after my return from Germany

Chapter 27

What now?

Anne gave a party to celebrate my return and for Honor and Peter who were engaged and shortly to be married. Honor was just nineteen. The tooth that had always hung a little over her lower lip had been corrected. I rather missed it and she said she did too but her mother had insisted. At the party I met another Michael and learned that if you had once been kissed it seemed Open Sesame and other people wanted to kiss you. We had danced for a bit and then went outside in the garden where there were drinks and chairs and before I knew it, I was kissed. I gasped and said "We don't know each other. Can't we talk a bit?" "It is much easier to kiss," he replied. I had to laugh; it was for him but not for me. To my amazement I found I enjoyed kissing him just as much as the first Michael at Oxford whom I was going to visit. I wondered if I were a Scarlet Woman. He asked me out again and I guiltily found myself agreeing.

I was surprised that my parents were quite content that I should visit the first Michael at Oxford, and I felt very grown up. I fell in love with Oxford; it was more beautiful than any town in Germany even though it had no window boxes. The college gardens were full of flowers and the curving High Street had spires and bells. Michael was at Merton, the cherry trees were out with bluebells underneath. We danced, we went on the river, we strolled down Addison's Walk; the chestnuts were coming out, I was enchanted, but did I love him? Evidently not for I had a horrible shock when he said to me "I really want to have an affair with you, but I don't suppose you would, would you? It is done a lot up here." I most certainly would not and was amazed that he should ask me. Did kissing someone mean that you would have an affair? I could not imagine how he came to that idea and felt I needed advice, but whom to ask?

For the first and last time I asked my mother on the question. "Never kiss a man till the ring is on your finger," was her pronouncement. I hooted, "You can't mean you kept to that?" "Well," my mother admitted, "as near as could be. Anyway never let a man kiss you the first time he takes you out!" She said that with such authority I thought it might be true, but felt I would seek another guide. I soon went down to Manor Farm and asked Donald who was then at Cambridge. He admitted that Michael was right, people did have affairs, but he did not hold with it, "and nor do you, do you?" he asked. "No, I do not but did not know if kissing someone involved an affair." He assured me it did not. He had kissed several girls with no intention of an affair. I was somewhat relieved.

He had a friend from Cambridge down for the weekend, I forget his name, but he fell for me and I rather liked him. He had just graduated with a Second in English (which was good, hardly anybody got a First) and we had a great deal in common. He was working in his own bookstore. He asked me out and I looked forward to it very much. We went dancing and I enjoyed it more than with either of the Michaels and was quite looking forward to kissing him goodnight when I remembered my mother's dictum. That was the most stupid thing I ever did; I did not let him kiss me and he did not ask me out again. I learned then to play it by ear and not to ask my mother for advice.

Honor had a very quiet wedding. Her father married her in his own church and the reception was in their garden. There were no bridesmaids, only her sister as Matron of Honor, Princess Imeritinsky, who had married the white Russian. Honor and Peter seemed very happy. He had been given a job up North for a year and they were to go there right after their honeymoon so we would not see them for some time. I had not seen Honor for many months but we always picked up where we left off and laughed a lot.

Chapter 28

What now?

The big question for me now was what was I to do with my life? I had thought that my aunt had paid for my expenses in Germany and indeed she was willing, but Daddy did not like being a poor relation and Mummy told me he had sent her a check for my expense. I was upset about this. I never minded accepting from Auntie Dora for I knew she was wealthy and that she loved me as a daughter. I was concerned that Daddy had spent a lot of money, the new house, the beautiful car for Bettina, Germany for me and the Bristol Oil Wharves which he kept mentioning. He did not bring up the question of the university and I thought enough money had been spent on me, "finishing" me off in Germany and giving me a new language. College was very expensive in those days, and I only knew one girl, Dulcie Edwards, who went. She had now graduated and was teaching at a girls' school. At that time I thought all you could do after the university was teaching and I was not sure I wanted to do that.

If I had not been given Germany I thought I would have liked an Art Course at the London Polytechnic. I loved water color although I had not done it since Threave House. Of course it would have been much better for my future had I gone to London University on my return from Germany. Later I wished I had but at the time I felt I should get a job using the gift of the German language which I had been given. Luck, Chance or synchronicity produced one.

For some time people in England had been aware of Hitler's persecution of the Jews and Jewish committees had been set up to help Orthodox Jews to get out of Germany. Bertha Bracey, a Quaker who had lived a long time in Vienna, felt something should be done to help the *Mischlinge* (people who had just one Jewish relative, were not Orthodox, some were even Christian) but still they were persecuted. Long before the *Anschluss* (when Hitler annexed Austria) she left Vienna and started a Quaker Committee in London in order to help these people. I saw an advertisement in the paper that the Quakers urgently needed German speakers as interpreters, and so applied. I felt this was something I should and could do. I remembered from Miss Le Pla how good the Quakers were in their humanitarianism.

I was accepted at once and put to work the same day in a room with another 17—year old girl. Our job was to interview refugees already in England who wanted to help relatives or friends get out of Germany and Austria, for Austrian *Mischlinge* were already discriminated against even before the *Anschluss*. We were immediately dubbed the "Kindergarten" and felt very abashed interviewing distinguished men of letters, professors, doctors and many musicians. It needed a certain sleight of hand or mind. I found the best way I could manage it was to translate their German immediately into English and write it down in shorthand and then type it up later to hand to a case-worker. The case-workers often had worked with Bertha Bracey in Vienna and some knew German, but their job was to decide from our notes who were the most needy cases and also to find rich Quakers or other English people who would give guarantees of support to the refugees. They had contacts with the Home Office, Civil Service and even Members of Parliament. I was paid three pounds a week which was quite good in those days. It was the first money I had ever earned.

I worked with a case-worker called James, who was in his upper twenties and had studied singing in Vienna. He had a lovely voice and would sing a capella Schumann's *Dichterliebe* at the drop of a hat, which was usually once a day at my request. I was sorry he did not sing Schubert but I loved especially one of his songs which ended "*und vor deinen Fenster soll klingen das Lied der Nachtigall*" ("before your window shall sound the song of the nightingale") and thought "*Nachtigall*" expressed much better than "nightingale" the bird's song, even to the echo quality in it. There was another song about the Rhine and Cologne Cathedral. I remembered the cathedral where we had heard an organ recital and had seen the Gero Crucifix, a 10th-century wooden carving which expressed suffering, and also a painting of a Madonna in a rose garden. I was glad to recall that.

We often worked long hours, not the usual office day, and it was anything but the usual office. I was plunged into a world of music and suffering, sometimes above my head. The Rose Quartet, led by the concertmaster of the Vienna State Opera, had been brought over as refugees and they gave a recital of Beethoven's late quartets. I gave out programs at that concert; I had never heard music like it, it was not earthly. I did not understand it but floated along hoping it would never end. Dr. Bergmann, a refugee I helped, was a fine musician, and obtained a position at Schotts transposing Telemann's figured bass. He said it was a shame I did not play an instrument since I loved music so much and taught me the recorder from Bach's Little Magdalene book transposed for recorders. I was very grateful.

I found my German was adequate but I had problems with translating all the German offices and bureaus, and asked James for help. He advised me to go to a Student Language Club near St. Martin's-in-the—Fields and there I would find a man in the German section who could help. I went there and found all the help I needed. There were students of several languages there and after about an hour or so classes stopped, a gramophone was put on and we started dancing. It was there I met Howard.

Chapter 29

Howard.

He was an American pianist who had just received his B.A from Yale and had been awarded the Ditson Fellowship for one year's study in England with Nicolai Medtner, a Russian composer and pianist who was well known at the time. Unfortunately, Medtner did not speak English so Howard had to learn French. He had studied for a month in France before coming to England and had learnt French in school but was having difficulties understanding Medtner and was therefore coming to French classes. Howard said he fell in love with me the first time he saw me; perhaps he did. I was slower but he was certainly the most interesting man I had met, although our first two dates were disastrous. He invited me to the circus, which I did not like ; it smelt and although the acrobatic turns were beautiful they scared me and my heart beat too fast. The next date was to Hampton Court and this sounded better. I was interested to see an English palace after all the German palaces and I preferred it to them, except for Charlottenburg Schloss with its mirrors and open windows filled with flowering chestnuts. Hampton Court was simpler and it had some good paintings including a Breughel entitled, "The Massacre of the Innocents"; it was not babies but turkeys being slaughtered. I have not forgotten that painting.

Afterwards we went into the garden; would we had stayed there! Howard wanted to go into the famous Hampton Court Maze although there were signs posted: "Enter at your peril." The hedges were about ten feet high. Now they have keepers outside to help anyone who cannot find the way out and start yelling, and maps inside, but then they did not. You entered at your peril. I was most reluctant but Howard said he had a good sense of orientation and he was sure he could find his way out. He was dead set on going in, so most unhappily we did and became lost and could not find the way out.

I think my claustrophobia started then. It seemed hours before we found what seemed to be the center and a seat there. He said, "Now you sit there and I will find the way out and I shall call your name occasionally and you return my name. There are four paths leading out of this place. I will take the one to the furthest right first and make a map of it, and then the second right etc. I will keep calling." He gave me a kiss and said not to worry. I was impressed by his attitude but scared to death. He went off and I was left alone; it was getting dark. I still remember the horror. He returned after the first path, showed me the clear map he had made of it, and said he would try the second right. It was not until the third path that he found the way out and returned triumphantly with a map of right and left turns clearly marked. We found our way out although I felt more dead than alive and at the time was not anxious to see him again, but I did because he was interesting.

The next time he took me out was to Kew Gardens. He knew the old song "Come down to Kew in lilac time." It was perfect, the lilacs were out and the cherry trees with bluebells beneath. He had never seen the latter and he liked flowers more than any man I had ever known. He knew the names of quite a number and was anxious to learn the names of those he had not seen before, which impressed me.

We then started going to concerts together and heard a memorable Beecham concert. Sir Thomas Beecham was well known for his outspoken language and his rudeness to everybody. He had a running row with Ernest Newman, a well known music critic. Newman did not care for Mahler and made a statement: "England has no need of Mahler." Sir Thomas was determined to show that England did and he performed Mahler's Second Symphony, "The Resurrection," which I had never heard before and think many had not. It was superb with its alto aria and the vocal chorus at the end, "Resurrection," and the audience gave him a standing ovation, which was not usual in England. He hushed the applause. "Ladies and gentlemen, in being here this afternoon you have shown yourselves to be the most intelligent of the British musical public." More applause. He spoke again. "No need for applause, that is nothing much to be proud of." Everybody loved that and applauded again. Howard laughed so much he had tears in his eyes; he had never heard anyone like Beecham.

I was anxious to hear Howard play but it proved to be difficult. He had a practice room at Wigmore Hall but visitors were strictly forbidden. I told him we had an electric Duo-Art piano at home and asked him to dinner but he was rather dubious about it. He remembers well the first meeting with my mother; Daddy was on the continent. He said Mummy gave him the first wine he had ever drunk. He played some Chopin, the E Flat Nocturne and also the Military Polonaise which Bettina loved, and ever after asked him to play that. He did not want to play Beethoven. Mummy asked him if he knew the Charleston which she had discovered when she and Daddy paid a visit to America during the Risdon years. Howard said his elder cousin had taught him but he had never danced it except with her. Mummy found a record, put it on, and soon to our amazement they were kicking out knees and elbows in the most amazing dance we had ever seen. My mother was delighted with Howard and when he told her he lived in a house for music students with a piano in his room on which he practiced, but that the landlady would only permit girls in their rooms if they had a letter from their mothers, she was quite willing to write one. "I am sure you would always behave like a perfect gentleman, Howard," she told him. What a different world!

After that I often went to dinner at his boarding house. He told me the food was dreadful, they always had Brussel sprouts, but at last I heard him play Beethoven.

He was studying the Waldstein and the Appassionata at the same time and I had trouble distinguishing them but was overwhelmed by the power he displayed and became more and more attached to him. I always cared most for people who could teach me something or make me laugh and Howard did both.

Howard took me to meet his teacher, Nicolai Medtner, who seemed glad that I could speak French. He lived in Hampstead and had a beautiful garden of many kinds of chrysanthemums which he named after composers. He told Howard I had the soul of a musician for I guessed correctly on Mozart and Schubert. Howard did not and we both failed on Beethoven. Howard played Chopin there and one of Medtner's Fairy Tales.

Ralph Vaughan Williams invited Howard for a visit which impressed me. People always ask me if he pronounced his name "Ralph" or "Rafe." In his lifetime he was always known as "Ralph." After his death it was his wife who insisted he be called "Rafe" and I can only think it was because she had read Nancy Mitford's famous book on U and Non-U people. U people were the upper class who said "dinner" and "napkin" instead of "supper" and "serviette" which was non-U or middle class; they also left out the "l" in "golf," and so I suppose it was for this reason that "Ralph" became "Rafe." We said "dinner" and "napkin" but we never left out the "l." Everyone discussed the Mitford book. Vaughan Williams was very kind to Howard, and congratulated him on his style.

Howard also taught me a lot about architecture and he was a great admirer of Christopher Wren. Previously I had cared more for Gothic churches, but Howard took me around and showed me all the city churches Wren had built. He was enthusiastic about how simple they were except for the spires into which Wren had put all his ingenuity. He had known, said Howard, that the city would grow up around the churches and only the spires would be seen. He showed how great Wren was in designing St. Paul's in that he realized columns were no longer necessary to hold up the arched roof. I thought of this in the war when the Guildhall at Windsor was bombed and repairs had to be done to the ceiling. Wren had built the Guildhall but the city fathers had refused to pay him until he put in columns, so he did but he stopped them two inches short of the ceiling. This was only discovered in the war. It made headlines.

Howard made sketches of several of the spires of the city churches and it turned out he had been undecided whether to be an architect or a pianist, but he had great success with piano recitals in Newport, R.I., and was offered a scholarship to Yale in music. His parents were very poor, and this was the only way he could get to college. "Also," he told me, "since I was eight I have practiced four hours a day in order to become a concert pianist." I was astonished; four hours a day since he was eight! "Supposing it doesn't work out?" I asked. "It must," said Howard, "it is my life." I felt scared for him. He was a magnificent pianist, but there were so many. Schnabel had said his son, with whom he played

Schubert Duos, would never be a concert pianist "for he could not make the contacts.in the music world."

We went to art galleries and the British Museum where we saw the Elgin Marbles. Howard was also interested in oriental art; he gave me a Hokusai print he had found in the Charing Cross Road and "The Silent Traveller in London" by Lin Yutang who was Chinese. He opened my eyes and mind to a lot of things besides music. We studied the paintings in the National Gallery together and went to hear Shakespeare. I became a Londoner under his guidance. He loved standing on Westminster Bridge and looking down the river. He said he had found his soul in England.

Meanwhile I continued at the Quakers, interpreting, translating into English and transforming into shorthand which I then typed for the caseworkers. More interpreters were added including Doreen who had studied singing in Germany and who became a friend and taught me Lieder. Howard came with me to concerts the refugees put on. We heard *Drei Groschenoper* which impressed us both but not as much as *Die Winterreise* sung by a wonderful baritone. I remember someone quoting from the song "*Der Wegweiser*" (The Signpost), "*Eine Strasse muB ich gehen die noch keiner ging zurück.*" (I must follow a road that no one returns) and saying "that is the song of the refugee."

Chapter 30

Tragedy.

Before the news on the radio they gave police bulletins. One night I heard, "If anyone knows Harry F. Robertson will you please contact Westminster Hospital. He was knocked down by a tram on the Embankment and is now in critical care." Daddy's Club, The Army and the Navy, was near the Embankment. I rushed up to Mummy and Bettina and we phoned Westminster Hospital. It was Daddy. In those days one did not carry I.D. cards, but he must have had his business card on him but without home address or telephone. Bettina drove us to Westminster Hospital. They told us that Daddy had been knocked down by a tram and was suffering from laceration of the brain and not likely to live. He had been hit by a tram which had come from his blind eye side. He lived six days, groaning all the time. We stayed with him, spelling each other. I remember Bettina and I were on the Embankment looking over the river and I was muttering to myself "Friends, Romans, countrymen, lend me your ears/ I come to bury Caesar not to praise him."

I was not aware I was saying it aloud until Bettina said: "Oh, do shut up!" I was not thinking too clearly at that time. I remember thinking that if his brain were lacerated he would not want to live and I would not want it for him. He had such a good mind. He died after six days of agony.

Bob Fletcher, his good friend who played golf with him and sometimes rode with him and Bettina at Richmond, came to me and said: "Your mother is not capable of making a decision. You are the eldest daughter. Do you want the body brought to your house?" I did not know what to say. I felt the body was not Daddy and did not want the dead body with the bloody bandages in the house. I said no but felt I had done a dreadful thing. Bob Fletcher said: "Well, I will then have to go and say goodbye to my dear friend in the morgue."

Mummy knew Daddy wanted to be cremated. I did not know about that and was always afraid of fire. I would rather he had been buried in the earth in an old churchyard. Instead we had a ceremony, a church of England burial service, but at Golders Green crematorium. I was conscious of flames all the time, even felt I saw them although I do not think that possible.

Auntie Dora was there and I was thankful for her for after the funeral more horrors evolved. My father had not left a will and all his money was in Bristol Oil wharves, which his partners would not release to his widow, so there was no money. Jimmy Wilding, a lawyer friend of my parents, wanted to contest it but Auntie had already sent a lawyer to investigate the position and said it was hopeless. I felt dreadful for Bettina. Not only did she love my father the most but she lost riding at Richmond, and she had to give up her beautiful car, the Lincoln Mercury. My aunt said she would look after us but Mummy did not like her very much, and she wanted Jimmy Wilding to contest. It was a miserable time. At least I had my job; Bettina had nothing and she was not trained for anything except driving. After a while Ronnie found her a job driving an old lady who had "stabled" her car at his garage but was not happy driving anymore, so Bettina had something to do.

Howard was very helpful to me and would play Beethoven for hours to me which seemed the only comfort. I did not want to talk, only to listen to music. The Fletchers were very kind to Mummy and after about a month they took her out to the theatre once a week and she stayed with them overnight. One night when she was gone I was due to go to a concert but developed a terrible headache and so came home. I was surprised to see a car in the driveway but even more surprised when I entered and saw Bettina and Ronnie sitting close together on the couch with the remains of a bottle of wine and a dinner a *deux*. I do not know who was most startled but I pulled myself together and said "Hullo, Ronnie, how are you? I have come home with a dreadful headache and must go to bed at once, forgive me," and vanished upstairs. So this was the reason Bettina had no boyfriends !

In the morning before Mummy came home I asked her, "Does Mummy know?" "No. Daddy liked him," Bettina said defensively. Yes, but . . . . in this homogenous age it is impossible to convey the class structure in England before the war. "How long has this been going on?" I asked. "Since he taught me to drive, about two years," said Bettina. "We are friends. He knows I will always have to look after Mummy, but I will never love another man but Ronnie." I looked at her. I knew my sister. She probably spoke the truth. "You don't always have to look after Mummy," I said, "she may get married again." "Oh no, she won't, she doesn't want to," said Bettina. "Ronnie knows, he understands." "It hardly seems fair to him," I said, and then I thought, Bettina always marched to her own drum but so did Daddy. If he had lived and made the money he hoped, it is possible he would have bought them a garage in the country which they could have run very happily together; as it was I did not know. "Do you think it would help at all if I met him and said I was on your side, his side, whatever . . . ." Bettina smiled. "Yes, it would. He thought you were fantastic last night." "How do you meet him? How do you see him?" "I meet him on Wednesday afternoons, his day off, and since Daddy died he has been driving over here when Mummy stayed with the Fletchers," said Bettina. "Well, I don't want to crash in on the little time you have together but perhaps I could meet you both for a cup of coffee or something." And so it was agreed.

We got on well together. Ronnie had joined the same Public Library I had and had learned a lot, not only about mechanics, but politics and history. He was an interesting person. I liked him. I do not know when Mummy found about him.

Auntie suggested that we rent the house so that some money would be coming in and that we should come and live at Blackheath the other side of London, near, in a small house she owned. She needed someone to drive her for Uncle had developed angina and needed the chauffeur all the time. She would buy a small secondhand car for Bettina which she could use for herself and Mummy when she was not driving Auntie. It seemed the only solution although my mother was not happy about it as she and my Aunt did not get on too well together.

Chapter 31

Howard and Honor.

Howard's scholarship was up. A year had seemed such a long time and had gone by so fast. We were both sad. He said he might try and come over next summer on another scholarship but first he had to get his M.A. at Yale before applying. I remember the last night before he left we strolled on Primrose Hill. He had always liked the names of the suburbs of London, some of which were now Tube stations, like Chalk Farm where he lived. Then there was St. Johns' Wood. These all harked back to when London was surrounded by villages; I had not noticed them before. I had learned a lot from Howard, not only music but architecture and odd bits of history like that. The evening light was in our faces as we walked down Primrose Hill. He told me he would always love me; I thought I loved him, especially when he played the piano, but it seemed to be the end.

A few days later I heard from Honor. She had a three-month-old baby and they had returned from the North as Peter now had a job in London and they had rented a house in Brent, the next station from Hendon. She asked me to visit her and to come the next day. She sounded strange on the phone.

When she opened her front door and saw it was I, she burst into tears, and we hugged each other. Where was the lively sprite I knew? She had put on a lot of weight and had a look of her mother. Why was she crying? "What is the matter, Honor?" I asked. "I am so miserable," she said. I gasped. "But you and Peter were so happy at the wedding, and now you have a baby!" "You try getting pregnant on your honeymoon, the first week, the first night. I was sick all through the honeymoon, all through the pregnancy and still feel dreadful. I can't bear for him to touch me." She shivered. "Was sex so terrible?" I asked. "I never had a chance to find out, I got pregnant and sick right away, I can't stand the thought of it. His parents luckily love the baby and when she is six months old they are going to take care of her and I'm going back to the Cordon Bleu." "And Peter"? She burst into tears again. "Oh you will hate me, my mother does, my in-laws, no one understands. Everyone hates me." "Oh, Honor." I was not demonstrative, but I put my arms round her again. "I shall never hate you, my first friend, my best friend, but you always wanted a baby!" "Not right away," she wailed, "he should have known better." I did not know how to cope with this situation other than by telling her I would never hate her, and her mother would not either. "She does," sobbed Honor. "She will get over it," I assured her. "But the baby? Wont you see her, visit her at your in-laws?" "I suppose I shall go down for weekends," said Honor, "but I'm leaving Peter as soon as I earn enough money at the Cordon Bleu to get a room for myself." I felt so sorry for them both, they had been so happy at the wedding and the years before. "Soon," I suggested "you'll feel better about him, it is just everything has been too much for you, perhaps later?" "No," said Honor firmly.

In the next room the baby began to cry and Honor went to fetch her and handed her to me. I do not know if I had ever held such a young baby. She seemed sweet. I gave her the bottle and she quieted down. Honor did not know of my father's death and when I told her she became her old self, full of concern for me. She remained adamant in her decision to go back to the Cordon Bleu, to hand the baby over to her in-laws and to leave Peter as soon as she could afford it.

Neither Honor nor I knew anything about post-partum depression and there were no counselors in those days that I recall; I do not know if anything could have saved that marriage. I visited her regularly until I left Hendon, but when we went to live in Blackheath it was a two-hours train trip both ways and we lost touch for some years. Honor was never one to write.

Howard wrote regularly. He told me before he left that he would write on board ship and post as soon as he reached New York, about five days, and then it would take about a week in the mail. We wrote each other every week and his letters were a great joy; we could communicate well by mail.

I vaguely remember the move and the little house at Blackheath. It had a chestnut tree in the garden and when it bloomed I took out my handwound 78 r.p.m. gramophone and played Mozart's "*Exultate, jubilate*" under the chestnut tree, and it seemed to me that Mozart must have composed it under a chestnut tree in bloom. I had bought a book with a description of all Mozart's works and when I heard one, ticked it off. I looked up the date of the composition of "*Exultate, jubilate*" and it was not at the time that chestnuts flowered, which surprised me.

It took a bit longer to get to work from Blackheath, which was not on the tube but on the suburban line. That was all right in the mornings, but in the evenings I often stayed late for various reasons and Blackheath was scary to cross at night. In the train I had a good view of Westminster from Charing Cross Bridge but then saw miles of jerry-built houses that degenerated into slums around the docks in the river, until we came to Greenwich which was filled with shipping. There was a great deal of talk of war, and my mother was scared that if it occurred we would be the first to be bombed because of our nearness to the docks. My uncle's firm was down there.

It was in 1938 that I received the letter from Howard asking me to marry him. It was a beautiful letter. He said he would always love me; he knew how hard it would be for me to leave England especially with the threat of war. He could somehow come over to marry me in England. He had his M.A., he had a good job in the music school at Columbus, Ohio and he hoped that he could make me happy there. He wished he could get a teaching job in England but it was not possible. Mummy was quite delighted, she always liked Howard. Bettina was horrified at the thought of my leaving

England. I consulted Auntie Dora with whom I was perhaps the closest. She said "I always hoped you would not marry a business man." (She had.) I said I couldn't leave England with the threat of war. She suggested that she send me on a trip to America for a month, so that I could visit Howard and see how I felt. Chamberlain had been to Munich and war seemed a little less imminent.

Chapter 32

America and Switzerland

I do not remember much of the Atlantic crossing. I was introduced to orange juice which only children under six had had in England. A Dutchman at the table said: "The only way to drink orange juice is with gin." I met a very nice American girl who asked me to stay with her in Washington D.C. and she would show me the sights. Her name was Ginny; I did not know it was short for Virginia and was amazed that anyone would call their daughter that.

It was very generous of my aunt to send me to America but she had not thought of consulting Howard as to when would be the most convenient time for him. It was not easy for him, in his first term, at Columbus, Ohio, to make time for me. He arranged to put me up with friends, but I first spent a week in New York with Louisette. She was the sister of Aline, my mother's French actress friend, with whom we had always kept in touch. I knew Louisette from her visits to England. She was an excellent seamstress and worked in some exclusive salon; she was very kind.

I liked New York, especially at night when the lights came on in the skyscrapers against the sunset. I went on a river trip round the Statue of Liberty and then to the top of the Chrysler skyscraper. I also went for a few days to Washington D.C. to visit my shipboard friend Ginny and fell in love with Washington, the Lincoln and Jefferson Memorials and, above all, Mount Vernon. I had never seen anything like the color of the maples in the fall around the elegant house, with the river beyond; it was beautiful.

I then took the train to Colombus, where Howard met me. It was in the middle of a football weekend and I was quite overwhelmed by the noise. He did not like football but he felt he should introduce me to an American pastime. He bought me a corsage which impressed me. I don't think I had ever been given flowers. Unfortunately he got us seats on the opponent's side of the stadium. All around people were screaming and they didn't like us. I did not enjoy the game, of which I could understand nothing; it had no relation to the soccer games my father had taken us to at Chelsea. Howard had tickets for a concert by Rachmaninoff but unfortunately I can remember nothing of it except the splendid reception the School of Music put on for him, where for the first time I saw an ice sculpture.

The whole visit passed by in a daze; it seemed I was seldom alone with Howard. I asked if we could not go for a walk in a park or somewhere green and I do recall a pleasant walk on the campus. That and the few times he played for me recalled the old magic. The threat of war seemed imminent again; no one believed Chamberlain any more. I felt how terrible it would be if war were declared and I were in America. Howard understood how I felt and that was so touching. He had hoped to give me a ring but I could not say I would marry him, just wanted to get back to England before I was cut off. He said if there were not a war he would try to get to England next summer; he gave me a watch. Years later someone opened it and it had "I love you" written inside.

I felt dreadful about the whole thing and that I had disappointed everyone, although it was only my mother who hoped I would marry Howard. Bettina was delighted I was not going to leave England, and my aunt as usual was very understanding. She was sending my cousins to Switzerland for a week's skiing as a Christmas present but unfortunately Rita had broken her ankle, was in crutches and could not go. My aunt suggested I should take her place. "I have already asked your sister, but she does not want to go. She is a strange girl." So I went and it did lift my spirits.

We went to Wengen; the mountains in snow were overwhelming. My elder cousin, Jean, had often gone skiing and was quite an expert but Donald was a novice like me; my younger cousin Gordon did not go. Donald and I had an instructor on the nursery slopes and in no time we were skiing down gentle slopes. We had to go down a sled ride and the instructor told us to lean out or we would fall over into soft snow. The sled ride was carved out of ice and arched up high at a certain point. Donald was in front. "Lean out," yelled the instructor. I saw him trying but not hard enough for he vanished over the top; I felt sure I would do the same and land on top of him. I prayed and leaned as far as possible to the left and sailed round the curve and reached the bottom of the sled run safely. Donald was all right but very relieved I had made it without falling right where he had.

It was strenuous fun. After breakfast we put on our skis and stayed on them till a smorgasbord lunch at the hotel and back again till "*the dansant*" time. It was the age of "dancing teatime"; we danced in our ski boots. Then we went and bathed and changed and came down to a wonderful dinner and more dancing. One day Donald opted to go on a long snow shoe hike up a mountain but I decided against. I met two very nice German boys with whom I talked in German and asked about Germany. They said they were not Nazis but were afraid of war; they invited me to their chalet for tea a little way up the mountain from the hotel. I had not been there very long when there was a knock on the door and a red-faced Donald stood there who said gruffly: "I've come to take my cousin back to the hotel." I was very embarrassed, but touched at the same time that Donald should take such care of me. He was quite upset. "How could you do such a thing?" he asked. "You didn't know them and they were German." "They weren't Nazis," I replied, "I asked them." He felt I was quite crazy to have gone, but I had no such feeling. However, we made up and I danced mostly with him after that.

I loved skiing. The only thing like it was the time my horse ran away with me on the Five-Mile gallop; first of all fear and then the glory of flying. I never made it beyond the nursery slopes and the sled run but it seemed I went very fast.

Chapter 33

The Quakers and War.

When I returned from my leave of absence from the Quakers, James had left and I worked for a new case worker, a brilliant young Austrian refugee who spoke perfect English and knew several MPs, one of whom, Sir Harold Nicholson, gave affidavits for many refugees. E. told a fascinating story of how Sir Harold had helped him get his friend and tutor, Stefan, who was also Jewish, out of the country after he had been taken by the Nazis. Stefan had telephoned E. from Vienna on his way to the Nazi hotel. E. went straight to Sir Harold who immediately gave him the necessary exit papers, but said it was up to him to get them to Croydon airport that night. (It was long before Gatwick or Heathrow) Sir Harold knew a diplomat was flying to Vienna that night but he did not know who it was). It would be up to E. to pick out the diplomat and in Sir Harold's name ask him to deliver the papers himself; he would be carrying a briefcase. E. said he examined carefully the faces of everyone carrying briefcases; there were many. He could not ask "Excuse me, are you such and such?" for he did not know the name of the diplomat. In the end he intuited aright who it was and gave Sir Harold's message. The diplomat realized the gravity of the situation and went right to the hotel where Stefan was detained and got him released at once.

I became friends with Stefan and he told me he and five other Jews had been stripped naked by the SS men and forced to stand in the snow and had been whipped with icy water from hoses. He was the last. "How did you stand waiting?" I asked. He was a violinist and said he had gone over fingering of a Mozart quartet. Stefan was Hungarian and I tried to teach him English and he taught me *Faust*. I learned more from him than he from me; he seemed to have much more difficulty learning English than the Austrians did. I had never read *Faust* and found the famous lines when the protagonist says that if ever he found something to content him, he would be ready for death and to pay his debt to Mephisto for his gifts of youth, knowledge and love. "If ever I could say to the moment 'O stay you are so fair!'" Stefan smiled ruefully, "You can say that, Audreylein, because you are English. Really one can't say it in German anymore." I realized then it was as hackneyed as "Friends, Romans, countrymen . . ."

Stefan also showed me how to read the score for a quartet, just by following the top violin line. I knew the treble clef and had no difficulty and great enjoyment doing this. He also taught me something of classical musical form, so that I could follow the music.

I made many wonderful friends, among whom was E. He was a very dashing young man and had a beautiful steady girlfriend, a Swede, whose name I could never remember. He also, according to the secretary in the office, slept around. She said she had spent the night with him and "it was very nice." Definitely not my cup of tea but when he discovered I knew the poet Rilke, he became interested in me for that reason. He asked me what I had read. I had bought all the German poems available in England at that time with the excellent translations of J.B. Leishman and Stephen Spender on the other side of the page. He knew them and said they were very good. He asked if I had read "*Malte Laurids Brigge*," a prose work or any of Rilke's letters. I had not and he said he would lend them to me and then we could discuss Rilke, so we began meeting after work.

He wanted to know what I liked best in Rilke. I said it was his concept of death, that one could build one's own death in life by concentrating on the things one held most dear; I quoted from *The Sonnets to Orpheus*, "*Tanzt die Orange*" (Dance the Orange), and also from his poem on a tree in which he "became" the tree. E. could quote further from these poems which he also knew by heart. I said it seemed to me it was like the idea of the Kingdom of Heaven beginning on earth. He was impressed and said he would like to read the Duino Elegies aloud to me and then we could go through them, analyzing them. I had never heard Rilke read aloud and it was overwhelming in its music as well as its meaning. E. was a poet himself and showed me some of his poems; I showed him some of mine. He said it had been suggested to him that he write a sonnet sequence, i.e., three sonnets each starting with the last line of the previous. He said it was good discipline. I did this although I had to use the penultimate line of the previous sonnet in one. Two of these later were published. 1939 rolled on. More and more countries fell to Hitler. War became inevitable and England started to prepare. Everybody had to register for a gas mask and a ration card. Chamberlain became disgraced and Churchill, although not yet Prime Minister, was the man of the hour. He had spoken in no uncertain terms for years against Hitler and told England to re-arm; now it almost too late. I think blackout started before the war; everyone had to have blackout curtains in every window so as to conceal any light from future bombers; it took a lot of preparation to install them. I wonder there was enough material; many people machined their own to get the correct requirements. Blimps went up on Blackheath Common and all over London. Nobody quite knew what good they would be or what they were meant to do.

Bettina at seventeen volunteered as an ambulance driver and was told she would be called up as soon as war was declared. Children were evacuated in droves from London; their pictures were in the papers every day. They were sent to the countryside, some to Canada. Aunt Dora was anxious to establish a children's home in the country for the children of people in Uncle's works; she felt parents would be more likely to send their children to someone they knew. She was right; a lot of people kept their children right in London fearing to send them to strangers. It was decided to close our little house; my mother and aunt would go down to Manor Farm to examine the feasibility of establishing a children's home there. I would go to Uncle's house on the heath where he and my cousins were staying. Donald was down from Cambridge and being trained to take over the Works; he hated it and wanted to join up but Uncle had angina spells and needed Donald.

Everybody was called up at eighteen unless they were in a "necessary" position. As an interpreter I apparently was "necessary," at least for the moment; no one knew how to cope with all the refugees in the country. If Hitler invaded they would be in great danger. I soon left Blackheath and found a room in a house run for refugees in Paddington; I did not fancy crossing the Heath in the blackout. I was rather lonely in this house for everyone was shacked up with someone else except me, but Dr. Bergmann lived near and came to give me recorder lessons and I went to the farm at weekends and E. and I read Rilke together frequently in the evenings.

I remember September 3rd when war was declared. In a way it was a relief; we had been expecting it so long. We worked late at the Quakers and several of us went to eat at Lyons Corner House, Trafalgar Square. There was a small orchestra of refugees led by a brilliant Hungarian violinist. At first they played waltzes and café music of the day but then the conductor stood up alone and started to play with the solo violin, shorn of all its pomp and circumstance, "Land of Hope and Glory." One by one in silence everyone rose to their feet, no one sang, they just listened. I met E.'s eyes, mine stung, I knew he felt the same. It was no jingo patriotism, it was just of England that we all thought and what had to be faced. Years later when I heard Elgar's "Pomp and Circumstance" march played at college graduation, high school, even kindergarten graduation, I wished they had chosen another tune.

Bettina was called up as an ambulance driver and sent to Chatham, a Naval dockyard, where sporadic German bombs were dropped before anywhere else. At seventeen she was very young to be picking up bodies and bits of bodies. Ronnie had joined the RAF and went down to see her and persuaded her to join the WAAFS (women's RAF) where women were needed to drive a 32-seater Dodge bus to transport troops. Few women could do it, but he was sure she could, after training, and they were in such demand, he felt sure she could get stationed near Mummy. It was good advice and she took it.

When the Battle of Britain started my aunt and mother were in the midst of it at Manor Farm, only fifteen miles from the sea with many airfields around. At weekends when I went down I saw dogfights right over us, so near one could see the RAF circles of the Spitfires and the black iron crosses of the Messerschmitts. It was hard to tell which one went down in flames . . . Every night the announcer on the BBC told how many planes were down. There were always more Messerschmitts down than Spitfires, but the losses were tremendous. Churchill said "Never in the history of mankind has so much been owed by so many to so few."

A time bomb fell in the orchard at Manor Farm and they were ordered to leave. It was no place for a children's home, right in the middle of the Battle of Britain. My uncle's heart problems grew worse and he retired and he, my aunt and mother drove up to North Wales to try to find a place for a children's home. The Piggotts stayed to look after the farm and I still went down occasionally for weekends. Uncle had a dugout built near the tennis court. The house in Blackheath was closed and Donald stayed at the Works.

I did not know what to do. For the moment I was still needed as an interpreter, but E. confided in me that he felt if England were invaded, which we all expected, the Home Office would probably intern the young male refugees and send them to the Colonies, for their fate would be dreadful should Hitler be successful. We still continued our Rilke readings and one night he took me to the Tube through the darkened black out streets. Snow was starting to fall and a lovely voice was singing Gustav Holst's melody: "In the bleak midwinter/frosty wind made moan/ earth stood hard as iron/ water like a stone./ Snow was falling, snow on snow, snow on snow . . . . / in the bleak midwinter long ago." The words "snow on snow" were enveloped in the melody so perfectly that we stood still to listen, holding hands, and the snow fell around us. When the song ended we walked in silence to the tube. Soon after that he came and visited me in my Paddington room. I played a record of Schubert's B Flat Trio. He stayed late and I urged him to go because the tubes stopped but he didn't. Then he asked me if he could stay the night. I loved him with all my heart but I knew he had his beautiful steady girlfriend, I did not think he loved me and I was still a virgin. Perhaps because my parents had had an unhappy marriage, perhaps because of Honor's dreadful story, I just knew I couldn't. In today's world maybe I lost the great experience of my life. He never asked me again.

We still met every day and then he asked me to move in with his family. His mother and sister did not speak English well and he was worried how they would manage if he and his brother were interned. I did. We were all having dinner the night the first bombs fell on London. One fell two doors away and the plaster ceiling fell down on us. The sausage on my fork was covered with plaster. We were on the third floor and felt the house was falling in on us, so forgetting our gasmasks we rushed for the staircase just as the wall opposite cracked. It seemed as if it were going to fall in on us but it fell outwards, the other way. We ran down the naked staircase in the midst of the most awful din, crashing glass, falling masonry, distant bombs and then our guns began. We reached the street and it was at least two feet high with broken glass. I wondered if one could run on broken glass or would it leap up and tear your legs; girls still wore skirts. We found we could run on it. Every block had an air raid shelter which was really nothing but a basement, the kitchen quarters in old houses, the windows covered with sandbags, and the steps left open for entrance and we all knew where it was for our block. Dreadful bits of jagged metal were falling all around, the shrapnel from our guns, but we reached the shelter where we were greeted by a cheerful Cockney: "'ere's a cuppa tea, ducks, where was your bomb?" Quite a few people were already there, someone had a mouth organ.

I spent nights for four months in that shelter. The German bombers were very punctual, coming at 6 p.m. so we were let off work early to go home and get something to eat or take to the shelter. They left at 6 a.m. We slept on rubber mattresses, no plastic in those days, and men blew them up when we were ready for bed, if not sleep. Some people could sleep. They always kept dim lights on. Our guns seemed to make as much noise as the bombs. People tried to reassure me, "Those are ours, the ack-acks," but they all made the same dreadful noise to me. I could not believe that women were manning some of those guns, but I had heard that the A.T.S trained women to fire the ack-ack guns.

There were about thirty in that shelter, most of them cockneys, and very funny. One was a great wit. If a bomb fell far away he would say "nah, that's only a tuppeny (two pence) one." If it were nearer it might be "a tanner's worth (sixpence)." One night a bomb fell on the gas main near us and we felt what we had most dreaded had come to pass, gas! The lights went out and a creeping miasma seemed to fall on us, so he came up "Well, that's a bob's worth!" (the old shilling) When torches (flashlights) were switched on we realized what had happened. The bomb had released the soot in the old chimney which probably had not been swept for years and we were all black with soot, that was the creeping miasma, and the gas came from the main outside. No one could ever get the soot out of the clothes we were wearing that night. They had to be thrown away.

We sang a lot in the shelter. I learned "Green grow the rushes, O" and the "Twelve Days of Christmas" together with another lovely song, and "St. Peter let her into heaven for her yellow, yellow hair, with the refrain "all in yellow, all in yellow" which I never heard before or since.

E. was right. The young men refugees were rounded up and sent to Australia; I hoped it was for their own sake. E. did not have to go; he went to look after his brother who was a pianist, hoping he could help save his hands. In London the moonlit nights were the worst for landmarks were lit up. Buckingham Palace was bombed on a moonlit night. Queen Elizabeth, George VI's wife, became very popular for saying she felt closer to the East End after she had been bombed. The East End, the Docks, were the worst hit. The gas and electric mains were often damaged, but men were at work on them at 6:30 am and they seemed to get them working so that we could always get tea or something warm to eat at night before going to the shelter.

I grew fond of E's sister, Hanni, who was very funny. She could knit well and started knitting socks and gloves for the troops while her mother read to her from *Gone with the Wind,* hoping that in this way they would both improve their English. I asked her how she liked the book. "*Ein Wunsch, ein Mann, Rhett!*" she said. (One wish, one man, Rhett!) Friends of theirs found them a small cottage in South Wales where they could live and get out of the bombing in London. They took me to meet these friends, the Polaks, who were very wealthy Dutch Jews who had lived in England a long time. Their children had been born there and all spoke perfect English, but also French, German and of course Dutch. They had helped a lot of refugees and their house was always full of musicians. They were also very good to me, inviting me to music evenings from the first time I met them.

My family had moved to North Wales where my aunt had found a house suitable for the children's home. My mother went with her to help. At first they stayed in an old stone house. According to Welsh tradition if one could get enough friends to help and build a house of stone in one day it belonged to you. There was no mortar in the houses, they were just built stone on stone, like the walls. I went up for a weekend to see them and slept in the attic and saw a star through a crick in the roof. I wondered what would happen when it rained but was enchanted by this star. The walls downstairs were of many layers of stones. They did not stay there long; my aunt bought a beautiful house overlooking Cadogan Bay with a view of the mountains and sea, so peaceful. My mother had a small flat in the village.

My sister had taken Ronnie's advice and had joined the RAF as a driver. She did very well and soon became a Corporal with several women drivers under her. She could drive the large 32-seater Dodge coaches but many women drivers just drove cars to get the big wigs around. She told a wonderful story of what had happened to one of her drivers. She was driving a General through the night to some far-off destination, and the call of nature became urgent. She stopped the car, got out beyond the headlights, and nipped smartly back. She arrived at her destination without the General. He had nipped out too, and she left him stranded!

Bettina always told new drivers this story and warned them always to check that they had their passengers in the back.

Bettina had obtained a "compassionate" posting to be near Mummy in Wales and by working extra hours in the week could visit her for Saturday nights. She had kept the secondhand car Auntie had given her. She called it "the old lady" and I am sure only she could have made it go. I do not know how she scrounged the petrol. Actually she was posted at an airfield not too far from Mummy. Wales was very different from England with a different language and the place names were hard to pronounce. Bettina was phoned one night by a Canadian group who wanted transport. She asked where they were: "I was afraid you were going to ask me that, sister," said the Canadian, "as far as I can make out it looks like "Peelyweely." It was Pwhylli, pronounced Perthelly.

I did not know what to do. The Quaker Committee folded and I was sent to the BBC as an interpreter, but did not think it was contributing much to the war effort. One night I was too late to get to the shelter and a friend, Laura, asked me to come to her flat near Regents Park. There had been no bombs near there. She sometimes acted as an Air Raid Warden and she had a tin hat for which I envied her. It was not pleasant to walk through the streets without one because of the falling shrapnel. Her flat had no protection whatsoever. The bombers came with their grim thrumming noise and I wished very much I were in the shelter where the sandbags dimmed the noise somewhat. Laura suggested that we read out aloud to each other to calm our nerves. I usually played the second movement of Beethoven's Op 59, no 2 before going to the shelter and missed the comfort of that. It had the feel of a peaceful starry night and the music swung from star to star. Someone had written on the back of the record jacket that "it told of unaccountable angels/ telling of sorrow and light." I did not care for her selection of poetry; it was Macauley's "The Lays of Ancient Rome," but I still remember the refrain, "This year the must will foam/around the feet of dancing girls/ whose sires have marched to Rome."

Bombs seemed to be falling a way off, probably down by the Docks, but suddenly the sky was lit with flames. We saw across London to St. Paul's which was ringed with fire. It was the night the Germans bombed the publishers and booksellers all around St. Paul's. They were probably hoping to hit St. Paul's, and it was amazing that they did not. I was always afraid of fire since a child and the sky was red all over with St. Paul's standing out with the flames around it. It was the worst night for me not to be in a shelter. I shall never forget those fires.

Shortly after I had tea with a friend and she was killed that night by shrapnel that came through the window and killed her as she lay in bed. Not everyone went into shelters. I started having hallucinations with falling bodies and bits of bodies. My finger which had been cut did not heal. I had to go to the doctor and he said it was a whitlow and I should get out of London for a while. How long had I been in the shelter? "Four months." "You should get out for a while," the doctor said, "where is your mother?" I told him in North Wales and he said that would be a good place to go. There was no reason to stay. The Quakers had folded. Hanni and her mother had been found a safe place in the country. I told them at the BBC the doctor had said I had to get out of London for at least two weeks, and that I was going to my mother in Wales. When they heard that, they asked me if I would consider a position as secretary to the Head of the Light Program which was in Bangor, Wales. They assured me it was helping the war effort to keep people's spirits up and the Director was in urgent need of an intelligent girl. I said I was an interpreter, not a secretary. They told me the Director had not been able to find anyone and to think it over after I had had my two weeks' sick leave. In the few weeks I had been at the BBC in London, I had not been asked to do any translation. All I remember of that time was that we had to present I.D. cards when we entered the building. I noticed they were not closely checked and two others had apparently seen this and handed in two cards with "Adolf Hitler" and "Hermann Goering" on them and were not stopped. There was quite a to-do over this!

Before I left London I had a letter from Howard, forwarded from Blackheath. Since the war started our letters had become infrequent. He wrote me a very sad letter saying he would always love me but he did not think we could ever get together again with the war. He had met a woman who cared for him and he was going to marry her. He would always love me. I felt bad I did not answer the letter. I had often thought about Howard in the shelter, and generally with the feeling that I would marry him one day, after the war, if ever there were an after the war and

I lived through it, which I doubted. Now that was not to be and I quite understood his position, but I was tired of writing letters. I had typed so many letters on behalf of E.'s mother, to M.P.s, especially to Sir Harold Nicolson, about her sons and she had received a very kind letter from Sir Harold, assuring her that once the danger of invasion were past, her sons would be brought home and he would see to it that they were among the first. I had written to them in the shelter and received replies from E. and Stefan from Australia in which they reported they were well off, and not to worry. Stefan said they were forbidden to whistle or hum the funeral march from Beethoven's Seventh Symphony as it was such an infectious melody that it went on all day and drove people mad! When he was released he would join the Pioneer Corps, composed of refugees on England's side.

I remembered the time that he and I had sat in St. James's Park during the Dunkirk days when it was not clear if the British Army would be rescued after the French had surrendered. I had gone to the movie *Gone with the Wind* and came out into Leicester Square to see a crowd gathered around a newsboy. In those days they wrote the news on chalk on boards. The boy had written "France" on the board and the crowd was still and expectant. Under it he wrote "has" and then on the bottom line "fallen." A great sigh went up from the crowd. They knew what that meant. That night Churchill spoke: "We stand alone. We have that high honour."

The next day Stefan and I were sitting in St. James's Park and, as everyone else was, watching the weather. By a miracle the English Channel was calm and Churchill had sent out a call to everyone who had a boat, a sailboat, a dinghy, a dory, a paddleboat, anybody with a boat should go across the channel to Dunkirk where the remains of the British Expeditionary Force were stranded. Of course destroyers went too but they couldn't get in close enough to land, so the small boats were needed and all depended on the weather. Usually the Channel was much too rough for small craft; they would be capsized; but by a wonder there was calm water. The newspapers got hold of the word "halcyon" weather which had been used by the Greeks to denote calm weather when a kingfisher could build his nest on the waves. The small craft did not only bring the soldiers to the destroyers; those who could not get on the big ships were ferried back in the small boats. It was a miracle. I think 30,000 got home and the RAF kept off the Luftwaffe. Stefan said, looking around at St. James' Park, "I think this is what the English are fighting for, this elegance of the 20th century together with the rococo grace of the 18th." I thought of Manor Farm and the dog fights above it. We wandered around St. James's and saw the Artillery Monument from World War I in which the battles were carved around the base. Stefan said: "I saw the same battles, Paschaendale, Vimy Ridge, carved on a monument in Vienna." My watch had stopped. Stefan opened it and saw the words "I love you" that Howard had inscribed inside. I had not seen them before.

Chapter 34

Wales.

When I went up to Wales with two suitcases that carried all my worldly goods and Howard's letter, I thought of all these things but somehow could not write any more letters. I just wanted to be quiet and look across to the mountains and the sea and feel the stillness. I listened to Mozart and read Rilke and gradually my hallucinations ceased and my finger healed.

My family did not want me to return to London and urged me to take the job offered by the BBC in Bangor, an hour's bus drive over the mountains. I wanted to join the Services in some capacity but did not know what, and the BBC job was "protected," i.e., I had to enlist to leave it, could not be called up as most girls were at eighteen and sent anywhere. The bus drive over the mountains blew my mind; sea and green hills covered with gorse, stone walls, stone cottages and jagged peaks in the distance, and cloud shadows scudding over all, changing the hills from blue to tawny gold, and so peaceful. I was disturbed by seeing a gun at the driver's seat but no one demurred when he stopped the bus to shoot a rabbit; everyone cheered and started singing. It seemed a very casual sort of life after the rigors of London.

The Director of the Light Programme of the BBC implored me to take the job. The Welsh had different spelling (I had seen that from the villages passed on the bus trip); he had not found a girl who could spell, much less type or do shorthand; he offered me twice what the Quakers had paid and assured me I would be a blessing, darling. Everybody called each other "darling" which amazed me. He told a young scriptwriter called Cliff to show me around and make me feel at home. Cliff told me I was much too highbrow for the job but he would make me feel at home by quoting Shakespeare, which he proceeded to do. He wrote the most dreadful scripts, he said, and it would be a sign of their success if I loathed them. I found myself laughing and enjoyed it; it seemed I had not laughed for a long time. I agreed to take the job for a few months and was introduced to Mrs. Roberts, 5 Maes Isalow, with whom I would stay Monday to Thursday night. She would give me a cereal breakfast and I would eat lunch and dinner at the BBC canteen, return Friday over the mountains to Portmadoc and stay till Monday morning when I would catch the 7.30 am bus to Bangor. "I'm glad to have you, me dear," she said. "I'm sure you don't have BBC washing." I asked what that was and she raised her eyebrows to the next garden where a black bra and pants were hanging on the line. "BBC washing," she muttered darkly. I told her my underclothes were white. "I knew it, me dear," she said, "we'll get along fine."

The BBC Light Programme turned Bangor upside down. They used the chapel halls to rehearse their skits. Vera Lynn sang from there and Tommy Handley in "ITMA." At first Bangor was outraged but soon they began to enjoy the programs and crowded in the halls where the seats were so close together one had to get up to let anyone pass. Cliff wanted me to hear his skit and I agreed but refused to spend the whole evening listening to such drivel. We pushed past angry muttering people to get out, and then I found I had left my gloves! "You'll have to get them, darling," he said, "they would lynch me for certain and there's a fifty/fifty chance for you." No one ever made me laugh so much. We fell in love.

I remember the night he told me he loved me, no lights in the street but searchlights swinging across Cadogan Bay. "You are the only girl I have ever loved," he said. This was expected. "It was always boys before." I reeled. Thank heaven I had read Plato or I would not have known what he was talking about. No one discussed homosexuality in those days. He told me how dreadful it was, one was always outside looking in, but I could save him for he truly loved me. I really cared for him too; he wanted me to marry him and I considered it until the day he said he hoped I would not want children. "I would not want you to lose your neat little figure." That finished it. We remained good friends but I thought no more of marriage for I knew I wanted children more than anything, children I could bring up myself without nannies or governesses, but I did laugh with Cliff more than I had ever laughed with anyone. He came to spend a weekend at Portmadoc and stayed at the local pub. On Saturday night it was tradition in Wales that the men should sing in the top of the bus. The women remained silent. I always liked the top of the bus for the view was better. The conductor asked Cliff: "Is it a tenor that you are, we have enough baritones." Cliff said he was a tenor but he did not know the Welsh. "Ach, never mind the Welsh, if it is a tenor you are, just sing along. We have enough baritones." It seemed very funny then.

I wrote two poems in Wales.

BANGOR

Beyond the street the dandelions
strode fiercely to the sea,
but still the town was in the clouds
and smoke from many chimneys rose,
slow fountains that would never fall
and gulls wove through these scattered strands
their wild embroidery.
With clouds for sails and rigged with smoke
and decks of dandelion
the town sailed on the sea.

7 am Bus Portmadoc

How beautiful the chimneys in the morning
as birds pour through the dawn,
in glinting slits of sunlight
their icy chill cascades.
A darkened door, firelit within,
a red-haired child runs down the street,
a streetof morning shadows
where even stones are long and thin,
her hair first flame then copper leaves
but softer than all these.
The village ends, the road goes on,
through javelins of yellow gorse
to splendor of the tawny hills
a lion's crouching paws.

It was my sister who found the announcement in *The Daily Telegraph* that the Navy wanted girls who could speak German; they would enter as Petty Officers and train for Intelligence, MI5. "This is for you,' she said, and I knew it and told Mr. Watt, the Director of the Light Programme at Bangor and he quite understood. I liked him and never forgot the first letter I had to take in shorthand and type for him. A producer's programme had bombed (gone all wrong) and he wrote two pages in explanation, blaming this, that and the other, himself, the lighting, the casting, etc. I wondered if my shorthand would be sufficient to interpret

Mr. Watt's reply. I need not have worried. "I do so see what you mean," he wrote. Period.

I wrote to the Admiralty and sent my credentials in German and was told to apply for a test in German at the Admiralty any day between 9 and 5 p.m. My Dutch friends, the Polaks, had told me if ever I wanted to come to London I had a home with them, I could share Lida's room, they would welcome me, they had a secure dugout and they lived in Hampstead which was a little outside the main bombing area of London, so I asked if I could stay with them while I made my application. I did not realize that would offend E's mother. They were her patrons, she had introduced me, and I did a wrong thing. I did not realize this. They were safely out of London, I thought they would be glad if I had a safer refuge than the shelter. I had stayed in the shelter for them and typed dozens and dozens of letters to the Home Office for the return of her sons and their friends, which she could not have done herself. I don't think she ever forgave me, which upset me very much. The Polaks welcomed me with open arms. Dr. Polak had bought an extra ticket for me for Bach's St. Matthew Passion at the Albert Hall on the Sunday before I applied at the Admiralty. I had never heard the Bach and was overwhelmed. Dr.Polak told me, "Once a year, for a little while, while I hear Bach, I almost believe." I tried to convince him of the afterlife and we argued. I remember him saying: "Well, my dear child, I shall be so glad if you prove me to be wrong." Dolf, the younger son, who became a great friend, took me to an exhibition of Paul Klee and we both enjoyed it so much, we went back twice. Klee was so witty and he painted so many nuances of green. Later I found that he'd written that green was the hardest color to paint. Lida had been a year at Oxford before the war but had resigned to volunteer at the Dutch Army Headquarters in London. I never forgot what she said to me: "You know quite a lot about music and art but you are full of holes. You miss the benefit of a University education." I never heard truer words. The Polaks however did educate me and if ever I became a good Humanities teacher, much of the credit goes to them and what I learned in that lovely Dutch room with oriental rugs on the tables and angel wing begonias, with their drooping rose colored blossoms, in the conservatory beyond, and always music.

Chapter 35

The WRNS

About a week after I had taken my German Test at the Admiralty I was called up and told to report to Mill Hill for Basic Training. If I had joined up a few months earlier I would have had this training at the Royal Naval Hospital built by Christopher Wren on the river at Greenwich. My friend Nan had been there and said it was beautiful but very dangerous as it was so near the docks where all the shipping was, and that was probably why they moved the Basic Training Unit.

Mill Hill was hideous and grim. We spent most of the day scrubbing floors with lye soap and no plastic gloves. We had to learn all the parts of a ship so in this house the kitchen was the Galley, the toilet was the Head etc. I remember one day I was so tired I sat down on the floor to give my knees a rest from scrubbing and an officer loomed up and said "Robertson (my maiden name) you are sitting on the Quarter Deck!" Apparently this was a sacred place. I shared a double bunk with a sweet girl who had been married one day to an RAF pilot who was killed that night.

After Basic Training we were sent to Portsmouth and trained in signaling and drilling. This was better. I recall a church service on board ship in a huge hall filled with sailors who sang the Naval Hymn: "Eternal Father, strong to save/whose arm hath bound the restless wave/who bids the mighty ocean deep / its own appointed limits keep. / Oh hear us when we cry to Thee for those in peril on the sea." It was magnificent to hear all those men's voices, and to realize how appropriate the hymn was for them; I never forgot that sound.

After that those of us designed for Intelligence were sent up to MI5 and bound to the Secrecy Act. I never told anybody anything of what I did during the war. Long afterwards when a film came out giving in great detail our role, I believed, with others, that we were then released from our vows. We worked with Radar which the British discovered before the Germans. It was a great help in winning the Battle of Britain, when the RAF fought the Luftwaffe to save England from invasion, and did, although with great losses. Radar enabled the Britons to see the German planes coming from afar. "Never," as Churchill said, "has so much been owed by so many to so few," one of his great lines.

We, German speakers in the WRNS, were trained to listen on VHF (very high frequency radio) to German submarines in the Channel and around the coast. With our left hand we twiddled the radio dial very slowly until we came across German. We then wrote down with our right hand everything we heard in German. Left handers did the opposite. There were always two radio technicians on duty in the Watch Room, as well as a WT (wireless technician for Morse) and an officer. When one of us heard German, the other RT would phone the Radar Tower and give the frequency which the Wren in the Tower would then phone to headquarters at Dover. The Radar Tower was apart from the watch room with even clearer access to the sound. In this room was a sort of television screen in which sounds were recorded as blips. Dover could then get a "fix" on this sound and ascertain exactly where the U-boat was.

We kept a 24-hour watch, but it seemed that German was more often heard at night. Usually it was just chit-chat, news from home, where could one get laundry done, sometimes directions and codes, but whatever it was it located the U-boat's position. Code and directions were important but we had to write down everything for we could not always tell what was code.

We kept the line open to Dover, one operator relating the German while the other wrote it down at the same time. It was difficult to recognize some of the German accents; the Bavarians were the hardest. I was glad I had heard so many accents during my stay in Germany and while working for the Quakers. I was able to cover most of what I had heard. I did not know German shorthand but devised a way of eliding "ge" in verbs and so was able to transmit most of what I had heard to Dover. As a result my writing became perfectly illegible. I remember receiving a letter from my cousin Rita which said, "Audrey, what has happened to your writing? It used to be so nice; now it is pretty well illegible," and so it remained for the rest of my life.

At some stage we had to do a stint at Dover Headquarters, 240 steps down into the white cliffs of Dover until we reached the watch room. We stayed down there a week with no elevator, eating and sleeping and working down there in the depths of the cliffs. The Watch Room was awesome. We saw the results of our radar watching. There were blips on the big television screen indicating the positions of U-boats according to the last time we had heard from them; these changed frequently, of course. We also saw blips of our own E-boats, which tried to destroy the U-boats. I did my stint at Dover after I had been listening about a year with a girl from my station called Lallie, who was engaged to an officer in one of the E—boats operating from Dover. Somehow or other she knew his position in the formation; he was the third blip and we were watching on the screen when the third blip blew up. It was a dreadful moment. Lallie screamed and had to be taken from the Operations Room. I cannot remember whether she was supposed to know his position in line, but she did and she knew he'd been killed at that moment. There were very few survivors in E—boats or U-boats.

A friend of mine at another station was listening in to German one night when she heard the speaker suddenly break into the message he was giving with the words "*Wir sind getroffen!*" (We have been hit) Usually we did not experience such drama; we constantly heard two U-boats talking to each other identifying themselves as Gustav

Eins, Gustav Zwei. It is amazing: I've just now suddenly remembered these names. We became accustomed to their voices. When I was at Dover I asked if they knew which of the Blips were *Gustav Eins und Zwei* and they were pointed out to me, not far from the coast of Kent where we listened in to them. While I was at Dover, deep down in the cliffs, there was suddenly a great boom. We were told this was Big Bertha, a cannon from World War 1, shooting across the Channel at us from Calais. It never penetrated the cliffs but it did do damage to the town of Dover and to anybody who happened to be in the streets at the time. I did not enjoy my time at Dover; I was rather claustrophobic, perhaps a result of the Maze at Hampton Court, and hated not being able to see out of a window. I was glad it was only for a week and not a permanent station. It was interesting to see how radar worked but I was never very technological.

We all had to learn the Morse Code and I did but never became qualified as a Morse operator. I was always anticipating what was coming next. If "satis" came through in Morse I jumped to the conclusion it would be "satisfactory" whereas I should have waited to find out whether it was that or "satisfaction."

We entered the WRNS as Petty Officers, the equivalent of sergeants in the Army. To become an officer one had to be proficient in Morse as well as in German but I had no such ambition. My first station after VHF (very high frequency) training was at the west point of West Wales, at St. David's Head. It was at the end of nowhere and we heard no German the month I was there which was disappointing.

It seemed to me that I had gone back to prehistoric times. It was not like North Wales with its green covered hills sprinkled with gorse. It was bare rock and pre-Cambrian rock, I later learned, the oldest rocks in the world. There was a cathedral there, St. David's Cathedral, a beautiful Gothic building with 15th—century glass, built before the church divided and Wales became not only Protestant but "Chapel," very anti-images and stained glass. There was no Evensong held there as at many cathedrals in England. It was deserted except for an isolated college of seminarians who must have tended the place. It had some of the most beautiful 15th—century glass I have seen, but nobody was there except the seminarians. I went for a walk with one of them and he saved me from being wind-blown off the cliff. The winds were ferocious; I was in the air, but he caught hold of my raincoat sleeve and pulled me down. It was quite a startling experience, hardly what I expected. I think the Navy decided that no U-boats were operating off that coast and after a month I was transferred to Ventnor in the Isle of Wight, across from Portsmouth and a likely place for Hitler's troops to land in the invasion.

Typical of the Service, I served on night watch, midnight till 4am, before I left at 8 am to travel across Wales and England to Portsmouth, where I took a ferry to the Isle of Wight, and then a bus and arrived very weary at Ventnor to be told I was due to serve on night watch that night. I was introduced to many girls with fantastic names that I have never heard before or since—Vibeke, Petronel, Myrtis. When I appeared on night watch, Joy, who had a sophisticated way of talking, said: "As I tottered along the corridor just now, nausea tapped me on the shoulder." It must have been the Greek connotation of Myrtis that made me think of Nausicaa, so I said: "Nausea? I don't think I've met her yet." It took me a long time to live that down. I did not help myself the next morning for when I came off night watch I was told to take breakfast to Nan who was in my bedroom and not feeling well. I was given a tray with toast and marmalade and a bowl of cornflakes. We made tea ourselves in the house where we lived. It was a glorious morning; the sea was peacock blue and green with white caps and the white cliffs and the downs of Ventnor looked like Sussex. I felt very cheerful but arrived at Nan's bedside with one cornflake in the bowl. They had all blown away. Nan and I looked at each other and laughed; we became the best of friends and never forgot our first meeting and that one cornflake. Of course I went back to get her some more with a plate to cover them this time.

I also made another booboo on my arrival at Ventnor but that was hardly my fault. The Wrennery was about to mutiny about the poor food we were given. They wanted the officers to keep chickens so that sometime we could have a fresh egg. By 1941 there were no real eggs, only dried eggs but if one kept chickens one could sometimes have a real egg. I was told I must mutiny or I would be a blackleg. By this time I had been up 24 hours so just went along with what I was told to do. I met my officer for the first time and told her I had come to mutiny as I did not want to be a blackleg. She laughed. "You must be the new Wren. You've just arrived. You haven't had a meal here yet, you don't know what the food is like. How long have you been up?" I told her 24 hours so she said I should go to bed at once and sleep till dinner tonight. She added that we were going to keep goats and ducks to improve the food somewhat. "Goat milk and duck eggs will be used for cooking as everybody is sick of dried milk and eggs." I thought she was very nice and always stood up for her, even when she made a mistake during the Parade for Savings Bonds.

The Isle of Wight was full of troops, Naval, Air Force, Army with its various regiments and Marines. The Navy was the Senior Service and we, the WRNS, were given the honor of leading the Parade, the aim of which was to sell Savings Bonds for the War effort. There were bands and flags and it was quite a do. Our two officers led the parade, and we WRNS followed behind them. They turned to the right and we smartly followed them. The rest of the parade went on down town. Apparently our officer had been given the wrong map, but it was hard to live down.

A Petty Officer from Portsmouth was sent to inspect our drilling. I was in the front row between two tall girls and felt they would take larger steps than mine so made a big effort and landed up two feet in front of everybody else. The Petty Officer looked me up and down. He was all of six feet. "Even I couldn't get as far as that," he said. "Two steps backward, march!" Most WRNS, attached to naval bases, had far more practice in drilling than we did. We were stationed way off on the edge of cliffs so as to be away from as much electricity as possible, and we did not drill very often.

I think we were the only girls on the island; the inhabitants had been evacuated as it was thought that Hitler might make a landing there. We were very popular with the troops and were always invited to dances at Officers' Messes even though we were only Petty Officers. There was also a dance on the pier every night, so those were really my dancing days. It was customary to dance before night watch, and of course, after morning and afternoon watch. A young officer named Edward from the Somerset Light Infantry fell in love with me and I enjoyed dancing to his regimental band in the Officers' Mess, but I did not fall for him. Nevertheless he asked me to marry him after about a month. The threat of invasion was still with us, and there was a sense of "carpe diem" in the air.

The second night on watch I met Ray. She was a singer and had trained in Germany before the war and loved the Lieder of Schubert, Schumann, Brahms and Wolf as much as I did; we became great friends. She should have joined ENSA which provided music for the troops, but for ethical reasons she became an RN as she felt nurses were needed more than singers. She developed trouble in her legs from the long hours standing, but was not allowed to leave unless she joined the Intelligence in the Navy. She did, however, sing a great deal for the troops and was accompanied at one time by David Wilcoxs, who became the Director of Kings College Choir at Cambridge. Of course the Lieder she had learned in Germany were not in great demand by the troops; she also sang songs like "A Nightingale sang in Berkeley Square" and old English airs. To me she sang Lieder a capella, she had a voice a bit like Kathleen Battle's, only warmer, but the same silken sound. We went to the end of the garden where there was a picket fence where an occasional white goat appeared. She sang Reger's "A bird all in gold in a pear tree." Mostly she sang Schubert, especially when we lay on the cliffs overlooking the sea and "the seagulls flew back and forth." She waved her hand to indicate how they merged in with the music of "*Am Meer*" (By the sea). There was another Schubert song I loved, "*Nacht und Träume*," and there was a phrase, "*Sie beleuchten sie mit Lust*" (they are alight with desire) where the vowels "eu" and "*Lust*" modulated into the minor in a way which sent shivers up my spine. I was enchanted and very happy. I would rather have listened to Ray sing than to have danced the night away with Edward.

Somehow or other we got on the same watch list so we were off at the same time and could go with our free pass on the railway up to London to hear the concerts that Myra Hess, the famous pianist, was performing. We were not always at the same station, but over the years we managed to hear all the quartets of Beethoven, and performances of Mozart and Schubert, including Schubert's two great song cycles, "*Die Winterreise*" and "*Die schöne Müllerin*." These concerts were held at the National Gallery, where all the paintings had been removed except Botticelli's "Mars and Venus," left, we supposed as a symbol that love triumphed over war. I remember being surprised that Venus looked so cheerful and Mars so tired.

When we were both at Ventnor, we came off night watch at 8 am and caught the morning ferry to Portsmouth on the way to London. It was often foggy and we heard a bell from a buoy through the mist. It was an eerie sound. When we came home to Ventnor in the evening, the engines on the ferry shut off so we floated in, as in a rest in music, as Ray once said.

Once when we came to a concert at the National Gallery we found it had been bombed during the night. We were told the concert would be held at the basement of St. Martin's in the Fields. It was January and bitter cold. Myra Hess was due to play. It was icy in the basement. Myra Hess came in and said: "I do not know if I will be able to play as my fingers are so cold," but she did. She played "Jesu, joy of man's desiring." We stood up and cheered and then we left; we were shivering and found it was warmer outside. Myra Hess did a great deal to make London the music center it later became. She gave refugee musicians the opportunity to play, and those lunchtime concerts became an inspiration to a city that suffered nightly bombardment. Ray never sang at the National Gallery but she did sing at many lunchtime church concerts and to the troops in the Isle of Wight and the south coast. I look back on that time at Ventnor as enchanted. Nan had a record of Tchaikovsky's "Andante for Strings" and it always reminds me of that spring and summer. Bikes had been donated to the WRNS and Ray taught me how to ride downhill without holding on to the bars, but using your arms as wings. We saluted the syringa at the bottom of the hill. There was a Saxon chapel that was filled with primroses for Easter.

Ray and I were walking on the cliffs one day when suddenly two Messerschmitts swooped down and started strafing us. Ray flung me down into some stinging nettles and I yelled. "Are you hit, Audrey?" she asked. No, I was just stung. Nobody at the WRNS would believe that we had been strafed. "Why didn't you bring some bullets?" they asked. Later that day Messerschmitts zoomed down again. Nan was walking with an ex—boy friend whom she had to tell it was over. They were strafed and he flung himself gallantly down over her and got a bullet in the butt. Everyone thought that was funny. I didn't; I felt sorry for him. Nan said she was thankful she had told him it was over before he was hit.

Chapter 36

The War goes on.

Peter and his brother and Stefan were among the first of the refugees to be returned from Australia, helped, I liked to think, by the many letters I had typed on their behalf to the Home Office and various M.P.s They stayed for a while with the Polaks and both brothers soon found jobs at the BBC. Peter played the piano and talked about music and became quite famous. His brother became a writer on a radio news program. I went up to London to see them and found them both cheerful. They had been treated very well and had probably had an easier time than if they had stayed in London. They thanked me for all the letters I had written on their behalf and for staying in the shelter with their mother and sister. I had a long letter from Stefan. He had been knocked down by a truck his second day in the Pioneer Corps, which was the British Army Refugee Unit he had joined after his return. Apparently he was going to be medically discharged after his two days, but this meant he would qualify for free University tuition, board and lodging.

As he already had a degree in Math and in Chemistry from the University of Vienna, he could study for a Ph.D. in either and "they need no English, thank God," he wrote. People had been good to them in Australia, and he had joined a quartet as soon as they got there which was very pleasant. "To think I might have broken my arm and not been able to play the violin any more; I have been very fortunate, and I will let a mathematician friend I have met teach me English." He did get his Ph.D. at the University of London and eventually obtained a good job with the British Army in Salisbury.

I went up to Wales quite frequently after I had joined the WRNS. One could travel free with a naval pass. On Saturdays Bettina came over the mountains in the "old lady," the Morris Auntie had given her to drive in Blackheath. She had found a pub that had a stash of French champagne and she brought a bottle every weekend. We had a cheery time. Mummy sang songs censored by my sister and she cooked an Irish stew, composed of lamb, barley, potatoes, carrots and onions. I did not know my mother could cook; she had learned this dish from her own mother. She must have saved her entire meat ration for the week for neither my sister nor I could bring her anything as our ration cards were held at our stations. It was very tasty. My mother made us laugh saying in her inimitable way, "Of course it is lovely to see you darling, but it does mean I won't have my extra glass tomorrow morning." Apparently she and my sister had two glasses Saturday night, and Bettina corked it so that Mummy could have the rest Sunday morning. My aunt and uncle had made friends with a middle-aged Welsh couple, Clara and Stanley Richards, with whom they played bridge. Stanley took my uncle out fishing and they gave some of their catch to my mother, so for this reason we accepted the Irish stew without demur. It was about the one meal I can remember during the war; food was just dreadful and one forgot it as soon as possible. The thought of dried eggs and dried milk makes my mouth pucker even today.

My mother had a bedroom, bathroom, sitting room and kitchen with Mr. and Mrs. Morris in the village of Portmadoc. My aunt and uncle lived up the mountain in the most beautiful house called "Hafon" looking over Cardigan Bay to Harlech. Sometimes one could see the castle across the water. It was very peaceful. My aunt had started a children's home there in a house donated by the actress Sybil Thorndike who helped my aunt with the children, as did my mother and many people in the village. Mummy made a good friend of Jean Freeman-Smith who had evacuated out of London but loved the theatre and was dying to get back to see some shows. They all seemed quite happy in Portmadoc and it was to me one of the most beautiful places on earth. The way up to my aunt's house was called the Garth, with the mountain of Moel-y-Gest on the right and the sea on the left with Harlech and its mountains. The only person I ever met was the village idiot and we stopped halfway for a particularly beautiful view. I never minded him; he never talked. The villagers were very inbred; there were only a few surnames in each village—Williams (of which there eighteen), Roberts, Jones and Pugh.

I did not stay long in Ventnor. Both Ray and I were soon transferred. This often happened. Fortunately we landed up not far from each other, she above the cliffs at Dover and I at Kingsgate near where the Mulberry platforms were to be built for D day. We stood on the cliffs to see them pass, waving, but that was much later.

Ray and I managed to meet at least once a week at the lunchtime concerts in the National Gallery. We had free rail passes and for each of us it was only an hour to Charing Cross station. After lunch we would walk in St. James's Park and I would help her learn new songs by saying the words and she would then sing them; she said it was easier than just reading the music; perhaps she was being kind. I remember her learning Mozart's "*Non so piu.*" It was autumn and the leaves were falling in St. James park like the merry little notes in the Cherubino aria. I often was able to go and hear her sing to the troops. I went once to Canterbury for a concert, and afterwards we went into the cathedral which I had never seen. It was so beautiful we did not want to leave and nearly got locked in for the night.

After we left Ventnor, Nan married Ken, the major in the Parachute Troops for whom she had left that poor one who had the Nazi bullet from the Messerschmitts. I lost touch with her for about a year, but strangely enough while walking in London one day by chance met Honor. She had left Peter and was living with someone in the RAF called Nigel. "I am sure he will get killed," she said, and he did. I asked about her baby; she saw her occasionally. She said that Peter was going to get a divorce and marry someone else and then take Jane and bring her up. "Will you ever be able to see her?" I asked. "I expect so," she said, "I can always visit her at her grandparents." She promised to write but I did not have much confidence that she would.

I did a strange thing upon arriving at my new station at Kingsgate. A beautiful fair haired girl opened the door and said: "My name is Allison Anne, I am just leaving." The room behind her was full of light and irises and I thought if ever I had a daughter I would call her that. Another girl came to the door, tall, dark and rather commanding and announced her name was Audrey. This was a shock; I had only once as a child met another Audrey. I did not relish sharing the name with this very opposite-to-me type of person. When the Navy sent us to a new station they gave us papers with our surname and initial. Before I really gave it much thought I said "My name is Anne." I had always liked the name from Anne of Green Gables . . . and so I lived for four months with the name of Anne. I felt I developed a new personality, rather more frivolous.

I made no such friends as Ray and Nan at the new station, but became fond of Lallie who was the most beautiful girl I had ever met and knew it so she was not very popular with most people. She amused me. Soon after I arrived I caught the flu and looked very poorly for some time. Lallie said to me, "Anne, you look dreadful tonight. Would you go in and talk to Guy until I come in so that I can make more of an entrance." It tickled me, and I agreed. I got my own back in the most unexpected way. When new officers arrived, they usually invited four WRNS to dinner and dance so that they could become acquainted. This happened shortly after my arrival. Lallie and I were among the four WRNS to meet them. Lallie was engaged to a submarine officer at Dover but it did not stop her turning any heads that were around. Only one officer arrived, the other three had had to go on exercises but would be back for dinner. "Watch me get him, girls," said Lallie. To her surprise, to everybody's and most to mine, he did not fall for her but for me. His name was Terry, he was Irish, and evidently Lallie was not his cup of tea. We had several happy months together; he always knew me as "Anne" and he took me to London to a Hungarian night club to dance very often. I spent the night at the YWCA and he at an officer's club. It was a merry time. I received a letter from Donald asking me to meet him in London. We had not seen each other since I had joined the WRNS and that seemed a long time. He looked tired and older and he was miserable. His father had threatened him with a heart attack if he joined up as he was needed at the Works. Uncle Sydney had what was called "angina" for many years and took a lot of pills. Donald wanted to join the Army and be with his friends instead of middle-aged men who could do the work he did and asked if I thought his father would have a heart attack if he enlisted? People at the Works making munitions were "protected" as at the BBC. I hesitated; I did not know what to say. I felt very sorry for Donald, who was cut off from his contemporaries. He had learned all he needed to at the Works and it was true older men could do what he did now. He said he could better serve England in the army. I knew that, as he had been to Cambridge, he would be commissioned right away and had read that the life of a 2nd lieutenant in France in WWI was the shortest of any. People were saying that there would have to be an invasion. His life would be in great danger. "I could meet with a bomb in Greenwich any day," he said, which was true. "I would rather meet death with my friends doing what only a young man can do."

Donald was always so brave. I remembered how once I had been chased down a hill by a cow, and instead of facing it and yelling, ran, and Donald who was ahead came back and seized the cow by the horn. I saw how hard it was for him. I said I had seen Uncle lately and he was having the time of his life in Wales, going fishing and playing bridge with the Richards several times a week. I had not seen him taking pills and he looked better than he had done for years He probably would not have a heart attack if Donald enlisted. Of course if he got killed in France, it might be another matter.

"We both could easily be killed by a bomb in London," Donald said, "but in the meantime you are doing an important job for England, and you seem to be having a high old time, dancing several times a week. I haven't been to a dance since the war." It was true, since I had joined the WRNS I had enjoyed life very much, and felt for Donald that he was missing out on his youth, but also that if I encouraged him I might be sending him to his death. I remembered the owls and shivered. I could only repeat that his enlistment probably would not cause Uncle a heart attack as he seemed in better health than he had been for years. Donald would just have to do what he felt was right. It was true death might come to him in London, but it was not quite so likely as if he were sent to France. I felt then what I have felt since; when people ask for advice they have usually made up their own mind, but I was not happy about our meeting: I had not discouraged him from enlisting.

Soon after this, the Audrey and many other WRNS were moved and Terry was also stationed elsewhere so I thought it was time to return to my own name. I could not live the rest of my life masquerading under another, so made a clean breast of it to the officer, who laughed and thought it very funny. I also asked if I could have a top bunk; I could not sleep if somebody climbed over me in the night. Most people wanted the bottom bunk, so I did not think it would be a problem. I did not expect what occurred; the officer said there was a small empty attic room with a single bed in it which I could have if I liked. "We could probably rustle up another electric heater for you," she said. My life changed. I could sleep through the night and could see the sea from the little window in the attic. The electric heaters were no good. As Stefan said of them, and it loses in translation, "one's shins burn in front and behind one chatters with the teeth."

I don't think anyone was sorry to see the other Audrey go; she was bossy and complaining. But the little Cockney cook and maid of all work we had to look after us was a match for her. I remember Audrey complaining that the salt cellars were all bunged up again. "What's wrong with yer tie pin?" was the rejoinder, which tickled me.

Chapter 37

Humphrey.

It was very cold that winter; we were on the southeast coast and when the east wind blew it came right from Russia. The watchroom was fairly warm although we always wore sweaters; the only really warm places were the pubs. There were many more pubs along the east coast than in Ventnor. I only remember one there with a tree growing through it, but along the Kentish coast were many old smugglers' inns, paneled in black oak with brass bedwarmers hanging on the walls. Before the era of hot water battles, coals were put in brass pans to warm the beds. They were of embossed brass with long handles and were shining attractions hung against the black paneled oak. There were also old brass ornaments which used to decorate the harnesses of horses. As soon as spring came the pubs were full of daffodils, then tulips and afterward the summer flowers of lupins and delphiniums. It was said we had nothing left except beer and flowers. I learned to drink a half pint of beer; there was no wine left. It had all come from France and we were cut off. After dancing it was usual to go for a nightcap to one of the pubs and there I met Humphrey who was one of my loves. He was standing in front of the fireplace as I came in with someone else who had taken me to the dance. He came over and asked us both what we would like to drink. I said I would have half a pint in the faceted glass. He said: "You mean bitter, but why the faceted glass?" When it came I showed him. I took two swallows and then the rim of the glass with its facets reflected the shining brass, the fire and the flowers, all glittering. He smiled and I knew I liked him. Next day he asked me out to dinner and a dance and we both fell very much in love. I always felt drawn to someone who could teach me something, and Humphrey was an ornithologist; he knew all about birds. He grew up in Dorset, and knew the names of every tree and all the birds. He had not read Hardy which surprised me as Dorset was Hardy's county. He did not care for books except Gillbert White's *Selborne*, which was written in the eighteenth century and described all the birds of Dorset. He asked me if I liked woods;of course, I told him, I had grown up in the woods of Sussex and liked nothing better. He took me walking in the woods, which did not differ much from Sussex, and he taught me the names of all the birds; the finches, the chickadees, the migrants, the willow wren whose song descends. Nightingales did not sing near the sea. They preferred beech woods further inland.

After we had known each other some months he asked if I would come on leave with him to his parents' home in Dorset so we could hear the nightingales. His father was a Canon of Dorchester cathedral and was vicar of a small church at Fontmell magna, a village which was very old. It sounded as if it went back to Rome. I realized I would have to get confirmed so I could take Communion with him. I had always been religious and had read all the books of C. S. Lewis, but had not been confirmed at school or by Canon Raven as I had questions to which I had not found answers. Ray told me I could get confirmed by a Chaplain in the Navy. Her brother was a Commodore and she knew all about the Navy. I wrote to the chaplain's office at the Admiralty with my request and the times I was off watch and could come and was sent an appointment. When I arrived there were about a dozen sailors and WRNS; the chaplain asked if anybody had any questions or problems that they would like answered. Nobody said anything, so I put up my hand and said I had read C. S. Lewis in his entirety but still had a problem with Adam and Eve. I thought it was noble of the Jews to put the fault for evil on man and to emphasize the righteousness of God, but did not see if He were also all-powerful how He could allow such evil in the world. The Chaplain said "I think I had better take you by yourself," so for six weeks I went up once a week for a session with this very learned devout young Chaplain who had been to Oxford. He did sort me out a bit but it was not until years later when I read Rabbi Kushner's book *When bad things happen to good people* that I really had the answer I wanted. Kushner believed that God was good but he was not all-powerful in this world, as is implied in the Lord's prayer which states "May Thy will be done on earth." In the Latin the subjunctive makes it very clear that it is not done on earth. In my youth a great many people still believed that everything that happened was the will of God, the death of a child, the war etc. I learned a lot and was glad I had waited.

I was confirmed in the Saxon chapel of Westminster Abbey which had been built by the last Saxon king before the Norman Conquest. It was deep down under the apse and felt very holy; prayers had been said and chanted there for centuries. Ray came to my first communion which was typical of her. Years later I tried to find the Saxon chapel along with the flags of Agincourt which I had seen as a child in the Henry VII chapel. Even the oldest guide knew nothing about either. I suppose the flags had been taken down in the war and as they were so transparently thin they had just collapsed. I don't know why nobody knew the way to the Saxon chapel.

I went on leave with Humphrey to his parents at Fontmell magna. Being a Canon sounded imposing so I was surprised to find they were very poor. They had no maid and Agatha, the daughter, did all the shopping, cooking and house cleaning. His mother was frail and old but she cleaned the carpets with dried tea leaves which she then swept up; they had no vacuum cleaner or even a carpet sweeper. They were a very old English family; they had portraits in the dining room going back to Humphrey's great-great-grandfather and they all looked a bit like him. I was thrilled about that but distressed they had no vacuum. Humphrey said many people in Dorset did not have one. I was also disturbed that with all the work his sister had to do, Humphrey let her clean his shoes and I protested that he could help by doing that. He said he had chopped up enough logs for them to keep warm through the next winter, and he did not know how to clean his shoes; his batman always did it or at home his mother or sister. We had a great time in the woods listening to the nightingales and all the other birds. One day we identified by sight and song forty-three different birds, and I loved the service in the little church filled with primroses. We were going to a dance in Dorchester and I suggested we take Agatha with us. Humphrey was a bit glum. "That means I will have to dance every other dance with her instead of you." "I'm sure she will find someone there," I said. Humphrey was not so sure but she did. She found someone in the Paul Jones where everyone danced with the person next to them and she danced with him the rest of the evening.

The spring before the invasion was beautiful, and we were very much in love. Humphrey told me he was many times. Once under a wisteria in bloom he asked me if I would wait and see if he came home. "I do not think it right to ask you to marry me now," he said, "I might come home a cripple and you would be landed with me, or if I were killed you might think you had to be true to me and that would not be fair on you." I rather wished he had given me a ring then, but said I would wait for him. It bothered me that he never read a book and that when he took me to a concert he looked at me and not at the music. Ray met him and said he was not a musician but he was very handsome. I suppose he was. He was tall and dark with a moustache;

he had a nice smile and looked every inch the captain he was, and very like his grandfathers. I was happy with him in that respect.

We knew the invasion was coming for the Mulberry boats which took the troops over the Channel were built near us on the Kentish coast. Donald had joined up and came to meet me in London. He looked very handsome and cheerful in uniform and I took him to meet the Polaks. "He is just the sort of cousin I should have expected you to have," said Dr. Polak, which pleased me. Donald was delighted to be in the Forces and enjoying his training. He told me he had met a girl he rather liked, called Dorothy. I told him about Humphrey. He was glad he had joined the Services and it had not upset his father too much.

The week before the invasion Humphrey and I were walking along the cliffs at dusk and we saw a strange light in the sky coming over the Channel. "That is not a plane," Humphrey said. "No plane flies like that. It must be one of the rockets I have heard the Germans were making." It flew always in the same direction "towards London" Humphrey said, and he was right. It was the first of the VI rockets. They came in droves and the ack-ack guns went into action on the South coast and brought down many. There was a lot of action near us night and day but many reached London and wrought havoc, more destruction than the 1940 Blitz. People still went to the Underground shelters at the tube stations, but shelters such as I was in earlier, which were only sandbagged basements, were no help against the rockets. It was not long before the V2s came along, which were even more dangerous. They came with a horrible thrumming and when it stopped people said you knew it was overhead and would come down on you. It always seemed to stop overhead, then one could hear it whistling down exploding with an almighty crash which seemed on top of you. All this was in the future but is symbolized in that first VI rocket coming before the invasion.

I suppose Humphrey knew the day he was going but was not allowed to say. Each evening might be the last. He told me he would pass the cliffs where I was. "I will stand on the cliffs and wave the next day if you do not come one evening," I told him. He did not go on D-Day One but very soon after. Many of us stood on the cliffs waving to all the Mulberry boats. It seems to me they were open, but I cannot really recall. We saw the men from a distance but they may have been under cover. I just remember the endless waving, not knowing to whom.

Chapter 38

Donald, the Invasion and afterwards.

I had letters from Donald and Humphrey that they had survived the beachhead. Donald wrote that the fields and woods of Normandy looked very like Sussex and he felt quite at home. Humphrey said he thought he saw me waving from the cliffs. They both reached Caen, but there Donald was killed. His commanding officer wrote my aunt that his troop was covered by a hedge but then they had the order to advance and Donald stood up to lead his men and was shot by a sniper; he had recommended him for the Victoria Cross. "He will never get it," my aunt said. "He was just doing his duty as every officer is supposed to do" and she was right. I received compassionate leave and went up to Wales. I did not know what to say to my aunt, we just held each other. Then she said, "When the postman got the telegram he knew what it was and gave it to Clara Richards. She handed it to me, wish he had." I did not understand and puzzled over this quite a bit. My mother thought it was perhaps because Clara had two living sons. Uncle went to pieces; he did not have a heart attack but he became very absent minded and probably started what we would now call Alzheimer's. I confessed that Donald had told me he wanted to join up and asked me if I thought Uncle would have a heart attack if he did. Aunt Dora told me he had told her he wanted to enlist and she had told him he must do what he thought was right. She gave me his prayer book when his things were sent home. I told her he had met a girl he liked called Dorothy and perhaps she should be given something. He had told her too, but she said the girl was so young it was better she forgot him. In the last letter he had written he said he was mentally and spiritually ready to die.

Paris was liberated and everyone thought the war would soon be over. My aunt began making plans; she was always a great organizer. They would sell Manor Farm. It was Donald who cared for it most and it would be too large to run after the war; three miles from a railway station and no cinema for fifteen miles; they would never get staff. I was shaken; two lights went out from the world. I returned very subdued to the WRNS on the cliffs at Kingsgate to learn that they had had no submarine traffic since the invasion; the officer felt we would be closed down. Soon we had confirmation from the Admiralty. There was no longer any need to man the radar stations along the coast; there were no more U-boats in the Channel. We were still there when the news of the abortive attempt to assassinate Hitler came through. If only they had been successful it would have saved so many more lives.

Those of us who knew Morse as well as German, such as Ray, were to be sent to Shaef. They were envied; they would be working with Americans and therefore probably entitled to their PBX, with wonderful food. The rest were to go to MI5 to translate either captured German documents, or file. I wrote an impassioned letter that I should be used for translation, citing all the translations done for the Quakers. I could not stand the thought of London with all the V1s and V2s just for filing. We were sent to an office to be assigned for our translation skills.

To my great delight I found Nan there. I had not seen her since Ventnor but knew she had married Ken, who was a major in the Parachute troops and therefore in the forefront of every battle. We had always laughed together and tried desperately to continue to do so. We asked to room together and were able to do so with another girl called Jean. We were tested for our translating skills, in groups of three, which was not a good idea. Nan and I were landed with a daft girl from Scotland who did, however, make us giggle. Either one of us would suggest a translation of first sentence and Ellen would say "Nay, nay, ah dinna like that." The other would try to amend it but again all Ellen could come up with was "Nay, nay, ah dinna like that." In exasperation we would say "Well, Ellen, how would you translate it?" Her reply was always the same "Well, tha' ah canna tell." In the end we just skipped her and her last sentence became a byword with us for all the problems that came up. She was with us in the lift (elevator) one day at MI5 and an admiral got in. We saluted him and he returned it, saying "Thank you, my dears," which thrilled Ellen. "Ay, isn't it great to be in the hoob (hub) of things." It hardly seemed the hub to us; in fact we felt the Admiralty did not know what to do with us now the coastal radar stations were closed.

I met a young sailor named Peter who had been employed on a submarine listening on radar to U-boats. He loathed submarines; he said that one did not own one's own hammock, one just used any hammock to snatch a few hours sleep, and there was no place to keep books. He loved poetry and taught me some lines of Tennyson which I did not know, about the eagle. "He watches from the mountain walls/ the wrinkled sea beneath him crawls, / then like a thunderbolt he falls." I thought "the wrinkled sea" was very good. He asked me to go to a concert at the Albert Hall with him, "Child of our Time" by Michael Tippett. Ray and I could no longer meet for lunchtime concerts at the National Gallery as we only had the bare hour for lunch, no longer being on watch time. I accepted for I was hungry for music and probably should not have done so. Afterwards he kissed me underneath the Albert Memorial and I was horrified to find that I enjoyed it. I tried to tell him about Humphrey but he said he was only going to be around for a few weeks. Then he would be sent to Germany, and possibly trained for the occupation forces. He gave me Shakespeare's Sonnets and suggested we go for a walk and read them to each other. I felt very guilty about this, but it was so wonderful to find someone with whom to discuss music and poetry amid the dirt of London and the V2 bombs. Humphrey was not a good letter writer, and he did not want me to become too "airy" as he called it. "You know I don't read books, "he wrote. I found myself thinking that if I had found Peter before Humphrey, we had very much more in common, but of course I was going to be true and wait for Humphrey. Peter was sent to Germany very soon.

Chapter 39

The War goes on, Nan and Ray.

The autumn of 1944 was very grim. After the liberation of Paris things seemed to bog down and meanwhile the V2s kept falling over London, doing more damage than the Blitz. We really did not know how things were going in France. Nan's husband, Ken, was in the forefront of every battle for he was a Major in Paratroops. Humphrey wrote me he was the only officer left in his regiment; we did not know where they were. It seemed to rain every day and we were tired, tired of war and waiting and bombs. We had two uniforms, one for best, and both were frayed at the cuffs and there was no material to make new ones. The war had lasted five years and we were tired. Both Nan and I could not sleep and suffered from nerves and indigestion. We tried to make each other laugh. Nan taught me the lyrics from Gilbert and Sullivan operas. I knew the music but had not realized Gilbert was so witty. We realized we shared a love of Robert Louis Stephenson from childhood. She taught me "In winter I get up at night/and dress by yellow candlelight/ in summer quite the other way/ I have to go to bed by day/ . . . Oh don't you think it's hard on me that when I like so much to play/ I have to go to bed by day. "She knew the Lamplighter poem and recalled a line which enhanced the loneliness I had felt in his poems. He asks the lamplighter "to see a little child and nod to him tonight."

We were on the bus one day and two Cockney women were in front of us. One got up to leave and said, "Well, bye-bye, ducks, ever so bye-bye." We enjoyed and remembered that. The newsboys wrote headlines on blackboards and during the Battle of the Bulge which went badly for us one headline read "Patton takes bite out of Bulge." Nan unconsciously gave us our greatest laugh. We both were sent to MI5, I to translate and she to file. She said she was so tired she was glad she did not have to translate. It was not much fun. Most of the letters were drenched in seawater and many were written in the old German script, so it was very hard on the eyes to read. At the end of the day we were both exhausted, and sat on the bus together not saying a word. We were stationed in Chelsea at this time in an old house, and the Mess Hall was in another. After washing up we walked over to eat dinner in the Mess; it was cold meat, the then English apology for a salad, a wilted lettuce leaf, a slice of tomato, and baked potatoes. We started eating in silence. At that time I did not eat baked potato skins so cut them off. After a while Nan asked, "Don't you eat potato skins?" "No," I replied. After a few minutes I felt called upon to say something. "Do you?" "Yes," she said and after a little while added "Sometimes I eat other people's skins." Of course that gave us a great laugh.

We went by bus every day from Chelsea to MI5 off Piccadilly and the queues were long, but the English were patient and jumping the queue was unheard of. Nan and I were at the head and we had been standing in the rain a long time. The bus eventually came and the conductor said, "Room for just two." We both jumped on but a man behind us did too and pushed Nan off the bus. I turned on him, he was quite large but I was furious. "You pushed my friend off the bus," I said and with all my strength I pushed him off and saw Nan's face wreathed in laughter as he came tumbling off. She saw me push him and stepped back.

A V2 bomb damaged a lovely old church in Piccadilly which was near MI5 and also near the American Embassy. A wealthy American had been going to services at that church and donated a large sum of money for renovations. The following story became a great success. At the dedication service the vicar used the archaic word "succour" for "help" and said "We thank you, O Lord, for this timely succour." The American of course thought he meant "sucker" and was understandably at first not amused. I heard it from an American who was.

We lived for anything that could make us laugh. It was a hard winter. Nan had been married over a year and Ken had been given leave several times. The Parachute troops were given extra leave because of the extreme danger of their jobs. Each time Nan hoped to get pregnant; she wanted a baby and she feared Ken would not get through. He wanted a child too so that Nan could get a medical discharge and get out of London, but they did not have any success and Nan grew despondent.

I did not see Ray so often, but one day I had to phone her. I was going upstairs, the bombs were falling, and a girl I did not know ahead of me was singing something I had never heard, so beautiful. I grabbed her as she was about to enter a door. "What are you singing?" "Mozart's 'Ave verum'," she said and vanished through the door and I never saw her again. I phoned Ray, she knew it and we met in St. James's and she sang it for me a capella. There was still the occasional V2 falling somewhere, but I floated away on Mozart and felt perfect peace.

Nan had Christmas leave but I did not get leave as I had been given it earlier after Donald's death. I intended to go to the Polaks for any time off, but Jean, the girl who shared our bedroom, approached me.

Chapter 40

Nightmare.

She had not been looking well for some time; she had lost her boyfriend in France in August. She asked me if I could possibly lend her thirty pounds, saying she was in trouble. We were paid three pounds a week and while we were on the radar stations that was ample for toiletries as we had all meals and rail passes free. Since we were in London, however, we had to pay for buses and for lunches and I had under ten pounds in my Post Office savings bank and no other bank account. Auntie Dora had told me if ever I wanted money just to ask her and she would send it. I told Jean I could get the money in a couple of days from my aunt. She was most grateful.

It was hard to make trunk (long distance) calls during the war. One had to go outside to one of the red telephone boxes and have the exact coins and be ready to drop more in whenever told; otherwise one could be cut off in the middle of a sentence. It was difficult to find out how much it was from London to Portmadoc in Wales, but I gathered together a number of sixpences and some shillings and waited for at least ten minutes in the cold till I heard the familiar Welsh lilt in the voice announcing Portmadoc and gave my aunt's number hoping she would be in. She was. I asked if she could send me fifty pounds, not for me but for a friend in trouble, and not ask any questions. "Of course, darling," she said. "I'll post it tonight." Did anybody ever have such an aunt? I was so glad to be able to tell Jean I would have the money in a couple of days. She would not take more than thirty pounds, although I offered her the fifty and told her she need not bother about paying it back, for Auntie had said that.

She burst into tears then and related the whole sad story. She had to have an abortion; her father was a clergyman and her parents would put her out of the house if they knew and she had nowhere else to go. It seems hard to believe in this age but so it was in the forties. "Where are you going?" I asked. "Is he a doctor?" "Oh no," she replied, "no doctor would do it. He is going to use a coat hanger." I reeled in horror." How did you find him?" I asked. She told me she had heard of him through a friend who had gone through the same experience, and had come through it all right, although it was dreadful. "Where do you have to go, and when?" I then asked. "Christmas eve" was the reply, "after dark. He is in Holland Park somewhere; he has given me directions from the station." Christmas eve and after dark! It was unusual for a girl to go out alone at night for there were no street lights, no buses, and black out curtains over all the windows. A few taxis crawled around; they had dim headlights that could not be seen from above. One was allowed dimmed flashlights but it was very hard to find your way anywhere you did not know. "How will you get back to Wimbledon?" I asked. Our quarters had been moved from Chelsea to Wimbledon, further out where not so many V2s fell, but it was a long way from Holland Park. "He says he will get me a taxi to the tube station afterwards," she said. There were lots of steps at Holland Park tube station.

I made up my mind. "'I'll come with you," I said. "I will keep the twenty pounds and that should be enough to get a taxi all the way from Holland Park to Wimbledon." Twenty pounds was an awful lot of money in those days; it should be enough, I thought, even with the tip. She cried again and thanked me. "But it is Christmas eve; he said fewer people would be around then; also fewer people to ask questions at the Wrennery. Aren't you doing something for Christmas?" "I'm coming with you now," I told her.

It seemed such an irony that Nan, safely married who wanted a child so badly, could not get pregnant, and poor Jean who had lost her young man in the war, could. There were few WRNS who remained over Christmas and nobody noticed when Jean and I slipped out Christmas eve. We had a hard time following the instructions from Holland Park, and it was even harder to find the name of streets in the blackout with our dimmed flashlights. They were dingy streets and I did not like the look of them a bit. We eventually found the address and the door was opened by a tired looking woman. I asked her to be sure and call a taxi when it was over and she agreed and said it should be about an hour. I had a brought a long book to read. It was *Anna Karenina*, not very appropriate reading, and I could not keep my eyes on the text, I was so worried about Jean. It was longer than an hour until Jean came back to report that the first attempt had not been successful and it had to be done again. I sat there waiting; I am sure I prayed for her; it seemed a long time. Eventually she returned looking dreadful and groaning with pain. There was some trouble about getting a taxi but eventually one arrived and I asked in trepidation how much it would cost to drive us to Wimbledon. "Fifteen pounds," I was told and I breathed a sigh of relief. I would have enough money and some for a tip. It seemed forever till we reached the Wrennery. Jean looked dreadful and was in pain. She wanted to go to our bedroom but it was upstairs and I insisted on taking her to Sick Bay where there was always a nurse in charge. It was a nice young nurse who seemed sympathetic. I told her Jean had cramps and was bleeding badly and she said she could give her something to stop the pain and the bleeding. There was no one else in Sick Bay that night, and she would stay by her all the time. She was a blessing. I do not know if she knew or found out what had happened but she never said anything When I went to see Jean in the morning she was sleeping and slept most of the day and in the evening she looked much better and was so thankful it was all over. The nurse said she should stay in Sick Bay a couple of days and I was thankful. It was the worst Christmas I ever had, but it was even worse for Jean. I felt no man was worth what she gone through.

Chapter 41

Marcel's Story.

There were about a dozen WRNS left in the Wrennery over Christmas and on the day after, Boxing Day, one of them rang up a convalescent home for wounded servicemen nearby to ask if there were a dozen convalescents who would like to come and dance to the gramophone The offer was accepted and I was told I had to come to make up the dozen. I was not very keen. I had not danced since Humphrey had left for the invasion but had to comply. I had visited Jean and she was doing well. As I came downstairs I heard Fred Astaire music which Donald had loved and to which I had taught him to dance. I entered reluctantly and heard someone ask if there were any Wren who spoke French because there was a Belgian patient among them who could not speak English but who had escaped from forced labor in Germany through France and Spain and was anxious to tell his story to anyone who could understand him. I put up my hand and was introduced to Marcel who was blond and blue–eyed and overjoyed to find someone who could speak French. He had his left arm in a sling and limped a bit and asked me if instead of dancing we could sit down somewhere where he could tell his story. We sat on a sofa in an anteroom where we could still hear the music, "The way you look tonight," and see the people dancing. He told the most amazing story I had ever heard.

He was a musician and played clarinet in the village band and was living with his parents when the Germans swept through Belgium in 1940. They killed his parents and took him off to forced labour in a munitions factory in Germany. He did not know where it was, he never learned German and tried to be as unhelpful as possible, and he was often moved.

After several months or years he said he was billeted with a woman who spoke French. Her husband was at the front but she had originally come from Toulouse. She engineered his escape from Germany. They must have been in love for she took dreadful risks for his sake. He said she was "*tres gentille*." She gave him her husband's old German uniform, bought his ticket to the nearest border town to France and produced papers for him, and gave him German money and also some French. I reeled. "How could you travel in a German uniform through Germany if you knew no German?" He said she tried to teach him some but gave up. He had no talent with languages, he said. She told him if he were stopped and interrogated he was to give the Nazi salute and say "Heil Hitler!" and with a bit of luck he might get through. He did. He was asked to produce his papers and gave the Nazi salute with "Heil Hitler!" He reached the border town to France; I cannot remember which town it was, but it must have been towards the South. His difficulties were not over. He had to dispose of his German uniform; she had given him peasant's clothing to wear beneath and a small suitcase. He changed in the toilette at the station and put the German uniform in the suitcase and disposed of it bit by bit in various ash cans.

He was to try to get to Toulouse where he should say he hoped to find his parents. Actually he hoped to find hers. She did not know if they were still alive but if they were, they would help him. Her father knew of a way over the Pyrenees on to the road to Barcelona. Marcel said it was a long way to Toulouse, he ate a lot of apples, and he found work with farmers who gave him something to eat and sometimes helped him by truck on the way to Toulouse. Mostly he walked. "Why didn't you join the French Resistance," I asked. He wanted to get over the Pyrenees and find a ship from Barcelona that would take him to England where he would find an army capable of defeating *les Boches*. I gather he did not think too much of the French as fighters although he said they were kind to him in helping him get to Toulouse. He had to get through to the west side of the town. His friend did not want to give him written instructions in case he were stopped and interrogated. It was hard for him to remember the streets she told him but eventually he found the address she gave him and her father was still there. He was very glad to have news of his daughter for he had not heard from her for years. He gave Marcel a coat, gloves, and cap and went with him part of the way. "Was there not a border crossing into Spain?" I asked. He said there was not; there was just a path over the mountain and the main thing was to keep out of sight of anybody. There were few villages and few people around but if he saw anyone he should try and hide.

Spain was supposed to be neutral in WWII but everyone knew they were pro-Nazi. If they found an Englishman they were supposed to direct them to the British Consulate in Barcelona but if they found a French or a Belgian they would know they were escaping from the Nazis and would return them. There was no way Marcel could pass for an Englishman for all the English he knew were the words of a popular song he played in his band in Belgium long ago ("Tiptoe through the tulips, through the garden where the lilies blow"). It was therefore expedient that he keep out of sight. The only people who might help him were the local priests. Again he was given no written instructions. His friend who had helped him said it was important to get to Toulouse and over the mountains while it was still summer for the snow fell early in the Pyrenees. He was later than he had hoped in arriving at Toulouse, it was already early autumn. He had to learn by heart the names on signposts that he should pass.

Marcel was a born raconteur; I felt was listening to a modern *Odyssey*. Apparently he went quite a way without meeting anyone but then he saw a troop of soldiers with guns. They shot over his head and he knew they would interrogate him. He was on the top of a hill so he rolled down the side away from them and in doing so he hurt his arm but rolled to the bottom of the hill where he had the luck to meet a priest. Marcel had been an altar boy and knew some Latin, so he said "*Salve me*" (save me) and the priest did. He took Marcel to his home and tended his arm. He was afraid it might be broken but there was no doctor near and too dangerous to use if there had been. He kept Marcel for several days and fed him up and gave him something to ease the pain. They conversed in Latin, but Marcel said he was not very good in that, had no talent for languages, but that he would be forever grateful to that priest. I cannot remember all his adventures, the saga went on for hours, but I think he was directed to someone with a truck who eventually drove him to Barcelona, again without passing a sentry. I do not know how this was possible, but I suppose one could not have sentry posts all along the Pyrenees. Marcel's French became quicker and quicker and I had difficulty catching every word. I urged him to slow down and he tried.

Once in Barcelona he found his way at first to the American Consulate, but no one could help him there, probably because there was no one to understand him. He was directed to the British Consulate and at last he found someone who could speak French and was willing to help him. By this time he had got frostbitten in two toes for snow had fallen, and before he found the truck he had had to trudge across some snow.

The British Consulate took him in and gave him medical attention and kept him there until there was a ship stopping at Barcelona on its way to England. I did not know there was any trade between those countries during the war but evidently there was. The Consulate gave him English papers, a ticket to England, and money to go by metro to get to the port. The danger was that he might be questioned by the Spanish authorities as to whether he was English; they might know English and he could not speak it. That happened. He was stopped by a Spaniard who asked him to speak English to prove that he was. He spoke the only English he knew: "tiptoe through the tulips to the garden where the lilies grow." This was the most incredible part of the whole story to me. The Spaniard did not know English either and he accepted those couple of lines as proof that Marcel was English and he was allowed on board! I was gasping by this time; truth was certainly stranger than any fiction. I heard the last waltz playing and thanked Marcel and told him he would soon have to go. He put his arm around me and gave me a passionate kiss. I was so dazed by the story I accepted it. As I tottered up to bed I realized he probably did not know my name; I did not remember being introduced, only that he had started off "My name is Marcel."

He did not know my name but as he had the ingenuity to traverse the Pyrenees, he did not let that stop him. A couple of days later there was a letter addressed "A la plus petite demoiselle des Wrens" which was handed to me. He thanked me with all his heart. He was now back in the hospital, would I visit him? Of course I did. On his pajama pocket there were a few music notes. I asked him what they were. He had made up a melody and had no paper to write it on. That pricked my heart full sore. I went out and brought him some music paper. I visited him in hospital and later when he was better we took walks on Wimbledon common. He was very grateful to England but he was afraid he would not be able to fight *les Boches* with England. The war would be over before he was well enough to fight. He was told he would be repatriated to Belgium when the war was ended. He fell in love with me: I was the only one with whom he could talk. I was drawn to him, his amazing story, his blue eyes. He was sent to a convalescent home in the country and asked me to visit him there. He could find a room for me. I was torn. I had promised to be true to Humphrey and felt that I could not keep Marcel at bay as I had Peter. I could perhaps have been happy with either of them, but was determined to remain true to Humphrey, so I told Marcel I could not visit him in the country.

Chapter 42

1945 and Howard.

After Christmas both Nan and I became ill, stomach flu or something. Nan was in Sick Bay but I was in a WRNS hospital with strangers who did not like me. Next to me was an Irish girl who kept singing "One more martyr for olde Ireland, one more murther for the crown." I told her I hated Cromwell for what he had done for Ireland, but she would not speak to me. On my other side was an old Cockney cook. (I tried to remember her tirades for Nan) "You my (may) or not 'ave 'ad trifle wot disagreed, but as soon as you come in, I sez to 'er I sez, I sez, You're three months gawn" (gone=pregnant). There was also a long story about a "ringer." I asked what a ringer was. "Ark at 'er," she said, "oos never gone out with nothing but!" I could have said that was not true, I had gone out with Peter who was a Petty Officer, but there seemed no point; I had never been with people who seemed to dislike me so much.

Ray came to see me and it was a breath of fresh air. She had short curly hair and looked like a face on a Greek coin.

She hummed "*Ave verum*" to me. She was very happy. She had had a fling with a Polish officer who had introduced her to Sim, an older Pole, who before the war had worked as a journalist in Vienna and also sung Polish songs in a cabaret. He had taught her these songs by ear and she very much wanted to add them to her repertoire. She was singing quite a bit around London and to the Poles and these songs were delightful, but she could not find anybody to write a piano part for them. She had sung them to me before a capella and I knew how unusual they were. When the Anschluss came to Vienna in 1938, Sim was surprised to hear his friend in the cabaret announce the Nazi take over. He had not known his friend was a Nazi sympathizer and he realised he had to leave Vienna immediately for his colleague knew he was Jewish. He came to England in 1938 through the Quakers although I never met him then. He obtained a good job at the BBC writing for and talking to Radio Poland. I had met him through Ray who had now moved in with him; they were married later. I was worried when she did this because of my experience with Jean, but she was not. I had never seen her so happy or singing so well or so much.

I remember the first time I met Sim. He knew I was coming and opened the door to me with open arms prepared to give me the Viennese-Polish embrace but I was holding a pair of shoes I had picked up from the cobblers and did not know what to do with them, drop them or give them to him or what. We laughed, I laughed a lot with Ray and Sim; he was a very witty man, and I was introduced again to the magic of those who had known Vienna, although his Viennese accent was tinged with Polish overtones.

I was waiting in hospital for Ray to give me an answer to an ethical question. She was much more ethical than I was. I knew this when I first met her at Ventnor and she was handing out sheets. Most people kept the best sheets for themselves or their friends; she kept the ragged ones for herself which impressed me very much. The doctor had told me he could give me a medical discharge on the grounds that I was a nervous wreck from the V2s, could not sleep or eat. Did I think I was essential to the war effort? I did not think that translating love letters in German script sodden in seawater was essential, but wanted to know what Ray thought. She told me to accept the medical discharge, that it was no disgrace, that indeed the Admiralty wanted to get rid of us now the radar stations were closed. She was only still employed at Shaef because she had some place to stay in London when her Wrennery was closed. The doctor had told me that I needed rest from the V2s in order to be able to sleep again, and fresh eggs and fresh milk to ease my stomach pains. Did I have somewhere to go in the country where I could get these? I said my mother and aunt were in Wales where people did keep chickens but they had to give all the eggs to the Egg Board for people in hospital who needed them. He said he could give me a letter recommending that I get fresh eggs and real milk. Was I justified in taking this? Ray told me to take the medical discharge, that it was no disgrace. I was worried about leaving Nan, but she was given the same opportunity. It was hard to leave Nan. For six months we had been together day and night, but we promised to write and we did.

When Aunt Dora heard of my medical discharge she suggested I come and stay with her at Hafan for a week where she could give me a room looking on the sea and Elizabeth, her old cook whom I had known for years, would look after me during the day she was at work with the children. And through the Children's Home she could even get me the fresh eggs and milk the doctor ordered. Mummy agreed for she had only a small bedroom with a double bed which she and Bettina shared at weekends, with a mattress on the floor for me whenever I had leave. I could never stand sleeping with anybody, their legs seemed to get in my way; I wondered sometimes how I would manage when married.

I remember waking up in the little room looking over the sea to Harlech. It was March and early spring in Wales. The sky, the sea, the hills were blue; even the air seemed shining blue. I had slept for thirteen hours and Elizabeth brought me the most perfect scrambled eggs made with real eggs and butter and milk. They were on toast and it was the most delicious meal I had ever tasted. Mummy and Auntie visited me often but mostly I slept. When I was awake and alone I looked over to the mountains and thought about Donald.

I thought about how he had written that he was mentally and spiritually prepared for death. It must seem strange for anyone in this day and age to realize what he meant but I knew. Donald was among the last in many generations who had been brought up in the classical tradition, *dulce et decorum pro patria mori* (it is sweet and fitting to die for one's country), and he was ready to die for England. England meant to him what it meant to me, Manor Farm and the hills and woods around it and the views over to the distant Weald of Kent. He had written me that Normandy reminded him of Sussex so that he felt at home. He knew the Sussex villages which each had a memorial to those who had died in WWI. By the Vietnam War this feeling had gone, but in WWII we did feel it was a righteous war and Hitler had to be stopped and Donald was ready to give his life. By "spiritually" he meant "religiously." He was religious as I was; we never spoke about it, one didn't, but I knew he believed in an afterlife where he would see his loved ones again. I felt with C.S. Lewis that each one brought his own heaven with him, the best he had known on earth; Rilke felt the same way and so did Keats who wrote that heaven contained "the happiness known on earth repeated in a finer tone."

Lying there, looking over mountains to Harlech, I considered reincarnation. It did seem unfair that Donald had missed so much of life. Plato believed in reincarnation. In his Myth of Er, in Book lO of *The Republic* he suggested that one chose one's next life on the wisdom learned in this. On the other hand I think it was a Greek who said "Whom the gods love, die young." Donald would be spared much grief and disillusion. I felt very near to Donald, then and all through my life. Whenever I ate celery I would remember how he would get up from the dinner table to fetch it if it had remained by someone's plate and not reached us. When I heard Fred Astaire music or Paul Robeson I would remember him; whenever I saw a ping pong table or heard owls. Visually I could see him in my mind's eye better than my mother, sister or aunt. Auntie Dora had an oil painting made of his last photo in uniform which captured him very well at 24, and at that age he looked much the same as he did in his teens, so he remained forever young whereas we others changed.

It is hard to remember the last few months of the war; they are very confused in my mind. After a week at Hafan spoiled rotten by Elizabeth's cooking, I went down to my mother's flat in the village and went through my case with my pre-uniform clothes. It was strange not to wear a collar and tie and I did not like anything found in the case, but I did find Howard's letter which to my shame I had never answered. It had arrived during the Blitz and I had not known what to say. Now I did and wrote with many apologies wishing him every happiness. I told him I had come through the war, that Donald had been killed and that I was waiting for Humphrey's return. I hoped he was safe and happy and sent it to his parents' address in Rhode Island which was on his last letter and to which I had always written in the past and then forgot about it.

I wrote regularly to Humphrey but his letters became less frequent. I knew he had been through a terrible time; he constantly referred to the fact that he was the only officer in his regiment who had not been killed. He was glad I was out of London; apparently they did hear of the V2s although we were never allowed to mention them in letters. He thought he would be demobbed two months after the end of war. He would go home for a week and then drive in his car to see me. It should be possible by then to get petrol.

Aunt Dora was a great organizer. Apparently she had contacted an agent in Sussex to try and sell Manor Farm. It held too much of Donald for her and also it was now too large to run. Elizabeth was getting old and would have to retire. The agent had found someone interested. Somehow or other the agent had also found a smaller house and garden near Wadhurst Station for herself and Uncle, Rita and Gordon when they came home, and had rented a bungalow a mile down the road in Ticehurst village for my mother, sister and me. As soon as the war ended which now seemed inevitable, we would go down for a few weeks to Manor Farm to clear out things. Our house and my uncle and aunt's house in Blackheath had been badly damaged by bombs at the beginning of the war and Donald had stored our furniture at the Works. Life was changing so fast it did not seem possible. I was greatly cheered by the gift of a dress from Aline's sister in New York who evidently had been sent my measurements. It was blue with white trimming round the collar and cuffs and it remains in my mind as one of the few dresses I remember.

Bettina was demobbed early; her airstrip was closed as it was used mostly for Canadians coming over for training in Wales, and there was no need of them anymore. I know at least two men had fallen for her but she was always faithful to Ronnie, who had been shipped out to India in 1943 to train mechanics there. I think she had a soft spot for the Colonel for whom she worked. He must have been instrumental in obtaining for her the drop of petrol she needed to drive over the mountain to see my mother. Before he left for India, Ronnie had persuaded Bettina to get away from Chatham driving ambulances and into the WAAF (Women's RAF) with compassionate posting near our mother. Bettina worked extra hours during the week to get the time off on Saturday to visit her for the night. She was one of the few WAAFs allowed to drive at night, and she was on constant call during the week as most of the Canadians arrived at night. She drove the 32-seater Dodge coach over the mountains in the night which was some feat. The Canadians were always very impressed when they met their small driver. It was fortunate she was there and able to drive us in the big car down to Sussex. My uncle had not had a heart attack on hearing of Donald's death, but he had become confused and was not capable of driving any more. It seems that everybody knew the war was ended before it was officially declared. Parents came up to get their children from the Home that Auntie had run for children from Greenwich where the Works was situated. The Home was closed and it seems to me that we drove down to Sussex a few days before the end of the war because I have a memory of hearing the news of the end at Manor Farm and also seeing it on Uncle's TV, one of the earliest, which stayed at the Farm. I remember seeing Churchill with the King and Queen and children on the balcony and the thousands of crowds; I was thankful I was not there, I always hated crowds. It was strange to be at Manor Farm again; the nightingales were singing, it was May. Auntie would not come with me to hear them. The Farm to her was Donald, and she could not wait to get away.

A week or so after the end of the war, still in May, Auntie came from answering the phone with a strange look on her face. "For you, Audrey, an American. He says his name is Howard and he is in Portmadoc. You had better take it in the study." I don't know how I reached the phone. It was Howard and he was in Portmadoc. He had taken one of the first planes from France and somehow found his way to this remote Welsh village from which I had written him, and then I was not there. "I must see you," he said, "I've come so far." "But you are married!" was all I could find to say. "It's nothing of a marriage," he said. "It was a disaster from the start. I always loved you. I haven't seen her for two years. When I had a chance for home leave, I chose instead to go to France. We never write. Please see me, I've come so far." That really hit home to me. How could he have got over from France? I did not know any planes were flying between the two countries. "How did you know I was here?" I asked. "I went to the address in Portmadoc from which you had written and found you had left, and the woman said I should go next door to Mrs. Clara Richards who would know where you were. Mrs. Richards told me and kindly let me use her phone." Clara said later she was dubious if she were doing the right thing but he seemed such a nice young man, and he had come so far. "Please see me," repeated Howard. My mind seemed to get into gear again. I could not ask him to the Farm, we were just about to leave for our new homes and all was chaotic. I thought of Ray; she had said I always had a room with them. It would be easier to meet Howard in London and I was sure she would put us both up. I had just looked up trains to London, for Ray had asked me to come and hear her at a lunchtime concert. The earliest train from Robertsbridge at that time did not arrive at Charing Cross till 1.30 pm, which was too late for the concert, but I knew the time of the train and also that the London train left Portmadoc at 8 am and arrived in Paddington at 1 pm. I gave Howard this information and said my friend, Ray, would put us both up. "I'll have time to get from Paddington to Charing Cross and I'll meet your train and we can go to St. James's Park," Howard said. I was touched he remembered St. James's Park was near Charing Cross Station and certainly it would be better to talk there than in a station, so we agreed to do this.

I went back to my aunt, mother and sister and was in such a daze that I repeated verbatim all our conversation. My mother and sister looked stunned but my aunt took it in stride. "Of course you must meet him," she said. I phoned Ray and she could put us both up.

My sister drove me to the station in the morning. "I always knew you would do something strange," she said. I don't know how I got to London, but when I saw Howard at the end of the platform, I suddenly knew everything was all right and coming out as it should. I forgot all about Humphrey and my intention to be true to him, and ran towards Howard and we kissed long and sweetly, until I drew back, shaken. "You are married." He repeated what he had said on the phone, that it was a disaster of a marriage, he had always loved me but it seemed so hopeless when my letters grew scarce. She wanted to get married but it never worked. He hadn't seen her for two years and when he had the chance for home leave, he chose France. They never wrote, they would get a divorce, it was easy in America. "Then will you marry me?" On Charing Cross station with all the crowds I suddenly knew it felt right, I belonged to him and not to Humphrey who never read a book or listened to music. I remembered what I had already shared with Howard, music, architecture, Shakespeare, flowers, and I agreed. We went into St. James's Park, had tea and sandwiches at a little kiosk and then went and sat on a seat, and he put his arm around me and it felt so good. He said he had been traveling for days and it was dreadful to find I was not in Portmadoc, but he had found me now. He said tomorrow we should go to the American Embassy and find a lawyer, so that I would know the whole situation. He planned also to go to London University where he had applied for a Ph.D. program in Piano Pedagogy and been accepted, "so we will have two years in England, but then I will not be able to get a job here, even with an English Ph.D. much as I would like to, because there are already so many refugee musicians here. The Board of Musicians will not agree to any Americans. Do you think you could stand leaving England?" I said it would not be so bad now there was no longer war and fear for my family; also I had lost Manor Farm, which to me was England. I could accept the thought of it now.

Howard wanted to go to an American PBX so he could get some food to take to Ray, but I told him there was a PBX near the Embassy where we were going tomorrow and we were going out tonight, but I was impressed he thought about it. He then asked if we could go on the top of a bus to Ray's, as he remembered I liked doing that rather than going by tube. "Is it still tuppence?" he asked. I really did not know. This was the first time in years that I would have to pay a fare; for so long I had just shown my Naval Pass. I think it had gone up to fourpence for central London. It seems incredible now that it was so little.

On the way back to Ray's I had a sudden thought. I knew how much she wanted to find someone who could write out a piano accompaniment to her Polish songs and it occurred to me that perhaps Howard could. He was glad that he would be able to do something for her and said it should not be too difficult if it were just folk songs and she could sing them to him. I was delighted about this. Ray and Sim greeted us with wine, but Howard said he would rather write down the piano accompaniment for her songs first. Ray was so happy about this she gave him a kiss and they sat down at the piano right away. Ray asked me which one and I said "Rosmarian," which was the only one I could pronounce. She sang it first and then he played along with her and asked for manuscript paper so he could write it down. It did not take long and he insisted on doing another one before a glass of wine. It was a very happy occasion. They then asked him to play. He said he had been two years in the Army without a piano, playing the organ at services, and had only just started again but he would play something short. It was the Chopin E Flat Nocturne. Tears pricked into my ears that he had remembered I liked that. He turned round and kissed me and we all had another glass.

They wanted to know how he had got over from France so quickly. The war had just been over two weeks. I never quite understood how he had managed that. Apparently he had put in for it as soon as he received my letter in March, and arrived somewhere in Wales and then had a hard time getting to Portmadoc only to find I was not there. Mrs. Morris, Mummy's landlady, told him to go next door to see Clara Richards who could tell him where I was. It was really a synchronicity that he arrived when he did. A few days later we would have left Manor Farm and the telephone had not yet been installed at our cottage. It would have been very complicated for us to have found each other. If I had been in Portmadoc when he arrived it would not have been so easy for us to talk as it was in St. James's Park. It was all rather amazing friend and then Simmy's rich Polish friend said we should drink again to romance and then invited us to eat at the Polish Club. I was glad I was wearing my one nice dress sent to me from America. We danced and I realized Howard did not dance as well as Humphrey but it did not matter, I was very happy to be with him and we had a wonderful evening. Ray sang the two songs and Howard accompanied her; it was all magical.

The next day we went to the American Embassy and saw a lawyer. I felt embarrassed but the lawyer was very kind and said Howard was right to bring me along so I would know the whole situation. Howard repeated what he had already told me, that he had not seen her for over two years, that when he had been given the chance to go home on leave he had chosen to go to France, that they never wrote and that the marriage had been a disaster from the beginning. He thought she would be glad of a fresh start and would agree to a divorce. The lawyer asked if she had a job and when Howard said she did not he looked grave and said that was unusual, most young women in America were doing war work, and she might want his money. Howard said she lived with her parents and they were comfortably off. If she would agree, the lawyer said, it would go through easily. If she did not he would have to wait till they had been separated three years and then go to Reno, where it would definitely be granted but would cost him an arm and a leg.

The lawyer then asked when Howard hoped to be demobbed and Howard said he had a contract at the University of Biarritz to teach piano until Christmas. He had done this as the Army was looking for teachers with degrees in order that the thousands of Americans now in Europe would learn something while they were waiting to go home, which was not so easy for them as for the Britons. They needed ships to take them and only two Cunard liners were available, capable of taking a thousand at a time. Of course, at this time the war in the East was still going on and it was not certain who would be sent there. That was a horrible thought; Howard did not think it likely in his case as he had been through the Battle of the Bulge and had the qualifications to teach. The lawyer said if his wife did not agree to a divorce he could stay on teaching at Biarritz University as he could not go to Reno until spring, and so it worked out. She did not agree, he had to go Reno, and it did cost him an arm and a leg, and he did not get over to England until the next summer. The lawyer said it would also be a good idea to go to the University of London and put in an application for the next fall term. So this is what we did that day.

All went well there; Howard even found a professor willing to take him and ready to be his major professor for his PhD dissertation on Piano Pedagogy, so he signed up to start next August, which seemed a long time away.

We then went to the PBX and Howard bought a lot of canned food and cheese which was still rationed in England. I saw a bowl of maraschino cherries which I had not seen for six years but remembered Daddy having for Manhattans and they looked so luscious I could not stop staring at them. "Take one," said the nice young man behind the bar, although we were not drinking there. "Have all you want." I took one and it was ambrosia, two and it was delicious, three, four and then I knew I would never want another maraschino cherry in my life.

Howard was very anxious to know when I would see Humphrey. I told him he expected to be home in June, and would spend a few days with his family in Dorset and then he hoped to find petrol for his car to drive to Sussex to see me. Howard said he would not feel at ease until I had seen him. I assured him not to worry. I was quite clear in my mind that Howard and I belonged together in spite of all that stood in our way. I told Howard I had been true to Humphrey for over a year in spite of having two interesting young men fall in love with me, but now felt sure it was with Howard my die was cast. It is hard today to realize how dreadful and how unusual a divorce was then. I knew of no one who had been divorced.

Howard had only a few days leave and he had to go back to his teaching job at Biarritz. He was optimistic that she would agree to the divorce, that he could come over to England and marry me and we would have some months together in Biarritz. I was not so sanguine. He did get over to England once again before he was demobbed and came down to meet the family. The atom bomb had fallen and we no longer had to fear he might be sent to the East so we were thankful for that. He wrote to me every day, the most wonderful letters, and we came to know each other even better through them. The postman at Ticehurst was most sympathetic and took an interest in our correspondence. If there were a day without a letter he would assure me there would be two tomorrow. "I hate coming without a letter," he once said.

After my first visit with Howard, Mr. Piggott picked me up at the station as Bettina and Mummy were over at the cottage getting things ready. He and Mrs. Piggott had stayed at Manor Farm during the war and were taken over by the new owners. He was the first one I told.

"I am going to marry an American." "Is he a gardening sort of man?" he enquired. I assured him Howard was. "Do they have the same flowers in America?" he wanted to know. I knew they had roses. "You will remember what I taught you about pruning roses, and soap and water for black spot." I assured him I would.

I found my aunt alone and told her everything. She was a tower of strength from the first. She advised me not to tell people about the divorce; there was really no need they should know and many would be upset for me. I had decided I would not tell Nan because I knew she would be shocked. I only told Ray and Sim and the Polaks and wished I had not told the latter for they were concerned. It was another age and I was stepping out of it. I do not know how I would have managed without my aunt.

Howard got on very well with my family, they all liked him. At our first meeting I asked him how much the war had affected his ambition to be a concert pianist. He said that of course it had thrown a spanner into the works, but now he was back to practicing four hours a day and was going to give a concert in Biarritz in October. He asked me if I thought I could stand the long hours of practicing; he had had problems with that with his wife but I was not a bit concerned. "Just tell me what you are playing so that I will learn which Beethoven sonata is which and I will do my embroidery and listen and learn and it will be wonderful." I was worried that taking the time for the PhD might hinder him, but he said it would be an asset. Times had changed, very few could live by just giving concerts, it would be an advantage to be on the piano faculty of a good university and an English PhD would be a help in finding a good position. We only had a few days each visit but the letters were a great bond. One had grown used to absence during the war.

Chapter 43

Ticehurst and Devon.

My aunt had rented a cottege for us near her at Ticehurtst. It was a delightful fourteenth-century village with an inn and a butcher's shop from that time and a church which the Vicar said must have been started in the thirteenth century, for it had a Lepers' Squint. By the fourteenth century leprosy was no longer a great problem in England. I wrote a poem about it which describes it:

LEPERS' SQUINT
Go back six centuries
to Ticehurst village church.
There still were lepers then
who lived outside in fields
or in deserted barns.
Perhaps the people left out food,
they must have done
for how could lepers work
with toes and fingers gone?

This Christian charity was cheap
compared to kindly touch,
contagion feared by all.
Outside the church the ground
was high towards the east
and here they cut the squint,
a square carved in the wall
that slid into a slit
above the altar and the Host.
When summoned by church bell
and all the rest were safe inside
through here the living dead
could see the wine and see the bread
that brought Communion.

There was also a thirteenth-century fresco which had been covered over in the Reformation and then re-discovered. It was of St. Christopher carrying the Christ child on his shoulder. St. Christopher was for centuries the patron saint of travelers; he was always portrayed as very tall, and in this fresco fish were putting out their tongues at his big feet. This proved that the fresco was early for by the fourteenth century such grotesque description was discouraged. I loved it. There was also some good fifteenth-century stained glass in the windows. The church was beautiful and we took to going every Sunday and then on to lunch with my aunt and uncle.

The plans for reunion with Humphrey had been set up long ago. He was due to be demobbed at the beginning of June, would spend a few days at home and then hopefully get enough petrol to drive his car to visit me and stay at the fourteenth-century village inn. We had no room at Little Pashley, which was a very small cottage. This was only two weeks after I had met Howard again. I was very anxious to see Humphrey. At this late date I had no intention of writing him a "Dear John" letter. I felt sure I would feel the same about Howard when I saw Humphrey but had to make certain. Howard felt too that this was only right but he was anxious the meeting be over. In the meantime he had written home asking for a divorce, had been given a categorical refusal, so it would have to be Reno. I never really expected it to be easy. Howard hoped it would be and that he could get over to England and marry me and we would have some months together in Biarritz; I was not so sanguine. I was eager to see Humphrey and get it over; I felt in a spider's web. His letters had been strained of late. I certainly could not write him, I had to see him.

It was agreed he would phone when he got to the inn. Mummy and Bettina would then retire to the kitchen and we would have the living room to ourselves. I saw him coming down the path, for the first time out of uniform, but he still looked distinguished and very English. I opened the door and the words rolled out of me somehow: "Humphrey, I cannot marry you. I have been true to you for over a year in spite of provocation, but Howard, the American pianist I told you about, flew over from France to see me and I just know I really belong to him." Humphrey stood stock still. "You are going to marry an American and go to America. I never would have believed it of you." He seemed more

275

surprised that I was going to America than that I was not going to marry him! The enormity of it suddenly dawned on me but I clung on to the closeness I had felt with Howard. "I know it is strange." "How could you go to America, you love England so much?" I did not know how I could but just felt it was inevitable. "I couldn't write you, I just had to see you," I said, "it only happened two weeks ago." "Let's sit down," said Humphrey, "and let us have a drink." There were drinks on the table.

"Your letters have been strained of late," I said. "How is it with you?" Then he told me had met a girl in Holland and had an affair with her, it was over, he would never see her again, and it did not mean that much, "but maybe I'm not the marrying sort of man," he said. I do not know if he said that to make me feel better, but it did. "How can you leave England?" he kept on. I told him I had lost Manor Farm, my uncle had sold it after the death of my cousin, and that had been England to me and I had lost it. "That is not true," he said. "Didn't you tell me that an old right-of-way ran through your uncle's property, and that it was not far from here. We could drive there tomorrow and at least see the lake. Did you hear the nightingales this year?" I said I had but that they were over now. "Never mind," he said, "We will go there tomorrow." I was amazed; I had not thought I'd see Manor Farm again and it touched me very much that Humphrey thought of doing such a thing.

We intended next day to drive through Sussex to Hastings to see Battle Abbey and the field of 1066, which Humphrey had never seen. We drove by Manor Farm and down the right-of-way and stopped at the wrought iron gate to look into the courtyard. There was someone in the garden so I had to explain I had lived there as a child, that it had belonged to my uncle and I wanted to show my friend the lake. The woman was most kind and invited us into the garden, so I saw again the Elizabethan bowling lawn, the sunken rose garden and the view from the terrace over the hills. She asked us into the house but that I did not want, asking instead if we could go down to the orchard. She told us to make ourselves at home so we walked past the old well covered in honeysuckle where glowworms hid at night and down to the stream which divided the garden from the orchard. "This is where you heard the nightingales," said Humphrey and we stopped and held hands for a moment for we had shared something perfect. Indeed, I think my first view of heaven will be the last light on the bluebells and the nightingales beginning to be heard above the thrushes, blackbirds, and warblers.

We drove down to the lake, walked around it, and then on to Sock'nersh, another Elizabethan manor and on to Burwash where Kipling lived and so through Sussex to Hastings. We had dinner there and danced. No one danced as well as Humphrey and I remember thinking "this is the end of my dancing days." But that was all right. I realized I belonged to Howard and wrote him so that night. The next day I took Humphrey to the church and a long walk through the woods at Birchinwood Farm. He said, "These woods are very fine but of course the ones you grew up in will always be the best." We parted as friends; he asked me to meet him in

London, but I was not sure about that. I realized I was right to have met him. We belonged together in the woods, but life was not lived in the woods or on the dancing floor.

When Howard found out that he could not get a divorce until after three years 'absence, which would be in March, and that he would have to go to Reno to get it, he wrote me that he thought it best not to apply for early demob but to stay at Biarritz University as long as possible for he was earning good money there as a teacher as well as his military pay and the divorce would cost a great deal. He had heard from University of London that he would have to be in attendance there in August to start his two—years Ph.D. program. He hoped to get back to England by early summer and I should think about where we should spend our honeymoon. He thought the G.I. Bill would provide enough for us to live frugally in London for the two years of his doctoral work; he did not want me to work. I had written him that I could get a job as a translator or secretary.

I told my family these developments and my aunt said she and my uncle had decided that the best thing they could give me as a wedding present was a rent-free flat for the two years we would spend in England. She was negotiating with a real estate agent in Blackheath to purchase a house that had sustained some bomb damage in order to provide a retirement home for her old cook, Elizabeth, and also for Mrs. B. who had been manageress at Uncle's works for a very long time. The large living room at the back with conservatory attached she thought could be adapted as a flatlet for Howard and me. She was a ambitious organizer, nothing daunted her. She decided the conservatory could be altered to become a kitchen/bathroom. There was already water there and a bath could be installed with a kitchen table hung above it which could be lowered over it. There was already a sink and room for a stove. "But isn't it all glass?" I asked. Yes, it was, but she thought I could make curtains to draw when we were taking a bath and it looked out into quite a large garden which would be ours, but she supposed we would occasionally invite Elizabeth and Mrs. B. to enjoy it. We went up to town to try to find materials for curtains but in all the stores there was still only blackout material. She bought that and Mummy had some red ribbon, yards of it, which I machined in two rows on the bottom. Auntie said Howard could have the piano from her old house at Blackheath, which had been in storage at the Works since the house was bombed out in 1940. It was a good piano and she had it properly retuned and renovated. The curtains in the living room were fine and heavy and would keep out the cold and we had a real fireplace. We would have a small bedroom upstairs and a toilet we would share with Elizabeth. It all sounded very exciting.

After the war Uncle made a Settlement for Bettina and me which I felt she deserved more than I did. She had to drive Auntie and Uncle around, and Uncle proved to be quite a problem. He must have had Alzheimer's although they did not call it that then. He was very vague and would wander out of the house and garden at all times of day and night. My aunt found a wonderful couple, Mr. and Mrs. Hawkins. Mrs. did the cooking and Mr. Hawkins who had been a butler was landed with the task of keeping an eye on Uncle. On his day off it fell to Bettina.

Ronnie was not demobbed for a long time. In 1943 he had been shipped out to India to teach Indians how to become mechanics. He had saved all his money and when he came home he asked Bettina to marry him and thought they could start a taxi service together; Mummy could come along. But even though Ronnie was the only man she'd ever loved, Bettina did not fancy marriage. She often told me she did not see how I could stand having a man around all the time. She felt it her bounden duty to care for Mummy and they both were very happy together, though possibly my mother might have married again as she was only in her forties and very pretty, but I do not think either of them thought much of marriage.

Mummy's wealthy friend from Wales had now a flat in London and she was always urging Mummy to come up for several days and go to theatres with her, which she did about twice a month. Ronnie then came down to visit Bettina and eventually they became lovers and went away for holidays together. With the money he had saved Bettina encouraged him to grow chrysanthemums which he had always wanted to do and he produced the most beautiful blooms. He went to live with his brother and his wife and had quite a good job. I often met them for a drink; I felt sorry for him for he would have liked children, but Bettina was an unusual character and did not care for the usual things and one just had to accept it. Mummy did too and she was quite helpful, always ready to go up to London for theatres; I do not think she ever met Ronnie, who did not get home to England until after I left Ticehurst.

Bettina enjoyed village life. She became good friends with our neighbors, the Vidlers, who owned the farm next to us. She was one of the few who could understand Mr. Vidler, who spoke broad Sussex. It sounded a bit like Middle English. He came to see us soon after we arrived and we gathered was asking us not to draw water in the afternoon till after 4 pm as he watered his cows at that time and we shared the water. "My luvvies have to drink at four and canna bid them wait." When we realized his "luvvies" were his cows of course we agreed to wait for tea till 4.30 pm and never do a wash or have a bath in the afternoon. I asked him how he managed to get so much coal, which was in a big heap outside his back door. "Tidnt all for we," he said, which became a catchword with us. He was a thin wiry man and his wife was taller than he, a fine figure of a woman and aptly named Boadicea though he called her "Sissy." When Bettina was fond of someone, she gave them initials so they became Mr. and Mrs. V. This dated back to our childhood, I think, when she could not pronounce my name and called me "Olly." When I was nine or ten I revolted and she said she would then call me "O" and only "Audrey" in public. Mrs. V. became Bettina's great friend. There was a son called Bruce, about twenty, who had just missed the war and became rather sweet on Bettina. He had one of the new tractors and they both spent ages testing it out or just looking at it.

We had no electricity and Bruce showed us how to light oil lamps, at least he showed Bettina. Mummy and I never mastered the art and I liked to go to bed with a candle which shone on wild flowers by my bedside. I remember primroses.

"Flowers under candlelight/have caught eternity/So far beyond the world/ their enchanted spirits sail/ that to the eyes of angels/ their petals are unfurled."

Ray and Simmy were married shortly after the end of the war, and I went up to their quiet wedding. After their honeymoon in Devon, they came to see us and we put them up at the fourteenth-century inn in the village. Mrs. V. knew we had friends from London and gave us half a dozen eggs to give to Ray. She had not seen a fresh egg since before the war. Mummy made one of her classic remarks: "What I say is, you can always fall back on an egg!" Rationing remained, and I remember what we received: 2 ozs butter, 2 ozs margarine, 2 ozs lard, 6 ozs cheese, 6 ozs meat and two half pints of milk a week per person. Sugar was rationed but forget the amount; it was mostly kept for making jam. Clothing, material and shoes were also rationed and hard to find. In the country we grew fresh fruits and vegetables and even in London nearly everyone had an allotment but there was not enough protein. I was worried how Howard would cope with rationing but he wrote if we had stood it for six years he could stand it for two, and all he wanted was for us to be together. I asked him what clothes he had and he replied "Two suits and two split combinations." This gave us a good laugh for "combinations" in England are the same as long-johns or underwear; he meant two trousers and jackets that did not match. I wrote him that George Bernard Shaw had said England and America were two nations divided by a language. We wrote to each other every day and his letters were wonderful. We learned so much of each other from them.

Life in Ticehurst village was very friendly. We came to know the owners of Pashley Manor, and their Elizabethan manor house which had belonged to Anne Boleyn's family. It was rather in need of repair and the Forsyths hoped to be able to renovate it when things became better. Verity was an author, first I had ever met, and I showed her some of my poems. She suggested I submit them for publication so I did and two were published which bucked me up no end.

The Sawyers lived further down the road and he was very interested in Chinese porcelain. I longed to introduce Howard to him for Howard was the first to get me interested in oriental art. Geoffrey Sawyer had married a Belgian girl during the war who did not speak much English and was glad to speak French with me. She told me the first thing the Belgians said after being liberated by the Americans was "*Vous avez vu leurs dents?*" (Have you seen their teeth?) American teeth were a wonder to Belgians and English alike. In England if you had buck teeth before the war you were stuck with them; braces were unknown and the straight white shining teeth of the Americans were a wonder.

We were closest to the Vidlers who lived next door and Mrs. V slipped each of us an egg nearly every week. Apparently she did this to others too for a dreadful thing happened. She was summoned by the Egg Board to appear in court and account for every egg her chickens hatched. Mr. V. was incoherent in his Anglo-Saxon. "His Cissie knew not the Black market during the war but wherefore could she not give a friend an occasional egg now." Only Bettina could understand him and she came up with a stroke of genius. "Why doesn't Mr. V. go to the Egg Board? They won't be able to know what he says but he is a true Sussex farmer." Mrs. V. had always done the PR and dealt with the Egg Board, but she agreed this was a good idea. Mr. V. went; nobody understood a word he said and Mrs. V. was let off with a caution and no fine. Mrs. V. was famous in our family for coming up with the idea that there was always an extra drop in the bottom of the bottle. We called this a "Mrs. V" and passed it on to others.

In September 1945 Nan wrote me from Devon and asked me to come and stay for a week. Ken had been demobbed early but he did not want to work as an Estate Agent (realtor) with his father in law although he had found them a nice flat in Bristol. Ken had other ideas. Ken was Cornish, brilliant but a little strange. The first time I met him at a tea party in Ventnor I handed him a plate of bread and butter and he said: "No thanks, never touch it." I realized he was one with my father in never letting truth distort a good line, and laughed. As a Major in the Paratroops he been demobbed with a nice sum of money and with this he bought the Ford franchise to sell tractors in Devon (there had been no tractors in Devon up till this time). He also bought an old blacksmith's forge and with the help of a mechanic who had been with him in the war, set up the first repair shop for tractors in Devon. It was a brilliant idea; in five years he became very rich and eventually was elected Mayor of Crediton where the first thing he did was to abolish pay toilets for women. This made national news and eventually other towns followed suit. This was in the future; now Nan and Ken were living in a thatched cottage with a well.

Nan and I had corresponded since we were demobbed in March and she knew we were living without electricity and having to wait for the cows to be watered before having our afternoon tea. She hoped I would not mind having a bath every other day. Ken drew the water from the well but the tank which had to be heated by a gas geyser only held enough for two baths and water for washing. Ken had to have a bath every day as he became dirty working in the forge. They were very happy but she was lonely as he was working so hard and only came home for lunch. She wanted to know all about the Humphrey/Howard situation; she was still not pregnant and unhappy about that. She hoped I could come; of course I would have to bring my ration card but would be glad to hear milk was no longer rationed in Devon as there were so many cows and she could promise me a dish of Devonshire (clotted) cream for tea everyday with raspberry jam which she had made herself using all their sugar rations. I was delighted at the thought of seeing her and managed to find two bottles of whisky which I knew they liked. Bettina always seemed to know a place where such luxuries could be found.

I took the train down to Devon on a Saturday so Ken could meet me with the car at Exeter. Nan was learning to drive but only in the villages as yet. We passed Dartington Hall and other places they suggested for a honeymoon, not too far from them with a bicycle. Nan introduced me to hanging baskets of geraniums; I had seen those in Germany but not in England and I always think of her in connection with them.

The cream teas were even more delicious than anticipated. The kitchen had a big black stove which was kept on all the time; in the morning Nan put a dish of milk on the stove, without separating the cream, it cooked slowly during the day and was "clotted" enough to eat with a spoon at tea time on scones. This was the famous Devonshire cream. They ate their main meal at lunchtime with meat such as it was and vegetables, and had "high" tea about 6 p.m. The first day we had an egg with our tea but eggs were just as scarce as in Sussex and after that she gave us rhubarb. I noticed Ken made a face but said nothing and turned rather gloomy. The next day we still had rhubarb and Ken was so silent that Nan later remarked to me that he was often very moody. I said "Try giving him something else besides rhubarb for his tea, what about baked beans?" She told him what I had said and they both laughed and rhubarb was banished. Whisky cheered Ken up and he regaled us with the most fascinating tales; he had been in the Merchant Navy before the war and like my father never minded stretching the truth for a good line. I told them about Mrs. V. saying there was always an extra drop at the bottom of the bottle which we had come to call a "Mrs. V." and they took to that and quoted it to me years later.

After my return from Devon I thought it was incumbent on me to try to earn some money, but the BBC no longer had any use for my services. I found a job as a secretary in London but after paying for my room, meals and fares home decided I was not earning enough to make it worthwhile and I loathed being a secretary. One Friday evening in February when I came home for the weekend there was an almond tree in flower against a green sky. I realized this was probably the last spring I would see in the country, for Howard and I would live in London and only be able to come down for occasional weekends. I decided to enjoy this last spring in Ticehurst and did; I saw the snowdrops, the celandines, primroses and then bluebells. I walked in the woods nearly every day and worked in the garden at Little Pashley, and tried to learn some cooking from Bettina.

Howard wrote me of some of his experiences in the War. He had been present at the liberation of Paris and had seen several operas. They had been stationed at Chantilly, a little way away and an extra train was put on to get the troops back after the performances. He had seen Chartres Cathedral and hoped that we would be able to visit there and go further west to Mont St. Michel which he had not been able to see. In Belgium he loved Ghent and the van Eyck Altarpiece there, also Bruges. He had found wonderful friends in Holland who wanted us to come and stay and we could also see the art museums in Amsterdam.

He had been organist to the Chaplain of the Seventh Army and had seen service in the front line. He wrote me this story: he drove the Chaplain around in a jeep which held the organ and he had strict instructions never to remove the tarpaulin that covered the organ except during services. The Chaplain, however, one day ordered Howard to remove the tarpaulin and get in the jeep and fill in the holes in the floor which were there for the purpose of draining water that might leak in during a storm. The organ was on a little platform above the rest of the floor. The Chaplain wanted the holes removed as he wished to store some of his papers there, and pens and small objects might fall through. Howard was reluctant to go against instructions but the Chaplain was adamant so Howard left the tarpaulin over the organ and began filling in the holes in at the furthest corner from it. There was a sudden alarm, they had to leave immediately, the Battle of the Bulge had started and they were in the direct line of advancing German tanks. Howard hastily flung the tarpaulin back over the jeep but was unable to fasten it down securely except over the organ. The Chaplain had already put in some of his things; they had to drive madly through the night and a dreadful storm and his papers were sodden. It was not Howard's fault but he felt the Chaplain held a grudge against him on account of that incident. Howard received the Bronze Star but he would never give me details about that; he made light of it and said it was just for being in the Battle of the Bulge. He took part in the Normandy landings but after the beaches had been more or less secured by the Allied Forces.

Chapter 44

Howard and honeymoon.

At last he arrived in England. We said our vows very quietly in the old Ticehurst church where the fishes put out their tongues at St. Christopher's feet. Only the immediate family was there and we left the same day for our honeymoon in Devon. For our first stay I had booked Cumstock which was near a station so that we could take a cab to our destination. My cousin Rita sent our bicycles on next day and we walked to the station to pick them up. They were very useful; they had the new gears which helped on the hills. There were fifteenth-century churches all around which Howard sketched, and it was good he did as they are the only mementos of our honeymoon; we did not have a camera. We found a village which had an old epitaph carved in the walls: "Here stepped Brutus, the first Roman to enter England in? B.C." I have forgotten the date.

Howard also made a sketch of Little Hampden which consisted only of a medieval church, a Pilgrim's Inn and a tavern where they served very heady Devonshire cider.

There was a village further down the road. We were exploring the church which had an eighteenth-century organ with bellows when the Vicar came in. When he heard that Howard was an organist he begged him to play the organ on the following Sunday. The congregation had not heard it since the beginning of the war; he had two hefty lads who could man the bellows and it would be a great treat for the village. Howard said he would have to have a rehearsal; I think he was scared that the boys might not be up to the bellows. I tried to blow for him but could not last a bar; it was very hard work. The Sunday performance was a great success and we were treated to a wonderful meal at the Pilgrim's Inn where we stayed.

Howard and I were very happy lovers from the start but what I feared came to pass; I could not get to sleep with someone else in the bed, the legs got in the way. Howard did not snore but slept like a baby, but for the first weeks I could not sleep at all. I dozed during the day in the sunshine while he sketched the churches. Auntie Dora was furnishing the flat at Blackheath and wrote and asked me whether we wanted single or double beds. I knew Nan and Ken had single beds and thought it safer to opt for them. I was sorry later for after a few weeks I could get to sleep and found one of the sweet things of marriage was waking and finding an arm around me in the night. My aunt as usual was very understanding and found a double bed which could be used as a divan downstairs with cushions. During the winter we slept there all the time with the firelight flickering on the glass windows of my Globe Wernicke bookcase, which I had emptied of books and filled with Grandpa's rococo hock glasses and a tea set Auntie Dora had found for us. She knew I liked nice china but none was available so she went to a secondhand store and found a tea set which had the Crown Derby colors of red and blue although it had "Amherst" at the back. "You won't be able to entertain anyone for dinner anyway," she said, which was only too true.

We visited Nan and Ken. Nan and I were a bit leery as to how Ken and Howard would get on. Ken had not liked the Americans he had met up to now. Howard was upset at Ken's reply when he asked what the population of their village of Crediton was. "What do you want to know for?" asked Ken. "Was that a strange question to ask?" Howard wondered later. I assured him it was not; Ken was Cornish, and one just had to accept him as he was. However, Nan and Ken were impressed by Howard's playing. They were both musical and had a good piano, well tuned even in the thatched cottage, and Howard could not play enough for them.

Nan knew our flat in Blackheath would not be ready till September and her parents were kind enough to invite us for two weeks to Bristol to live in the flat that they had bought for Nan and Ken, which had been rented and would be again, but was empty for the last two weeks of July. That was a godsend for us and we had a wonderful time in Bristol. We both loved the Cathedral and the Saxon church there and also one of the oldest suspension bridges in Clifton, a suburb of Bristol. Nan's parents drove us around and we visited the Cheddar Gorge and other wonderful places in the west. I think they let Howard drive the car to Tintern

Abbey for I remember quoting Wordsworth to him, "the sounding cataract haunted me like a passion," which I would not have done unless we were alone. I remember Nan had left some of her china and glass there and I broke a crystal bowl pouring hot custard into it. We had a happy time in Bristol, and Nan's father, Mr. Davey, said Howard would have made a wonderful real estate agent for he asked all the right questions, which pleased Howard. He also impressed them greatly with his Beethoven sonatas.

We visited Ray and Sim in London on the way home. I had heard her sing in London quite a bit in the months before. She sang at lunchtime concerts in churches and various places, and she told us Howard's arrangements of the Polish songs always went over well. We four always had a good time together; they had a party for us while we were there. I was intrigued at what Ray served at parties, how did she manage for food? She said she concentrated on wine which one could get now and did little things with shrimps and sausages which could be obtained in the stores. I was looking forward to giving a party at Blackheath when we moved in but had no idea what to serve. We stayed with Mummy and Bettina for a few days and I was pleased that Bettina took to Howard enough to call him "H" which intrigued him greatly. I wanted to go for a walk in the woods; it had rained but the sun had come out. Howard did not care too much for muddy woods and asked "Is O going to carry H?" which made us laugh. We did laugh a lot. He and the Sawyers became fast friends from the beginning. They fought the war over together for they had taken the same route from Normandy. Geoff Sawyer had some lovely Chinese vases and we learned to distinguish the many dynasties. Of course we visited Auntie and Uncle and everybody got on well. Auntie Dora said she thought I had made a wise choice.

Howard had written to his old landlady in Chalk Farm to see if we could get a room for a few weeks until our flat was ready. Someone else answered for she was dead but they had a room for a short let. We did not know of anywhere else so we accepted and arrived there to find the one room apartment with gas ring was all in pink and a puce pink at that. It was dreadful but it was only for a few weeks.

I took Howard to meet the Polaks and he played for them on their beautiful grand piano. I had never heard him play on a grand and it was magnificent. They were impressed and liked Howard. All the family was there, Dolf from Cambridge, Lida, and Nol who had recently married and since the war had been interested in films and quite successful. He and three other young families connected with the films or stage had started what he called a cooperative house in Sevenoaks. Dr. Polak called it the Commune! Each family helped, either by cooking or looking after the children during the day, and in this way they could live in the country, commute to London, and the children could grow up in the country. Nol suggested Howard and I might find it a good place to stay when we visited England as he was sure we would, and I filed it away in my mind for future reference.

Mummy and Bettina visited us in our one room. My mother took one look around and said "Is romance dead?" Apparently she reported it to Auntie Dora for we received a letter saying we could move in earlier if we were prepared to paint the living room. Howard had done a lot of house painting with his father and said he could manage the ceiling and the upper walls; I would just have to do the floorboards and as far up as I could reach, so we only stayed about two weeks in the rented room and moved in to our flat in Blackheath and started painting.

Chapter 45

Blackheath.

Within a few days my Auntie Min came to visit us. She was Auntie Dora's sister but no sisters were more unalike. Auntie Dora was a tall commanding woman; Min was all elbows and knees with bony shoulders and a thin nose that poked into everything. She saw Howard on top of the ladder and some of the paint from the ceiling had fallen on his fair hair. "Was he that grey when you married him?" she asked, a typical Min remark. She made Howard laugh a lot.

Howard was very interested in architecture and I sometimes felt he would as soon have been an architect, but he was a child prodigy in piano and the rich people in his home town of Newport supported him in concerts at an early age, and then he obtained the scholarship to Yale in piano. After a year he had left and gone home saying he felt his true love was architecture. His major professor came all the way after him to Newport and told him not to be absurd; he was bound to get scholarship after scholarship in piano, even eventually probably the Ditson Fellowship to study in Europe (which indeed he did), so he returned to piano for he had no scholarship for architecture. I had always known of his interest in architecture and mechanical drawing so was not surprised when he suggested he should paint a black wrought iron gate on the white wooden doors that separated the living room from the conservatory–cum-kitchen. It looked truly wrought iron and made a great difference to the living room.

Auntie Min introduced me to cooking classes, where I would meet another of her nieces, Frances, who had married Cyril, who was the nephew of Min's husband, Alec. I had met him over the years at family parties and always thought him the shyest and the most handsome man I had ever seen. Frances invited us to meet them for a walk in Greenwich Park next Sunday afternoon and go back for a salad supper; a great friendship ensued. Cyril and Howard were both interested in gardening and Cyril had the most wonderful garden, not only vegetables but flowers. When he found out we were interested in gardening he told us not to worry about vegetables, he had more than enough for themselves, his mother and us; he gave us bulbs to plant for the spring, snowdrops, crocuses and tulips. Both Cyril and Frances were interested in music, she sang in a choir and they could not get enough of Howard's playing. A routine developed; we went for a walk on the heath or Greenwich Park Sunday afternoons, then back for supper; and we had them over for a meal one evening in the week.

Cyril was head draughtsman in my uncle's factory and would have liked to have been an architect. Frances said she had never seen him talk so much as he did to Howard and me. We all became great friends and nothing is more pleasant for a young married couple than to meet another with similar interests. Howard was fascinated by the Observatory at Greenwich with the date line, O degrees, for Greenwich standard time, and many instruments from Isaac Newton's age and earlier and Cyril knew all about those. Greenwich Park itself was delightful with its Spanish chestnut trees and the elegant Naval Hospital built by Sir Christopher Wren. From the stair window at Cyril and Frances's house you could see the many masts of ships anchored in the docks at Greenwich.

Two of the happiest years of our lives were spent at Blackheath. Howard only had to see his major professor once a week to report on the progress of his dissertation for the Ph.D. in Piano Pedagogy, which he wrote in the mornings and I typed. I learned very interesting facts about music which I had not known; the overtone series, the circling fifths and the Indian rajahs which changed according to the time of day.

I had always fallen for men who could teach me something and Howard was a wonderful teacher. He did not have to take any classes at the University of London, only write the dissertation and give a concert each year in the spring which demonstrated his methods of teaching. I felt later it was easier than an American PhD, which consisted of two years of classes in the subject studied and then one to two years for the dissertation. Of course the concerts demanded a lot of study but he could do this by practicing at home. Auntie had told Elizabeth and Mrs. B. he would be practicing four hours a day, never after 9 pm.

Elizabeth was delighted but I heard afterwards that Mrs. B. had complained; Auntie Dora just took no notice.

I remember coming home from cooking class, amazed at the joy I felt. Here was I, not in the country, but in a suburban London street where there was only a laburnum tree in bloom, as if on wings with happiness, knowing I was going home where Howard would be practicing. He would stop, we would have tea and "visit" awhile. I had had to learn that in America one does not have to leave home to "visit"; it just means "chatting." He would then return to practicing and I would get my embroidery and listen. Later after supper we would read aloud to each other, Shakespeare's plays or the *Iliad or Odyssey* or Robert Frost's poems, which Howard had brought from the States. I did not know those too well and enjoyed them very much.

In October Howard took off a week and we went to visit his cousins in Scotland. His mother had emigrated as a small child with her parents who left behind a married daughter who had two girls. These were the cousins, now elderly women who had never married but lived together in Glasgow, which was unfortunately a very ugly town. They lived in an old house with thick walls and the beds were in the walls for warmth and one drew a curtain across at night which intrigued us. They also served porridge (oatmeal) hot every morning with a dish of cream and a dish of brown sugar at the side which you dipped into, and that remains in my mind as most delicious, and how did they get the cream? We in London still had only two half pints of milk a week. I remember Dr. Johnson had said in scorn that in

Scotland men ate oats which in England were reserved for horses, but I thought the porridge was wonderful.

The cousins had made arrangements with other relatives for us to visit Loch Lomond which was very beautiful and I thought of Donald who had so enjoyed Harry Lauder singing that song. We went further towards the Highlands to Perth, pronounced "Pairth." The Highlanders had a very different accent to that of Glasgow; they aspirated the "h" in "where" and "which" and I found their speech beautiful. I remember a lovely valley between mountains and a suspension bridge. We did not stay long as we wanted to visit the Lake District on our way home and that exceeded all expectations.

We were lucky in having beautiful weather for it usually rains there but the sun shone every day. I think we rented a car or perhaps we went by bus and visited Wordsworth's Dove Cottage in Derwentwater and many other lakes. I remembered Keats had said on first seeing the mountains there that his "imagination surpassed was at rest." I told Howard I thought the letters of Keats had added greatly to my education and he said we should read them aloud and we did.

When we came home to Blackheath the first thing Howard did was to tape up the windows in the living room for they let in a great many draughts. Mrs. B and Elizabeth were horrified: "How will you be able to open them?" "We won't open them till the spring." In England at that time it was considered healthy always to have an open window at night. Howard said this was ridiculous; it lost the little bit of heat there was in the house. He was proved correct; the winter was the hardest England had had for years and our living room was the only warm place. We had sufficient coal and we kept the fire going daily. The rooms in the rest of the house just had electric fires and all the windows let in draughts.

We often went down to Little Pashley for the weekend to stay with Mummy and Bettina and to visit my aunt and uncle. The snow was on the ground one day and Howard was amazed to see all the windows open. We went to Pashley Manor to ask Verity Forsyth, the owner, if she would like to come for a walk. She was in the Elizabethan hall with fires at both ends; she agreed and Howard never forgot how she took off her leopard skin coat for it was warmer outside!

My younger cousin, Gordon, was demobbed before Christmas that year. I think he had been in the Occupational forces in Germany. He was engaged to a girl in Wales whom he would marry in the spring, but in the meanwhile he had a bedroom at our communal house at Blackheath. He could always eat at the Works but I felt the least I could do for Auntie was to invite him to dinner occasionally and to all our parties. I had never been close to him and he was very unlike Donald, but he enjoyed Howard's playing and having dinner with us. One evening I had him and Auntie Min and Uncle Alec to dinner. Frances had shown me where one could buy fish in Greenwich. I asked Auntie Min what she would be wearing to Gordon's wedding and she said: "Me voile" and Howard nearly died holding in his laughter. He had a vision of all her elbows and knees sticking out through the thin material.

Nan came to stay and to see the famous gynecologist in Blackheath; he was not able to help her but he recommended someone in Exeter. Nan said she prayed she would not be jealous if I became pregnant before her. I told her we had decided to wait to have children until Howard had a position in the USA. Nan was amused by Auntie Min who played Bowls and tried to get me to say I was pregnant so that she could get some white wool so she could make a new Bowling dress for herself. "But I'm not," I said. "You could say you were," said Min. Nan asked if she and Uncle Alec played tennis as well as bowls. "We used to," said Min, "before we were in an accident and broke all our legs." Nan had a vision of centipedes.

We had a party while Nan was with us and Ray and Sim came all across London for it. It took at least an hour both ways. We had lots of wine, sardines and little shrimp things and our cheese ration for the week. Howard had been invited to a gathering of American students at the London School of Economics and there we met Bob and Betty from Kansas City. Bob was a character; he had volunteered for the RAF in 1940 long before America was at war. He had just gone to Kingsway, the headquarters of the RAF and said, in his Midwest drawl, "Do you need any hayelp?" "What sort of help do you envisage?" was the reply. "Oh bomber pilot, navigator," said Bob, so they enrolled him as a bomber pilot and he made thirty bombing missions for the RAF before America entered the war and he was transferred to train American pilots. I had never heard of a bomber pilot who had made thirty missions; usually their career was cut short long before that. I asked him how he did it. He said he never flew home on the beam but underneath it for he felt the Germans would know the frequency. I did not know how this was possible but was very impressed with his sagacity. Bob had once said Howard was lucky to have married me and so gained an entrée into an English family. He and Betty had never been in an English home so of course I invited them frequently although they did not drink, which was a surprise. They were always delighted to come but never invited us back; they had just a one-room flat, not suitable for entertaining, and they said they would wait to do that until we all returned to America.

I remember the first Christmas with Howard in England. We went to stay at Little Pashley (cottage at Ticehurst) with Mummy and Bettina but according to tradition, since Grandpa died, we spent Christmas Day with Auntie Dora and Uncle Sydney. We were quite a large party with family and friends, about twenty at the table. Dulcie brought in a large turkey and unfortunately it slipped off the plate on to the floor. "Never mind, "Auntie Dora said with aplomb, "take it out and bring in the other one." Dulcie was rather gormless, "but there isn't another one," she said. Everyone roared with laughter. Mrs. Hawkins came in and took charge. "I'll see to it," she said, and minutes later brought in the same turkey but garnished all over with parsley.

That was not the only laugh we had at that dinner. Red wine was served and Auntie Min spilt some on the white tablecloth and with great agitation tried to sponge it away with water. Auntie Dora told her not to worry, it could be erased with salt, but she went on scrubbing away until Uncle Alec said: "Leave the table, Min." I thought Howard and my cousin Rita would explode with suppressed laughter but eventually everybody did. Mummy and Uncle Sydney sang their traditional duet "Come, come, I love you only" from "The Chocolate Soldier" and later Howard played. I was touched he played the Chopin Revolutionary Etude which Bettina particularly enjoyed.

The next day, Boxing Day, Mummy and Bettina, Howard and I were invited to a party at Pashley Manor. Before we went we had a little celebration ourselves and Mummy and Howard danced the Charleston. It was always amazing to me that Howard could do that, for he had not danced much in his life, but his cousin had taught him that as a teenager. Mummy said he was the best partner she had ever had at the Charleston. She was prevailed upon to do her class act which involved putting on a top hat and singing "Alexander's Ragtime Band" ending with a high kick.

Pashley Manor looked very grand and Elizabethan, all lit up, and with fires at each end of the Great Hall, and for once it seemed warm enough. There was a son, Alexander, aged twelve, who had curly hair like Howard's, and I wondered if one day I would have a son like that. Dancing in the hall was beautiful, and when we left to go home it started to snow.

That winter was very cold and I never regretted Howard taping up the windows. We had a fire going daily but I woke up one morning and the snowdrops I had picked were frozen in the water on the dining room table. "I couldn't get them out of the jar," I told my mother later. "What did you want to get them out for?" was one of her unforgettable remarks.

Howard gave a concert at the University of London in the spring and all our friends came and it was a grand occasion. I think that was the first time he played Mozart's "Fantasia in C Minor," which he did for me. I was concerned he did not play more Mozart and recommended this Fantasia as being dramatic enough for him. It became a favorite of his too and I never heard it played more beautifully.

Howard took a few days off and Bettina drove us up to Wales for Gordon's wedding. On the way we stopped with one of Mummy's old stage friends, Ivy, who had married Alban, the uncle who had taught us to fly kites as children and was a bell-ringer, and who was always a great favorite with us. I knew Howard would be fascinated by the English art of bell-ringing, chimes, which was mathematically, not musically oriented. The night we stayed with them in their village on the Thames it was bell—ringing rehearsal and one ringer was absent and there were four bells. Howard was asked if he would like to try. He was given bell number two and a chart something like this: 1234, 2341, 3412, 4123 and then it became more complicated. It had a strange name like Grandsire Bobs or Trebles. The heaviest bell was number four and was rung by an overweight schoolgirl. The ringers were sometimes lifted from the ground by the rope to which they clung to ring the bell; Howard often was. I was fascinated watching. I had always loved the English chimes better than the European carillon which played tunes. We both wished we could have stayed till Sunday when there were two services, Morning and Evensong. I remembered the chimes for Evensong which rang out over the fields at Manor Farm and they were different. Uncle Alban said there were many different chimes and when he was in the Navy whenever they landed he offered himself as a bell-ringer and was always accepted. Most churches had four to six bells; he said some cathedrals had eight but he had generally rung four to six. He showed us some of the mathematical combinations and there was an incredible number of them.

Ivy was very amusing. She had been with Mummy on the stage as a comedienne and was still very funny. She told us risqué stories which we had not heard before and I never remember seeing Howard laugh so much; the tears ran down his face. This joke is old but we had not heard it. A dark haired man and woman had a baby and it had red hair. The husband was worried and went to the doctor. "How often do you have sex?" asked the doctor. "Not very often." "Once a week?" "No," replied the husband. "No? Twice a month?" "No." "Well," said the doctor. "I can tell you the answer. Rust!" I can still remember Howard's laughter.

The only other thing I remember about the wedding except that the bride looked beautiful (and so did my cousin Rita, who was bridesmaid) was that we discussed the re-opening of the channel boat service between Dover and Calais. This was the spring of 1947. Howard said he would love to take me to France and show me Paris and Chartres Cathedral, and Gordon said he would lend us his station wagon in which we could put a mattress and sleep and I could make curtains for the car windows. He said everyone was so anxious to talk to anyone from England and as we both knew French we could ask to park in the farm orchards and we would be welcomed. Aunt Dora was interested; she wanted to see a photo of Donald's grave at Caen. She had written and had been told that Donald was buried at the English Cemetery at Caen but there was as yet no listing of the grave; it was one among hundreds. Eventually a catalog would be made of rows and numbers but now in order to find a grave since they were not alphabetically ordered one had to walk up and down the endless rows of graves. I was sure we could find it and Auntie would be happy to have a photo so the idea was sown.

Bettina and Mummy were dubious. How could we wash our clothes? Both Howard and Gordon said there were laundries in every village. How could we wash ourselves? That would not be so easy for me. Howard and Gordon had washed in army facilities and said the villagers washed under farmhouse pumps which Howard could use. Baths did not seem to be frequent in farmhouses. There were toilets in every village but it was doubtful if any hotels or guest houses were yet available.

Chapter 46

Trip to Europe.

We enquired at the British and American Embassies. There was only one channel crossing a week but we were assured we would be welcomed and if we knew the language would be able to stay at farms overnight with our station wagon. I made curtains, again with blackout material. Howard wrote his friends in Holland who had been so good to him and they wrote back enthusiastically asking us to come and stay. We were issued with petrol coupons which we were told we could sell very well on the black market if we did not need them all. We decided to go first to Paris; I had never been there, then on to Caen Cemetery and through Normandy to Mont St. Michel, visiting Chartres Cathedral on the way. We would return visiting Ghent with the van Eyck Altarpiece which Howard had seen and waxed eloquent over, and I wanted to see Bruges, which was near, because of Michelangelo's statue there of the Madonna and Child, and also because of what Rilke had written about its old almshouses. We would then go into Holland and stay with the Wobbes in South Holland at Heerlen. I hoped we might see Delft. Humphrey had brought me a wonderful reproduction of Vermeer's view of Delft. It was an exciting project. We had a mattress at the back of the station wagon with sheets and blankets, and took casual clothes which could be washed easily; I kept my one good dress at the bottom of the suitcase to wear when we arrived at the Wobbes's.

Howard took quite a few American dollars for we were told these could be sold for a great many francs and would help us more than pounds. We parked the first night on the downs outside Dover. It was a lovely morning in early June, the sea looked smooth. We had no cooking equipment with us. Gordon had said there was food and coffee to be had in every café in France. I looked forward to some good cheese; 6 ozs a week for seven years had mostly been used in cooking. We were still on wartime rationing.

In the morning Howard could not start the car; it did not make any of the necessary noises. We were aghast. We had to get down to the quay by a certain time in order to get the one boat to Calais that week. Luckily Howard had parked on a slight incline and was able to give it a push and then leap into the driver's seat. I could not drive at all. We coasted down to the quay and found a garage ; they could find nothing wrong and suggested we let them tow us on board and when we arrived in Calais we could find a garage where they would have time to do more. Luckily I had brought along a small French dictionary with directions for all sorts of mechanical repairs. Gordon had promised to have the station wagon thoroughly vetted and filled. We could

308

not understand it; the car had run well the day before. We were the last on board and the last off as we had to be towed aboard and then again in Calais to the nearest garage. I did not imagine that the first French I would speak in years would be about the mechanics of a car. The French could find nothing wrong and asked if we were sure the tank was full. Howard was confident about that; he had refilled it in Dover. Nevertheless I said, "Please test it." It was empty; someone had siphoned out the petrol from the tank as we slept! The French mechanic supplied us with a top we could lock and, minus quite a few of our American dollars, we were off to Paris where Howard felt sure he could get the best value for his dollars.

He had several contacts in Paris from the war. I felt I could do something with the garcon at a café so Howard left me at a cafe on the Champs Elysses. I just asked the waiter where I could get the best value for American dollars. He told me to put them under my plate and he would pick them up when he returned with my coffee. It was a very good rate. I finished my coffee, thoroughly enjoying the Champs Elysees and was asked if I would like a glass of wine by a nice looking Frenchman. I told him I was waiting for my husband. "*Bien sur,*" he replied, "but that is no reason not to enjoy a glass of wine with me." I felt I was truly in France and accepted and was glad I did for we had a very interesting conversation and Howard was gone a long time. We were on our second glass of wine and he was telling me his experiences with the Resistance and I was telling him of the London Blitz when Howard at last arrived, looking worn out. He had not been able to find any of his contacts from the war and in future he would leave it to me. The Frenchman told us where we could get tickets for the opera for Howard had not been able to do that either.

We decided to spend the night at Chantilly, a short distance from Paris, where Howard had been stationed during the war. Obviously we could not park and sleep in our station wagon on the streets of Paris, so we set off for Chantilly, where I knew a famous medieval manuscript, '*Les tres riches Heures du Duc du Berry*', was housed. We found that the museum was closed indefinitely. It was a delightful village, though, and we were welcomed by Howard's former acquaintances, and allowed to park in their orchard. They invited me in for a wash but I was dismayed to see the bath was full of books! We thought we would leave the station wagon locked in their orchard and go to Paris by train but unfortunately the last train which during the war enabled Howard to get back from the opera had been cancelled and we would have to miss the last act ! This was a bitter blow. I wore my best dress that day in Paris for the opera and it was "*Oiseau de Feu.*" I shall never forget the red gold scrim hanging down instead of a curtain which cast a glitter over the singers and dancers. I was entranced by the music, the elegant staircase and the macaroons during the interval. During the day we went to Notre Dame and St. Chapelle which were overwhelming with their glorious medieval stained glass. Howard had seen the Louvre many times and was anxious to see Versailles, which he had never visited. I was disappointed, had never cared much for palaces since Germany. However, it was the first time Howard had not given way to my wishes so felt I had to acquiesce fairly graciously.

Howard was an indefatigable sightseer. I think there were 365 Versailles rooms and I am sure we saw most of them. Of course the Hall of Mirrors was beautiful but that is all I remember. I collapsed on the lawn outside and refused to move. "But you haven't seen the Grand and the Petit Trianon," said Howard. "If Marie Antoinette herself came by just now, I couldn't get up," I replied, "you go and see them for me and I will lie on the grass and look at the elegant gardens and imagine the fountains are playing." I soon fell asleep.

The next day we were at the English Cemetery at Caen. The guide was sorry the lists of graves were not yet available. They would be soon with letters and numbers indicating where each grave was to be found; now we would just have to walk up and down, looking. Howard suggested he start at one end and I at the other but I felt sure I would find Donald's grave and I did very soon. We had brought flowers and laid them there and took a photograph. We had bought a camera specially. I did not think his spirit was there but at Manor Farm.

Our next stop was Chartres but on the way there we had a flat tire. Out came the little dictionary of mechanical terms together with the prices one should pay for flats, carburetors etc. We were charged an exorbitant rate and challenged them to no effect. Then Howard conceived the bright idea of offering them a petrol coupon which we had been given by the American Embassy. This worked wonders; they took it instead of cash and we realized that the reason there were so few vehicles on the road was because it was very difficult for the French to get petrol to travel. Howard said we had been given enough petrol coupons to travel throughout France and we were only going a short distance to the west and then back again though Belgium and Holland, and we would have more than enough to get us there and back to Boulogne where we had to be three weeks hence to catch the channel steamer, which was returning Boulogne-Folkestone instead of Calais-Dover. Pounds were not of great value in getting francs and Howard had only a certain amount of American dollars, so we traveled for the most part on petrol coupons given us by the American Embassy!

Chartres Cathedral was overwhelming. I had always loved the fourteenth—and fifteenth-century stained glass in England, but Chartres was built in the twelfth century and the segments of glass were smaller and glittered like jewels. We were told that they had lost the recipe for making the blue glass which shone like sapphires along with the rubies, emeralds, and pale sea-blue stones. Malcolm Miller had not yet started his lifelong devotion to Chartres, giving lectures in English, but the French guide was able to direct our attention to the statues outside which the jeweled windows echoed, Christ as King, Judge, Redeemer. The statues had such devout faces, so full of faith. Chartres had been built by the whole town: lords, ladies, masons, glaziers, all working together to build this superb cathedral; there was never again such a monument to faith.

We stayed in Chartres two nights in a small guest hotel and I was able to have my first bath in France. We also found a laundry and had all our clothes and sheets washed. We then continued on through Normandy to Mont St. Michel. We asked farmers if we could park in their orchards and they were most welcoming. Howard used the pump for washing and I brought my bowl and asked for water. I was followed into the orchard by children and chickens which was embarrassing but the weather turned warm and there were many streams and rivers in which we could swim. We had brought swim suits and I have a photo of Howard sitting on the bank of a river, looking so happy and so young; it is touching to see that photo. We had a wonderful time. Food was cheap, bread and the delicious cheese of Normandy, Camembert, also omelettes. There was also meat sometimes on the menu, expensive, we never ordered that, but when Howard with his American accent asked for omelettes, he was told "It is forbidden for Americans to eat omelettes, they must eat meat" so from then on I ordered. The French knew they had more food than we in England. Sometimes the farmers in whose orchards we parked asked us to a meal, and we had very interesting conversations, chiefly about the French Resistance, of which we knew little. They were interested to hear that I had been through the London Blitz and that Howard had participated in the liberation of Paris. Howard at first ordered Contrexeville or Evian water which was twice as expensive as the good red wine I had, so he soon switched to wine or apple cider. The apple orchards reminded me of Kent and Sussex as they must have reminded Donald. The difference in France were the poplar trees, marching alongside every stream and giving a severity to the landscape. Otherwise the wheat and barley fields were the same. I did not see so many oats and missed their silvery green and also the small yellow fields of mustard.

We saw Mont St. Michel from afar off with the sea seeming to divide it from the land. Howard said it had for many years but a low bridge had now been built so there was access to it at high tide. Before that it must have been impregnable and even now it seemed so, a church built on the top of a rock. It was one place where we met tourists; we had seen none en route, not even at Chartres, but there were many like us climbing the steep narrow way up the rock. There were cafes and tourist shops on either side. Every café proclaimed to have the best omelette and we could see the ovens from the street; the eggs were tossed into a pan and then disappeared into the cavernous ovens and reappeared as light as air and most delicious. They had been good all through Normandy but these omelettes at Mont St. Michel remain in memory ambrosial. The church was Romanesque with heavy round arches, older than Chartres. We were shown the refectory where the monks ate in silence with one monk on a dais reading scripture to the others; it must have been a hard life. They had latrines right at the top which seemed an improvement on some we had encountered in the villages. We saw the sunset from Mont St. Michel and then turned back east. We had a long way to go and hoped our petrol coupons would last out; Howard said not to worry, we had enough to travel all over France.

We had good weather all the way but it seemed a long way to our next destination and I grew tired of washing in orchards. We stopped two nights in a pension in Bruges, a beautiful small town which had remained medieval. We took a trip through the canals and visited the church with Michelangelo's Madonna and Child, the gentlest statue he ever carved, The child is standing holding his mother's hand and there is tenderness between the two figures. We visited the Beguinage, the oldest alms houses in Europe and some of the most beautiful of which Rilke had written.

Howard wanted to revisit Ghent, just a short distance from Bruges and for me to see van Eyck's altarpiece, the Adoration of the Lamb. I was overwhelmed. I had always liked van Eyck. "The Marriage of Arnolfini" in the National Gallery in London was one of the first paintings I remember and I liked the restraint of the Northern Renaissance. When the Ghent Altarpiece was closed it showed the Annunciation, the angel Gabriel appearing to Mary, and there were shadows in this painting for it had happened in this world. When the altarpiece was open it gave a vision of Paradise so there were no shadows, but light perpetual. I missed the shadows but loved the symbolism of the meadow flowers. I knew the flowers but wanted to know what they symbolized. The Flemish guide did the best he could but neither of us knew the names of flowers in the other's languages. I pointed as much as I could and did learn that the columbine symbolized the sorrows of Mary, but there were so many others I wished to learn; for that I had to wait many years, but I never forgot that Altarpiece. There were panels attached at the bottom of the central panel and these showed the knights, the judges, the cardinals and every guild coming to worship Christ, symbolized as a lamb. The guide told us one of the panels had been stolen and ransom was offered and accepted but only the back panel was returned. The Judges were a copy.

Howard's friends, the Wobbes, were delighted to see us and it was wonderful to have a bath. We had hoped to visit Amsterdam and to see the Rembrandt and van Gogh museums, but we were told they were still closed and the Wobbes were adamant that we should not try to go there. We knew Rotterdam was still in ruins but thought things were better in Amsterdam. It was a disappointment. Howard still wanted to show me the famous flower fields of Holland. When he had been there before they had been full of tulips; now in July the gladiolas would be out. Mr. Wobbes was afraid we would not find anywhere to park our station wagon. In 1940 the Dutch had opened their dikes to flood the land in order to try and stop Hitler; this was a heroic effort for it took years for the sea to drain and even longer for the salt to vanish. I had read about it but had not realized quite what a sacrifice the Dutch had made.

In spite of Mr. Wobbes' misgiving we set out for the flower fields. There must be farms there where we could park and the Dutch all seemed to speak English or French (German too, of course, but they did not like to speak it). Mrs. Wobbes said if we did get there could we bring her some gladiola bulbs. It was further than we thought and we had to use many petrol coupons which worried me but Howard assured me we had plenty. The gladiolas were glorious and we brought back bunches of them for the Wobbes as well as bulbs. It grew dark as we returned and we had to pass some of the flooded fields which seemed endless. The dykes stood about a table foot high above the water. There was plenty of room to pass on them but little room on either side. We found no farmland and Howard said we would have to find a subsidiary dyke and just park at the side of the road. We had encountered little traffic on the way there so we got into our pajamas in the truck and went to sleep. To my horror I was awakened about 6 am by a horn and Dutch voices saying something about "Shall we give them a little push?" I put my head out of the window and said, *"Kej ne douke, als U Bleeft."* It was two farmers in a truck. "Oh, a pretty girl," they said, "just a little push and we can get by." I tried desperately to wake Howard but he was always slow to awake. "It's the head," he used to say, "I can't get it up." I realized the front seat was full of gladiolas and they had to be moved before he could start the car so I prodded him again, put on my raincoat over my pajamas, got out the side door and into the front seat. It was not easy to move the gladiolas from the front to my side of the mattress, and Howard would not wake. I could not drive, but I could start the car and perhaps that would wake him. I hoped it would not jolt us into the water. It did the trick and the shock was enough to wake him. He leapt out in his pajamas and drove a little way down the road where it was wider and the truck was able to pass, the farmers cheering wildly and calling out "England, England." They saw the license plate at the back. I was a nervous wreck but it made a good story. Mrs. Wobbe was delighted with the bulbs and the flowers but I did not care too much for gladiolas after that. We had a wonderful farewell dinner and were especially happy that Mr. Wobbe, as a photographer, had been able to develop the photos we had taken of Donald's grave and others in France and Holland. It was hard to find anywhere on the continent or in England at that moment where one could develop photos.

We had two days to get to Boulogne from where the channel boat left that week. That was fortunate as Howard knew Boulogne. I grew anxious as I saw him coasting down hills and then starting the engine at the bottom and in the end he had to admit we were running out of petrol coupons, but he was sure we would make it. I do not think I have ever been so scared. Supposing we did run out of petrol coupons, there was no way we could buy petrol, and we had very little money left anyhow. How would we get back to England? It was essential we make that Boulogne boat. There were no phones between England and the continent at that time and the family could not have helped anyway. We had written a couple of postcards and found a letter awaiting us at the Wobbes, but that was the only communication we had had for over three weeks. We were isolated on the continent and everything depended on having enough petrol to get to Boulogne. I think we had one coupon left. We used that and still coasted up and down hills; I thought we would never get to Boulogne. Howard said there was a park above the quay where we could stop the night and coast down. We reached that park and the quay lay below. It was dark. I stepped out in my sandals and cut my foot on a broken bottle. Our flashlight batteries had run out. We could not see what I had done, it bled a lot. Howard washed it off with our last bottle of water, tore off his shirt and bound my foot as tight as he could. I took two aspirins which I had with me and we opened the bottle of Kummel we were taking for Mummy and Bettina and had a good swig and then waited for the dawn.

We were the first in line to board and when they found out our situation we were towed on again! Luckily there was a doctor on the ship. I was in great pain; he gave me something to ease it and then put in stitches. He asked how far Folkestone was from my home. Luckily it was only about two hours from Ticehurst. He said I should phone my family immediately we docked and tell them I needed a doctor with penicillin. This had been discovered and used for the troops during the war but I did not know it was available for civilians. The doctor said it was and it was urgent I should have it as the foot might already be infected. Luckily we had enough money for petrol to Ticehurst. It was not an easy call to make; Bettina had been against the trip and this last incident proved to her she was right, but I recovered and remembered Chartres and Ghent and the other beautiful things. However I did develop an allergy to penicillin and came out in hives. Howard had to leave me with Mummy and Bettina for several days as I could not step on my foot; he had to get back to register at the University of London. It was the first time we had been separated; he phoned every night since Little Pashley was by then on the phone. I remember him telling me everything looked as clean as a hound's tooth and not like home at all! He was always meticulously tidy and I was rather more happy go lucky. I recovered all right but I remember the Ticehurst doctor telling me that I should always inform any future doctor that I was allergic to penicillin. I was just so thankful to be safely home in England, but in a few days felt the trip was worth it.

Chapter 47

Last year in England.

The last year in England went by very swiftly. Howard was disturbed that all the American universities to which he had applied wanted an interview. They were impressed by his credentials, a Master's from Yale and a prospective PhD from the University of London, but before signing him up for the fall of they wanted an interview before June and of course he could not do this until he had obtained his English PhD at the end of June! Our American friend, Bob, was in the same position, but his wife had an apartment in Kansas City in which they could stay and he could work for the fall term in his father's furniture store and go for interviews and hopefully get a job for the spring. We were not in the same situation and I could tell Howard was getting very worried when one day he received a letter from Kansas City University, offering him a position, sight unseen. We immediately arranged to meet our American friends from Kansas City, Bob and Betty, to get their opinion. Bob pulled a long face; he said he realized we were not in a position to refuse but Howard would have to make up his mind to apply to another university for the following year, as Kansas City University had been blacklisted by the AAUP (American Association of University Professors) for the very low salaries they paid. Once in the States Howard could take a few days off at a weekend and go for an interview elsewhere. The fact that he had given two concerts in London with some fine reviews was not enough. Interviews were always required. "One good thing," said Bob, "my parents live in Kansas City and they would put you up and probably find you somewhere cheap to live" We felt this was too much to ask anybody, but both Bob and Betty said they had already written his parents about us and they would be glad to help us. This was my first example of American hospitality. Howard said we had no option but to accept Kansas City University and I was glad that Bob and Betty would be there. Bob said I would loathe the climate, fiendishly hot in summer and below freezing for several months in the winter and flowers only a few months of the year. I looked my last on Michaelmas daisies, dahlias and chrysanthemums which flowered until Christmas. During December we had bowls in the house with hyacinths and snowdrops appeared in January, crocuses in February, and of course daffodils in March, and then the full glory of the spring and summer. I made a point of enjoying them to the full.

Ray was pregnant and would have her baby before I left. In the two years after the war she had done quite a bit of singing in and around London. She was willing to give this up to have a child. Sim had lost his job at the BBC as the Voice of Poland closed after the war, but he was an excellent journalist in English, Polish, and German and his articles sold all over Europe. He and Howard had the same birthday which we celebrated together. It was a special one when the U.S recognized Israel. Ray's mother sold her house and helped them buy one in Hampstead which became a meeting place for people coming and going to Israel. Ray said there would always be a place for us when we visited from America and indeed there was.

Cyril and Frances were considering whether to have a child. They both wanted one but they were older than we were. Frances was thirty-seven and at that time it was thought late to have a first baby. However they decided to go ahead and Frances became pregnant before we left England. We were to be proxy godparents, and if a boy, the child would have Howard's name, and if a girl, mine. We were very touched. Nan was still childless; it made me sad to think of that.

I cannot recall the last weekend with Mummy and Bettina. Long ago I read somewhere that when one remembers the past one it is the golden threads that are recalled and the drab and sad fade away. I know Auntie and Uncle invited Howard and me to a weekend in Wales for we have happy photos of the occasion but I remember nothing of it.

The last time we saw the Polaks they gave us a lovely book of facsimiles of musician's signatures together with any scrap of music they might have composed. Mozart as a child visited the youngest son of Johann Sebastian Bach in England and wrote to him, "Don't ever forget your true and faithful friend, Wolfgang Mozart." When the Polaks had visited us in Blackheath they gave us a wedding present of tea spoons with the handles embossed with the cantons of Holland. They were a great delight too. Mr. Polak had visited Israel and he told us there were so many Jews there who did not speak Yiddish or Hebrew that the shop signs were mostly in a strange English. In a department store he saw a notice "Women can have fits on second floor" and outside a butcher was "Butcher slaughters himself every Wednesday." I took a sprig of angel wing begonia which flourished in their conservatory behind the living room although Howard told me it was forbidden to bring any plant into the States. I did it anyway but it did not live. I loved the graceful bronze leaves and the small rose like blooms that sometimes flowered.

I visited Ray in hospital when she had her baby and they had not yet named him so he was in a little cradle by her bed, "Male Wolf." Her surname was now Wolf. Cyril who was a wonderful photographer took a photo of Ray, Sim and the baby Nicholas, and I kept that to take to the States with me.

The one farewell I do remember was the last dinner with Cyril and Frances. During our two years in England we had seen the most of them, visiting back and forth generally twice a week. Both Cyril and Howard said they never had such a friend as each other; both loved gardening, architecture, and music and shared much. We lived across the heath from each other and could walk over. I remember them standing at their gate and waving farewell; I really felt it as such.

Both Howard and I felt our two years in England were the happiest of our lives, and indeed the photos show it, not that we were not happy once in America and with children, but there was always tension. Would Howard get tenure? Would he get good students, would they do well at their auditions? In England we were carefree and in love, and we were fortunate to have that time together and in recalling it I remember a happiness I never afterwards knew.

Chapter 48

Arrival in America.

Of all the things Howard had missed during the rationing in England, he had missed ice cream and milk most. Of the two half-pints of real milk we received a week, I gave him one to drink and kept the rest to enrich our dried milk. In 1947 ice cream became available every three weeks and anyone could get it who queued up. Mostly they were children but Howard stood with them in his teal blue overcoat; he did not seem a bit abashed. His teal blue overcoat made quite a splash among the dark demob suits of the English; he once asked me if there was anything wrong with him for everyone seemed to be staring at him in the tube. Indeed they might; he stood out like a peacock among crows, but he had never seemed to notice that people stared before. I remember little of the voyage except the cliffs of Dover receding into the mist. I held them in view as long as I could so that I would be able to recall them in my mind's eye. I don't even know if we went on the Queen Mary or the Queen Elizabeth. It was the ship that had a glorious mural of the Canterbury pilgrims. I recall the pleasure of the first taste of lemon meringue pie and the next memory was of the Statue of Liberty, which was very impressive. I imagined what it must have meant to the starving Irish and all the other immigrants.

We spent the first night with Louisette in New York and she gave me another lovely dress, which was a delight for the clothes and materials in England were still of a very poor quality, We then went to Newport, Rhode Island, to visit Howard's mother and father. I had met them ten years previously and had liked his father, who was shy and retiring. He was a draughtsman at the Naval Base in Newport and I remember Mrs. Wilson had told me that he actually designed an improvement for a torpedo that became standard in the Navy but that his boss had taken the credit for it and the prize money and had only confessed on his deathbed that it was actually John Wilson's idea. This had haunted me. The Wilsons found a friend of theirs with a car to drive us around, and the first thing they showed us was the statue of a chicken, the Rhode Island Red. I was a little surprised. Then as we drove on into New England I was struck by all the English names of towns, Bristol, Norwich, Ipswich; how homesick these first settlers must have been. I liked New England; the towns were set up as English villages used to be, with a church, town hall and village green. I hoped it might be our fate to settle there. Howard had told me that nothing he had seen in Europe was as beautiful as the New England fall because of the flaming colors of the maples.

Howard and his mother took me to see the renowned Cliff Walk built by millionaires in the first decade of the twentieth century. Renaissance palaces, Gothic ruins, classical mansions, all side by side; it took my breath away. I saw where Howard had developed his love of architecture but the juxtaposition of Renaissance, medieval, and classical made me gasp. I saw the Breakers built by the Vanderbilts, who had sponsored Howard's first concerts as a teenager, and did not know what to say, but apparently that was all right, for most people were struck dumb by the grandeur of it.

One evening at dinner the subject of astronomy came up and Dad grew quite excited. I found he had read Alfred North Whitehead who was a favorite of mine and the conversation became quite interesting until Mother Wilson flapped her table napkin and declared "Oh don't talk about such things, it makes me noivous." Dad replied, "I have waited forty years to talk about such things." I realized I had better go out in the garden to chat with Dad; he spent most of his time there, so I did. I asked him about the torpedo invention which someone had stolen from him and he said "Oh that wasn't the worst thing that happened to me." "Oh Dad," I said, "I am so sorry. Do you want to talk about it?" He then told me his parents had died when he was very young and he had been brought up by an elder married sister. They were very poor and she resented having to look after a young brother. He had no toys as a child; he very much wanted a wooden horse and cart to drag along with a string. He earned money as a child collecting ashes from furnaces and when he was ten he had enough money to buy a horse and cart. "But by that I time I was too old for it." Tears came into my eyes and I hugged him. He smiled. "I did all right," he said, "I did well at school and was trained as a draughtsman and had enough money to get the boys a horse and cart but I don't think they liked it as much as I would have done." Tears were running down my face by this time, and I seldom cried. He patted my shoulder. "I have never told anybody about that before," he said.

I remember little about the long train ride across America. It is strange I can recall so many details of childhood but of the voyage out and the train trek I seem to have retained little. I do remember the beauty of the Adirondacks and their strange name. We had decided to spend a few days in Colorado for an American honeymoon. It cost little more to get there and then we hired a car and drove over the Trail Ridge 12,OOO feet high I think to Estes Park where we rented a wooden cabin near a lodge that served meals. Howard wanted me to chill out before the sizzling heat of Kansas City. We contacted Bob Raymond's parents who were going to put us up for a few days. They suggested we just stay with them as they had room, but we did not think we could do that. They said they would have a room ready for us whenever we arrived and to just phone from the station and they would pick us up.

The mountains in Colorado were impressive, huge and white, but I missed the little villages of the Alps with their church spires or onion domes. The wooden cabins were on the side of a steep mountain and the floorboards ran downhill which made me feel dizzy and I was scared the bed might slide down. I saw my first chipmunk.

I was very touched by Howard's suggestion that we wait no longer for a baby. "I'll be at work away a lot and it might be less lonely for you if you had a child." I felt that was very thoughtful. There was no question that I might work for a while; Howard was old fashioned in this respect. Also we had no idea how long it might take; we might not be as lucky as Cyril and Frances. Nan had been married five years and still no baby. Our future was far from settled because we knew Howard would apply for a better paid job than Kansas City University once we were there, and we assumed we would move in a year, but we decided to wait no longer for we both wanted a child.

Chapter 49

Kansas City.

I shall never forget the arrival in Kansas City. It was over 1OO degrees and like an oven. I had never seen people sweat before and the sight of all those wet backs appalled me. In the English summer cricketers wore scarves and most people cardigans; here even the wind, when it blew, was hot for it came from the desert.

The Raymonds could not have been kinder. They were having a family reunion but they had kept a bedroom for us and we were to come right over. My first experience of American hospitality was unforgettable. Mrs. Raymond and I took to each other right away. She had never been out of the States but she had an adventurous spirit which she had bequeathed to her son Bob. He and Betty were there together with Roxie, his sister, Dave, her husband and their two little boys and also his brother Ted and wife Nina with a sweet little girl, Wendy. Mr. Raymond owned a furniture store in town and his grandfather or great-grandfather had provided coaches from Independence for those brave souls who had driven with their families to California. He was a true mid-Westerner and they all spoke with twangs like Bob, except his mother, who had a very gentle voice. We ate on the screen porch through which the hot wind sometimes blew, and Mrs. Raymond served the most delicious dessert; it was fruit salad with small marshmallows and whipped cream and it had been iced. I felt I had never tasted anything so good. There were trees around and they seemed to be filled with a screeching sound. I must have continually looked up to try and find what the noise was for Mrs. Raymond told me they were cicadas and the louder they were the nearer it was to the end of summer and fall. I could not believe they could get louder so hoped fall was near.

Many of the young people slept out on mattresses on the porch which seemed to go all around the house, but a bedroom had been reserved for us. Bob told us the only way to get cool was to take the sheets off the bed and run them under the cold tap until they were dripping wet, wring them out slightly and then rush them to the bed where they dried in five minutes to give an illusion of cool. There was of course no air conditioning in 1948. The cold tap trick worked and it was good to sleep in a bed that did not slope downwards.

The next day Mrs. Raymond showed me her wonderful quilts. I suppose quilting was known in England for it is mentioned in Jane Austen, but I had never seen any and the delightful shapes and colors and fine stitching entranced me. I thought it was truly art and told her so; she was pleased and said I should meet her youngest daughter Nadine, who lived in New York and was the only one of her children who appreciated quilting. She was most anxious that we stay with her; she had just retired from the furniture store and would love to have our company. We felt that would be imposing. They had a piano that was quite well tuned; I wondered how in the heat, but apparently it was a special kind of piano made for that climate. She knew from Bob how little Kansas City University paid and was anxious how we would get by. When she saw we were determined to try she suggested that an elderly widower down the street wanted someone to cook the evening meal for him for free rent, and she introduced us.

I was worried that after years of cooking with little I would not be able to cook well enough for this man whose name I have forgotten, but will call Mr. B. His stove was filthy and Howard spent hours cleaning it. I then put in a meat loaf with some trepidation, and baked potatoes. Howard made a salad. Mr. B said the meat loaf had not enough ketchup in it.

He insisted on taking us to his church on Sunday, which was Baptist. Howard and I would have much preferred to have found an Episcopal Church. It was a great joy to me that Howard had been brought up an Episcopalian which had the same liturgy as the Church of England. We had enjoyed going to a fifteenth-century church at Blackheath and when in Ticehurst to Evensong at the even older church in the village. The vicar there was "high" church and chanted the responses. The congregation were not up to chanting and mumbled until Howard one evening chanted the responses in answer. The Vicar was delighted and from then on asked Howard to do this. It was the only time I noticed Howard had an American accent. I knew he said "cawfee" and "ideah" in the New England way but it was not until I heard the responses and answers chanted in the liturgy that I noticed the difference and it rather intrigued me. I had never been to a Baptist service and was appalled at being called "Sister" Audrey and "Brother" Howard. The music was dreadfully strange to our ears and we decided we would find some way of getting out of going there again.

However the situation did not arise. As soon as Howard had left for work on the Monday, Mr. B. started pinching me on the behind. I was so astonished I stared at him in amazement. "Just a little pinch now and then," he had the nerve to say. I slapped his hand, "Not on your life," I said and rushed out the door, up the street to Mrs. Raymond. She was as upset as I was and said she would go down and give him a piece of her mind, and fetch my clothes, and Howard could fetch his in the evening. We had left our books at Mrs. Raymond's and most of our stuff at Howard's parents so we had taken very little to Mr. B. I got up to thank her and somehow came over dizzy. "It must have been the heat, and I ran up the street," I said. "Or you might be pregnant," said Mrs. Raymond. I stared at her; how was that possible? It was only three weeks since Colorado. She insisted on making an appointment with her doctor. She then rang up Howard at work and told him to come first to her house that night. She pressed us again to stay with her but Howard had found out from some of his colleagues at work that there were one room apartments very near the university for $80 a month. The bed let down from the wall and hung up when it was not in use. I would have liked to stay with Mrs. Raymond but did not know how Mr. Raymond could handle the music that Howard had to practice hours a day, for he was giving a concert that term, so we decided to try the one-room apartment and promised to come to lunch every Sunday.

The bed in that apartment was a joke. It was supposed to stay put until pulled down but it did not. It would come down of its own free will when it wished to and we spent a lot of time dodging it and calling out "Ware bed!" The manager was not helpful and suggested we should put something like a chair in front of it that would bear the brunt if it decided to fall on its own. We laughed a lot dodging it, which proved that we were still very young. If unimpeded it would fall on the kitchen table.

Four momentous events occurred while we were in the apartment. First I discovered I was pregnant. Mrs. Raymond took me to her doctor, who had delivered her three grandchildren. He dropped cigar ash on my stomach when he was examining me and I sat up and yelled at him, "How can you be so unhygienic?" He looked astonished but put aside his cigar. I did not tell Mrs. Raymond for I felt she would be as horrified as I was, but I did ask her daughter, Roxie, if he was in the habit of smoking during examinations. She said he had never dropped ash on her stomach but he did always smoke. Everybody did in America at that time except Mrs. Raymond. Mr. Raymond did and Howard smoked far too much. In England cigarettes had been rationed. I had never heard of a doctor smoking while examining a patient but Roxie and Nina had produced three healthy children so I hoped I would.

Both Howard and I were very happy about my being pregnant although Howard was afraid my family would think we should have waited till we had a home. I felt a baby would be company for me for Howard was away a lot. As we had no piano he had to practice at school so it meant a long day alone, and I did miss his practicing. He told me it meant much to him that I enjoyed listening. I felt I was struggling with him through the hard passages that he had to work through repeatedly and I really got to know the music and could in the end distinguish between the Waldstein and Appassionata sonatas, no matter which movement he practiced.

At about the same I time we learned I was pregnant we had a letter from Cyril with a photo of Frances and their baby son, John Howard. We were very excited about this and felt transported back to Blackheath and all the happy times we had had with them. We were to be godparents by proxy. I wished we had had a glass of wine to drink to them but Kansas City was dry. The Raymonds never drank and I learned I should not while pregnant, although an Italian doctor told me Italian mothers always did, it was good for the milk. I did not miss drinking and was anxious to do all a perfect mother should.

The next event was disastrous. I entered the hall of the apartment building one day and the manager handed me a cable. I had never had a cable; I tore it open and remember the dark hall as I did so. It was from Lida Polak telling me Dr. Polak had died of a sudden heart attack at 53. I was devastated; he had always been more than a father figure to me, a rock, a beacon through whom I had learned so much. It seemed to me that I had been educated in music and art and everything I cared about in their home. The Amadeus Quartet had started practicing there and Dolf was for a while second violin. The world seemed to grow dark at the sad news. I was very touched that they thought of me to cable as if I were one of the family, and struggled out to the post office to return cable my grief. Howard was very understanding and tried to comfort me but the one way he could have done, through music, was not possible as we had no piano.

I do not know if this shock had anything to do with the next event. At three months I had a threatened miscarriage and the doctor told me to go to bed at once and stay there for ten days, except for going to the bathroom. My husband would have to leave me a sandwich in the morning and cook at night. I could not get out of bed or carry or lift anything, so there I was, marooned in the tethered bed, seemingly surrounded by furniture with nothing beautiful to look at. I handwrote an air letter sheet to Bettina and Mummy telling them the typewriter was on the blink so they would not be hearing from me for a week or so. Since scrawling down German messages in the WRNS my writing had become illegible and nobody wanted a handwritten letter from me; I asked them to let Auntie Dora and others know. That tree outside the window was the saddest I had ever seen. Was this the glory of the American fall? It looked as though the noisy cicadas had eaten it away. It was dull brown and looked bitten. I had read all the books we'd brought along, but remembered one of Howard's that I took up again. It was called *Green Mansions* and it was soothing.

When Howard came home he was aghast. I assured him I had prayed and we would not lose the baby and he should go downstairs and call Mrs. Raymond. We did not have a telephone in the apartment, it cost too much, but there was a pay phone downstairs. Howard was not much of a cook and all we could think of was boiled eggs. This was before the days of "take-aways." McDonalds had not even started. Mrs. Raymond said she would be over in the morning and he should tell the manager to let her in.

I was never so glad to see anybody. She had brought me the fruit marshmallow salad which she knew I liked and ham and cheese. She was very determined. We had only taken the apartment by the month and we were to give notice right away. As soon as I was well enough to move we were to come to her house. She was already preparing a little apartment for us, a room with a screen porch in which she was going to put up plastic; we could put the bed there with just blankets in it in which we would sleep all winter, and only open it for sleeping. Bob and Ted could get the piano up to the inside room which would be our sitting room with desk and chairs. It was on the other side of the house to the kitchen and to the bedroom where she and Mr. Raymond slept. As soon as he came home he listened to the radio and he would never hear the piano. What could I say? I had never heard of such hospitality; I do not think anyone in England would have done it; this was truly American hospitality. We would eat the evening meal with them and then go upstairs to be by ourselves, as young people should, and Howard could practice as much as he liked. It was this that overwhelmed me; he would be able to practice at home so I and the baby could hear him. She would be able to teach me to cook and I would be company for her. She would not hear of rent. She told me that although Howard had taken out insurance it would not cover hospital expenses for the baby for that had to be ten months after the insurance was taken out! I must not worry about sleeping in blankets all winter, that is what they had done in the covered wagons, and we would be warm enough with the little heat coming from the other room at night. "It will get down well below freezing in a month," she said. I could hardly believe it; it seemed only yesterday that the temperature had been 1OO degrees.

Howard was as overwhelmed as I was but he was so concerned for me that he could not but agree. The fact of having a piano at home was a deciding factor, for he had come to enjoy my being with him when he rehearsed and even listened to my comments!

I stayed about three weeks in my furniture guarded prison and during that time Bob and Betty came to visit me. I was glad to see them for I was afraid lest they think I had presumed on their friendship to land on their mother, but Bob reassured me. He said his mother had been very bored since she had retired from the furniture store; she had always wanted to visit Europe but had never left the middle west. He had never seen her cotton on to anyone as she had to me, I was her great adventure. I asked about how his father thought about it and he said he liked us for he could retell his stories of the wagon trails that had left Independence of which the family had had enough. Bob had received an offer from a University in Ohio and was going to start there for the spring term as Assistant Professor of Economics. Howard had already sent in applications and had received an offer from Florida State University in Tallahassee for twice the amount he was paid in KC, but they wanted an audition. He was reluctant to leave me, but I encouraged him to go to Tallahassee.

Once we moved in with the Raymonds, life took a turn for the better. We grew accustomed to the Lone Ranger on the radio, which was Mr. Raymond's favorite. We knew to come down to eat when we heard, "Hiyo Silver." After dinner we went upstairs and Howard practiced. He was due to give a recital and I was able to go to it.

Three days before there was great excitement. Prof. Ernst von Dohnanyi, well-known composer and conductor of the Budapest symphony orchestra, arrived on a tour of the United States. He and his niece arrived and could speak little English. Howard told them I knew German and I was called in as an interpreter; they were glad to see me and I was drawn to them both. His eldest son had been killed in the abortive attempt to assassinate Hitler in July 1944. Hitler had not penetrated into Hungary as he had into Austria and Dohnanyi had conducted in Budapest during the war, but he was known as an anti-communist and when the Russians advanced he felt it prudent to escape to the West. He was found hiding in Vienna by a former student who was in the U.S Intelligence. It was only possible to find him a visa for South America and for two years he had been conducting there and trying to learn English with a view to getting eventually to the States. He was now touring America, visiting universities to which he had been invited, in order to decide where he would like to settle. He heard Howard's recital and was very impressed and said he was an excellent pianist, and what was he doing at Kansas City University? I explained our situation and that Howard had been accepted by Florida State University at twice the salary he was now paid, but he needed to go for an audition and he was reluctant to leave me in my somewhat precarious condition. Dohnanyi said Florida State University was one of the places to which he had been invited and he was more than willing to state that he had heard Howard play and he was an excellent pianist and perhaps that would save him the cross-continent trip for an audition. So it was that Howard was offered a position at Florida State University and by Christmas we knew that we would be going to Tallahassee, Florida, for the fall term next year. I remember Howard's recital and how enthusiastic Dohnanyi was.

While I had been immured in my furniture prison the election of 1948 had taken place and I had learned to keep my mouth shut when politics were being discussed. I was amazed when I arrived in the States to find that Roosevelt was not so revered as in England. Indeed my in-laws in New England had not a good word to say for him and his New Deal which had done so much to help the poor. Howard explained that New England had always voted Republican, and that Lincoln who had freed the slaves was a Republican. He told me that in England I had voted Conservative in the only election I could and that was similar. I disagreed but did not know enough to argue. When we arrived in Kansas City I learned that Truman had a bad name because he had worked for Prendergast who had concreted all the riverlets in Kansas City whether they needed it or not because he had stocks in concrete. All the Raymonds were Republican and voted for Dewey. I was a lone voice in the wilderness voting for Truman in my mind (I was not able to vote, of course) and Howard told me to keep quiet about my opinions. "But Truman stopped the war and saved you from going to the East and he acknowledged Israel," I pointed out. Howard could not vote in the election as he had not established a place of residence, and he was not sure how he would have voted. "My family has always been Republican," he said. I asked when was I ever going to meet a Democrat. He said we would meet plenty down south and at the University. I was confused. Did one vote according to geographical region rather than achievement? I celebrated Truman's victory on my own.

Mrs. Raymond's youngest daughter, Nadine, came to visit from New York where she had married Bill, a wealthy man on the Stock Exchange. She had studied art history at the University and had a position as "docent" in one of the New York galleries and could obtain free tickets to the Met and the Frick. We took to each other and became friends for life. She asked us to visit them in New York where she would show us around; I hoped this would be possible one day. She was very appreciative of Howard's music and said she expected to hear him in Carnegie Hall.

The winter was hard; snow lay on the ground and stayed there. I asked Mrs. Raymond when flowers would appear and she said not till May but I would see roses bloom before the end of the month, when my baby was due. "No daffodils in March?" She shook her head. The houses were kept very warm to me, 78 degrees, when outside it was below freezing. My face could not stand the contrast and my nose turned blue: I was determined to walk a little for the child's sake. My Aunt knitted me a soft woolen mask which fitted over my head and ears, tied around the chin and had holes for eyes and mouth; no hole for the nose; it must have received air from the mouth. I bought snow shoes and walked every day up the frozen street, thankful for the red splashes of color from the cardinals which were the only things not white. In my mind's eye I tried to walk through the Elizabethan sunken garden, up through the cherry orchard to the bluebell woods and on to the hills of colored fields, dark gold for barley, lighter for wheat, silver green for oats with small patches of bright yellow for mustard. Sometimes I could not remember them.

At Christmas a part of Kansas City, called the Plaza, which was built in the Spanish style, was floodlit and I enjoyed walking there; it was near the Raymond's house. We had had no Christmas lights in London since before the war, and the floodlighting seemed glorious. Mrs. Raymond did not cook turkey but roast beef. I made Yorkshire pudding, for which I found a recipe in the American cookbook. It was new to everybody and they liked it. I also made English shortbread from a recipe of Cyril's mother; equal amounts of flour, sugar, and butter and then baked as a pie in the oven and cut in pieces when warm. This was a great success, and I encouraged Mrs. Raymond to have a cup of tea with me in the afternoons and a piece of shortbread.

I often thought how fortunate we were that the only American friends we had met in England had such a hospitable family who would take us in in America, and that we landed where they were. Also, if Howard had phoned from Wales two days later we would have left Manor Farm and it would have been hard to contact me. When I studied Jung years later I understood what he meant by synchronicities, strange coincidences, and I discussed these with Mrs. Raymond.

My aunt had written me that the English government had lifted the embargo on sending any money out of England just for Christmas, and she could send a present up to fifty pounds. She was anxious to send Mrs. Raymond something to show my family's appreciation and suggested a teapot and hot water jug. I had told her we drank tea from tea bags, to which I had grown quite accustomed, so much easier, but thought Mrs. Raymond might like an English tea set, and she was very pleased with the one that arrived. Auntie embroidered me a large tablecloth with forget-me-nots around it. She designed it herself and I used it for years for parties once we had our own home.

I was anxious to get Mrs. Raymond something that was reminiscent of England and found a florist that had

Dutch bulbs and lovely bowls to plant them in. I chose white Narcissus for they would stand up to the heat of the house better than hyacinths. I bought an attractive bowl, buried the bulbs and kept them in a dark cupboard for several weeks. Fortunately they were ready to emerge and start blooming just at Christmas.

After Christmas the long winter of my pregnancy becomes a blur. Howard and I went to see the movie *The Red Shoes* with Moira Shearer, whom I had seen dance at the Sadlers Wells ballet. The choreography was by Frederick Ashton; it was beautiful and we came home on a high. Mrs. Raymond never went to the movies, which was unusual in those days; she also did not take out car insurance which worried me. I persuaded her to come to the *The Red Shoes* with me and she was overwhelmed. "You actually saw her dance," she said. "What a different world it must seem to you here." I told her it was much more comfortable here and no one in England would have done as much for me as she had. She fed and sheltered us, and she would not take any rent. She said it was a disgrace what Kansas City University paid. I do not know what we would have done without her. It was the only time I saw a three-generation American family.

The baby was due at the end of May and Howard was committed to teach at Kansas City University till July. The plan was that we would stay with the Raymonds until July and then go to visit Howard's parents a while. Howard was due to arrive at Florida State sometime in August, but it did not work out that way.

Chapter 50

John Donald.

The doctor warned me that I would have a long and difficult birth as my bones were small, and that I should not come to the hospital until twelve hours after labor pains had started. Mrs. Raymond sent us there after ten, and Howard read to me from C.S. Lewis. Mrs. Raymond came too, and after twenty-four hours insisted I be given something for pain. It took thirty six hours for the baby to be born and it was a forceps birth. He came out looking like a carrot and I screamed "I have a carrot baby." The wretched doctor tried to push his head down and said it would get flatter. I don't know why I didn't get a C-section and didn't think much of the doctor. The baby screamed all the time and the doctor said it was colic and colicky babies did cry. I tried to breast-feed which I thought was an overrated pastime but it was supposed to be good for the baby and I was getting more into the swing of it when we were sent home and then all hell started!

The baby cried all the time. The Raymonds had had four children and none of them had been colicky. Mr. Raymond could not stand the baby's screams. I tried to keep him awake during the day so he would sleep at night, but without success. He cried night and day. After a few days Mr. Raymond showed his pioneer stock and went round to the doctor's home when he was having his Sunday lunch and announced "If you don't do something to stop that Wilson baby from crying all the time, I aim to come and shoot you!"

The doctor responded quickly. He took the baby away from me and put him in the hospital, weaning him abruptly which was very hard on me. It was already hot in June and my breasts hurt abominably in spite of all the ice bags Mrs. Raymond gave me. It was decided that as soon as I was well enough I would fly with the baby to Boston where my in-laws would pick me up by car and drive us to their home in Newport. Mrs. Wilson said on the phone that Howard had been colicky and she knew all about colic. It was decided I could travel when the baby was three weeks old and had been in the hospital two weeks. Mrs. Raymond was most distressed but we could not subject Mr. Raymond to all this any longer, and the hospital would not keep the baby any longer. At least he would be used to the formula and bottle by then. As Howard was committed to teaching another four weeks at Kansas City University, I had to fly alone for the first time with a three-week-old infant.

We left at night and Mrs. Raymond drove us to the airport telling Howard to be sure and put the bassinet in the trunk. We arrived at the airport and the bassinet was not there! Mrs. Raymond gave Howard the baby and immediately raced home to get it. I was worried sick about her, knowing she had no car insurance. That was one of the worst things that happened. Poor Howard was so upset, and I tried to comfort him. I lost my reserved seat, Mrs. Raymond barely got there before the plane took off, and the only place for me was behind the pilot. I had a man on each side whose heads kept falling on my shoulders during the night and I had to heave them off with my elbows to protect the baby.

Actually I learned something about my colicky baby that night. He loved movement and the engine noise. He would have slept peacefully during the flight and I might have been able to do so to had I not had to fend off my neighbours' heads every few minutes. He finished one bottle, which he seldom did, and tried to sleep instead of crying. When we arrived at New York I found my luggage had not made it and all I had was the diaper and formula bag with bottles. They promised to send it on the next plane. I tried to explain that my in-laws were coming to Boston by car to fetch me and if the luggage were not there they would not be able to return to Boston to get it. I was promised it would be there, but I did not see how; surely I was travelling on the fastest route to Boston? Maybe not. I had to wait several hours in New York and encountered an even more urgent problem.

I had to go to the bathroom and what was I to do with the baby? There were no changing tables in restrooms at that time. There was no attendant in the restroom. There was no one to whom I could turn for help, no Mother's Aid or any help whatsoever. Flying was very different in 1949, definitely not arranged for mothers with young babies. If I thought I had had a hard time knocking my neighbors' heads off my baby during the night flight, that was nothing compared with the problems of going to the bathroom with a infant in my arms. I leave it to the imagination. I was a wreck when I got on the plane to Boston, but here I had a little help.

The stewardess must have thought I looked ill for she found a nurse among the passengers and put her in the seat next to me. The nurse took my temperature and said I had a high fever, did I have any pain in the breast? I certainly did. She said I was probably starting an abscess. She gave me aspirin and said she would come with me to meet my in-laws who must be told of the situation and get me to a doctor with penicillin immediately. I said I'd had an allergic reaction to penicillin two years before, but she assured me it was easier to take now and I had to have it. She held and fed the baby during the flight to Boston and came out with me to meet my in-laws.

Dad had borrowed a car from a friend and Mrs. Wilson was looking forward to a jaunt round Boston, because they did not get out much. I remember her disappointment. The nurse told them they should phone their doctor to have penicillin ready when we got to Newport as I was very ill. Mrs. Wilson took the baby who again enjoyed the ride and did not cry. The doctor was waiting at their home with penicillin and brushed aside my idea of allergy to it, said I must not climb the stairs but sleep on the couch downstairs. This upset Mrs. Wilson for she had prepared a bedroom upstairs but she rallied and for two days she took care of the baby. She certainly knew how to handle colicky babies; she insisted that the doctor prescribe something called paregoric which did enable him to sleep sometimes, although I learned afterward that it had opium in it. She had a rocker which meant that I could keep him moving. As soon as we got out of the car he started his piercing yells so I was very grateful to her. She showed me how to jab my shoulder bone into his stomach so that he hung face down over my back, and surprisingly this seemed to ease his discomfort and stop him yelling as long as I kept walking at the same time. I did not have an allergic reaction to the penicillin and recovered fairly quickly.

As soon as I could walk she and I went to town and I bought a canvas stroller which had a mattress in it (which could be removed later when the baby sat up). This was even better than the rocker. I had it by my bedside and would move it up and down during the night whenever the baby cried. He liked best being toted up and down on someone's shoulder and I remember doing this in the garden while Dad was working on his roses. He said "I don't know about children. I once had a boat but had to give that up when David went to Brown; had a car and had to give that up when Howard went to Yale. I think I would rather have had my boat and car." I said, "Dad, what a thing to say when I have your grandchild in my arms!" "I wouldn't have met you," he answered, "and I wouldn't have missed that."

He was very insistent that we call the baby John, the seventh John Wilson since the first had emigrated from England in the 18th century. I had always thought of

"Donald" but could not go against Dad's wishes. I wrote explaining to Auntie, and she thought "John Donald" a good name; we both agreed there was only one "Donald." Bettina immediately called him "JD" and he was always known as that by his English family. At length Howard arrived and I was never so glad to see anyone. He helped a lot with the baby, even trying to give him the bottle at night if I would wake him. That did not work as he was very hard to wake and I had to kick him so hard he fell out of bed and hurt his head, so I had both on my hands! After that I did the 2 am and 6 am and Howard did the rest.

The baby was christened when he was six weeks old in the same Episcopal Church in which Howard had been, and I have a beautiful photo of him in the robe Aline had made for me of Jap silk and Bruges lace. He must have had some paregoric for he looks very peaceful.

Chapter 51

Tallahassee.

Florida State University was in Tallahassee, the state capital. Nobody in England had heard of it and I was surprised that many in the States had not either. It was apparently a small town but growing fast after the war. Florida State College for Women had become co-ed and renamed Florida State University to accommodate the many veterans who were returning to college on the G. I. Bill, and there was an influx of new, young faculty.

I expected that Howard and I would travel down together for I did not fancy another long trip alone with the baby, but when Howard phoned the Dean he was told that was not possible. There were only two hotels in Tallahassee, and neither would take a two-month-old baby! Howard would have to come first and find rooms for us, and then buy a car in order to fetch me from Jacksonville and avoid a long wait changing trains; a car was essential in Tallahassee as there was no public transport. I was surprised a city could be without public transport but in hospital there was a girl next to me who came from a farm just outside Kansas City and they had no inside toilet, so I was learning that America was different from what we saw in Hollywood films. We had of course saved some money from my aunt's and then Mrs. Raymond's generosity, but had to spend a lot on hospital fees as the baby came too soon to be covered by insurance. My flight was expensive too, but we hoped to have enough to buy a piano and were disturbed that a car was the first priority. Howard had to break it to me gently that I would have to learn to drive!

We decided that I would take the baby with his mattress in the stroller so that I would not have to hold him all the time as my side and arm were still sore; Howard would take the bassinet with the rest of the luggage. The trip was not as bad as I imagined for the baby always liked movement and noise. I enjoyed what I saw of the mountains in North Carolina and wished we had landed there. Howard met me with a green used Plymouth car and I was introduced to the American system of buying cars. In England you paid cash but in the States you could pay by month by taking out a loan. He had bought it from a dealer who had promised to give me six driving lessons as Howard did not think it a good idea for a husband to teach his wife. I wished I had learned in England; I remembered how Donald had failed his driving test the first time.

Howard had found a nice one-room apartment for us in a boarding house; he had a hard time cleaning the stove again, he said. It was owned by a friendly woman who liked babies. After the long train journey and then the two hours' drive the baby was tired and went to sleep all through the night for the first time. We hoped this was a good omen and perhaps he was getting over the colic. It was much hotter than in New England but there were beautiful large trees around with a strange kind of mist hanging from them which Howard said was Spanish Moss. It looked weird but at least it was something entirely different from anything I had seen and the trees did not seem so loud with cicadas as they did in Kansas City. I did not see any flowers and was disappointed for I had been told Florida meant the land of flowers. I was told the camellias started blooming in December, followed by azaleas and then day lilies In those days there were not many flowers around in the summer, but there were decorative leaves, pink and white, called caladiums. There were ferns hanging in pots in the screened porch which surrounded the house. The windows were open and there were fans; it seemed very hot but not so overwhelming as Kansas City.

The new faculty and their wives were invited to a reception by the President of FSU. The kind landlady was ready to take care of JD who seemed ready to go to sleep at 6 pm and sleep till the lO pm bottle when we would be back. We met a lot of young people in their twenties and thirties who all seemed very interesting. There were two French girls; one had married a German refugee who was now a chemist and the other had married an American parachutist who had landed in her backyard; he was now a history professor. Then there was an American girl called Pat, who became my first friend. She asked if I were interested in forming a Literary Club; I was most impressed. She told me there was a library in town where one could get books. Later we found out that wives could use the University Library. We also met a meteorologist and his artist wife. Most of these young people were renting apartments in the former Army barracks and I thought it would be nice to join them there, although they said they were overrun by large black cockroaches called "Palmetto Bugs." I was appalled but they said these cockroaches were everywhere, in the classrooms at the university as well. It was the damp heat that encouraged them.

On the way to the president's house Howard took me to the Music Building which was the first building on campus to be air conditioned. There were no cockroaches there and it was refreshingly cool. Howard was against spending money on rent for a cockroach-ridden apartment and wanted to use his G.I. loan to buy a house right away where window air conditioners could be installed. Apparently as a veteran one could buy a house as one did a car and the monthly mortgage was less than the rent for the former barracks. I was confused for I would have liked to be among these new young friends we had made but did not like cockroaches. As I had done all my life, I wrote Auntie Dora for advice. She had been unable to send us any money from England as it was illegal, except for the Christmas allowance of fifty pounds.

She took the law into her own hands. A friend of hers was going to Switzerland and then USA, and she gave him a thousand pounds (about $4000 at the time) for us. With it came a letter saying she thought Howard was right. He should use his G. I. loan right away and buy a house on the mortgage plan. It had started in England and was called the never-never plan. She hoped there would be enough after the down payment for a piano, and after that she did hope we would be able to afford a maid once a week for me, to do the scrubbing of floors and help with the washing and ironing. She added, "I don't know what your grandfather would have said about Audrey being without any help." I did not know what Grandpa had to do with it. Times were changing; Frances had no help, nor had Nan, and Ray had only her mother, who'd died soon after her child had been born.

Sub-divisions were being laid out and we found a house on a lot with a 300-year-old live oak tree with masses of Spanish moss which cooled the front of the house. It was at the edge of town with fields all around and a dairy farm nearby. Howard was adamant we buy it for he felt in ten years it would sell for much more than we paid and he would be able to build the house of his design. I knew how much architecture had meant to him and agreed, although it was the only house on the street and there was no telephone. That worried me in case I needed to call the doctor for the baby. We had one neighbor, about five minutes away. She came around with a pie with the usual Southern hospitality the day we arrived. There were two window air conditioners for which everyone envied us.

I was very lonely and scared to be without a phone. One afternoon when it grew a bit cooler I put the baby in the stroller and walked over to the kind neighbor to enquire where the nearest telephone was. "Why, Mrs. Wilson, "she said, "you never came over here all by yourself. Thiemann (her son) will sure have to carry you home!" This was the first time I had heard the Southern usage of 'carry' for 'accompany' and assured her that would not be necessary! She told me not to worry about the phone, she had raised four children and could help with most troubles, and should a doctor be necessary one of her young 'uns could run up to the store another five minutes away. I met her fourteen-year-old daughter who was anxious to baby-sit and had looked after two younger brothers and knew all about changing diapers, feeding, and burping etc., so this was a good thing.

There was a concert nearly every week and Howard wanted me to go with him and I enjoyed this very much; there was often a party after it where we met the same young people as we had at the President's house. They all could drive. Pat came to visit me with an exquisite concoction of little marshmallows, Rice Krispies, and chocolate chips. She had a baby girl a month younger than John, but her mother was staying with her for a while for which I did envy her.

The dealer from whom Howard had bought the car gave me six lessons and surprisingly enough I passed the test. However, the first time I went out alone with the baby in the bassinet at the back (no seat belts or infant car seats at that time.) I could not get into first gear (of course it was manual transmission in 1949, and I never drove anything else). I was on a steep hill and started careering backwards. The handbrake did not help. There was a truck coming down on the other side of the road and in desperation I called out to the driver through the open window, "I'm going backwards!" "Well, carry on, sister," was the reply, "there is nothing behind you!" I was so grateful. I rolled to the bottom of College Avenue (I still can't pass it without a shudder) and stopped the car. There was a young man and his mother walking towards me on the pavement and I leapt out and implored them: "Can either of you drive? I've just nearly killed my baby at the back because I was not able to get into first gear! Could one of you drive me home? It's near here, and my husband will take you anywhere you want!" They were surprised but agreed, no doubt because I was in such a state. After that, Howard said he would accompany me in future till I felt more secure. Thank goodness there was not much traffic on the road in those days, but there were cows, especially near the farm by our home. The next Governor of Florida was elected on his slogan that he would get the cows off the road.

Auntie Dora got into trouble for illegally sending us money. It was forbidden to send money out of England in 1949. She knew she might but she did it all the same. She was visited by someone from Scotland Yard and she wrote us that she rounded on him, saying "Yes, I did send my beloved niece some money. She is all alone in America with no one to help her, no telephone, no neighbor on her street, and she has a three month old baby. I should think you gentlemen would have something better to do than to interfere in a family concern such as this." She said the detective bowed and said "I agree with you, Madam," and withdrew. The money enabled us to get a Sanforized (pre-shrunk) upright Baldwin piano which was built especially to stand the hot damp climate. A window air conditioner was installed near by and another at the other end of the house. It was not as efficient as later air conditioning but it kept out the cockroaches.

A few weeks after the beginning of the fall term we learned that Dohnanyi had accepted a position in the Music School at Florida State University. He arrived with his 'niece', who was now his wife, having received a divorce from her former husband. She was about thirty years younger than he and had two teenagers from her former marriage, a boy and a girl. Howard had of course written to thank him for recommending him for the position at FSU and it seemed they were glad to see us; they did not speak English any better than they had in Kansas City. I wondered how they would manage with no public transport, for I knew neither of them drove. Apparently rooms were found for them in a sorority house, but very soon they were in a home about half a mile from campus, to which Dohnanyi walked every day. Elena asked me to come and visit her; I explained I had a baby and was just learning to drive. She was most sympathetic; she had tried to learn to drive once in the Prater in Vienna but had to give it up. In order to avoid hitting a squirrel she had landed in a ditch and did not have the heart to try any more. She liked babies, she could understand them better than most people who came to visit her, she begged me to come so I did, feeling she was probably as lonely as I was.

I met her children who spoke a little English. The girl was going to study Art History at FSU. I also met 'Fraulein', who was a character. She had been with Elena since her birth, and had been instrumental in helping them escape from the Russians. They had apparently had to hide out in Vienna waiting for the Americans to come; both children had had the measles at that time. Fraulein helped by selling Elena's jewelry and her own pearls. I told them how I had worked with the Quakers in helping "Mischlinge" get out of Vienna and they knew what the Society of Friends had done. Dohnanyi had helped many Jewish musicians out and they had vouched for him on his arrival in USA. There had apparently been some questions raised as to why he had stayed in Budapest as a conductor. Elena explained he had never been a Nazi sympathizer but as he knew no language expect Hungarian and German it was difficult for him to find work in France or England. He had always been known as very anti-communist and was afraid of being captured by them. I think it was a relief for Elena and Fraulein to speak of what they had been through, for most people in America at that time had no idea. I wondered how they would get to the stores to find food as they had no car, but a kind woman came in her car to take them every week.

Soon after the Dohnanyis arrived they gave a party, chiefly for the Music School but also for those who had helped them, and for the first time since arriving in America there was something to drink! By this time I knew Elena well enough to ask how she obtained it, for Tallahassee was "dry" at the time and she told me that if one had money one could drive to the coast, thirty-five miles away, where there was a restaurant built over the water and therefore not "technically" in Leon county. There one could buy liquor, but no wine was available. Fraulein served the best punch and she told me the recipe: equal parts of apple juice, ginger ale and bourbon. A few years later there was an election as to whether Leon County should remain "dry." The bootleggers and the Baptists together put in a whole page advertisement in the local paper. "Temperance is health and safety; drink is sin and death." I cut it out and sent it to my mother who always liked her little noggin. By that time there were enough FSU faculty to swing the vote, and it became possible to buy liquor in Tallahassee, but there was still no wine for many years.

I was playing on the front lawn with John one afternoon when a black woman came across the fields, approached me and asked if I needed help. I asked her to come in to discuss it and offered her a glass of lemonade. Our dining table was in the kitchen and I sat down. She remained standing although I asked her to sit down. "I never sat with no white woman," she amazed me by saying. "Well, I said, that is ridiculous, we have only one table and of course you sit down." She did reluctantly, saying, "I can tell you're not from here but aint you afraid some neighbor might come by?" "So what?" I remember saying. This was my introduction to segregation in the south.

I had never engaged anyone to work before but I remembered Mummy asked for references, so I did. "Well," she said there is Mrs. So and So who still wants me come but she's too far, a three mile walk." I had already made up my mind I liked her. I told her I needed help scrubbing floors and vacuuming and that I hated dusting Venetian blinds. "Oh I got a padded fork for that," she said "I'll bring it with me." What a clever idea, I thought. I had found out from friends the going rate of maid service, and she seemed reasonable. "I comes myself," she said; "I walks over the field, just across the hill." I was grateful for that. We agreed she should come once a week for the day. "You'll have lunch with me," I said, "and sit at this table." "Usually I sits in the kitchen," she said. "Kitchen and dining room are one here, "I told her. She told me her name was Rosa Lee and we agreed she should come next Wednesday. I told her my name and that I had no phone. "I'll be here," she said.

During that first year she and Elena Dohnanyi became my closest friends. I loved to hear Rosa Lee talk. I never knew what she would say next. She told me once her sister-in-law was coming to stay and she was sanctified and "mighty ticklish about her food." "Why does being sanctified make her ticklish about her food?" I asked. "Oh Ma'am," she said," don't you know nothing? When you gets religion, you hollers, but when you're sanctified you gets the jumps, and my sister-in-law, she gets the jumps so bad, it makes her mighty ticklish about her food." I asked if she were married. "Yes and no, Ma'am, I've had two, both dead, and I don't want to be bothered by no more aggravation! I should never have married my second, it was along of his thumb. It was for all the world like Henry's, my first's thumb. Now Henry had a strange thumb, didn't think I'd ever see the like of it again, but there it was, on the pew next to me, a thumb like Henry's. I thought it was a sign. It was no sign or it was Henry warning me against him." I could think of nothing to say.

One day it was raining hard and Howard came back early and offered to drive her home. She was grateful and proceeded to get in the back of the car. I protested. "Oh no, the bassinet is there and toys, get in the front seat." She said "Ma'am, I knows you don't know no better for you aint from here, but I'm not aiming to get this nice young man into big trouble or me, for that matter, if anyone should see me sitting in front with a white man." Howard was as astonished as I was for he came from integrated New England; we both had to learn about segregation in the south.

There were two universities in Tallahassee: Florida State University and Florida A & M University, which was for the blacks. Howard made an attempt to contact the Music Dept at FAMU and was invited over where he met the President of FAMU, who I think came from Yale, where Howard went. We invited him over to dinner, and it was a very nice evening but there were repercussions; Howard was told by the Dean of Music in no uncertain terms he would never get Tenure if ever he did such a thing again! We were both appalled and so were many of the new young faculty whom we informed.

Before this happened, we had been invited to dinner at the Dean's house and there I saw the biggest cockroach I ever came across. The Dean saw me gazing at it and said: "Oh, you are looking at Bertie. He always comes out about this time." Cockroaches were accepted. However Howard got back into the Dean's good graces when we joined St.

John's Episcopal church of which the Dean was a member. We did not know this, but it was a good mark for Howard, and then he was invited to join the Junior League where he met one of the leading politicians who liked music and always came to Howard's concerts with many friends, and this also stood him in good stead with the dean. Also, we were close friends with the Dohnanyis.

Marian Anderson came to sing at FAMU and FSU faculty were invited as she said she would not sing to a segregated audience. She was already famous and had been championed by Mrs. Roosevelt. Quite a few townspeople came too, but they all sat at one side of the audience; we sat with the Music Faculty at FAMU. When Marian Anderson entered she announced that she had said she would not sing before a segregated audience and we were to mingle. We felt rather smug as we were already on the black side. It was a magnificent performance and she got a standing ovation from everyone.

Chapter 52

Dad's death. Visit to England.

In the spring of 1950 we had a shock; Dad died of a heart attack. There was no history of heart trouble before and he was not an old man. We were sad and Howard of course took a few days off and went up north for the funeral and to discuss with his brother David what was to happen to their mother. Howard felt she would want to stay with David who had a duplex in Seekonk, Massachusetts, just a few miles over the border of Rhode Island. She had all her friends there. This was what she decided to do. She had an immediate offer for their house in Newport, for it had been kept in excellent shape by Dad. She said she would come and stay with us for six weeks at the end of April, after the move.

As soon as Auntie Dora heard that she began moving. She had contacted Cook's International Travel Agency and found out that if there were a travel agent in Tallahassee who had contact with Cook's, she could pay in England fares for John and me; if we came before the baby was one year old he would travel for nothing even though his first birthday would be in England. She did not know what to do about Howard because of course he had to teach, but when she heard his mother would be able to be with him to cook and look after him, she begged us to agree to find a travel agent in Tallahassee who would play ball. The Dohnanyis knew one so that part was easy. It was not so easy to think of leaving Howard for six weeks but he was always so considerate and aware of how hard it was for me to leave my family and England. He was all for my going. I should just stay a few days after his mother came to show her where things were. Rosa Lee was horrified I was leaving Howard, "a poor lone man," for six weeks but agreed to come and help his mother.

It was two years since we'd left England, but it seemed like ten. When I thought of seeing the family and the bluebell woods and the nightingales, my heart lurched. I knew I had to go. I was hungry to walk in the woods. It disturbed me that there was nowhere to walk in Tallahassee, no sidewalks on the streets, and I had no contact with the land except for the sunsets over Lake Jackson, which did help, but I felt so estranged not experiencing woods and hills. I had nowhere to put down roots. Howard said we should not do much with our present garden (or yard as they called it) for we would be leaving in a few years and then we would have the flower garden I wanted. It was a hard clay soil we had now and apart from the old live oak in front nothing had grown there.

It was amazing luck that I could go to England in May although it was not so convenient for the family. Mummy did not like the countryside, as she said "it was too rural for her," and when Bettina had to drive Auntie or Uncle and other people around she felt too isolated at Little Pashley. It was very sad for Bettina who loved the place and the woods at the back and the Vidlers as friends. Mrs. V had become her best friend, but Bettina always put Mummy first. They were about to move to Tunbridge Wells. Auntie had already moved from Ticehurst to Sevenoaks where she had a lovely house with central heating at the edge of Knole Park, an Elizabethan manor house, gardens and ground to which she had access to walk. She had not been so happy in Ticehurst as she was on the main road.

Mrs. Wilson arrived and I introduced her to a few people at St. John's Episcopal Church. She liked the church but did not approve of much in Tallahassee, no sidewalks, too hot, but she seemed glad that she would look after Howard for six weeks. We had now been married for four years and were very happy together and disliked the thought of separation, but I knew he would write every day and I promised to do so too. He drove us to Jacksonville. John was already walking and starting to say, "Ma-ma" and "Da-da." I took a photo of Howard and told him I would say "Da-da" in front of the photo every day so the baby would remember him. He put us on the train to New York where Louisette would meet me and accompany us to board the Queen Mary. Louisette had crossed the Atlantic many times; it was old hat to her. She gave me another lovely dress.

On board ship we had a small cabin with two bunks with rails put across the lower one to act as a crib for the baby. He was very interested in the train ride, the taxi ride, and the ship and no trouble at all. He was already starting to eat adult food mashed and learning to drink from a cup; he came to the dining room with me and behaved himself very well. We arose early and walked round the deck before many people were astir, and then had a delicious breakfast of scrambled eggs and bacon and English tea. It was an uneventful trip except for one thing.

After our breakfast and lunch I installed myself in a deck chair next to the rail and had the stroller by my side so that I could push it up and down if the baby grew restless. I was the last chair in the row. Through the barricaded rails he could see something of the sea. One afternoon an incredible thing happened—the ship suddenly tilted, it seemed 45 degrees. The deck chairs beside me started crashing backwards, there were yells and screams of dismay. There is a little ditch, I do not know what it is called nautically, but it runs at the edge of each deck to catch the rain. It must have been mother instinct that impelled me to get the front wheels of the stroller over the rim of this ditch; then I dug my own heels in it, leant forward as far as I could on the deck chair, tried to grab the rail with one hand while holding on to the stroller with the other. We were the only ones who did not crash backwards. I realized with dismay that the ship was about to tilt in the opposite direction and all the deck chairs would return down on top of us, and the baby would be quite unprotected in his canvas stroller.

I was the last deck chair in the row and the covered gangway was not far away where we would be protected from returning chairs; I prayed and at the moment of what I hoped was balance rushed the stroller to the gangway and got its front wheels over the rim of the ditch separating the deck from the gangway. Thank goodness a sailor was there and grabbed the stroller and me. The chairs came crashing back outside with a dreadful din of breaking wood and screams. "What has happened?" I asked the sailor. "A sudden squall," he replied, "but I've never seen one so sudden that it wasn't logged on radar first so we could get the chairs in. You'll be safest in your cabin, it won't last long." He took me to the elevator which was working. Downstairs the motion was not so violent but I was glad of his arm and that we reached the cabin safely.

The squall did not last long but it caused quite a bit of damage and there were many bruises and a few bones broken during the deck chair crash. I felt very grateful I had been able to achieve safety. I saw the young sailor quite often afterwards and of course thanked him and then asked if he could show me where I could stand on deck to see the first of England. He asked if I were being met at Southampton and when I told him I was he took me to a small railed area jutting out from the main deck, I could stand there and put the baby's legs on one rail so I would not have his whole weight to carry. He held on to the top rail and so did I and squished in close behind him. The sailor gave me a table napkin to wave and said he thought my family would find me easily as there were not many babies that age on board. I thought I would see them first on the quay as I was long-sighted then and Mummy and Bettina would be the two shortest people.

I think, though, that they must have seen me first for I saw someone waving a large white handkerchief and knew it was Bettina. It was an incredible sensation; I realized the truth of the statement "My heart was in my mouth."

The young sailor got us towards the front of the queue down the gangway. Mummy was in tears and we were all quite speechless. The sailor helped us with the luggage and the stroller to the car which Bettina had parked very conveniently and in no time we were off on a spring morning through the countryside. Mummy wanted the baby on her lap and I knew all he wanted was to be in the front seat to see out so handed him over and he was quite happy and so was she. She was very good with babies; I had seen that in the children's home she worked in during the war in Wales. It was a shame she did not have the chance to bring up her own babies according to the mores of the time, but she and I became much closer after I had children.

I remember the arrival at Little Pashley. Someone had lent them a crib and playpen and Bettina won my son's heart forever by giving him two little Corgi cars which came in boxes. I had told her he loved cars but I'd found no toy cars in Tallahassee (I did later), so he had only blocks and rattles. These Corgi cars were famous in England, small duplicates of actual cars. He immediately started a car noise and Bettina started another and he was enthralled. He wanted to take them to bed with him but she placed the boxes on his bedside table and said they were garages and the cars had to be garaged at night and he immediately saw her point.

We stopped for lunch on the way and soon after we arrived home he fell asleep and I was urged to go out in the woods. The bluebells were out, so I went out quite serenely. I had never left him before. I knew what to expect, but I was still overwhelmed when I saw the seas of blue under the light leaves of the beeches with the faint scent of hyacinths; my heart seemed to stop. I stood and gazed; I would come back later for the nightingales. I knew Bettina had champagne on ice in the fridge and they were waiting. It was an occasion.

Next day we went to lunch with Auntie Dora at her new house in Sevenoaks on the edge of Knole Park. The grounds stretched off into the distance and we walked there. My cousin Gordon, his wife Beryl, and their little daughter Tricia who was six months older then John came to tea. She was an affectionate child and wanted to sit on my lap. My son had never climbed up voluntarily, he was not a cuddly child, but when he saw Tricia there he bounded up, pushed her off, and for the first time put his arms around me and climbed up, whether out of affection or feelings of ownership I do not know.

Bettina had dubbed the baby "JD" when they first received a photo of him, and he was always called that by his English family and grew up with that name. It suited him; he was a cheerful little chap with a wide grin, very independent and undemonstrative, but my mother told me that came from me for I had been the same.

Guided by Bettina, Auntie Dora gave him a truck in which to transport his cars and he was in hog heaven, inventing, helped by Bettina, suitable noises to distinguish the truck from the smaller cars. Nothing in life had prepared me for the difficulty of teaching my one year old son the custom of sharing. However, he played happily with his cousin, Tricia, who made no attempt to take his cars but listened, fascinated, to his car noises.

After two weeks at Little Pashley, I shared the next two weeks between Auntie Dora, the Akehursts, Ray and Sim, and Nan and Ken. I was shown the flat in Tunbridge Wells into which Mummy and Bettina were to move. It was in a Victorian house, divided into two flats, owned by an elderly couple who were very pleasant. Mummy would never be alone, and she could walk to the cinema, to which she had developed a great attraction in Portmadoc, and also to the shops by herself. Bettina would be freer and it was easier to meet Ronnie. They were happy but I bade a sorrowful farewell to the nightingales, doubting that I would hear them again. But I did, half a lifetime away, in Provence.

With Auntie I visited Knole Park house which I had thought was Elizabethan but was older. Auntie gave me an interesting book, *"Daughter of Time,"* by Josephine Tey, a detective story but an unusual one dealing with historical facts. The detective visits the National Portrait Gallery and decides that Richard III is about the only English king who does not look like a thug and he does not believe the Tudor propaganda put out by Holinshed, and used by Shakespeare in *"Richard III"*—that Richard killed the little princes in the tower. It was far more likely, he thought, that they had been murdered by Henry VII, for they barred his ascent to the throne. The detective obtains access to old documents and finds out that their death was after Richard III's. The book became famous and was taken up by historians who confirmed the facts. In Knole House there was a letter prominently on display from the fifteenth century, by Lady Bessborough, saying that she could not understand how they were saying Richard was crookshank. "I danced with him as a girl," she wrote, "and he was straight as a wand." Of course Holinshed was a Tudor propagandist but Shakespeare believed it and so did the world after "*Richard III*."

After Auntie I visited the Akehursts and missed Howard horribly for we had always been a foursome. Their son John Howard was nine months older than JD and under supervision, sharing was achieved, and we had a good time together. Cyril had a car by then and took us to the Downs. Ray had had a daughter in January that year, and her son Nick was not interested in cars. I feared that with two children she would not achieve a musical career. For three years after the war until Nick's birth she had sung and toured quite extensively, which was essential, but nowthat was no longer possible. Sim was a free-lance journalist, writing all over Europe, but money trickled in only spasmodically. Ray took me to a concert and afterwards we walked in the Temple Gardens where we were alone and she sang me a new song, a capella. It was Brahms "*Wie Melodien zieht es mir, leise aus dem Sinnm*" which translates roughly, "like melodies it arose gently from my mind," and I had that peculiar sensation, which I only had when Ray sang, of happiness falling around me. I wished time to stop.

They had a party for me. I had brought everyone whisky from the Duty Free shop on board, and it was welcomed as it was very expensive and hard to get in England. When Ray sang the Polish songs I missed Howard very much. Sim told me again that I had a beautiful profile; he'd told me that once when Howard was there and had said, "Yes, doesn't she?," but he had never told me that himself, so I was grateful to Sim for it is always nice to hear.

We visited Nan and Ken last. I felt bad going there with a baby when she did not have one yet, but she begged me to come. They were still in the thatched cottage but leaving soon for Ken had become a rich man with the Ford Tractor franchise. Nan touched me again by telling me she had prayed she would not be jealous if I had a child before her as she had been of so many others, and happily she could tell me the news that she was expecting in October. I was so thankful. She had found a doctor who told her she could become pregnant only a few days a month and to have sex on those days, and it worked. She had never looked prettier or happier and they were to live in a lovely old Georgian house in Crediton with the most beautiful garden grown over centuries. I told her how I missed flowers, that in the hot summer with tropical rain showers I couldn't get anything to grow. She told me to grow geraniums in hanging baskets under the eaves and only water them occasionally and I took her advice. We had a happy time although JD had his first disaster there. I had bathed him and placed him on a table by the bath to dry him. The ceilings were low and suddenly he jumped up and his head went through the plaster. I was terribly upset but Ken took it calmly and said it could easily be replaced and thankfully John was not hurt.

JD had another disaster visiting Mrs. Polak. He was drinking out of a cup but he had not been given a glass before and bit a piece out of it. Luckily Nol was very speedy in action and got the glass out of his mouth, but I became a bit unnerved and wondered what he would do next. Nol repeated his offer that we as a family could stay at his co-op, St. Julians in Sevenoaks, if we could come again. Lida had gone back to Oxford to finish her degree, which she had given up during the war to join the Dutch services.

I spent the last two weeks in Tunbridge Wells. The flat was attractive but I did not like the town; it was on the London coast road and very crowded, but Mummy and Bettina both seemed happy with it. Bettina took me to meet Ronnie and, if it meant they could see each other more, I agreed Tunbridge Wells was a good thing. Rita was coming back with me to Tallahassee and also to visit friends in New Orleans and North Carolina and I was glad of her company on the trip.

Chapter 53

Return to Tallahassee.

It was not so hard to leave England the second time, for I was longing to see Howard. Again I tried to impress the white cliffs on my mind so that I could recall them at will but they soon became a blur. My cousin and I had not seen much of each other since Germany. She was very attractive and had had many suitors. She had been in love with a Czech officer, but when he asked her to marry him after the war she refused. "It was bad enough for you going to America," she said, "but just imagine not knowing the language, and then the Cold War . . . ." I wanted her to join the dancing at night but I would not leave J.D. though the stewardess said she would keep an eye on him. I did not see how she could find me quickly if he cried. I did keep him up for a concert for one night where Rita met some young people and agreed to stay on for dancing. There were no squalls and we made it through the Customs and to the train, which seemed very long. Howard was there waiting for us at Jacksonville, and poor dear, he had been given a ticket for speeding! JD obliged by calling him "Da-da" which pleased Howard very much.

Rita stayed with us about two months and went with us to concerts that Howard gave in town and in Jacksonville and Pensacola. She came to me one day and said: "Audrey, this town is impossible. There is no place to walk!" She was right. There were no sidewalks, and nowhere to go had there been. In England everyone went for a walk every day, and in New England it had been the same, but there was nowhere to walk in Tallahassee. Newport was built around a village green with a church and town hall, and then there was the Esplanade by the sea and the famous Cliff Walk. It was not that the Americans had forgotten the English "constitutional," but it had been the railroad that had forced towns to grow up alongside of them with no form or shape and with no parks or gardens. However, that very same fall Maclay Gardens were opened in Tallahassee. They were built by an Irishman who had come over in the twenties and had bought land with a lake in it surrounded by dogwoods and azaleas and then he added an Italian garden in which he had planted cypress on either side of a long pool with camellias beyond. He had paved it with old brick so it was an elegant place to walk and everybody from the university, most of them from the north, rushed to enjoy it.

We went there every weekend and I sometimes took Howard to work and kept the car so I could take Rita there during the week. At one of the university parties Rita met a professor who had invited her to audit her lectures on Political Science, and Rita was interested in doing this. I hoped that perhaps later I could audit some Philosophy or Art History lectures. Everybody was so astounded I did not have a college degree that I grew embarrassed. I had given a lecture in the Literary Club on the origin of nursery rhymes which was a great success and I was made the President for the following year and told that I must apply to teach at FSU; and then came out the embarrassing fact that I had no college degree. All my friends had gone to college, but Howard said I would never need to teach; he was the old-fashioned type that felt women belonged in the home.

I'd brought from England LP records of "The Abduction from the Seraglio." They were hard to pack and I could only bring one opera. My favorite was Mozart's "The Magic Flute" but I felt they would have that in the States, was not sure about "The Abduction." Dohnanyi was very impressed and gave me "Rigoletto" on records for Christmas; he said I should have some Verdi. It turned out that JD simply loved that opera and it was how we found out he was musical. He was given a little drum, and very soon he was picking out "*la donna* e *mobile*" and calling it "my tune." Once he said he could not come to eat as his tune was about to play.

Chapter 54

The Fifties.

Next summer Howard was invited to teach at Brevard Music Camp in North Carolina. Several faculty members had already taught there and said it was a beautiful place, although the living quarters were just log cabins. It was in the mountains, and it was the first time that JD and I had really "bonded." One afternoon Mahler's "*Das Lied von der Erde*" was being sung (The song of the earth) and I longed to hear it. I only knew that one Mahler symphony that Beecham had conducted, I could not find a baby-sitter and told my two-year-old son that I wanted to hear "my tune" and would he please sit quietly on my lap and listen and he did through the whole hour-long performance. I was awed, especially by the aria "*Abschied*," ("Farewell," . . . the beloved earth blooms out in spring . . . .").

I was already pregnant with my second child, and we both hoped it would be a girl and wanted to call her "Allison Anne" after that fair-haired girl who had opened the door to me at Kinsgate, showing a room beyond full of light and purple iris. "I am leaving," she said, and went out of my life forever but left her name. I thought it was so musical. "Allison" sounded as though it were played by violins and echoed by "Anne" with cellos. I had no trouble with pregnancy this time and continued to go to concerts. There was a large mirror in the foyer which I shuddered past for years afterwards, fearing to see my rotund reflection.

The day before the baby was due I lost a filling in a tooth with great pain. The dentist was reluctant to treat me fearing it would bring on the birth in his office, but he listened to my plea that I could not stand the tooth pain on top of what was to come and filled the tooth. The doctor had told me not to come to the hospital for several hours as I had had such a long birth with JD. By this time there was a neighbor next door and she came in and saw me clinging to the bathtub and said to us "Get to the hospital at once or the child will arrive." We barely made it and I still think the head nurse delivered the baby for I don't remember seeing the doctor. When I visited the hospital later to see friends having babies, she always asked particularly about my second son. We did not get our girl but a very sweet good baby we called Andrew. From the first he was an angelic child. There was no colic with him. He seemed to sleep through the night at once as soon as we came home, and we could dispense with the woman to help me who kept on singing about "the sunshine in my soul," which drove Howard quite mad. From the first Andrew was no trouble. JD was doubtful what to think of him but thankful he was not interested in cars, though later he wished he were.

In the summer vacation when Andrew was six months old Howard wanted to drive up to Massachusetts to visit his mother, stopping with friends in North Carolina, his cousin in Staten Island and Nadine (Mrs. Raymond's daughter) and Bill in New York. They had a lovely house in Queens and they had room for us; they already had two sons. I remember the trip only vaguely but the return was a disaster. Everything went wrong with the car until it finally conked out in Columbus, South Carolina. It was the back axle or something disastrous, and there was nothing for it but to send a telegram to our bank in Tallahassee and buy a new car. There was only one car available at the garage at which we landed. I felt we should drive around in it and inspect other cars, but this went against Howard's Puritan ethics; that would not be kosher. The car available was O.K.

We had to wait for hours in the garage, the baby was feverish, and I was very concerned. Howard and I each thought the other was keeping an eye on three-year-old JD. He was drawn to the grease pit and to my horror got into it and then came screaming towards me and the sick baby, black with grease! The only thing I could think of was to strip him naked, leave his clothes there, and then, with him yelling at one hand and the baby in my other arm, run down the street till I could find a motel to take us in.

Years later when I taught the *Aeneid* to students I used this as an example of Virgil's psychology when he tells his shipwrecked comrades who have lost everything that "years afterwards these memories will make you smile." The class always roared with laughter at my story and I had to smile, remembering.

I soon found a motel and they were very kind and Howard came along with the luggage and we found some more clothes for JD. The money came eventually, and the car turned out not to be a lemon but was very serviceable for years and it made a good story to illustrate JD's propensity for disasters. As a grown man he was in charge of Disaster Preparedness for Lee County, Florida, and I felt it was very appropriate.

Chapter 55

Rita's Wedding. Wigmore Hall Concert.

I can only recall the years by remembering the trips to England. In l953 my cousin Rita wrote that she had become engaged to Brian, who had been a prisoner of war of the Japanese for six years, from the fall of Singapore. He had taken part in the notorious Burma Road horror and was not demobbed for quite a while, and then had to spend some time in hospital. He was one of the few to survive and said later he felt it was because he was more of a vegetable than many. He was quite O.K. now and had a job as a solicitor in Huntingdon. Rita had known him quite a while and they were going to live in Cambridge. She hoped we all could come for the wedding and Auntie would provide the flight, as Howard could not take so long away.

I was nervous about the flight and with reason. It was always difficult to make connections from Tallahassee and we had to drive to Jacksonville and take a bus to the airport there to get the Atlanta-London plane. The bus driver drove us past the airport twice. As he attempted this a third time I screamed at him: "Turn!!" Andrew looked at me reprovingly and said "You shouted at him Mummy." It was lucky I did for we barely made the plane.

For the first night Auntie put us up at an old hotel in Sevenoaks and thereafter we stayed with Nol at his co-op home at St. Julians. The hotel had no built-in closets but a huge wardrobe. Before we could stop him four year old John opened and started swinging on the door and the whole thing came down on top of him. It took six men to get it off. He was not hurt but only scared.

It was decided to get a baby sitter for the boys for the wedding. Bettina was bridesmaid in dark red taffeta and looked beautiful and very happy. Rita made a lovely bride. She had asked me if I wanted to be matron-of honor but I did not; I preferred to sit with Howard. The service was at the village church, and the reception was in the family garden. It was a beautiful day, all the summer flowers were out, lupins, delphiniums and stocks with their lovely scent. I was embarrassed that my little fur stole that I had taken from England and never worn in the States, started to shed during the service, it had not been mothproofed enough. I managed to hang on to it long enough for Howard and me to be photographed but then dropped it in a waste paper basket; it was a ruin.

When Dohnanyi learned we were going to England he asked if Howard would like him to recommend Wigmore Hall to put on a recital for him and make all the arrangements. It was very kind and flattering and of course he accepted and we had the excitement of this after the wedding. I had written my old Austrian friends and they contacted others I had helped while working for the Quakers; the Polaks had a large acquaintance also, and Dohnanyi's recommendation brought in many. There was quite a good audience and a number of reviewers who were complimentary, so it was a great occasion for us. Someone gave a reception and I met Martin Esslin who afterwards became Head of Drama at the BBC and later visited Tallahassee for a theatre gala at FSU. Stefan had married Hanni and they lived at Salisbury where he had an important job with the British army; they came up to London for the concert. It was good to see them again and they asked us to visit. Ray and Sim were there with all their Polish friends. The program started with Schumann, then Mozart's Fantasia for C minor, and after the interval Beethoven's Waldstein and Chopin's E flat nocturne for encore.

Howard was always happy in England. He loved visiting Salisbury and old Sarum and I enjoyed seeing the cathedral again. Howard and Stefan played Mozart piano and violin sonatas together and we had a good time. We went to see Nan and Ken and their son Richard, who was about a year younger than JD. He was a serious child, devoted to his mother. She told us she had been caught for speeding and Richard asked the policeman if he could go to prison with her. They were settled in their beautiful Georgian house in Creditor and had even installed central heating, so things were going well for them. Ray had now given up singing which made me sad; she had become a guide for the British Council. They came down to St. Julian's at Sevenoaks to visit us where Howard played on Nol's grand piano and Ray sang the Schubert lieder and of course the Polish songs. We spent a few days in a country cottage with the Akehursts and the children played well together. Cyril hoped to visit Canada some time for the firm and to visit us at the same time although it was at other side of the continent. John Howard had a huge red motor car he could drive and he kindly let JD have turns, which impressed him greatly.

Chapter 56

Children, Civil Rights, Friends.

My mother was very astute. She noted that Andrew liked to play with a ball and spent a long time throwing a ball back and forth to him. She said he threw astonishingly straight for someone not yet two and he would take after her football brothers. I recalled my days of throwing ball and taught him how to bounce and catch a ball. On the way home at the airport in Gatwick we had to climb a moving staircase, an escalator. Andrew looked around in surprise and said "I'm not used to this kind of life." Howard was very attached to him. He said to me "This is a sweet one," for Andrew liked to climb up and sit on our laps, something which JD never did voluntarily. Andrew was not as musical although he made little tunes for himself. He amused us once saying after Howard stopped practicing, "Are you going to be unselfish now, Daddy, and let me play my record?" Of course Howard complied. Andrew was always anxious to help me so I let him lay the table and he must have done it once when the Nutcracker Suite was playing for he made up a little tune to the Arabian dance. He could not pronounce his name and called himself "Ahie" so he fitted the words "Ahie put the forks down, Ahie put the forks down" and ever after he sang that little tune as he laid the table. I think the consonants "dr" must be difficult for children to pronounce, for Bettina could never pronounce "Audrey." When we arrived home I showed him an empty side of the house with no windows where he could throw his ball and learn to catch it and he spent hours doing that. I made it clear that was the only wall he could use!

I took JD to Sunday School once he was three and I could have put Andrew in the nursery, but he was such a quiet good baby I thought he might enjoy church with me and he did. He snoozed a bit during the sermon but in the Episcopal Church there is so much kneeling and standing there is not much time to fall asleep. He seemed to enjoy the music, the candles, and the procession.

Howard gave up coming every Sunday for he was so tired. He had twenty-two students for two half-hours each every week. He said he found it hard to adjust to a different personality every half-hour; he was not as social as I was, and he found he had to urge them to the piano or they would start telling him about their private lives. I worried that he was not getting the concert career for which he had spent his life preparing. He told me somewhat sadly that the day of the concert pianist seemed to be over. With so much radio available and now with the advent of television not so many concert pianists were needed. People preferred to hear and see Van Cliburn over and over. He was thankful to have had the Wigmore Hall recital. I felt very bad about this, but what could one do?

The world was going through the upheaval of civil rights in the fifties and sixties. In Tallahassee the blacks staged a sit-down in Woolworths to protest that though they spent money there, they were not allowed to be served coffee. Governor Leroy Collins challenged the existing code. He published a letter in the paper saying he thought if they spent their money in Woolworths, they were entitled to a cup of coffee. His own mother did not speak to him for three months. Many students and some faculty at FSU wanted to sit with the black students to show their support, and I did, but Howard told me he would never get tenure if I did so and I realized he was right and just went by and wished them luck. Many white students were jailed along with the blacks and a good friend of ours, Jack Ice, ran into trouble with the mayor for visiting his students in jail. The city manager, Arvah Hopkins, went to Dr. Strozier, the president of FSU, and demanded he fire Dr. Ice; the President refused to fire Jack and shortly afterwards he had a heart attack and died. The atmosphere was tense on campus and in the town. I wrote to Leroy Collins thanking him for his letter and received a wonderful reply, saying it meant a lot to him knowing some people supported him. Later I became acquainted with him as he was a member of our church, St. Johns. The church was divided as the Southerners found it very hard to change their attitudes. We had a wonderful minister, Dr. Barrett, who was very much in favor of Civil Rights. When he left he wrote a book *Farewell to Halitosis*, of course a play on the name Tallahassee which a lot of us enjoyed. Our new minister, Lee Graham, was of the same mind and gradually quite a few black members joined St. Johns. I always remember a sermon Dr. Barrett preached on angels. He was devoted to trains and accumulated a set that duplicated the New York-San Francisco line. When he finally obtained the last carriage remaining for his set and then was given a seat in this particular carriage on a railway trip to a conference, he told the congregation the next Sunday that he knew the Almighty had more to do than bring about such a happy coincidence for him, and this was why he believed in angels: it was they who were responsible for such serendipities. I felt his 'serendipities' were very much like what I called, after Jung, "synchronicities," those times when coincidences seem magical, as when Howard was able to reach me at Manor Farm after he had flown from France, whereas if he had called two days later, I would have been gone from there and not accessible by the telephone. Also that we landed in Kansas City, the home of the one American student we had met in England, whose family was so amazingly kind and hospitable.

As a faculty wife I had access to the FSU Library, which was a godsend. I found Chaucer's "Troilus and Criseyde" and decided to learn Middle English to read it. Going out I met a faculty member who asked what I was reading. "You should be taking that for a class," she said, "so when your boys are grown you can apply for a position at FSU." Again I had to explain to my chagrin that I had no college degree.

Jack Ice, who was a Philosophy professor from Harvard, was also insistent that I should take classes for credit, for I might indeed wish to teach later on. We felt we did not have the money and Howard was always against the idea that I might have to work outside the home. Jack offered to let me audit his classes and he would grade me as if I were a real student. I jumped at the chance, and once JD was in kindergarten found a friend who would baby sit Andrew for me with her little boy, so I could go to class and I would do the same for her. I took six philosophy classes with Jack: Plato, Aesthetics, Logic, Ethics, Paul Tillich and Modern Philosophy, and aced the lot. How I wished later I had taken them for credit, eighteen hours! However, they did help me; not only did I learn a lot but I felt if I could understand philosophy I could do most things except math. Jack was at the top of his form as a teacher, and through him I met Paul Tillich when he was on a lecture tour at FSU.

By this time we had made a lot of friends and started a Pot Luck group which met at a different house each month. Geneva and Dave became very close friends. Dave taught choral music at the boys' school which was attached to the university, and Geneva taught piano and conducted a children's choir as well as a choir she organized among the faculty. That was the only time I sang in a choir. I made Howard laugh by saying that I was trying to learn to sight read by singing a fifth when turning to the right and a fourth when turning to the left. "I'd be happier about that, honey," he said, "if I were convinced you were sure of your left and right." I had to agree; it was a weakness with me.

One year the Dean of Arts & Science joined us together with two new friends, Patricia and Bill, who were classicists and archaeologists. We played very intellectual games. Steve, a geology professor, was excellent at devising them.

Patricia had a PhD in Classics and Archeology and had been with Bill on many digs in Greece. She really lit up my mind and she was very insistent that I take classes at FSU so I would be able to teach one day. I had a dream about her one night. She was a fantastic cook and in the dream she gave me a fish dish covered with orange and lemon slices. I knew her well enough to say that I did not think it was her best and she said in the dream "I am surprised you didn't like it, it was the fish dish Cosima took with her when she ran away from von Bulow to throw in her lot with Wagner." I said "Nobody takes a fish dish with them when they leave their husband to run off with another man." Patricia said, "She did, it is well known. She hid it under her cloak." I do not know what Freud would make of that dream.

Chapter 57

Our house. Third Garden. Carnegie Hall.

As soon as Howard obtained tenure he wanted to sell our house and buy a lot on which he could build a house of his own design. I was afraid we did not have the money, but he insisted this was the time and I knew how much it would mean to him to draw up the blueprints and build his own home. Architecture had always been his second love, and it did not look as if he were going to fulfill his lifelong dream of being a concert pianist; there was just not the demand any more with radio and television. Some wooded lots came on the market on the second-highest hill in Tallahassee, San Luis Ridge, where the first Spanish fort had been built in the 17th—century. They were owned by Governor Leroy Collins who kept the land adjacent and gave it to the city for a park. So if one built there, one would never be threatened by surrounding apartments. We chose a lot that overlooked the lake in the park with an orchard of Tung trees beyond; in the spring they were pink with blossom, looking like apple trees, reminiscent of England.

The lot had thirty-four flowering dogwood trees on it. Of course we could not keep them all but we kept enough to make a background for purple, lilac, and pale pink azaleas instead of a front lawn. The soil was good, fertilized with leaves for hundreds of years, not like the baked clay we had known. I looked forward to a flower garden. San Luis Ridge was among the highest places in Tallahassee, preferred by Howard because he had noted flooding in lower areas in the tropical storms of summer. In order to get the best view of the lake and tung orchard and to avoid the western light, we had not chosen the crest of the hill, so the house was somewhat down from the road. Howard designed drains to carry the rain around the house and into San Luis Road, which was fifteen feet below the house. One of our archaeological friends said they were the best drains he had seen since Corinth. Another friend gave us jasmine sprigs to plant, which he said in a year would be a tall hedge to shield us from the road and also to stop the children falling over. We started planting before the house was finished and by the time we moved in the jasmine hedge was flourishing, because everything grows so quickly in Florida.

Howard drew up the blueprints himself and the house was really his triumph; it was much admired. I left it all to him. All I wanted were bookcases on either side of the fireplace in the living room, like those I remembered from the Merchant Taylors School in London where I had taken my Junior Oxford exam.

Howard had all sorts of clever ideas including a fluorescent light under glass in the mantelpiece, which showed up the Bristol glass bottles displayed there and shone on the painting above; vertical slots in kitchen cabinets for trays, and a Lazy Susan in the corner of the kitchen cabinets. The kitchen and bedrooms were small. The boys' rooms had desks built in under the windows by their beds and a sliding door which they could close. He also used sliding doors for their rooms and the bathroom into the hall to save space.

The living room and the boys' rooms were paneled in gold cypress which was quite inexpensive at the time but later became rare. The gold darkened to a rose-brown which was very attractive. There was a cathedral ceiling in the living room with beams which Howard insisted should be painted black at the sides so as to coincide with black shelves along one wall for books and *objets d'art*. The painters jibbed at this and said they had never painted the beams in cathedral ceilings black but Howard insisted and the black emphasized the richness of the paneling.

I loved the house and what I admired most was something rare in most houses—the windows were low to the floor so that everywhere you could see out to trees and flowers. It was like being up in the trees. The few windows to the west had low eaves and little light came through them. On one of the black shelves in the living room was a model of a sailing ship Dad had made; he was a skilled craftsman. Above were two German swords from WWI that Howard had brought back from the war, and on the porch was the head of a little 14th-century angel that he had found in the ruins of Ulm cathedral about to be scooped up by a bulldozer. I never understood how he could have carried anything so heavy home, but I loved the little angel.

The new house took months to build. In the old house in the very cold winter when Andrew was three, we had been shopping and I had my arms full of paper bags and struggled with the key to open the door. Evidently some frozen cans of juice had not been wrapped in plastic and they broke through one bag, scattering cans all down the steps leading to the front door. I dropped the other bag and said to Andrew "Oh help me gather up the cans !" He was usually the most helpful child but he was shivering with cold. "Can't, Mummy," he murmured, "so cold." I pulled myself together. "Of course you are, my poor little Florida cracker, go inside, you are not used to the cold. I come from a cold country and can manage." He went in and shut the door. Seconds later his little face peeked out. "I'm asking God to help you, Mummy!" Everybody loved that story.

Before we left the old house, a TV tower was built at the end of our street. At seven, JD was quite independent and for two years he had been catching the school bus at the top of our road. The neighborhood had built up and our road was full of houses, most of which held children with whom JD played on return from school. Those were the happy days when it was quite safe to let children play together in the street. He had a watch and was home by 6 o'clock.

In the TV tower at the end of the street, Jack Ridner hosted a birthday party on children's TV every day. JD had been invited to one and was sold on TV ever afterwards. He was most upset that we had no intention of buying one.

Many people in the neighborhood had TVs and I assumed JD was watching the children's hour with friends. I could hardly stop that, but to my amazement a friend who had TV said to me, "Your son seems very popular. I see him on every birthday party with Jack Ridner." When asked JD said happily, "Oh yes, me and Jack Ridner are friends, he lets me in every day!" The child had been walking to the TV station and entering with other children! "Didn't any of the mothers question you?," I asked. "No," he said, "I don't think they knew all the children there, but Jack Ridner knows me and it is he who gives out the cookies!" We put a stop to that of course and explained to JD that one could not gate-crash other people's birthday parties, it was a no-no.

Both Howard and I were against TV. We felt it would hinder the children reading or doing homework, but fate was against us. A month before we were due to move, JD caught the mumps and gave them to Andrew and eventually to me. I had not had them as a child and had them very badly, and we were due to move in ten days! The doctor said I would have to stay in bed, only getting up for the bathroom. It was he who told us we must get a TV to keep the children amused so I could have peace and quiet or I would never be able to make the move! TV was censored then; the boys went to bed before adult shows. From four to seven when they watched it was mostly cartoons and birthday parties and of course cartoons and commercials all Saturday mornings. I was amazed to hear "*Vesta da guibba*" on a cereal commercial. Both children learned to sing "no more rice crispies" to Pagliacchi's lament and I survived the move.

Howard was very much admired for the house and that he had designed it completely himself and drawn up the blue prints. Our friends Jack and Betty had bought a lot and were also building in San Luis ridge, and had found a builder with a plan they liked who seemed reasonable. We asked the same builder for an estimate and Howard was content with it. My only contribution was to suggest a second estimate from the best builder in town, Carl Ferrell, who came up with an estimate $1000 cheaper. We had obtained a good price for our first house and were able to put $10,000 down and so had a 30-year mortgage payment of $67.00 a month which was a great blessing and seems unbelievable today.

Things had changed at the FSU School of Music. Dohnanyi had often told us that he had had an American-born Hungarian student who had been sent to study with him in Hungary when he was twelve, and who had lived with the family. He had won the prestigious Prix de Rome prize for piano in 1940 and had just started on a concert career when America joined WWII. This was Edward Kilenyi, who had enlisted in the U. S. Army and joined the Intelligence Corps. After the war he was sent with the Occupation Forces to Germany and had been instrumental in saving Dohnanyi from the Russians and getting him a visa to South America and later to the States. He had been for several years in New York attempting to continue his concert career, interrupted by the war, but by the middle of the fifties, he had decided that the day of concert pianists was over and he asked Dohnanyi to try and find him a teaching position at FSU. Dohnanyi was able to do this and Kilenyi arrived with his Welsh wife and her two parents who lived with them in Tallahassee.

Kilenyi was an excellent pianist with a repertoire of Liszt, Bartok and other pyrotechnical composers, and all the newly arrived best students wished to study with him. None of Howard's students left him, for he was a very good teacher and popular, but it did make a difference. Howard told me ruefully it was not much help as a pianist to have a name like Wilson, and he became rather depressed. He had started a while before to compose and had a Flute and Piano sonata performed at FSU which was a great success. He played the piano part. He also composed songs for two of my poems and a Piano and Violin sonata; it was rather difficult and the resident violinist was not interested in playing it. Dolf Polak's old violin teacher, Peter Bornstein, was touring the States, and I thought he might like to perform it. I invited him to come and stay and he was very impressed and said he would like to play it at his Carnegie Hall recital next year and invited Howard to accompany him. This was a distinct boost to Howard's morale.

Chapter 58

Camping trip.

The boys were now nine and six years old. Many of our faculty friends went camping with their families and offered to lend us camping gear, so we decided rather rashly to go in our Volkswagen bug with rack on top holding tent, stove, and lantern. I remember Steve, the geologist, explaining to me the niceties of lighting the lantern. We were going to stay first of all in North Carolina, and then on the Blue Ridge Parkway. Afterwards we planned to continue up north and to stay with Howard's cousin in Staten Island, with Nadine and Bill and their two boys in New York, and then with Howard's mother, and end up in Arcadia Park in Maine. Our friends had done much longer trips out west, but although I longed to see the mountains, I was a little fearful.

I recall our stay on the Blue Ridge Mountains, looking down on the lights in the Shenandoah Valley below. That was a high which stayed in my mind together with the difficulty of lighting fires, the tremendous problems with the lantern although I had written down instructions, the times it rained and drops appeared on the inside of the tent, which if one did not touch them, remained there. In spite of dire threats they were too much temptation for JD and indeed I understood it. They were fascinating. He became somewhat damp but there was no way to move him as the tent was only designed for four. I was impressed by the facilities at each camping site, hot and cold water, showers, picnic tables, much less primitive than the conditions on our European trip. There was an umbrella over the picnic table at one place, and I remember Andrew sitting under it in the rain, eating a slice of bread with nothing on it. However, it did not rain often and we enjoyed the cool weather.

While we were with Howard's mother in New England, Howard rang up his old professor at Yale, who invited us to visit him there and then to stay at his weekend cottage at a lake nearby. He had a speedboat we all enjoyed very much, also the sunsets over the lake. We were sitting talking one evening of Howard's student days at Yale, and his professor (whose name I have forgotten) said "Of course you would not get in now." I date Howard's depression from that remark; I remember his face. I was furious and snapped back, "How can you say that? Didn't you drag Howard back when he wanted to leave for you needed a good student? Didn't he win the Ditson Scholarship for study in Europe and England? He has given a recital in the Wigmore Hall and will in Carnegie Hall next spring." I could have killed him. He was somewhat abashed and said "Oh yes, the Ditson." "Wasn't that for the best pianist of the year?," I asked. He agreed and I don't know what happened next, but I could never forget Howard's face. It haunted me as I remembered how often he had told me that from the age of eight he had practiced four hours a day to become a concert pianist and now to be told that by his professor!

I remember the ice cold water in Arcadia Park in Maine which only JD could face, also that the sun seemed to be setting in the right half of the sky when I felt the west should have been on the left. Howard explained it was because we were on an inlet.

We decided to go a little out of the way home and visit Howard's great friends at Yale, who were now in West Virginia where they taught at a small college. He was a violinist and she a pianist. They had a brilliant daughter of fifteen, named Pravda, a pianist who had been taught by her mother and had perfect pitch and incredible skill for one so young. They were paid very little and were worried about Pravda's further training at a university. I said, "But surely she will get a scholarship." Her father looked at Howard. "We both had scholarships at Yale, but Howard's father had to sell his car to keep him there, though Howard waited on tables. We have no car." Apparently Pravda was academically gifted as well and was due to graduate; there was no place they could afford.

That night I said to Howard: "what do you think about offering Pravda to stay with us free. I am sure she would get a scholarship for tuition and books, and you would have a student who could compete with any of Kilenyi's?" At first he was doubtful about having her around all the time, and would it not be too much for me? Where would she sleep? I said the boys could sleep in double bunks, and she could have the other room, and so it was decided. Pravda and family were delighted. Everything went as planned and she obtained a scholarship and was due to arrive in the fall of 1959.

Chapter 59

The great surprise.

What we did not know at the time and what came as the greatest surprise was that next spring we were astounded to learn I was pregnant! We were amazed, we had no intention of having another child, and were always careful, but I suppose on New Year's Eve we were not. Where would we put the child? Our bedroom was small, we fell over each other as it was, there was no room for a crib. We would have to glass in the screen porch, but until then the baby would have be in the living room or kitchen.

We were both thunderstruck but soon I began to have a feeling of serenity, I did not know why, for the future months looked fraught. What complicated matters was that Howard was due to play his Violin Sonata with Peter Bornstein in April in New York. My physician was adamant that I should not fly as I already had had a threatened miscarriage at three months with my first child. Howard was desperately disappointed and indeed I was too, but I was feeling so sick I did not really feel up to the trip, also there was the problem of where to leave the boys.

About the same time we had a letter from Auntie Dora. Uncle had died some time before. She wrote she was not feeling well and wanted to see us all and could make arrangement through Cook's for us to come on the Holland-America line which was family orientated with special facilities for children. She was sure our friend Nol could put us up at his communal house, which was near her at Sevenoaks, and we all needed a holiday; she knew Howard could get two months off in the summer.

All I could think of was that I would be pregnant in England! I loved my two little American boys but I thought if I were pregnant in the country, in the Kentish Weald, with its colored fields of barley, wheat, and oats, would it not mean that the child would have something of England? I asked the doctor if I could make the ocean trip. He said that I could fly and sail safely between five and seven months; after that he would not advise it The return would be well into my eighth month but I decided to risk it.

Auntie was the first I told. I asked her not to tell Mummy and Bettina because I knew they would worry; I would inform them just before arrival. Then I wrote Nol explaining the situation and asking if he had available any of the two bedroom cabins he was building on the hill when I was last there; they would be more suitable than the brouhaha of the big house. He wrote back quickly to say that he did have such a cabin with tea kettle and bathroom, and we could sign up for meals in the dining room when we needed them. He also said he was away filming a lot and we could use his big bedroom to put up friends, and Howard could practice on the grand piano in the beautiful living room overlooking the Weald. If Howard and I wanted to go away together for a few days the boys could be accommodated in a dormitory while we were gone. He was always so considerate.

Howard was thrilled at the thought of that grand piano and decided he would give a Beethoven concert in the fall and practice the last two sonatas, 110 and 111, on that lovely piano. I thought of looking out on the Weald while I listened, and that the baby would be listening too. There would be activities for the boys with other children. Andrew was a bit upset at missing the baseball season but I said it would give him an opportunity to learn cricket and started preparing him for it. We let two graduate students stay in the house over the summer for a very low rent.

Howard's concert at Carnegie Hall went well and he had some good reviews of his Piano and Violin sonata. He got a raise and the thought of going to England for the summer compensated for the fact that I had to miss the recital. We did not manage to find anyone to glass in the porch before we left, but we would have a month before the baby arrived on our return.

Chapter 60

Visit to England, 1959.

The summer in England was ideal, glorious weather. The boys took to the social life at St. Julian's. We invited Ray to stay with their children, Nick and Cesca. Sim could only come for the weekend. I was horrified to find that Ray's hair had turned white; she was just in her forties. She said it was common in her family but I felt that life had done it to her. She was a guide for the British Council traipsing all over London with tourists and she looked very tired. She loved the country as much as I did and making music with Howard. She sang the Schubert songs, and it was a glory to hear them again. The Akehursts also visited, and we all went to stay with Nan and Ken. We saw Mummy and Bettina or Aunt Dora every day.

I remember one incident when we went to have dinner in Tunbridge Wells; the flat was in a Victorian house with a garden and high hedges, usual in England. As we came up the path a tennis ball flew over the hedge. JD caught it and threw it back and a small face peeked over to say "thank you." Bettina groaned, "That means we shall now have to say good morning." She carried the love of privacy to an unusual level and was quite appalled when I told her there were few hedges between houses in Tallahassee. "You mean children and dogs can run across your garden, and you want me to come and stay with you!"

We took advantage of Nol's offer and left the boys in a dormitory for a few days while we visited Rita and Brian at Cambridge. Their house was only a few minutes across buttercup fields to Kings College chapel, which held Evensong each day. The fan-vaulted roof, the Northern Renaissance windows, and the early English music took us to another world. We went every day, much to the surprise of Rita who had never gone. When we were in Germany we had visited a church that had incense which made her feel very sick, and ever after she only went to church on rare occasions. While we were in Cambridge she had to go to the 1000th anniversary of the founding of Ely Cathedral in 959. Brian's father was Canon of Ely. Howard and I had never seen that cathedral and looked forward to it very much. It had an unusual architectural feature—a lantern in the center mounted on eight 6O-ft oak trunks with a cupola on top. Stained glass windows at the sides streamed flashes of color through the nave. A procession of bishops and even archbishops in medieval robes led the choir singing Gregorian chant. It was a moment never forgotten, my heart lurched, and then I realized it was the child kicking inside me. "You are experiencing this too," I said. Then immediately a feeling of sadness came over me.

Would the child ever see such glory? With three children it seemed unlikely that even Auntie Dora could afford the fare, and then I got another little kick and it seemed to me the child was saying "I'll make it!" I told Howard and he was very touched.

We had a wonderful vacation. With the boys taken care of, I sat for hours listening to Howard play the last two great Beethoven sonatas, llO and lll, while looking out over the small colored fields I loved so well. I realized the child was hearing it too. It seemed Howard had never played so well.

While we were there I asked Bettina to drive me alone over to Manor Farm. I remembered how Humphrey had done so. I knew we could go down the right of way and I could walk around the lake. The bluebells and the nightingales would have vanished in August but I could remember them. She stayed in the car by the road and I walked three times round the lake repeating "This child shall have something of England, this child shall have something of England." I felt very sure it would.

The return home was uneventful. I informed the ship's doctor that I was four weeks off my birth date and said I hoped he had anaesthetic on board. The Dutch doctor was unsympathetic. "Anaesthetic? You won't need that for a third child! It will be good luck for the ship and you will be given a layette." I was not reassured and longed to get home.

Howard's Beethoven recital went well. It was a little overshadowed by Kilenyi who also decided to give a Beethoven concert that fall, although he knew Howard's had been scheduled long before. He was a showman and announced he would play any three Beethoven sonatas the audiences wanted, unless they decided on the *Hammerklavier*, opus 106, which was very long, in which case he would only play two. I told Howard he knew the audience would decide on that one as it was seldom heard and most other people did not know the names of the Beethoven's sonatas, except the Moonlight, so he really only had to learn two, and I was proved right. It was a tour de force and a great success.

Chapter 61

Arrival of Keith. Children. Auntie's death.

Three days after our return Pravda arrived. Of course we had informed her parents of my condition and they were concerned, but everything was set. She had been accepted with a scholarship. She fitted in well with the boys; they accepted her as an older sister. She would do her own wash; I wished I had a dryer. Many friends could not believe that I brought up a family for fifteen years with no dryer, but I wanted most a dishwasher, which I thought the greatest discovery since the wheel. We had also bought a second Volkswagen bug for me so that I would not have to take Howard to the Music School, return home to take the boys to school with the baby, and fetch Howard just when I was preparing dinner. I did not mind hanging out the wash, which I did every day. If it dried, which it often did in the Florida sun, well and good. If it rained I left it on the line till the sun came out and dried it. It tires me to think of it now.

Howard was a little disturbed having Pravda around all the time. He was a very private person, not nearly as social as I was. I did not realize it would be hard for him. She did her practicing at school, so Howard had the piano at night. The house was crowded, we could not find anybody to glass in the screen porch before the baby arrived so the bassinet had to be in the kitchen! Our bedroom was small; also Howard slept badly and he needed all his strength for the big recital. I had the bedroom and kitchen door open; I slept lightly and I could hear every sound.

After two sons we had hoped for a daughter, Alison Anne, after the fair haired girl who had left with the lovely name. I cried a little when the nurse told me but as soon as I had the baby in my arms I was content. Instinctively I knew he was a child of joy. He came quickly, only two hours and I did not need stitches. He always tried to make things easy for me. He seemed to smile as soon as he was born. Howard said he had a face hung around a smile. The boys were delighted with him. We called him Keith.

It was the first time JD had shown any affection for anyone. When the baby was about six weeks old, he offered to warm the 6 am bottle for me. I was grateful and showed him how to take the formula bottle out of the fridge, place it in water in the pan to heat and then to be sure and test on the back of his hand that the milk was just lukewarm. Evidently the milk was far too hot so JD poured cold water on the bottle, which was still a glass bottle, and it exploded with a loud bang and milk and shards of glass shot all over the kitchen. JD turned in horror to see the baby grinning with pleasure at the sight and waving his hands. Fortunately the bassinet was far enough away from the sink that nothing fell on him. I heard the explosion and came rushing in. "I just love that kid," said JD. "Look at him grinning!" After that we put the bassinet in the living room and it was still there over Christmas under the tree. Friends had German biologists to visit, and years later they came again and the wife told me she had never forgotten the paneled room with a fire, the Christmas tree and the baby beneath in a basket. It was the most beautiful Christmas she had seen.

The porch was at last glassed in by January. It was not an ideal room for a baby as the floor was tiled but we bought a large smooth mat for him to crawl on. JD crawled with him and produced his most precious cars which previously only he had been allowed to touch and gave them to Keith, showing him how to push them along and make car noises. This went on for years and the brothers vied with each other in producing suitable car noises. I was touched for in England he had been "the wild American cousin." This was because my cousin Gordon and his wife Beryl had invited us to tea with their four children. I knew this would be a gala tea and explained to my boys the routine: first of all a piece of bread and butter, then a cucumber sandwich, chocolate biscuits, a piece of jam sponge cake, and only then came chocolate cake. Andrew memorized it and duly followed it. JD and his cousin Tricia, who was nine months older, got on rather well together, and when we sat down at the table, JD grabbed a handful of chocolate biscuits and said "Trish, let's get out of here!" Fortunately Beryl had a sense of humor and told me that Tricia rather liked her wild American cousin.

Auntie Dora had been impressed with him too. She arrived one day to buy the boys presents but Andrew was on an expedition of some sort. Auntie said to JD "Well, we will go" but he replied "Can't we wait till Andrew is here?" Bettina also told me that when she and Mummy were taking the boys for a walk in a park she told JD, who was apt to run ahead, that if he stayed with them he would get an ice cream at the shop at the park exit. He accordingly slowed down, for both boys loved the English Ice cream choc bars. When they got there the shop was closed in the haphazard way English shops do close half-days on Wednesday, Thursday, or Saturday. JD just said "you couldn't help it, it wasn't your fault." Bettina was shaken that he made no fuss.

Andrew loved the baby too but he was not home so much; he was always playing baseball, either with neighborhood boys or in Cub League or Little League to which I had to take him. It was hard for him that his father could not watch his games, for they started at 5 pm and Howard was not home till after 6 pm. I don't know how all the other fathers were able to come; I was a poor substitute for I knew little of the game, but learned chiefly from the fathers who were intrigued by someone who knew nothing of baseball. They found it hard to believe. From them I learned that Andrew was the best pitcher, but as he was small and pitchers were supposed to be tall he was not put on till the situation was desperate and all the bases were loaded. "Put on the little pitcher," yelled the fathers until eventually Andrew arrived, stared all around the diamond at the loaded bases and then faced his opponent, stern and determined, and struck them all out! I was a nervous wreck, it was as bad as a recital. I had to have a stiff drink when I got home. I took the baby of course in his stroller and sat on the lowest of the bleachers pushing it to and fro. I wrote a poem to Andrew

Child that was you throw the ball
cut off behind the years,
from a photo your eyes startle,
a forgotten grace,
the ball, thin arm and serious face
irrecoverably lost,
Lacrimae rerum.

Auntie Dora died in 1960. I felt like a tree with a branch lopped off, but was not able to mourn her; I had no time. All mothers of young children know this feeling, but I think it is more complicated when you have teenagers that require car pooling as well as toddlers. I feel dizzy remembering those days. I was first up in the morning to have my bath, then tend the baby, make breakfast for everybody, take the boys to school with the baby and then generally go shopping for something, then back home to do the daily wash and hang it on the line. Keith enjoyed this part. Then I had to make some preparations for dinner, for after school and snacks would come baseball. I discovered the crockpot, the slow cooker, but it did not always work. Then lunch and Keith sometimes took a nap afterwards, not always, and I did the housework. If luck held, the wash was dry and I could put it away before fetching the boys from school or before baseball. After baseball came dinner, baby to bath, read to, and sing. I tried to get the boys to bed earlier than most Americans so I could have a little time with Howard, but it was difficult. Andrew wanted to be sung and read to for quite a long time, and he would make up songs and tell me things about his day which I felt important to hear.

I was exhausted when I tottered into the living room where Howard had been practicing for hours without me. Maybe I came in for the last hour and then sometimes I thought of Auntie but I was so tired, and I felt she understood. She always had. She had left money to all of us and Mummy decided she would like to come and visit.

Chapter 62

Mummy's Visit.

Bettina who had waited on her hand and foot for years had no intention of accompanying her, but Mummy still had the same intrepid spirit that had led her in teens to the Far East. The porch was glassed in for the baby, and the boys were back in their separate rooms. Pravda had left us after one term having been given an extra scholarship that paid board and lodging. She wanted to be with her friends and to practice in the evenings and one bathroom among five was a bit hard for a teenager with a need to prink. There were no hard feelings and she often visited.

We had no spare room. We had to give Mummy our bedroom and Howard and I slept on the sofa bed in the living room which we had not yet slept on. Louisette had, and she had not complained. But it was not comfortable; the mattress was very thin with a board across the middle. For years Howard had smoked heavily and he had developed what he called "a smoker's cough." The doctor did nothing to stop him smoking which infuriated me, but everybody smoked in those days, except me. Howard did not smoke in the bedroom for that reason, but everywhere else was full of smoke, and nobody thought anything about it.

Mummy came on the Queen Mary and loved it. She was put at the Captain's table and Louisette met her in New York and put her on the train to Jacksonville, where I met her with Keith in the car. She was delighted with the baby and he with her, for she had new songs to sing. At two he did not talk yet, which worried me a bit. When I went to visit Pat, her two year old greeted me with "Have you come in your Volkswagen?" while the best Keith could manage was "Ma-ma and Da-da."

At first everything went well for Howard was very fond of my mother; she made him laugh, and it was good to hear him laugh, but it did mean there was not much peace and quiet in the house, and Howard needed that to compose. When the porch was glassed in we put the TV there and the boys watched it for half an hour before supper, and on Saturday mornings watched children's cartoons which they delighted in, and so did Mummy. Even though the porch door was closed you could hear the TV in the living room, and Howard needed quiet. He told me he thought he would put the money Auntie Dora had left him towards building an addition the other side of the porch, with a small bedroom for John (Keith needed a room of his own other than the porch), a bathroom and a front room which we could use as a spare room and he could work in. Later, he said, when the boys left home, we could rent the addition to a graduate student and it would be a source of income.

He seemed more excited and happy over the project than he had been for some time. For years at weekends he had taken the boys and me to see new houses being built and he had met most of the builders. Carl Ferrell would not be interested in an addition but he knew a small builder whom he admired who would do it reasonably. Howard was thrilled at the thought of drawing up plans, and I was happy to see his lifted spirits.

Mummy had to come with me to Andrew's baseball games, and she enjoyed that very much. She had always said he would be an athlete. However she was not used to driving with me and that made me a bit nervous. Once when just she, Keith, and I were in the car I backed into a ditch at the baseball game. "Oh, oh, oh," she wailed. "What shall we do now?" She was quickly answered. Four men just picked the VW up and deposited us on safe ground. She was very impressed with the gallantry of the Americans, also with their dry martinis and crispy bacon. Friends were very kind in inviting us out to cocktail parties and she had a fine time. She also enjoyed playing draughts or checkers with Andrew which she had taught him in England. I remember when we were there and he was learning John said to her once "Let Andrew win, Granny, it means so much to him." "Not on your life," returned my mother, "he has got to learn to win." Later, I remembered that remark with regret that I had not beaten him in table tennis when I could.

Howard had taught him to play chess in England, and it was something they still both shared, which I was glad to see for though Howard had participated with John in Scouts, he had never been able to watch Andrew's baseball. We were all astounded when after Andrew had been learning chess for a few weeks, we were in a railway carriage in England where two men were playing chess opposite us. When they had finished, Andrew, who was then seven, slid from his seat and said to the man who held the chess pieces, "Would you please give me a game?" Andrew was shy and backward in coming forward so this was an astonishment to us. The man was tickled and agreed at once, and invited Andrew to sit on his knee, and afterward said to Howard "He has been well taught." Any game intrigued Andrew.

Mummy noticed a difference in Howard. She said he looked much older, and she did not like his hacking cough. She also thought he was depressed; I told her there was no one in Tallahassee who could help, for we had tried several doctors. She became very worried and that made me even more so. However he did enjoy drawing up the plans for the addition and when she left his builder started on them, for the Raymonds wrote they would like to visit us in the fall (we had often asked them) but now their son Ted and his wife Nina had moved from Kansas City to South Florida and they wanted to see us all at the same time.

Mummy and I had rather a sad farewell. She left from Jacksonville on a Sunday and Keith stayed home with Howard and the boys, for Mummy said she would like to take me out to a nice lunch with champagne which I had not been able to give her in Tallahassee. We could get wine and spirits, but champagne was not available in Tallahassee at that time. Unfortunately we did not know that Jacksonville was still dry, at least on a Sunday, and we were both bitterly disappointed. She returned to England on the Holland-Amerika line which I liked better than the Queen Mary for there was more deck space to walk, but she did not like it nearly as much as the regal splendour of the Cunard line.

The house addition proved a great success. My only regret was that the builder said our existent electric wiring would not be enough for a big appliance like a dryer so I still had to hang washing on the line. However, the boys profited greatly. The porch became their room with the addition of a ping pong table which I too enjoyed. The table was very convenient when we hosted potluck supper for it seated twelve.

Chapter 63

80th Birthday.

Dohnanyi's 80th birthday was coming up and the Music School was doing nothing to celebrate, so we decided we should and invited all the Music School faculty. Dohnanyi said he would rather have just a cake and my iced coffee (made with ice cream) instead of wine so I served using my English tea service which Auntie had given us. I made four cakes with twenty candles on each and Dohnanyi blew them all out. Albert Spalding, the famous violinist and his wife, had come to visit his old friend, so I invited them too. We had already heard them play the Kreutzer Sonata together. Dohnanyi had not played it for many years so he used the music and Zachara turned pages and unfortunately knocked the music to the ground three pages before the end, but Dohnanyi went on playing! He remembered it from years ago! That was the kind of pianist he was.

Mrs. Spalding was astounded at the tea service; she said it was 18th century Crown Derby. I pointed out that it had "Amherst" at the back, but she had the dinner service and said it had been made specially for Lord Amherst and she thought it was the only service made for him by Crown Derby in 1780. Everybody hastily put down their cups. "How did you get it?" she asked. I explained there was only white china in England after the war, and my aunt had found this in an antique shop but neither she nor I knew it was Crown Derby. Since Blackheath days I had always kept it in my glass bookcase where I remembered it glittering in the firelight. Her announcement made quite a sensation, particularly as Andrew in his pajamas was picking up the dirty plates and putting them in the dishwasher. He had been doing that since he was seven and I was grateful for the help although my mother had reprimanded me for exploiting the child. He went to bed at his usual time but woke up about 11 pm when I suppose he heard cars going off. I told her Mummy she had had two maids and a cook to help her! I needed his help.

Chapter 64

Howard.

Pravda was coming up for her senior recital and chose to do a Liszt concerto for which Howard had to play the orchestral part which was very hard for him as he did not like Liszt. I rather dreaded it but now can remember nothing about the actual performance. As usual she did very well. She had a scholarship for a few months' study in England and Howard suggested she write and ask Myra Hess because he thought she needed the profundity Myra Hess could give her as well as the brilliant technique she already possessed. Howard also had two other very good students graduating, so it was a very busy time.

I brought the boys home from school one day and to my surprise found Howard's VW bug in the driveway. He usually did not come home till 6 pm. I felt something was wrong and ran in and found him in the back room, unconscious and breathing heavily. I rang 9ll for the ambulance and then Pat to ask her to come and get the boys. Andrew said he could stay with a friend in our neighborhood so it would be only two for Pat and I agreed. As long as Keith had John he would be fine, and he knew Pat, because he often went to play with her son.

The Emergency Room took Howard in at once but I had to wait hours for news. I rang my minister and he said I should inform the Music School. I eventually found out that Howard had taken an overdose, but would recover. He would be in the hospital several days. The boys were all right and I stayed with Howard all night. What was so dreadful was that he said on coming round, "I couldn't even succeed in that." I tried to assure him that maybe there was a reason and life still held something for him. He had his family, did not that count for something? We all loved him. He kept on saying he was nearly fifty and he would not succeed in his life's ambition and we would be better off without him. We could go back to England, my family would take care of us. I told him I loved him just as he was and wasn't our love enough. The day of concert pianists was over, he had told me that himself, but it was not the end of the world, we still had each other and the boys. He said the only happiness he had had in life was with me. I prayed to God to help me and was given help; I seemed to be able to convince him that our love for each other had value and made life worth living.

The news had got around. The Dean of Arts & Sciences who was a great devotee of Howard's, came in with his wife and said they lived just near the hospital and when Howard fell asleep I was to come to their house for the night and could be back early in the morning. I rang the boys and told them. It seemed the best thing to do; Howard needed me now. He fell asleep at last and I went to Paul and Rebecca's. They gave me a book to read, "*Letting God help you*" by John Redwood, which outlined various passages in the Bible that gave strength. I had always been religious and learned many phrases off by heart. "God is a very present help in time of trouble" was one among many I still remember.

For several days and nights I stayed with Howard, but there was nothing they could do for him in Tallahassee; there were no psychiatrists here at the time. He had to go to Shands Hospital in Gainesville, and I was to visit him once a week. Luckily for me our musician friends, Dave and Geneva, had moved over there the proceeding year when Dave was offered a better position at the University of Florida. When they heard the news they asked Keith and me to stay the night, and Geneva would look after Keith while I was at the hospital, another synchronicity. I was so grateful. I hated driving and although it was only three hours it was a strain for me and wonderful not to drive back the same day, and great comfort to have their company after a trying day.

Howard and I had to interview several doctors. I liked one of them but was distressed to learn that he advocated electric shock therapy. I felt that would be terrible for someone sensitive. Howard, however, was willing to try anything that might make him feel better. He said he felt it was "a chemical imbalance" but the drugs that helped such conditions had not yet been invented. I had to leave him there.

Chapter 65

What now?

For three months I drove to Gainesville once a week, leaving the boys overnight with friends and taking Keith with me. He was three years old and not yet talking but he liked me to talk or sing to him. It was easier to sing the nursery rhymes although I grew tired of "Old King Cole was a merry old soul". I felt anything but merry but very grateful to Dave and Geneva who put us up for the night and looked after Keith while I went to the hospital. I had to be interviewed by five doctors before I could see Howard, and was exhausted. I did however manage to get out of Group Therapy where the spouses of those undergoing treatment were supposed to discuss their situations. I said nothing and was reproved that I was not contributing. I told them I feared if I said anything who knew it would not get back to my husband and make him feel worse. Two men got up and said they felt just the same way. I was asked to leave as I was disrupting the group. I was thankful to have one less hurdle before I could see Howard.

Howard said he felt better but he looked far from well and was still coughing, although he said the doctor had told him to try and cut out smoking as he had emphysema. He missed me and the boys and for therapy was making a woolen rug with beautiful butterflies. He was an artist in all he did, and I was touched because he used to call me his butterfly. It was a sad time and I did not know what would happen after our three months of insurance for mental illness expired. Keith was a help. One day just before we had to leave to drive to Gainesville I caught my thumb in the lazy susan and it was bruised black and blue. I said aloud, "How shall I drive?" and the child bent over and kissed the thumb. I was very touched and somehow managed the drive.

I wrote home about the situation but did not know what anyone could do. My cousin Rita came up trumps. She had made enquiries and found out that the best treatment for mental illness in England was at Guy's Hospital in London and they did not approve of shock treatment. She had also found out that Andrew could go to the village school at Seal where the young children at Nol's cooperative home went but John was too old at thirteen. She said that she would send John to her husband Brian's prep school at Eastbourne for the summer term and she suggested that we come over in March when our insurance ran out and that I ask Nol if we could not all stay at St. Julian's in Sevenoaks where we had stayed before. She would pay the airline tickets as her mother had done before. I was dumbfounded. To be honest my first thought was—oh the glory of seeing England in the spring.

I felt new life arising and knew Howard loved England. For the first time I saw a flicker of hope. He could go from St. Julians from Sevenoaks to Guy's every day; it was possible.

Unfortunately it did not turn out to be quite so easy. I wrote to Nol explaining the situation and suggesting that I help in the cooperative system by manning the nursery at night. I knew he had a problem getting mothers to do that, but I would be there anyway with Keith. I could also do gardening, and looking after children in the daytime. Nol as usual was as helpful as ever but unfortunately Howard could not stay there as they had their own psychiatrist and rules forbade anyone under any other psychiatrist's care staying there. Rita had already made arrangements at Guy's. I then wrote Ray and Cyril and Frances. I knew Ray took paying guests and asked the Akehursts to do the same and they were more than willing and Howard was happy to stay with them. He would have preferred to have been with us as at St. Julian's, but I would go up at weekends to be with him, and this was the best we could do. We were so grateful to Rita.

Chapter 66

England again.

When I wrote to thank Rita she wrote back that I was part of the family and closer to her then her own sister. She had become very wealthy and her mother would have wanted it; the whole thing was obvious and not to think any more about gratitude but to concentrate on getting to England.

The boys had realized the gravity of the situation and had frequently asked me what would happen if Howard did not get better. They knew their relatives in England, the only relatives they did know, and they accepted the situation, but Andrew was upset at missing the baseball season and I was also concerned for JD. How would he face leaving the family and going to boarding school? He was always good in an emergency; he was stoic about it. A teacher at their school in Tallahassee who had taught in England gave them special lessons in English money which was a great help. We rented the house for the summer term to graduate students whom Howard knew and we set off.

The flight was uneventful except that Keith threw up and I had no change of clothes on board. BOAC gave us a blanket and JD carried him in it till we found our luggage at Gatwick and I was able to change him before meeting the family. Rita was a great organizer. We all met for early lunch at a hotel in London. Mummy and Bettina were there to take JD down to St. Andrews in Eastbourne. Brian sat next to him at lunch and when he heard he was interested in track said he would do well at the school for they had a good track team. Frances Akehurst had been invited to go with Howard and me to Guy's hospital where we would meet his doctor and afterwards she would take Howard home with her. I would then go back to the hotel where Rita and Brian were waiting to drive Andrew, Keith and me to Cambridge with them for a few days until Bettina could fetch us and take us to St. Julian's. It was quite an organization. It was a strange parting with JD but I was pleased he and Brian seemed to get on. Both Howard and I liked the doctor so we could only hope for the best. We were used to partings.

I was very tired and may have snoozed on the way up to Rita's; I woke suddenly to the glory of the daffodils on the backs at Cambridge, and they gave me a lift. On arrival I fed Keith and put him to bed where he fell asleep immediately. I changed and went down to dinner where Brian gave me a stiff drink for which I was grateful. They had pheasant for dinner and I was a bit embarrassed when Andrew said "there is something wrong with this bird." Brian laughed and said Rita should have known better than to have given pheasant to a child who had only had chicken.

Next day I asked Rita if I could take the boys, with Keith in his stroller, across the fields to Evensong at Kings. She was surprised that I would take the baby but I explained that he was used to going to church with me and would enjoy the music, so we went. We sat at the back and saw the fan roof lit with sunset from the west window and heard the boys' voices sailing up there. Andrew did not seem as impressed as I thought he would be, but he had an earache from the flight.

Bettina came to get us in a couple of days without Mummy, which disappointed both boys but it was a long drive to Cambridge and then down to Sevenoaks. She explained she would bring Mummy to see us the next day. I was glad to see my sister; nobody gave me such strength.

I did not think Nol would be there when we arrived at St. Julian's for he usually stayed in town in the week, but he had driven down specially to greet and introduce us. He was grateful that I would be in charge of the nursery at night for he had difficulty filling that post, and anything I could do in the garden would be appreciated. Could I prune roses? I was glad that was something I could do. He said there were some plants that he had bought weeks ago but nobody had planted so if I would like to put them in anywhere it would be a good thing. I gathered there was no head gardener. He said I should use the spare room in his flat for my clothes and to take a nap there in the daytime if I wished, and I was free to bring my family into the flat at all times, which was a great joy as there was a lovely view over the Weald. He took us in there for a drink and I was delighted to see from the window crocuses around an almond tree just coming in to bloom. We agreed I would man the nursery Monday to Friday nights, leave to visit Howard on Saturday morning, and he would meet the 7pm train at Sevenoaks on Sunday evening to bring me home as there were few buses on Sundays. He could not have been kinder. He said that Howard was welcome for a weekend, perhaps at John's half-term, and he was sorry he was unable to put him up all the time.

Bettina left saying she would bring Mummy in the morning. They were welcome for meals any time as long as I signed up for them, and I paid for meals weekly, but otherwise I did not pay anything. I had trouble remembering to sign up and Andrew took over that job. Mummy was delighted to see the boys and it was a momentous occasion. Keith made his first speech. Mummy and Bettina had taken him up a little hill to a summer house. Away across the fields he saw a tractor but one of them got in his way so apparently he announced loud and clear: "I can't see!" I was not there to hear it but it was apparently an Open Sesame for he spoke in sentences from then on. He said to me, "Am your byby, Mum?" I reeled in horror. I had been waiting years, so it seemed, for him to speak and now he spoke Cockney! I said "You are my bayby although now you are a little boy, but you are never my byby." One family had cockney accents, but Keith did not develop one. Bettina spoke crossly to him one day when he was slow gathering up his toys. He wailed, "Aunt Bettina was mad at me!" To soothe him I said, "Oh no she wasn't, she was trying to help me get you to clear up, she wasn't mad." "She wad" he said firmly. I laughed and it became a family catch phrase for an emphatic assertion.

I could not wait to tell Howard and John/JD the great news. I'd had a letter from John which cheered me. The track was good, there were great hikes to Beachy Head and beyond, he met a boy called Tony who was his roommate and friendly, and he liked the history teacher although there was a lot of English history to learn. I had felt very worried for him, but apparently unnecessarily. He was doing all right. Keith fit right into the hurly burly of life at St. Julian's, everybody made much of him and he seemed quite at home. It was hardest forAndrew; he was in a room with four boys about his age and they shared a bathroom with no lock on it, and a little girl had walked in on him in his bath which upset him very much. However cricket was played after tea every day, when teenagers came back from Sevenoaks School; fathers played, girls too, and he enjoyed that. The man acting as coach told me he was a "natural."

It was still the Easter holidays and I had an appointment to take Andrew to meet the headmaster of the village church school, who was also the Vicar. Andrew liked him. He invited Andrew to come to church on Sunday although he told him no one from St. Julian's came but there would be children he would meet in class from the village. Andrew said he would come. I had a pang thinking of him going all on his own.

It was a joyous meeting with Howard. He already looked better and was smiling. I realized it was a long time since I had seen him smile. He was happy with Cyril and Frances and liked his doctor. When I said I seemed to be the official gardener at St. Julian's and had carte blanche to do what I liked, Cyril offered me several plants to take back. Howard was thrilled to hear of Keith talking and pleased with the letter from John that I had brought. We had a long walk in Greenwich Park which recalled old times and I felt perhaps it was best he was in a quiet place with friends he knew. St. Julian's was anything but quiet.

Bettina brought Mummy over to St. Julians to be with Keith but Bettina spent the day with friends in Sevenoaks. When I arrived back on Sunday everything seemed to be all right. I had been concerned, it was the first time I had left Keith for a night, but he seemed quite at home there and I was relieved.

I had a strange experience the second week. I stayed with the babies until they went to sleep and then sat outside for a while enjoying the almond tree in the evening. Next day a young woman asked me if I would like to come in for a cup of coffee after getting the babes to sleep. Her room was just next door and I would hear if anyone called. I thanked her and agreed but what was my surprise when I knocked on her door and found the room in darkness except for firelight and she naked in front of the fire! She looked very beautiful but I was stunned and shut the door quickly. Was she a Lesbian, was this a come on? I don't think I have ever been so surprised in my life. When we happened to meet afterwards, we smiled at each other and never referred to the matter. I never told anyone of the incident.

St. Julians was certainly Bohemian. I remember Mrs. Polak telling me she did not like the place. Of the four families that had started it, all had changed partners. There were several other families there now, indeed it was a rabbit warren of a place, but I kept to the dining room, the nursery and Nol's flat. I was concerned for Andrew but he was at school, with us for tea, then played cricket, came to visit with me a bit in the babies' room and then went to bed. He seemed happy enough and glad that his father was getting better.

John came for half term and Howard stayed for the weekend and we shared the spare room in Nol's flat. John slept in the teenager's dorm. He loved St. Julian's but was happy at school and seemed to be doing well. We were all to go down to his Sports Day at the end of term. Howard seemed much better and enjoyed playing chess with Andrew but I remember it chiefly as the weekend when the Beatles broke into our lives. We all listened to them on the television, then someone played records. Howard said they had used the modes in their melodies; I remember "The Octopus's garden in the shade" and everyone singing their songs and playing the records again and again.

I saw the spring again, through the crocuses, the primroses and wild anemones, through the daffodils to the glory of the bluebells. Keith loved the daffodils; there were so many thousands each child was allowed to pick one and hold it as a trumpet. I gathered them up from their hot little hands and put them in water in my room. I wrote this while in England.

And after many years,
the pale green fields and charcoal trees
with glints of silver where the willows

have caught the pallid light.
Afar among the trees
a house blooms
a petal of the sky, a pearl
re-echoed in the puddles
that glitter the hillside.
Four poplars stand –a pleasure—
and like the crocus blades
as bold and cold as birds.
A primrose caught in light
is unforgettable
forever in the mind,
but seen again
champagne.

The whole family gathered together to go to John's Sports Day. I think Brian and Rita were there as well as Howard, Mummy and Bettina and the two younger boys. It was amazing. John had a triumph. He won the 1OO-yard dash and the long jump. Andrew had won trophies for baseball but John had never won anything as track was not held in such esteem in Tallahassee, but this was his day of glory and I was so happy for him. Howard told the headmaster he understood how someone had said Waterloo was won of the playing fields of Eton. I remember the drive back over the Downs in the evening and how beautiful it was.

Rita and Brian gave a luncheon party for us to meet my cousin Gordon and his family. Tricia and John had met as babies and then again as children when John grabbed the chocolate biscuits and broke up the tea party by saying "Trish, let's get out of here!" They met again as teenagers with pleasure it seemed and went for a walk together after lunch. John never mentioned it but apparently they corresponded for years afterwards and we only learned this from Bettina who visited Tricia in hospital after her appendicitis and was astonished to see a large photo of John on her bedside table. They never met again.

I saw Ray frequently when Howard stayed with her. She had had to give up singing except privately for she had to help the family budget by guiding VIPs for the British Council which was a very tiring job. Sim wrote for newspapers all over Europe and earned quite well but the money did not come in regularly. I felt sad about this; "*ach der Erde, wer kennt die Verlusste*" Rilke had written, which loosely translates "Oh who knows the losses of the earth." That is what I felt about it.

I saw a lot of the Akehursts. Howard started playing again while he was with them. They had a piano which was always in tune. He continued when he went to Ray and they made music together. Rita and Brian were so impressed with how well Jon had done at St. Andrews that they urged us to let them send him to a private school in the States. They had no children and they wanted to help John. Howard said private schools in US were for wealthy people and he would be out of place but he felt a military school would be good for John, he would have the discipline and the band which he missed at St. Andrews He knew someone who had a son at Riverside Military School outside Atlanta. Enquiries were made there and there was a doctor's son there who came from

Tallahassee. I was horrified at the thought of a military school, remembering Rilke, but apparently this was different. We contacted the doctor who was impressed by the school and offered to drive us up there. Howard was not up to it and I did not relish the thought of a six-hour drive, so it was agreed. John seemed content; it was only I who was reluctant.

Before we left England Howard and I had a few days together in the Cotswolds. The boys were accustomed to St. Julian's, John was there for the holidays, and Mummy and Bettina came every other day. I had driven through the Cotswolds to Wales but had never stayed It was beautiful summer there every day, gardens full of delphiniums and lupins, buttercups in the fields and wild roses in the hedges. We slept in a four-poster bed which delighted Howard and we met a couple at the guest house with a car who invited us to drive around to see the cathedrals of Worcester, Hereford and Gloucester which were a delight.

One of them had bosses in the roof and a long table with a mirror on it underneath in which you could see in detail the carvings. Evensong was still given in those cathedrals. It was our last happy time.

I had seen the doctor at Guy's and he told me Howard was much better and he thought he would do well if he stayed in England. He was doubtful about the return to the place of his breakdown but what could we do? We had exhausted our medical insurance for mental illness; my family had provided the best England could give. There was no possibility of a job in England. It was fortunate that FSU had kept his place open. Howard felt he could manage it and so we returned.

Chapter 67

The End.

Guy's had recommended a psychiatrist who visited Tallahassee twice a week from Shands Hospital in Gainesville He was a kind man and Howard liked him. I was distressed that no doctor had insisted on his stopping smoking although he had been diagnosed with emphysema. All they did was to say he should cut down. It is incredible today that smoking was not outlawed earlier but we had to wait many years for that, too late for Howard. His cough grew worse and worse but smoking was allowed in the classroom, in restaurants, everywhere. My sister smoked and said she could understand how it relieved stress for Howard. I gave up trying to stop him for it only increased tension, which Guy's doctor had said was bad for him.

He grew more and more exhausted. He no longer practiced in the evenings. He enjoyed chess with Andrew and playing with the baby. He had found that Keith liked sitting in the car while it was being washed, watching the water splash against the window. That is one of Keith's memories of his father. "I could never understand why he watched my face instead of the water," Keith told me. He also took Keith under the overpass and hollered as he had heard the boys do in order to make Keith laugh. He was stopped by a policeman who let him go with a smile when Howard said "I was trying to make my baby laugh." He seemed to get more pleasure out of being with Keith than with anyone. He no longer wanted to meet with our play-reading group or Potluck.

I consulted with his doctor and I still recall the room, the desk, when he said, "Your husband is going to try to commit suicide again, there is no question about that." I could not believe it. "Is there nothing you can do to stop him?," I heard myself asking. The doctor said that work was being done on a drug to combat depression but it was not ready. (It would be several years before Prozac came on the market.) I must prepare myself for the inevitable. "At Guy's the doctor said he was better," I said. "That was in England; it was fatal to return to where he had had the breakdown but there is nothing you or anyone can do; it is not your fault or anyone's, it is just the depression which we can do nothing now to lift. I tell you this so you will be prepared." How can you be prepared for such a thing? I went to see my minister and he tried to be helpful, but I realized there was no help for Howard. I prayed for him.

Friends realized he was very ill. Dr. Irish asked me if I would like a job as her secretary. Howard was interested in this possibility but it was an eight-hour job and Keith was only in kindergarten. I had to fetch him at noon and then

441

take Andrew for his baseball games. Andrew suffered most from his father's illness and baseball was his great solace; how could I rob him of that? There were no authorized daycare centers at the time, in fact there were dreadful stories of children being abused by non-qualified day carers. How could I subject Keith to that? Dr. Herndon, an English professor at FSU, gave me an idea. She was starting a Program of Humanities to include art, literature, music, philosophy of Europe, and she knew I had studied French and German literature; I would be an ideal teacher if only I had a degree. She suggested I start an English degree, and perhaps could CLEP (exempt) quite a few hours, and get a degree in two years, and then get a teaching assistantship until I had my Master's or PhD. It would be little money but it would mean I could be home for my boys by 3 pm. I was intrigued by this idea but stymied by the thought of having to take Math and Biology which involved cutting up a frog. I realized I could never do that. I prayed, "God I feel I could do it except for Math and Biology, help me."

One night in bed I realized I had my Matriculation papers from the University of London in Grandpa's wooden jewelbox in the bottom drawer of my bookcase. I had taken Math and Botany, English, French, History and was sure the papers showed that I had covered more than one year of university study in US and I had my diploma. Why I had brought those papers when leaving England was only because they were in Grandpa's box along with *billets doux* etc. It was a synchronicity. I took them to the Dean and he advised me to take them to heads of departments; he felt sure they would confirm they were the equivalent of one year's university study. They did. Botany was accepted instead of Biology so I did not have to cut up a frog. I felt it was an answer to prayer.

I told Howard that I would enroll at FSU and hoped that Auntie's money would help us till I obtained a Teaching Assistantship. I have terrible feelings of guilt about that for I think it impelled him to kill himself so he could get his pension and life insurance for me. In his suicide note to me he wrote that all the happiness he had had in life was with me and he was glad he could now help me get what I had always wanted, a college degree. He had found out I would get Social Security and Vets benefits for three children under 18, which would get me through. For years I could not bear to think of this note and tried to shut my eyes and mind to it, but the fact remains it was his death that gave me the money to pursue a college education. The money Auntie had left us might have paid for the tuition but it was not enough to keep us till I could start teaching and earn enough to support the family. Howard realized this and found out I could get money as a widow which would support us until I was able to do so. He was too ill to work and the doctors held out no hope for his recovery, so I think it was a noble thing to do. I am sorry at the time I was not able to make this clear to my boys; I should have shown them the note he left me. It is him I have to thank for giving me the college education I had always wanted and a way to support our sons.

I could not bear to think of it, and just hung on to Daddy's dictum, "Throw your mind, Kid." I could not even cry; it depressed the boys so and I had to keep going for them, so I did try and throw my mind and not think of Howard but of them. It is only now in writing about it that I recall the love and tenderness I shared with Howard, and the happiness. It is an unexpected blessing.

It happened this way. Howard did not come back from school at the usual time. I waited an hour and then drove my VW bug down to his parking place at the music school. His VW was not there. I knew what had happened. He had driven somewhere else where I could not find him and there committed suicide. I felt that he had suffered enough and if he were ready to go it would be cruel to try and find him and bring him back again to a life he did not want. I did not call the police at once. I called my closest friends and they came at once and I am still so grateful to them. They were religious people as I was but when I told them what I felt had happened and why I did not call the police at once, M. said "I agree." I waited till the morning to call the police and my minister, and then it seemed all chaos descended. Howard was found at Macon, Georgia, dead of an overdose with suicide notes to many of us. In England when someone dies the family is left severely alone to grieve so I was overwhelmed by all the friends who came bringing food and staying. I did not know what to say to them, but I think it is better than the English way. I just had to get used to it. Keith, aged five, went to the telephone, lifted it and said, "I have just spoken to God. He said Daddy is all right and well again." It was a great help.

My dear philosopher friend, Jack, volunteered to go and identify the body so I would not have to do so. I could not thank him enough; I could not imagine doing that but I would have had to if he had not stepped forward to do so. Jim K., a neighbor, a wealthy middle-aged business man who had decided to quit the commercial life and get an M.A. in history, with whom I had become friends and watched TV intellectual question games, apparently had a private plane and offered to fly Jack up to Macon so he could bring the VW back. It all reeled past me, but the kindness of everybody touched my heart. Two faculty members with whom I was not very close sent me checks for $100 for they realized I would not be able to get any cash from our joint account until the death certificate was produced; so did Mrs. Raymond.

I was advised not to call John directly but instead the headmaster, who would break the news to him. He arrived the next day. I had to plan the service at St. Johns and when I asked that "Abide with me" be sung for I knew Howard liked that hymn, I was told I should get some singers from FSU to help. My artist friend, Artemis, offered to keep Keith during the service for I felt he was too young to understand it, and she did me a painting of blue hydrangeas during it. My friend, Betty, helped me with the funeral director. Howard was entitled to a Vet's funeral and he was buried near Dohnanyi who had died two years before.

Larry, the Dean of Arts and Sciences, told me he had registered me for two classes next term, which would be counted for my B.A. He felt it would be best for me to start classes at once, and I realized it would be a lifesaver to have something else on which to concentrate. I would have to take the 12th-grade math test before the year was out, but I could not think about that for the moment although it did loom grey on the horizon for it included algebra and all I ever knew I had long forgotten.

My sister was so touched at the kindness everyone had shown to me that somehow she got a letter of thanks to the local *Tallahassee Democrat* newspaper written from my family in England; this impressed people very much. I gave a cup and saucer from my 18th-century set to those who had helped me most.

After the funeral the weeks stretched endless grey but Keith provided a few laughs. One day at breakfast he asked for ice cream and I said that was not a breakfast food. "Oh no, Mum," he said, "you forget I am a big boy now and go to kindergarten and there I learned that in North Carolina and Japan they have ice cream for breakfast." It was such a good line and gave me the laugh I needed that I let him have it. His brothers were aggrieved.

Another time Andrew's fifth grade teacher came and fixed dinner for us, one of the many kindnesses we received. She asked Keith what I drank for dinner and he replied: "When she has any, Scotch." I was glad the teacher was not a Baptist; she enjoyed a laugh and a drink with me.

A tremendous kindness I received was from Dr. Fleet, the children's orthodontist, who had tested Andrew for braces which would cost over $3000. I received a letter from him. He was a musician himself and always came to

Howard's concerts and was a devoted admirer. He wrote that he had discussed it with his wife and they decided as a tribute to Howard as a musician he would forego the fees for Andrew's braces. I told as many people as I could for I felt such generosity should be known.

After a while I did receive money from the Vets and Social Security for three children under eighteen, and this enabled me to pay the mortgage, utilities, insurance and upkeep for the house, and with Howard's GI insurance I was able to pay the college fees. It was tight going but we had never had much money so I managed. Pat and Maury helped me with clothes for the boys for they had two sons a bit older and taller than my two youngest and John stayed on at Riverside Academy through the generosity of Rita and Brian. I decided I would rent the addition to a graduate student during term time when John was away, but would wait until after Rita and Brian had visited me which they planned to do in spring next year. I did not buy any clothes myself for many years except necessities from Blair's catalog to which Howard had introduced me.

I realized the Dean was right; it would help me a great deal if I could start studying. I consulted with Dr. Herndon who headed the Humanities Program. She advised me to CLEP(exempt) what I could after it had been decided that my Matriculation at London University exempted me from Freshman English and French besides the dreaded Math and Botany I decided to take two English classes, Shakespeare Tragedy starting with *Hamlet* and Victorian Literature, and try to CLEP World History my first term. I found it hard to exempt the History. I had to read the textbook and had no means of knowing what the professor concentrated on; I managed it but decided to take courses in the future. I would major in English, with German as my language, and was not sure whether to take philosophy, which I had studied, or Art History as a minor.

Chapter 68

Student life.

My first class was Shakespeare, *Hamlet*. I thought I knew something of Shakespeare having heard Gielgud seven times as Hamlet when I was fifteen. I found out I knew nothing except the words. I had not studied any criticism so did not know, for example, that the contemporary audience would know that the Ghost was evil as he came from below the stage. This was because the Mystery Plays, acted out in wagons, had conditioned the audience to know that the wagon represented earth, a ladder above heaven, and any body or thing who came from below was from hell. I had always thought the Ghost was good for Hamlet loved him, but he did come from below the stage. The class was taught by a brilliant young professor in his thirties who opened a new world. His name was Dr. Faber and he told us he had served on the Suicide Squad in Los Angeles and written his dissertation on "Suicide in Shakespeare," drawing a great deal from Hamlet. I listened fascinated, stars coming out of my head. Dr. Faber pointed out the crucial passages which he read, but we went through it practically line for line so he asked if anyone else would like to try and read aloud. A few boys, a girl, and I volunteered. I went into another world completely.

Our first term paper was on "Why did Hamlet delay?" and I could not wait to write it. Dr. Faber had given us some criticism to read and I used that and what he had told us, but I added that I found the imagery very Catholic. I knew that Shakespeare's parents grew up under the Catholic queen Mary and although Shakespeare was not born until after Elizabeth came to the throne, felt that his childhood might have had Catholic influences. I cited the references to purgatory and the tenor of Claudius's prayers. When Dr. Faber gave us back our papers he said he always read out an "A" paper to show the other students that it could be done, and then he said "I have another paper to read, one that a teacher dreams of receiving. This student has studied Hamlet well and read the criticism I advised, but she has also added her own ideas and she can write." He started to read my paper. I recall the moment as if it were yesterday, the room, the desks, my heart beating like mad. I sat there while the others filed out and he said "I thought it would be you." I was so moved, so emotional, I don't even know if I thanked him. I said "You wrote your dissertation on suicide; my husband committed suicide."

He asked me to come to his office and to him I told my story. I did not break down, just related it and said that I was concerned that it might be a sin. My minister had advised me not to tell his elderly mother who had been brought up a Baptist, but to tell her it was heart failure. I also told him I had delayed in calling the police. What did he think? He said it was the church not Christ who had decided that suicide was a sin, because so many early Christians were leaping to the lions and they were losing their converts. In Roman times it was considered brave and noble to commit suicide: it was the church who had made it a sin. I said there was still "thou shalt not kill" in the Commandments." He said in Hebrew "kill" meant "murder." The Church had wished to keep its converts, and in somewhat the same way they had decided that priests should be chaste, because if a man had a child he would leave his money to his heir rather than to the Church. He felt I was right to have done as I did. He made me feel better about it. I think he told me that in one of the hymns there was a line "the heart of the Eternal is most infinitely kind." I thanked him then about my paper, and when he learned my position he said I was doing the right thing, I was where I belonged and would be a good teacher, and would get through. He was most encouraging and we became good friends.

The Victorian Literature class was ho-hum after the Shakespeare so when I had studied the History textbook and with difficulty exempted World History I thought I would go to the German Department and see if I could CLEP Freshman German. I met a tall, slim, intelligent young woman, Ingrid Tiesler, who told me years afterwards that she remembered my asking if a class on Rilke were given. We talked a while and she assured me she would exempt me from Grammar and Vocabulary and Conversation, two classes. I was not so sure about the former as I was never clear on the adjectival endings that changed with gender and usually spoke very quickly so as to gloss over them. She said she would give me a book to study that would help me and indeed it did. She suggested I take "*Minnesänger*" which she was teaching next term. I was delighted and impressed with the standards of American students. She told me that it was also for graduates who had to do extra work. They were usually Germans who came to the U.S. for the PhD and earned their way as teaching-assistants for Freshmen German. She said a different Literature course was taught each term by professors and Rilke might be given at some future date.

I finished the Spring Term with two "A's" and enough credits to qualify me as a sophomore for the next term. I took off for two weeks when Rita and Brian came to visit. They tried to persuade me to come to Cambridge where I could study free as a vet; they would send the boys to boarding school. John, always independent, had indeed done well, but I shuddered at the thought of sending the two younger boys away. Andrew had suffered the most from the death of his father; baseball was his life and I could not deprive him of that. I also realized life was much easier in the U.S. I had a car and with care could shop just once a week instead of schlepping every day. I had just enough from Social Security and the VA to keep Howard's house and garden which I loved, and my independence. "But supposing you fail?" asked Rita. "You have to take all sorts of courses like Physics and Geology, don't you?" I said I had by luck avoided Math and Biology and felt I could do the rest. Brian was very understanding about not depriving Andrew of baseball; he had watched several of his games. I was touched and grateful and we parted amicably.

In the summer, courses were shortened into six weeks, with classes every day. I stupidly took two hard courses, Geology and Medieval Art. In Geology I learned about Continental Drift which I did not know, Nansen's discoveries, and that houses had been built too near the Mississippi, which changed course now and then. I found it all interesting but the fossils one had to identify according to period were a strain in the memory. I was undecided whether to take Art or Philosophy as a Minor. The latter would be easier as I had already audited eighteen hours and could do them over again for credit, but I felt Art might help me more in getting a job eventually in the Humanities Program. I could identify cathedrals but found difficulty in deciding to which school a manuscript belonged for they all seemed much alike.

Nevertheless when I was invited to a party by the Music Faculty to welcome Elena Nikolaidi, a Greek Met star who was retiring to teach at FSU, I decided to go for she would sing some Lieder. They turned out to be Schumann's *"Frauenliebe und Leben"* and I was looking forward with bated breath to *"Du Ring an meinem Finger"* with its glorious modulation on *"Ringelein."* To my horror she stopped at the song before and said "that is enough." I could not help it, I was so wrought up waiting for that modulation I called out, "Oh no, you can't stop now, please. *Du Ring an meinem Finger* !"

She was dressed as a diva with a long skirt and train. She swished the train around and announced: "Well, if somebody knows it, I will sing it" and sing it she did, far better than the previous songs and it brought the house down. I was standing transfixed when a grey-haired professor whom I did not know approached me, introduced himself, and in a charmingly familiar Viennese accent, asked "Do you know anything of German besides Lieder?" I said I did not know much German literature but knew something of Rilke. "*Ach*," he said, "*Reiten, reiten, reiten, durch den Tag, durch die Nacht/ und der Mut ist so müde geworden, und die Sehnsucht so gross*" (Riding, riding, riding, through the day, through the night, / and strength has grown so weary, and longing so great). These were the opening lines of "Cornet," a neo-Romantic poem of love and death that Rilke had written when he was very young, and it was said, later regretted. It celebrated the 17th century when the youth of Europe had surged to Vienna to save it from the Turks. It was rather as if someone had mentioned Shakespeare and another had countered with "Friends, Romans, countrymen . . . ." I was so wrought up with Nikolaidi's singing of the song I had been awaiting, I am afraid I was rather rude. "I hope you know something of Rilke besides that," I said. He told me later he realized he would have to catch up on his Rilke. We were waiting in line to thank Nikolaidi and by this time I had reached her. She was most gracious to me and I was very grateful and then made a quick getaway for I had an 8 am class next morning.

A few days later my Greek artist friend, Artemis, was giving a soiree for her compatriot, Elena Nikolaidi, and invited me. She asked me if I would pick up Dr. B., a visiting professor in Meteorology, who had known Nikolaidi in Vienna. He was staying at a motel and had no car. Of course I agreed. It was the same professor and he seemed very glad to see me. "I looked all over for you the other night, but you had vanished," he said. I explained I was a student and had to make an 8 am deadline. "I made enquiries about you," he said, "and applaud your noble effort. You will make it." I don't know why, but I told him I had to make the 12th grade test that year which was a requisite for a B.A. and it involved Math, Algebra which I had completely forgotten and never understood. "I can help you in that," he said. I stared. "You probably start with calculus," I said; "this is Undergraduate Math which I have exempted through my London Matriculation, but still have to take this 12th grade test which involves Algebra, and don't know how I am going to do it for I have forgotten all I knew, which was little."

He said, "I have to tell you something about my life. When I received my doctorate in Climatology from the University of Vienna I was not allowed to teach for I was of Jewish blood. I could coach undergraduates in Latin, Greek and Math. I know several nice little bridges in Algebra that would help you." I had to smile at the "nice little bridges" but it caught my heart too, for I realized something of what he had been through. I told him I had worked with Bertha Bracey's Quaker Committee getting *"Mischlinge"* out of

455

Vienna. He asked me out to dinner the next night "at the best restaurant in Tallahassee." I said I did not know it for my husband and I had never had money to eat out other than at Morrisons' Cafeteria. He said he would make enquiries, and I agreed to go for it would be a Saturday night.

Chapter 69

Dr. Biel.

The next night we went out to dinner at The Silver Slipper which his colleagues had recommended as the best restaurant in town. It was a disaster, a political old boys hangout specializing in steaks. We were led to a booth with a large photo of a steer above. We were both horrified. "If it were Vienna, I would have taken you to Grinzing; have you heard of Grinzing?" It seemed somewhere I had heard the name. It was a small village of wine gardens outside Vienna where visitors sat out under the trees and musicians sang old songs to them of love, death, God and wine. "All together?" I asked, surprised. He told me that in nearly every garden there was a plaque thanking God for wine. I liked the sound of that. "Not Strauss?" I asked. "No, not there, more melancholy than Strauss which is played and danced elsewhere. In these gardens a green wreath is hung before the entrance when the new wine is ready and the people go to celebrate; I will try to find a record for you of the songs."

He asked me about my studies. I said I was taking a major in English, German for language, and a minor perhaps in Art History, because there was a possibility I might be found a position in the Program of Humanities after I had my degree. I was finding Medieval Art History hard for one had to identify from which school the manuscripts came and they were mostly of the same figures, Matthew, Mark, Luke and John. "I could help you there," he said. "Those from the School of Reims are mostly done with a frisson, you understand frisson?" I did. "Those from the School of Aachen are more influenced by the classics and have solider figures." I stared amazed, that was a help. "How do you know that?" I asked. He told me had studied medieval manuscripts at the Monastery of Melk in his youth for pleasure. After he had to leave Austria and the mountains he loved he had studied art as a solace. New York was a wonderful place for art and there were galleries during the war that had sold beautiful prints very cheaply and he had bought and studied them. He had been asked by the head of the Le Moyne Art Gallery in Tallahassee to give an exhibition of his prints next spring; he had Braque Picasso, Durer, Redon, and many others I did not know.

He had been sent to Tallahassee by the Ford Foundation to teach Science at the black university of FAMU for a term, but the Head of Meteorology at FSU, who was his former doctoral student, had invited him to teach two classes in his specialty, Climatology, in fall and spring, alternating with his duties at his university, Rutgers. He was leaving next week on St. Johns day but would be back in the fall and hoped I would allow him to see if he could help in my studies. I asked him if he were a Catholic, knew Mahler had converted for his career. "A lapsed Catholic," he said, "I found it hard to pray except in beautiful churches and I could only seldom go to St. Patrick's in New York." He told me he had converted at age eleven for he found all the art he loved was Catholic, the cathedrals, the carvings, especially the wooden carvings so special to Austria. His mother was a lapsed Catholic, his father was Jewish but of no religion and did not mind.

I told him there was a new Catholic church near the University. The windows had been designed by the French artist who had supervised the removal of the windows at Chartres and their reinstatement after the war; most were abstract but of that beautiful unforgettable blue of Chartres; the west window was of Christ risen. "Could we go and see it?" he asked. I did not know if it would be open at night. "If it is Catholic, it should be" he said. It was. I had never been at night and the colors were not so brilliant except the West window which was beautifully lit. It made up for Grinzing.

Next day he sent me flowers. I asked him to dinner before he left and he came bringing a record of Mahler's Fourth; he had not been able to find the Grinzing songs, and I had told him I liked Mahler. We sat in the garden afterwards and Keith was delivered by a friend. He rushed down the drive. ""How old are you? How old are you?" he burst out to my horror. He had never seen a grey-haired man. Dr. Biel was amused and told him. He looked younger than he was. He told me later that as a child he had sung in the

Kaiser's celebration of his anniversary in 1910. "It was what they called a glittering occasion," he said, "all the crowned heads of Europe were there and ten years later there were hardly any left."

Andrew came in to dinner so we spoke English. Dr. Biel could be very funny. He told us about teaching at FAMU. There were no clocks and he had not been told how long to lecture. "Where's the clock?" he asked. A big black man arose, "I's the clock," he said, "when I gets up its over." Dr. Biel supposed the lecture should be about an hour and it appeared to work that way, but one day he was teaching about the hot-weather cow, how the Jersey cows brought from England had not weathered the heat of the South, so that they had been crossed by Brahmin cows from India to produce a cow giving the milk of a Jersey but able to withstand heat. He lectured well over an hour and at last said, "Where's the clock?" "I'm enjoying myself today," was the reply, "you go on!"

Thanks largely to Dr. Biel's advice I managed to identify correctly all the medieval manuscripts and received an A in the class.

In the fall I took my first German class with Dr. Tiesler, the Minnesänger. She had a beautiful voice, I felt I could listen to her recite poetry for hours. I took another class with Dr. Faber and introduced them both to Dr. Biel. Dr. Faber knew German, so we could all speak that language. He was fascinated by Dr. Biel. "I always felt there must somewhere be such a scholar, such a 19th-century gentleman, but I had never met one." I said he was a 17th-century man and he agreed and said it was lonely living outside your century but delightful to meet someone else who did. I said Dr. Biel knew of 20th-century art and was teaching me. "He could teach you of the literature of earlier times," he said, which was true. When Dr. Biel told me stories of Austria I felt was living in another century, sometimes in a fairy tale. He loved Stifter, a 19th-century Austrian. I knew Dr. Tiesler taught a course on Stifter and determined to take it.

From the first Saturday onwards in the fall term Dr. Biel came to coach me in Math so I could take the 12th-grade test that term. We spoke English for the problems were in English. He started out with what he hoped was a basic question I could answer: "What is three cubed?" Unfortunately I did not know whether it was nine or eighty-one; his face was a study. Obviously he was appalled at my ignorance but did not wish to show it as I was already so nervous. He cleared his throat. "Would you be familiar with how many inches there are in a foot?" he asked. I had to laugh and so did he from relief. We got on quite well with the problems, geometry, which I could see, and graphs, but as I feared I had great difficulties with Algebra in spite of his "nice little bridges." He told me there was generally a choice of questions and to choose other than Algebra when possible. He felt after a few weeks I was ready to take the test and he wanted me to do it and get the results while he was here. I passed, thanks to him. He told me we would have to have much further study before I was ready for the Graduate Record Exam but not to worry about it now.

Dr. Biel did not talk much about his experiences but he told me later that he had been saved by an American meteorologist whom he had met as a mountaineer. As a student he had climbed the highest mountains in Austria. He told me he had once left Vienna in the Christmas vacation to climb over the Alps to Italy. "Weren't you afraid of getting lost in all that snow?" I asked. He said he had a map and there were little villages all over the Alps where farmers were willing to put up students in hay barns. There were also refuge huts here and there for the *Wandervögeln* (wandering birds). He told me one time night had come on and he had not reached a village as expected, and he was climbing in the dark when he heard the Angelus from a church in the darkness ahead and climbed towards it and found the village On one of such trips he met an American meteorologist who offered to try and find him a post at Rutgers, his university. He eventually did and Dr. Biel had the invitation in his pocket when he was rounded up by the Gestapo. It was enough to save him but he had to leave Vienna for Budapest with only a schilling in his pocket and he had to leave his father. He never got over that but his father said his escape was the only joy he had and he must go immediately. He arrived in Budapest with nothing and having spent the schilling on a cup of coffee. He asked for a watchmaker (his father was a watchmaker) and was allowed to use the telephone to call a friend who came to get him and who kept him for several weeks until the American visa arrived.

Soon after he arrived at Rutgers Dr. Biel was asked to give an introductory lecture and it was thought it would be on the subject he was to teach, Climatology. Instead he gave a lecture on the history of Rutgers for he said he found that most professors he had met were unaware of it and bewailed its lack. He had done some research and found that the famous duel between Aaron Burr and Alexander Hamilton had been fought on what was now the campus of Rutgers. He had examined old maps and determined the exact spot of the duel and it was in the middle of a parking space. He then made friends with a policeman and with his aid uncovered an old marker which was deep in dirt. He felt sure the death of a famous politician would have been marked somehow and indeed it was—the date 1804, the names of Aaron Burr and Alexander Hamilton and a cross. Consternation ensued; it made all the newspapers. A suitable marker was installed; the parking place had to be enlarged to hold all the people who wished to see it, and Dr. Biel's classes were filled to overflowing. That was only one of his stories.

He told Ingrid Tiesler that he had become a climatologist through studying Adalbert Stifter, in particular his story "Bergkristall." This was a tale of two children who after a snowstorm wandered off the track and became lost in the high mountains. He said there were details given, a stilled stream below in the valley, details he had noticed but had never read of before, that led him to study climatology in order to understand the mountains better.

I still took as many courses as I could with Dr. Faber and he gave many on Shakespeare; comedies, histories, individual tragedies, sonnets. Once while studying with him I had a strange dream of Shakespeare which I told him. I dreamt I was bombed out of the 20th century into the 17th and was married to a London nobleman to whom I did not divulge this. All the details were very clear, lavender strewn on the floor, a comfit box on my wrist. I knew Shakespeare was playing at the Globe and ladies did not usually go there but only saw Shakespeare if invited to court, but I persuaded my husband to take me. It was very clear in my dream, the orange sellers, the noise, the groundlings. Then it shifted the way dreams do and I was entertaining Shakespeare in my house and told him I was bombed out of the 20th century and he was fascinated to hear that he had become so famous, that more had been written about him than anything else other than the Bible. He could not hear enough of his fame and I was a little disappointed until I recalled his sonnets and what fame meant to him. He then wanted to know all about the 20th century, how did it differ? I tried to tell him of the telephone and Dr. Faber was interested that he wanted to know about communication, psychologically that pleased him, but my dream faded as I could not explain the telephone. It was the clearest dream I had ever had up till then, and it is still in my mind.

After two years of study I had a great blow. Dr. Faber told me he was leaving, having been offered a better job at the University of Victoria, a university in the clouds, he said. He had published eleven articles while at FSU and was not given a raise. I think it was because of jealousy; he was the best English teacher I ever had. I was very upset. Dr. Faber said he would write but I knew Americans did not keep up communication as I had with Ray and Nan. My dear friends the archaeologists had left and though Patricia made a special trip to see me after Howard died, she did not write. She was teaching and had two children; she had no time. I realized it would be the same with Mel Faber.

Before he left, Mel Faber gave me one of the best compliments I ever had. I told him I was looking forward to being in graduate school where I would not stick out so much as older than the rest, a student in her forties when all the rest were in their twenties. He said: "I never think of you as old, you are always golden afternoon."

I had to take Physics or Chemistry. I was told Chemistry was easier, but I was fascinated by the ideas in Modern Physics and had studied them a little in Philosophy. The then-head of Physics, Steve Edwards, was an usher in our Church, St. John's. I told him I had read Alfred North Whitehead's *Science and the Modern World* and had been fascinated by his idea that quantum physics was like a circular railroad where sometimes the stations were there and sometimes they were not. "I can make you understand that," he said. I told him I was terrified of the math involved and he assured me he would get a graduate student to coach me and I would do all right with High School Math. I told him the problems I had had with the Twelfth Grade Test in Math, but he said not to worry, so I took it. I was fascinated with the concepts; for a while I thought I understood Einstein's Relativity and had an inkling of quantum physics and I liked the fact that one had to believe far more difficult things than the miracles in the New Testament. The String Theory and Heisenberg's theory of Indeterminacy led to a magical world. Dr. Edwards very much wanted me to get an A but I only achieved a B because of stupid mistakes in rudimentary math. Erwin, Dr. Biel, told me it was because I had not been taught math well as a child, and I remembered the year and a half after Miss Risdon left and before we went to school when as far as I could remember I learned nothing,

Chapter 70

Keith.

Keith was my great delight; he enjoyed life so much. When I first started studying, he was in Kindergarten at Florida High, while Andrew was in Seventh Grade. The school was affiliated to Florida State University. One had to sign up for one's child at birth and the school consisted mostly of the children of FSU and FAMU professors. Keith's great friend in kindergarten was a little black girl who later became a famous doctor. They were both nominated as president of the kindergarten class and she won. Andrew asked Keith for whom he voted and he said he voted for her. As they were tied Andrew explained he should have voted for himself. Keith did not agree.

The music program was very good there and once a year they had a musical program to which the public was invited. I asked Erwin to go with me to hear it. He was rather reluctant but later said it was the laugh of his life. It was not done chronologically. I remember the high school band was playing in the middle of the arena and the kindergarten class did a skip dance around them ending up in the front where the little girl curtsied and the little boy bowed and the audience applauded. Keith was in the first couple and apparently the applause pleased him for he stayed behind to join the second couple instead of retreating as he should have done. The program was really rather boring except to the parents and Keith's breaking the routine pleased the audience and they applauded loudly which delighted him so he stayed on through the third, fourth, right through to the twelfth couple, bowing with them. It wowed the audience who were laughing and enjoying it. Erwin said Keith was a born actor with a flair for the stage, tears of laughter were running down his face each time Keith failed to retreat with the couple but remained bowing and smiling. Andrew was embarrassed. I enjoyed it and thought it was funny.

At the beginning of my senior year I had a letter from Patricia telling me that she and Bill had been given the wonderful position of archaeologists in residence at the American School of Archaeology in Athens and inviting me to come over for two weeks and stay with them there. She knew I would be getting my BA next spring in 1968 and thought I would be going to England for a visit and she had found out there were cheap flights from London to Athens. It would cost nothing to stay with them and I could go on a dig with them and then go to Delphi myself and take the island trip. John would then be nineteen going to TCC and Andrew sixteen. They were both very reliable and I had no hesitation letting them take care of the house and pay the bills for two months. Keith who would then be eight would

468

come to England with me. I wrote Bettina of the plan and she told me she had a friend with three children who took in youngsters whose parents were abroad, and she thought Keith would be happy with them. He would go to school for six weeks as the summer holidays started later in England. He would stay in Bidborough, a village ten minutes from Tunbridge Wells where she and Mummy lived, but it was right overlooking the Weald of Kent, a lovely place. They would see him often while I was in Greece. I consulted the boys and they were all in agreement.

I graduated Summa cum Laude and the boys wanted me to walk. It disturbed me that they played "Land of Hope and Glory" as the processional for I remembered hearing the solo violinist play it on the night war broke out. Keith and I left soon after for England on one of the first B 747s. There had been a ghastly story in the papers how a door had flown open on one of the new planes and I was rather scared, particularly as we had to wait four hours while a man hammered on the door just in front of us. Keith was angelic about the wait.

We stayed with Ray for the first few days and I remember Keith's astonishment at coming out of Charing X station into Trafalgar Square. He stared up at Nelson on his column and asked "Who is that?" I told him it was the statue of an admiral who had won a great victory for England at Trafalgar in 1805. "What is he looking at?" Keith asked. I had never considered this but answered "He is staring south, out to sea?" Keith was enchanted with Nelson and could not hear enough. We visited Cyril and Frances and they took us to see the Cutty Sark, an old sail ship and then to Greenwich Naval College where Nelson's uniform was displayed and a special knife and fork that had been made for him when he lost one arm. Keith was fascinated and I was delighted to have a son who was interested in English history.

He also wanted to know where I had lived as a child and Ray and I took him to the Whitestone pond on Hampstead Heath where Bettina and I had sailed ships. I bought him a little sail ship but unfortunately it was a lemon and keeled over all the time. He was not discouraged and fiddled about with it till it eventually achieved balance and set sail. "Ah, the moment of truth," he said. Ray was impressed. "Of course he got that from you but to use it so appropriately, how did he hear it?" I told her that Erwin had given me a large pen and ink drawing of Agamemnon with his sword drawn, wondering whether to kill Iphigenia for a fair wind, and I must have used it to describe that moment. It was typical of Keith to remember a spoken phrase, although he never cared for reading. He loved hearing the history of England and was very happy at Bidborough.

I remember standing with him overlooking the Weald and telling him, as Miss Risdon had told me, that the fields of dark gold were barley, the lighter gold wheat, and the silver green oats. "What are the bright yellow little fields?" he asked. "Mustard," I said," and the dark brown are fallow, ploughed up and left empty a year." He told me he liked hearing the church bell ring the Westminster Chimes quarters through the night. I told him I had heard them as a child at Eastbourne. "Don't they keep you awake?" I asked, knowing the answer.

"Oh no, I'm asleep before the hour rings." I took him to school the first day, down a lane and over a stile and then we were in the woods and they were awash with bluebells. I did not have to shake him as I did Andrew once so that he would remember the bluebells. We stood still, holding hands, and I realized he experienced them as I did.

While we were in England in 1968 it was the 800th anniversary of the village church at Bidborough, which was Norman and built in 1168, and they had a memorial service and a church fete Keith gave me a little jug which he had bought at the fete, and I still have it. The church was older than the Ticehurst church, with round arches and a lepers squint which interested Keith. Mrs. Corbould was very good at taking the children to historic places. She took them to Hastings where the Bayeux Tapestry had been on loan for two years since 1966. I had never seen it except in slides but Keith actually saw it and never forgot it. He thought it was unfair that the Normans won for they were in armour and held swords while the Saxons just had arrows, and Harold, the last Saxon king, had had to march all the way from the north of England where he had defeated the Danes.

She also took them to Calais on the Hovercraft to see the Rodin statues of "the Burghers of Calais" which I had never seen, but Keith never forgot. "I remember the man with the key," he said, "he looked so sad but he was ready to die to save his city." I seemed to remember that their lives had been spared. Keith was also fascinated by the Hovercraft, which he said seemed to fly over the waves, just hitting them occasionally.

I also took him to Cambridge to visit Rita and Brian and to visit King's College Chapel where the boys sang Evensong. He said he would like to join St. John's Choir when we went home. We queued up every day for evensong and watched the boys as they entered for rehearsal. Keith waved to them but I told him they were not allowed to wave back. To his great delight, one small boy did. I took him on the Cam in a canoe and we were rather late for lunch, which was unforgivable to Rita, so I hailed what I thought was a taxi. It was black. "Madam," I was told in severe tones, "I am a hearse."

Keith delighted Brian by silencing my cousin Gordon who was pontificating on American football. "Oh no, sir," he said politely, "you are wrong there. American football goes like this." He demonstrated with forks and knives and Gordon for once had nothing to say except "I expect you'll go far."

Chapter 71

Greece.

In 1968 Athens may have been gathering pollution but the air seemed clear and glittering— *claritas*—and one was still allowed to climb the Acropolis. Although it was over 100 degrees, after the heavy heat of Florida it did not seem hard. Bill and Patricia accompanied me showing me the many sculptures that still lay around. I felt it was a good thing that Elgin saved what he could in the 19th century, and that they were displayed in the British Museum so the world could learn of the glory of Greece and save them from the Turks who had already blown up the Parthenon. I know that some people think they should be returned to Greece but their National Museum is already so full. It was in the British Museum that the civilized world first knew of them; had they been left in Greece they would have disappeared.

I had taken many classes in Classics during my last year knowing that, if I were lucky enough to get a job in the Humanities Program, I would have to teach classics. I was aware that the columns in the Parthenon were not the same width all the way down, they swelled in the middle, entasis, and this somehow gave the building a lift. The platform on which they stood was not straight but rose in the middle, and the outer columns standing against the brilliant blue sky were wider than the central so that they would appear the same. I had not realized the marble held iron ore within it and the Parthenon in the sunset appeared to glow from within because of this. I learned a great deal from Bill and Patricia. They took me on their dig at Sounion, mentioned in Homer, and also to Corinth; they showed me the wonders of the National Museum. I remember especially the boy taking a thorn out of his foot, and Zeus or Poseidon glorious in bronze. They were so alive. Egyptian art from which the Greeks had learned was static.

From the terrace at the American School of Archaelogy one could see the Parthenon, and there we sipped ouzo every evening watching it glow in the sunset. I liked ouzo, which was absinthe, better than the Greek wine, retzina, which had the taste of turpentine, and also one was given ice with ouzo. We did not eat until 9 pm, which was the custom, but Patricia made us appetizers for which I was grateful. For lunch we bought moussaka, which seemed to be minced meat wrapped in grape leaves. They were sold on the street.

Bill and Patricia took time off to take me to Corinth and Mycenae but they had to go back to work and I went to Delphi alone. They said I must stay overnight in order to see the sunset over Olympus from the rose mountain, and the sunrise on the Gulf of Corinth, from the gold mountain. I went on a bus which climbed up steep hills, not green in summer as in England, but showing the rock although festooned with the silver green tutus of olive trees and the Mediterranean below. The guide announced the crossroads where Oedipus had met and unknowingly killed his father, Laius. There was no commercial exploitation; I doubt there was even a cairn. At Delphi I was overwhelmed by the wideness of the distances, Mt. Olympus above the Gulf of Corinth, the stadium at Delphi. I stood by the Delphic charioteer; I had seen it on slides but was not prepared for the amazement in his eyes—he was so young but he had won the race.

It was the dawn of the world at Delphi; I wished I had Erwin or Mel or Patricia to share it with but perhaps it fell deeper because I was alone. I still can see it clearly in my mind's eye. I remember an ancient woman dressed all in black with a spindle in her hand; I had never seen a spindle but knew it must be one for she was spinning thread from it. I first saw men dance and one could see it was not originally for entertainment but as a ritual introducing drama. They were very serious as they danced and there were no women. Later on the island trip I saw women and even tourists join the dance, but it then did not have the solemnity, nor the ritual quality, that it did in Delphi.

I returned to Athens in a daze and Patricia said "I was right to make you stay overnight?" and of course she was. I then left for a four-day island cruise, Mykonos, Delos, Patmos, Crete and Rhodes. Mykonos was covered with white houses, white churches with gold mosaics within, and windmills. I recall the wide beach at Delos where Apollo was born, so full of light and the sea, azure and emerald. I recalled a talk by a Classics professor who said he thought the Greeks saw differently from us for they always talked of "the wine-dark sea" whereas to us it is the epitome of light. He thought the ancient Hebrews saw the same way for in the Kabbalah they distinguish color by its brilliance not its hue, and "sapphire" and "crystal" are frequently interchangeable. He said the colors of green and red were interchangeable in the Greek language for they both emphasized the quality of "flowing" whether of blood or the light green foliage of the spring.

Patmos is where St. John is supposed to have written Revelations. I do not think it was the same St. John of the Gospels, and found it hard to believe that that chaotic book could have been written on such a serene isle as Patmos. There was a huge fall from the mountains to the sea that took the breath away. Again I saw men dance in solemnity and saw there one of the first Christian monasteries with its tremendous-eyed icons. Crete, Knossus, with its Minoan art, seemed somehow much more modern although it was an older civilization. The women with their graceful clothes and jewelry might have been Parisians. I bathed in the Mediterranean at Crete; the water was so clear I saw the shells around my toenails, and the sea was emerald.

I arrived back in Athens in time for the farewell party for the American students who had just finished their classes and were returning home. The party was held in an open air café with the mountains behind and the sea below and one boy with a good voice sang in Latin "*Gaudeamus igitur*" which seemed very appropriate. I left soon after for

England and never saw Bill or Patricia again. I hope C.S. Lewis is right and that we will meet in heaven those who have touched our hearts on earth.

Keith had had a wonderful time while I was away. The Corbaulds had taken him and other children to the Changing of the Guard at Buckingham Palace and to the Tower and he had seen the Crown Jewels (which I never had). They had also been taken to Arundel Castle which is all a castle should be and then to the new site of Greenwich Observatory, which had had to be moved from London because of the effects of electricity and technology, and was now I think at Hever Castle. He was thrilled at all he had seen. I took him to the Changing of the Horse Guards at St. James's Palace. He saw the King Charles I statue, "alone in his own Whitehall" and years later took a photo of it for me.

Keith returned to US an Anglophile for life. He told me years later he never forget his first sight of Nelson on his column, so high above the world. Coming from Florida where most of the land was flat, it made an indelible impression on him.

Chapter 72

The M.A.

After I received my B.A. I could have taught English composition and grammar as a teaching assistant. It was very little money, and I decided to take another year and complete my M.A., for then I could teach Humanities for a little extra money, and I would be more interested in the subject matter, and it would be a step toward the Ph.D. which I now realized I would have to take if I hoped ever to teach at FSU. Jim Kobacker who had helped me so much over Howard's death had moved from next door, and a new family moved in. Dr. T. was Chancellor of the Board of Regents and he lost no time telling me that I would never get a job at FSU with three degrees from that University. I continued to pray for miracles such as I had had on finding my London University Matriculation papers in Grandpa's old jewelbox, enabling me to exempt math and biology in my B.A. Dr. Biel coached me for months in math to get me through the GRE, which I passed before leaving for England and Greece. That was a miracle. I passed in the lowest 5% in math, but my high verbal score enabled me to make it.

John was now at Tallahassee Community College and living at home to save money but I hoped next year he would get into FSU and a fraternity, which was what he wanted. The boys were most supportive and helpful, and had managed very well with the house and bills while I was in Europe. Keith says he remembers during most of his child hood going to bed with the sound of my typewriter and waking up to it.

I missed Mel very much. I took a graduate course on "A *Midsummer Night's Dream*" with a horrible professor who objected to my English pronunciation. At the end of term, besides the exams, we were asked to write a page on any aspect of the play. I wrote on how I had tried to find the ruby spots in the cowslip, as Shakespeare noted. "In their gold coats spots you see/ these be rubies, fairy favors." I knew he was always accurate in his descriptions of nature, but looked on the outside, then peered into the dim corolla, and could see no spots. I lay back on the downs and held the flower up to the sun which I realized Shakespeare must have done because then I saw the rubies with the sun shining through them at the bottom of the corolla. I wrote of this and of the delight I had in realizing I was doing what Shakespeare had done. Dr. M. was most scathing, but my good friend, Sister Maria, took the course the next term and he quoted my discovery without giving me credit. Sister Maria, who had heard the story from me, would not let him get away with it. "You heard that from Audrey Wilson, "she said, "and you told her it was ridiculous and of no interest." Another story of this Dr. M. His class was at 8 am and he locked the door at 8.03 am. One woman had to take her baby to day care and was locked out twice. I saw her in the library one day, and she was crying with her head on the table. I went over to her and she told me "I nearly committed murder. Dr. M. was standing by the open window low to the ground, and I could have easily pushed him out and I nearly did!"

There was a professor who taught Chaucer whom I liked. He told me I was the only student who had ever quoted Middle English in an exam. It was not a popular course and there was a horrible man in it who was often rude to the professor. When our papers were returned this young man had no grade. He complained. "Well," said Dr. C. "I read the paper and read it through again, and no grade occurred to me."

I was not well the year of my MA. I had the flu, indigestion, and stomach pains. The doctor threatened me with a hysterectomy. I explained I had no time to take off. I had to get my MA that year in order to teach the next for my Social Security money was running out. I did get something for two sons in college but not enough. The doctor said I was to come back in two months, which was before the end of the academic year, and he would decide. When I came back, it was the middle of the summer term and I still had four weeks before graduation. However, the doctor was insistent and said I should have the operation, and he would arrange it in two weeks time. I asked him to make it three weeks and went to my three professors asking them if I could do my term papers and take the final exams a week early. I had taken classes with all of them before and they knew I was a good student and in a bind; they gave permission and the notes for the last week. I had to write three term papers and take three finals in three weeks. I stayed up till 1 am typing or studying and arose at 5 am to do the same. It was pretty hectic, but I made it. I don't know how I managed to cook for three boys at the same time.

I had decided to take an extra course in Humanities and not write a thesis for the MA for I wanted to save my material for a dissertation on Rilke for the PhD. The day before I went into hospital I took my last exam for which one was supposed to be ready to write a synopsis on, as I recall, five out of a hundred authors which would qualify one to teach in Humanities, not just English, but Tolstoy, Victor Hugo, Balzac, Goethe, Dante etc. It was harrowing but I had no time to be worried about the operation.

My good friends, Pat and Maurie, took Keith with their family to the beach, which was very helpful as he was not allowed to visit me in hospital; the elder boys could. Keith had never been to the beach and it was a great excitement for a nine-year-old. I came through the operation and received the M.A. and I was told I could teach in the Humanities Program in the fall, which was six weeks away, as a teaching assistant. I was thankful, and very grateful to friends who rallied round. Dr. Gentry who was in charge of the Student Hospital at FSU let me stay there for two weeks to recuperate after I had been released from the Tallahassee Memorial Hospital after a week. That was a great blessing for I was very weak and for quite a while could not lift anything heavy.

Sister Maria Riley and her fellow nuns who taught at the Catholic School brought me a huge dish of pork chops when I came home, knowing my son John was there to put it in the oven. I remember it lasted us for days. Erwin was at Rutgers at the time but he phoned often, advising me to get to my notes on the *Iliad* which I had to teach in three weeks. I had already organized them and Erwin was a great help there. He told me to think when making the exams of how they would be easiest to grade. For instance, he suggested asking for ten characteristics of epic with examples from the text. It was a great help. He said I had a good memory and should learn the notes by heart as soon as possible in order to have eye contact with the students and to learn their names and use them From Ingrid, my German teacher, I knew the value of starting a discussion so as to get students involved. Andrew, my teenage son, gave me this advice: "Be sure and dress differently every day!"

Six weeks from my operation I taught for the first time. Here I was helped by my ham actress mother, for I really took to teaching like a duck to water. I could make them laugh, I could interest them in what I was interested in, and I took the trouble to learn their names. Apparently few teachers did and the students responded. First I learned the blond boys, then the blonde girls, then those with glasses. I told the class what I was doing and asked if anyone were going to switch to contacts to let me know, and it would help if they would sit in the same places. They were very cooperative and helped me when I made mistakes. My fellow teaching assistants told me they would probably confuse me deliberately but that never happened. They remembered my name; it had disturbed me as a student that a lot of my fellows did not know the teacher's name. I told the students I had something of value to give them, and, that being so, felt we should know each other's names. From the first term onwards my student evaluations were very good; I think it helped having an English accent. For some reason the southerners liked it. I wish I had kept my student evaluations for they certainly helped me those first few years. I can remember only one, which must have been from a football player: "this lady sure knows her shit."

As a teaching assistant I taught two classes (with the same material for the first year) and took two classes towards my Ph.D. I felt that Howard had had a much easier Ph.D. in England than I. He had only had to see his major professor once a week, and had had two years to write his doctoral dissertation. I had to take two years of classes for the doctorate and only then could start on my dissertation. I loved learning, however, and loved teaching, and was happy doing both, and the little extra money received as a teaching assistant helped.

My Chairman in Humanities was Dr. Goodman with whom I had taken Romantic Poetry and he was an excellent teacher. I thought I knew Wordsworth and Keats but he taught me far more and stretched my mind. He was a strange man; I was so impressed with his chronology of Keats's Odes that I asked if I could read his paper on it. "It was never published," he said, "I couldn't face a rejection slip."

I was a bit taken back. English professors had to publish but apparently he didn't care. He was the only American I had met who could quote as much poetry as I could and sometimes in the office when there was not much going on in the afternoon we quoted poetry to one another. I would have liked him to have directed my doctoral dissertation which I knew was going to be "The Development of the Concept of Death in Rilke's Prose and Poetry." He knew German and he knew poetry but he did not have a dagger against his name which would have indicated that he could direct a doctoral dissertation. Ingrid did not have a dagger either and anyway I was going to write the dissertation in English so I needed an English professor. I was in a quandary.

I asked for an interview with the Chairman of English with whom I had studied Victorian Literature and the Pre-Raphaelites. I asked his help in finding a major professor for my dissertation. He said he would do it. I was astounded. He did not know German and never taught poetry, but prose. I was a little dubious and suggested Dr. Goodman but Dr. S. said he did not have the dagger. "Do you know Rilke?" I asked. "I have heard of him," was the reply. I was not very happy about this, but what could I do? "You will have a German professor on your committee who doubtless knows Rilke and can check your criticism and writing. It is the best you can do if you want to write on Rilke; you will have to have a PhD in Humanities rather than in English." I said I knew more of Rilke than any other poet and also felt I had more chance of getting a position at FSU in Humanities afterwards than in English. He agreed.

Chapter 73

Teaching Assistant and Ph.D.

Those years still are very vivid. Dashing across campus from class to class; hoping the professor would not keep us overtime and so make me late for the next class. We only had fifteen minutes between classes and the campus was large. Would I have time to get ready to teach, to find the slides, to stack them right way up in the projector, did I remember where I left off yesterday? Thanks to the Dean of Graduate Studies I obtained permission to take for graduate credit some German classes taken before, providing I did extra papers, so I always had a class with Ingrid to look forward to. I had to do a great deal of reading, my eyes grew tired, and I needed glasses.

Erwin asked Ingrid if he could read some of the long German novels aloud to me. She said that was quite all right and so on Saturday afternoons we sat in the garden or in Maclay Gardens in a little pavilion overlooking the lake and he read Fontane's *"Effie Briest"* and *"Der alte Stechlin."* I remember those books better than others I read myself.

It was very relaxing and soothing to hear of the people of another century and their very different problems.

Apart from German, for my doctoral studies I took classics, philosophy, and art history, everything that would help me teach Humanities. Ingrid taught Rilke among other early twentieth century poets, but she did not teach a course on him alone. When she announced she was going to teach Kafka next term, Erwin became very agitated. "I beg you not to take that course; you will get a death depression and a B!" I told Ingrid and she laughed. "What would he like me to teach?" "Hofmannsthal," I said, and she agreed to do so. I had already studied Kafka with her among other writers in a course on the twentieth century. I hoped for the Hofmannsthal of "Der Rosenkavalier" but instead learned and enjoyed "Der Brief an Lord Chandos" which was almost as good as Rilke.

At last I was through classes and able to start writing my dissertation. I had my committee and of course Ingrid was on it, and then a dreadful thing happened. She had been suffering what she thought was toothache but it was diagnosed as a tumor on the brain and it had to be operated at once; she was told the chances of success were only 5O/5O. She and Heinz decided to get married right away; they could not before as they taught in the same department, but now they had to, so that he could make decisions for her. They were married the day before she went to the hospital which was Shands at Gainesville; nobody in Tallahassee was capable of the operation. Erwin and I were the only ones at the wedding ceremony at the Registry Office, and Heinz was so upset he forgot his wallet so Erwin paid for it and for a champagne breakfast. Ingrid asked me to bring the printed certificate she would have to sign once I had finished my dissertation. "I want my signature on it," she said, "I know Erwin will check your German." The operation would take at least five hours they were told and it was decided Heinz would call me when it was over so I could phone her mother in Germany. It took seven hours; at last Heinz called and the operation was deemed a success; the only problem Ingrid would have was that she could not shut her left eyelid and she would have do that by hand during the day and tape it at night. Her brain was not damaged. I was so thankful for that. She had one of the finest minds I had ever met. It seemed a long time till she came home from the hospital but she was able to teach in the fall term. Heinz obtained a position at Tulane University at New Orleans and next year Ingrid would teach at Loyola, the other university in New Orleans so they could be together. Their move was a great loss to me.

Most people took two years to write their doctoral dissertation, continuing as teaching assistants during that time. I was anxious to get it over and to know whether I would be taken on as faculty afterwards, and I was in need of more money. Erwin encouraged me by setting deadlines; abstract by September, first chapter November, etc. It was a grind as I was teaching as well but I tried to be free in the afternoons and evenings for research in the library and for writing. Computers were not yet available and one had to re-type pages in order to insert. I had a "corral" in the library where I could type. For five years afterwards I could not go near the library without a feeling of nausea. I became very worn out and suffered from nervous indigestion.

I had already the outline and names of chapters, which surprised my major professor, as he expected to organize that, as he did with my friend Anne. I had five chapters, each with a name of the country which had influenced Rilke in his concept of death. Dr. S. queried this: "How can a country do this?" I replied that the poems would illustrate that but indeed countries had different concepts of death. He raised his eyebrows, not having lived in Europe. I explained that Rilke grew up in Prague, the city of tombs and monuments to the dead, and as a result of his early years published "Cornet," a neo-romantic glance at history, when the youth of Europe surged to Vienna to defend it from the Turks. It was a tale of love and death.

Later Rilke learned Russian with the woman he loved all his life, and with her and her husband traveled to Russia at the end of the 19th century. He was impressed with the mystic faith of the serfs who had little in this life and looked forward to better in the next, and wrote that for him there was only one Easter, when he heard the Kyrie eleison on a Russian Easter morning. As a result he wrote "*The Book of Hours,*" full of mysticism and faith.

Later he went to France where he received a commission for a monograph on Rodin. The sculptor had a great influence on him and turned him away from subjective outpourings and to objective detailed information, carving out poems as a sculptor carves stone. *New Poems* resulted, which were indeed new in subject and treatment; also a prose work

The Notebooks of Malte Laurids Brigge, a study of a young Danish poet, Malte, who was appalled by the dying and the dead in the streets and hospitals of Paris. *Malte* was far more realistic than anything Rilke had written before, and presaged the Angst and depression of many later writers.

He was then invited to stay at the Castle of Duino, near Trieste, on the Mediterranean, where he started his *Duino Elegies*, and was surprised by the sonnets which came to him at the same time. He then visited Spain, and El Greco. After an enforced sojourn in Munich during the war he emigrated to Switzerland where he spent the rest of his life. Dr. Biel, a climatologist, was fascinated by the idea that geography had influenced Rilke's concept of death, and made a remark, which I cited, that it could be said that he moved always to a drier climate, and the Rhone Valley of Switzerland, where he landed, was one of the driest in Europe. It is in dry climates that you see the stars at their best, and Rilke was always fascinated by stars.

In the Seventh Elegy he wishes he were dead in order to know them at last. Rilke believed that in life an individual should concentrate on things that touched him and transform them to his inner world space and so build own his death which he could take with him to the next life. I concluded, "And does this idea differ very radically from the belief that 'the Kingdom of Heaven is within you' and that eternal life can start now on earth, and need not wait for death?"

I received my PhD in l972 and anxiously awaited a call from the Dean's office to know whether I would be taken on in the Program of Humanities as faculty. The Dean explained to me that he had tried to persuade Dr. S. to let me teach one course in English literature so I could be funded by the English Department and so enter the tenure system with full benefits but Dr. S. had refused to employ anyone in his department who had all three degrees from the same university. He of all people knew I had nothing but A's in all English courses except one B when I was ill. Dr. S. had told me my dissertation was the best he had directed so I was very disappointed.

The Dean said the best he could do was to offer me a job as Lecturer as an adjunct which meant I could be terminated at any time by a future Dean. I would be paid more but not as much as tenured faculty and was still hanging on a clothes line as it were, waiting every term to be confirmed. He had done all he could and he said I was urgently needed in the Humanities Program as the current teacher of the Junior and Senior Seminars for Humanities majors was a textual Shakespeare scholar who would doubtless leave if he were offered a position in Shakespeare criticism, and I should prepare myself to teach those as well as Honors classes for the undergraduate Program. I thanked him; he had done all he could. I was a Lecturer, and so counted as faculty but without the security of the tenure track.

My cousin Rita had offered tickets to bring Keith and me to England for a summer vacation and to take us on a Rhine cruise. She loved Europe but Brian, her husband, did not and so she suggested that Keith and I accompany her. Keith was now twelve and looked forward to seeing England again and to the trip on the Rhine. He would stay again with the family he did when he was eight for the time we spent in England.

Erwin had not seen Vienna since he had been forced to leave in 1938; He had visited Austria in 1952 and asked four of his friends to meet him in Salzburg, for he could not face Vienna with all its memories. His father had died in a concentration camp. The friends had come and met him at an appointed place, a wall outside a church in Salzburg. He felt now he could face Vienna if I came with him, and we agreed he should come to England where Bettina and I would meet him. He wanted to meet my sister. We could not put him up but he could stay with Ray while I visited my mother and sister and we would go together to Vienna, which I had never seen. This would be after our Rhine trip.

Chapter 74

The Rhine Trip, England, and Austria, 1972.

We started at Rotterdam, sailed down to Strasbourg, and enjoyed very much the scenery and the castles, but Strasbourg was the highlight. They had a performance of Sound and Light in English. A searchlight from either side first focused on the altar as a symbol of Strasbourg as the crossroads of East and West. Then various parts of the cathedral were outlined and the lecturer indicated when they were added with appropriate church music of the period starting with Gregorian chant and continuing with early and than later polyphony. It was a fascinating history lesson as well as illuminating the beautiful details of the cathedral.

Afterwards Rita suggested we go to dinner but I was always nervous about making deadlines and was afraid of missing the last bus. She pooh poohed that and said we would eat overlooking the square where the buses stood that went back to the quay. I saw there was only one bus waiting and we should get it but Rita said it was pointing in the wrong direction. I said buses turned round in the square and insisted we leave. Just as we were getting to the bus the conductor closed the door and blew the whistle, "*C'est deja siffle*," he said with fiendish glee and would not let us on. We looked around for taxis; none. A passer-by informed me there were none. We were in desperate straits; all our belongings were on the steamer. I suggested we would have to ask a passer-by if they had a car and would help us. Rita's French was better than mine as she had spent a year in France, but she could not accost a stranger with such a request. Erwin had told me to look at faces at the airport when trying to find a sympathetic teller. There was a teenage boy with father with a nice face so in desperation I asked him. "Excuse me, do you have a car and could you help us? We are on the Rhine steamer which is leaving shortly, we have lost the last bus, and there are no taxis. Could you please drive us to the quay?" He said they were strangers in town but he would drive us if we knew the way, since he did not know it.

The father broke in with a wail that he was extremely hungry, but the boy was more of a good Samaritan. He asked the way to the quay and was given a wave in the direction thereof, but Strasbourg was built in medieval times with no straight roads. We got in the car with the father grumbling about hunger and started off in the direction of the wave. The road soon led us in another direction. Our situation seemed hopeless when Keith exclaimed, "We passed that building on the way here." "Listen to the child." said the father, "the women know nothing and I am dying of hunger." By the grace of God, Keith recognized building after building to my great amazement for I could recognize nothing and we arrived at the quay. I thanked them profusely and regretted I could not ask them on board for a drink, but the steamer was just about to leave. I was very proud of Keith's sense of direction, which he inherited from his father. Keith and I were thankful to stumble into our cabin, to the strains of the schmaltzy violinist playing "Goodnight, my love."

The rest of the trip was uneventful. Keith won the prize for guessing correctly the number of castles we had seen, which was six. There was a Cook's tour on board and I made friends with the director. He asked me to dance for the Viennese waltz, which was my favorite, and I was very amused that both Rita and Keith would not look at the dance floor but kept their eyes down on their plates!

Back in England, Bettina was trying to sell her flat in Tunbridge Wells as the traffic in that town was growing appalling. It was on the mainline to the coast and the roads through town were bumper to bumper at weekends. Bettina told me that one day she saw the lights in front go red so she let in a florist van from the side. Immediately the cars behind screeched their horns at having yet another in front of them. In sight of all this the florist got out and with a flourish handed Bettina a carnation.

Auntie and Uncle were now no more so she did not have to look after them and they had left her some money so she could build a cottage of her own in the country somewhere. She consulted me as to whether it should be Wales or the Cotswolds. I thought the latter, though beautiful, would be too touristy for her and knew she loved

Wales. I did query how that would affect her seeing Ronnie. She said Mummy was no longer able to get away to London for theatre weekends as she had rheumatoid arthritis, so Ronnie and she were not able to meet so much. They had often holidayed together in Wales, and it would just be the question of the odd weekend. What I should have suggested was that she look at West Sussex. The traffic on East Sussex roads had blinded us to the fact that there were still little villages like Wilmington and Jevington in West Sussex that were unspoilt. She decided on Criccieth in North Wales, but first she had to sell the Tunbridge Wells flat.

Bettina and I met Erwin at Kings Cross station. He said he would like to take us to a rose garden for lunch. I started to explain there were no rose gardens in London but Bettina interrupted me by saying that there was Queen Mary's Rose Garden in Regents Park where she often went with Ronnie. She was more of a Londoner than I who had never seen it. She drove us there; it was an ideal summer day and we sat with roses all around us. Erwin ordered champagne and I was glad that he and Bettina took to each other; they were both eccentrics. He was to stay a few days with Ray, who had a guest house, for there was no room for him at the Tunbridge Wells flat. We delivered him to Ray's after a lengthy luncheon, and Bettina and I found ourselves driving past Fawley Road where we had lived as children. We both thought we should go and see the house. It was for sale and so we realized we could use the tradesmen's entrance and see the back garden and the steps where we had sat listening to the blackbird. We did and lo! the blackbird was singing in the same tree. We seated ourselves on the steps and listened for quite a while.

Erwin phoned from Ray's; he had seen the British Museum, and the National Gallery, and asked if there were not a small hotel at Tunbridge Wells where he could stay. Bettina knew of one in the old part of town and so we booked him there. We often visited him for lunch and invited him to dinner, although people were constantly coming to look at the flat. He was there once when two groups were there, a middle-aged woman and a young couple. Erwin said to Bettina: "Concentrate on the woman, she will buy it." Bettina felt it was too large for her, but I told her Erwin sometimes was prescient, and if he said she would buy it, she would. "Show her the garden," he said. Bettina had not done this as she felt it would be much too large for her, but the woman was delighted with it and said she would get someone to mow the lawn and offered to buy the flat then and there. Bettina had been trying to sell it for months, and she felt Erwin had brought her luck.

Erwin was very nervous on the plane to Vienna; indeed he was shaking. I realized it was traumatic for him. Back in Tallahassee by a miracle he had found in a store a record with the songs of Grinzing, the wine gardens outside Vienna; we had played them so often we knew them by heart. They were not at all like the oom-pa-pa German drinking songs, but rather melancholy, and often very funny. There was a particular singer, Hans Moser, who had nothing remarkable in the way of a voice, but his delivery was somehow unforgettable. He sang of angels getting permission from

St. Peter for a holiday in Vienna and going to Grinzing on the 38 tram; of an old man who had never married sitting by himself drinking wine; of someone taking his dachshund with him to Grinzing in order to be led home. We were to go to Grinzing the first night and take the 38 tram. I hoped this would cheer him up. At Schwechart, the airport, we found a taxi and Erwin asked him to drive to the hotel but not past Währingerstrasse; this was where his father had had his watchmaker's shop. From my window I saw St. Stephen's cathedral, *der alte Steffl* of the songs.

After dropping the bags, we left almost immediately for Grinzing, taking the 38 tram which ran past the hotel. It was a cluster of wine gardens with a church in the center. We first went to Heuermandl which had a thatched roof and sat in the garden surrounded by flowering vines that had a sweet scent. At Grinzing there was a green wreath hanging over the entrance announcing that the new wine was ready. People were singing and seated at long tables. Opposite us were two young men and by my side a little girl whose parents came from Switzerland. She knew no German so I talked French to her and she seemed pleased.

The waiter came immediately and Erwin ordered wine, which came in round engraved glasses with vine leaves on them; then the musicians strolled by and Erwin asked them for Hans Moser songs. There were three musicians, one played a harmonica, the second a fiddle, and the third a zither. They made a delightful sound and soon we were listening to songs we knew and the wine was having its effect. Nearby was an older woman with a heavenly voice, an opera singer, and she was allowed a solo after which we all clapped. "My children," she said, "it was long ago but once I was applauded by Toscanini."

Erwin asked the young men opposite if they were artists; they looked very Bohemian. "We are artists of life," they said. The little girl's mother came from Vienna and she had married a Swiss, but once a year they came back to Grinzing. Everybody talked to each other. I noticed a plaque on the garden wall praising God who had given us wine. The wine, though light, was very heady; I remembered the Devon cider that had surprised Howard and me. I certainly floated off on the music, the songs, and the scent of the flowers around us, which I could not place. Erwin seemed relaxed and happy, he had a good bass voice and the table applauded as he sang the Moser songs. We had a delicious Wiener Schnitzel and salad to eat, followed by *Apfelstrudel* and another glass, a Viertel, of wine. It was all I had expected of Grinzing, and more.

The next day we climbed the 240 steps to the top of St. Stephen's Cathedral with a fantastic view of Vienna spread below. One could see how the Ringstrasse had cut across the old wall and the palaces of Schönbrunn and Belvedere were clear to see. We visited them next and the White Salon at Schönbrunn was more beautiful than the Hall of Mirrors at Versailles on which it was modeled. The Mozart Boys Choir often sang there in 18th—century costumes but unfortunately they were not performing while we were there. We had a wonderful black coffee with whipped cream floating on it and lunch that day in a medieval tavern,

Griechenbeisl, where Beethoven and Schubert had carved their names with a diamond on one of the windows. I told Erwin how I had visited Shakespeare's birthplace in Stratford during the war and they had taken out the window on which Dr. Johnson and Keats had carved their names, and how the old caretaker had said: "If anything had happened to those signatures we could not get them again."

As we came out of the tavern it was raining and there was a taxi standing by so we climbed in. "Unfortunately I am engaged and waiting for a client but please wait inside while I call you another cab," said the very polite driver. Another taxi soon arrived and Erwin tried to give the first a tip but he waved it off. "Out of the question," he said. I was very impressed.

We went again to Grinzing as we did every night except once when we went to hear Strauss in the Hofgarten and danced a Viennese waltz. The next day Erwin was determined to show me the last of the Hapsburgs. It started with seeing all their funeral coaches which I found depressing; then we had to see their tombs and I frankly had had enough of death, but then we had to go to the Capuchin church where their hearts had been taken out of their bodies and encased in vials! I was not at all eager to see them but Erwin insisted. As we went into the Capuchin church I saw a statue to St. Rita "for the completely hopeless cases" and threw a prayer to her: "If you are for the hopeless cases, then help me, and save me from those hearts!" And she did. Erwin came back very disconsolate after having been told by the monk in charge that the hearts were not on view that day as it was Sunday! I told him I had prayed to St. Rita to save me from them and he was impressed and did not ask me to see them again. He asked me if I had ever prayed to her before and I said I had never heard of her before but might pray to her in the future. We had a St. Anthony who was supposed to help in the case of lost things but he had never done as much for me as St. Rita did.

I was very impressed with the Kunsthistorisches Museum of art, and saw a Breughel there I never forgot; it was "Return of the Hunters," a winter scene which was full of ice and cold and poor people. It was very different from the paintings of aristocrats and kings. The crown of Charlemagne was in that museum.

We took a trip on the Danube up to the monastery of Melk to see the Romanesque manuscripts Erwin had studied as a youth. I had never seen anything earlier than the Gothic. On either side of the Danube I saw my first vines, and the grapes green on them. Melk was tremendous, towering above the river, and I was delighted with the manuscripts and the clear readable Romanesque script so different from the twisted Gothic. On the way back to Vienna we stopped at Heiligenkreuz, a Cistercian monastery, where the monks did not talk but only sang. There were wooden carvings there, of faces, above the choir stalls, and the carved faces looked the same as the singing monks.

Erwin wanted me to see the Salzkammergut mountains, in particular the Traunstein which he had climbed; it had a lake below it, round which he had rowed his brother before his early death. His brother had had a heart defect and it was known he would not live long and Erwin had wanted him to see the glory of the mountains. We would stay at a place called Gmunden but it was difficult to reach; we had to change to a local train at Attnang-Buchheim after a long trip from Vienna.

It was early evening when we arrived at this station and from the train window I had an amazing sight of distant mountains—they looked as though they were of purple gauze, unreal. The sunset light was on them, which they reflected, rose and gold. They were limestone of which marble is made, not granite like the mountains round Vienna. It seemed at sunset that they reflected the marble within, which caused the *Alpenglühen* (Alpenglow). "Would we get there in time to see that light before it fades?" We did. The station was near the lake and we left our bags there and ran to the waterside. I shall never forget it. There were a few white sailing ships still on the lake, but a man was rowing a troop of them to shore for the night, followed by swans. Erwin said that the dining room where we were staying looked out on to another side of the lake where the light stayed longer, and he had booked a table by a window. We should take a taxi, our bags, and get to that table as soon as possible. We did. We saw the lake, an island with a castle on it, and beyond it the mountains which still looked as if they were cut of purple gauze, almost transparent, and the peaks turned rose and then gold and eventually silver and lights came out around the lake. People had been watching in comparative silence but then a waiter came up and asked if we wanted the window shut. The mountain air was suddenly chill but I did not want it shut.

There were lights in the castle on the island in the lake. "That is Johannort,"said Erwin, "there are all sorts of legends about it. They hold concerts there now; perhaps they will have a Lieder concert while we are here." I could think of nothing better than hearing Schubert there and we did. There was a statue to Schubert in the little town of Gmunden. Schubert was supposed never to have traveled but to have lived all his life in Vienna, but under the statue was written in very ungrammatical German, according to Erwin: "The never traveled Schubert here spent a holiday."

It was an enchanting place. We took a boat trip around the lake and to the next lake, Ebensee. Between the two, built on the mountainside, was a church, Traunkirchen, which we visited; flowering graves all around it. Some old women were climbing the steps with us, complaining of their feet, but when we reached the church they broke into song with very sweet voices, *Salve Regina*. It was an old chant to the Virgin. There was a pulpit there, with a wooden carving of a net full of fish, painted silver. They looked very real.

The Traunstein, the mountain—so magical at evening—was also majestic in the day. It was part of the Salzkammergut mountains where salt had been found for centuries. Next to it was another mountain called The Sleeping Greek Woman because one could fancy a Greek profile in the highest ridge of the mountain. Erwin had climbed both as a youth and the highest mountain around, the Dachstein, which looked grim.

The Traunstein looked beautiful at all hours. It had green woods half way up; the peaks glinted gold in the day, turning to rose at evening. We took a small open funicular up to the end of the woods, Grunewald. There were only two seats, opposite each other, and one hung on to the ropes, swinging way over the lake; it was the most birdlike flight I had ever taken, just hanging on to rope with the lake beneath and the mountains rising. There was no one at the top when we landed, but Erwin knew the way to an inn through the woods which was always open to travelers. The first thing we saw on the way up was a huge green tree and underneath, carved in wood and then polished, was a plaque: "When this tree was a sapling, Maria Theresa reigned." It must have been over 200 years old.

We climbed up through the green woods encountering more of these polished wood plaques containing legends of the place. Many referred to the castle in the little island in the lake, Johann Ort. I remember one in particular. "There was a giant called Erlaf who lived in these mountains who fell in love with a nixie (a water nymph) who lived in the lake. He built her that castle on the island and they lived there together happily a summer long." Erwin explained that the wood had been cut aslant across the bole of the huge trees and then polished. Another plaque carried on the tale. "But the joy of a nixie lasts only a summer long. As it began to be autumn, she paled and pined and eventually died. And Erlaf retreated to the mountains and is heard still lamenting when it thunders." It was like walking up through a fairy tale.

The inn was open with lovely refreshing wine. We sat outside and looked down through the trees to the island in the lake. We had Wiener Schnitzel and Apfelstrudel and dark coffee with whipped cream. It was quite a long walk and it was late afternoon when we swung down in the open funicular through the sunset over the lake.

We were rowed over to the castle to hear a Schubert recital there which was all it could be, and it was enchanting to be on the lake at sunset in a small boat. On the return we took the steamer. The tenor even sang "*Nacht und Träume*."

There was another surprise. One evening, as we were strolling after sunset along the promenade under the linden trees, there was the sound of a horn over the lake. "Oh good," said Erwin, "I hoped we would heard the *Echoblasen* (Echo Blowing)." Apparently in summer youths would go out in boats with horns and call to one another in most melodious phrases. He had not known if they still did it; often they waited for moonlit nights, and that night there was a full moon. People stood still and listened. It went on for about half an hour and when the boys returned someone offered them money, which was refused. "Oh no," they said, "We do it to honor our mountains."

I hated to leave Gmunden and the Traunstein, thinking I would never again see any place so beautiful, but Erwin wanted me to see Heiligenblut in the Dolomites and then cross over into Italy by the Lago di Gardo and then by train to Milan from whence we were catching the plane, he back to America, I to England.

Heiligenblut was indeed beautiful, and the Dolomites were higher even than the Salzkammergut mountains, not the glittering limestone but of a dark rock. Erwin had climbed those mountains too, and Heiligenblut was a little village down deep in a valley. It had a legend: the Prince of Denmark was bringing home a vial of Christ's blood from the crusades. "Quite naturally," said Erwin, "the Prince of Denmark instead of returning by sea from the Crusades would cross the highest mountains in Austria, get lost there, and die in the snow. Next spring from the holy blood a flowering tree would spring and the peasants would see it as a command to build a church commemorating it, and a village, *Heiligenblut* (holy blood), would grow around it."

It was only a small village but the guest house had balconies overflowing with flowers, begonias, and I was impressed that the owner was watering them himself.

"One cannot trust anyone else," he told me. The red flowers were bright against the dark mountains which were rather overpowering. Three youths at a neighboring table suddenly burst into yodeling. They were mountaineers, tackling the Dolomites. There was an impressive plaque beside a cairn of stones with an inscription in Latin: "The stones of our mountains honor those who died trying to conquer them."

The Dolomites had changed hands from Italy to Austria and back again and both languages were spoken there. I remember the crossing from Austria into Italy. It was a small station and an old crippled man had come there to see the event of the day, the crossing of the train at the frontier.

Erwin wanted to be on the platform to see the last of Austria and for some reason he waved to the old man, who went crazy. He moved his crutch from one hand to another and with all his heart he waved and Erwin waved back, rather moved, and said he would remember that old man.

In Italy we had our first setback. So far everything had gone according to Erwin's plans but there was a festival in the little village where we were supposed to spend the night before crossing Lake Garda and there were no rooms to be had anywhere. This was bad because it was essential we cross Lake Garda next day in order to get the train to Milan for the plane to go home. Erwin spoke fluent Italian and eventually found a taxi driver who was willing to drive us up the mountain to his brother's tavern, which had rooms, and he would fetch us in the morning in order to catch the boat. It sounded risky; suppose he didn't come back, and we would be stuck up on the mountain, but Erwin was serene, it would be all right. We started off and it grew darker and darker and there were no lights on the mountain and the road grew smaller and smaller.

Eventually we arrived, but where were we? It looked like the smugglers' tavern in Carmen; the village seemed to be this tavern lit within, brigands seated outside, a fountain, lamp and darkness all around. They had schnapps and cognac, but no food. We were hungry. I hastily gulped a cognac and lo! a young man appeared who had vanished into darkness but came back with ham, cheese and salad from his father's deli somewhere in the darkness, for which he would accept no money. "We seldom have visitors," he said, "and never from overseas." The cognac and food had its effect; it seemed a stage setting now, I could not believe it was real. They were very kind, produced coffee and rolls in the morning; the taxi driver arrived and we caught the boat.

Lake Garda produced "lovely, laughing Sirmio," the island where Ovid was exiled, many Roman buildings, Romanesque churches. It was as if we had gone back centuries. We caught the train to Milan with its wedding cake Gothic church, and we did see "The Last Supper" before catching the plane back to the twentieth century.

Chapter 75

After the Ph.D.

It was sweet to be called "Dr. Wilson." I did enjoy it. I taught three classes of different time periods, including the Honors class, gifted students who would be given extra work but would graduate with Honors. It was a delight to teach them, to see their interest when an idea was thrown out, to discuss it and see their responses. I grew to know them all quite well and quite a few turned into Humanities majors including a boy named James. He was interested in becoming a lawyer, not to earn money but to help poor people and the Law schools encouraged Humanities students to apply as they had more general knowledge than most, providing of course their grades were high.

I also sat in on the Junior and Senior Humanities Seminars taught by a very brilliant young man, Dr. Andrews, who was the textual Shakespeare scholar the Dean had mentioned. He chose *Mimesis* by Erich Auerbach as the text book for the Junior Seminar, and *Irrational Man* for the Senior in order to teach Existentialism, which had become very popular. I felt *Mimesis* though fascinating as a history of European literature was as hard as many graduate courses, and while I enjoyed it and learned a lot could see it was hard for the undergraduates, particularly as Dr. Andrews chose to teach it as a three-hour class once a week. It introduced the Humanities majors into literature that most had not read, Cervantes, St. Thomas More, Erasmus.

Erwin suggested he read Goethe to me. I did not know *Wilhelm Meister* or *Dichtung und Wahrheit* (Poetry and Truth) and so we agreed that on the weekends, which had been devoted for years to study, he should read these books to me. I did enjoy them, particularly *Dichtung und Wahrheit* in which I learned a great deal of European history that would be of use in teaching Humanities.

I particularly remember Goethe writing that when he was a young boy, Marie Antoinette came through Frankfurt on her way to marry Louis XVI of France. (Apparently this was the meeting place where her Austrian entourage left her and the French troops took over). She was presented with a wedding veil with an acanthus pattern, like the one described in the *Aeneid* as being given to Dido. Goethe as a boy felt this was an evil omen. He somehow managed to make the eighteenth century come alive.

Chapter 76

Family

My eldest son, John, graduated in Geography and obtained a position in the State Department of Transportation, and later a graduate degree in Urban Planning. It was a very long and hard MS degree, as hard as my PhD I often thought. He was married very young to Nancy who was the most beautiful girl and became more like a daughter than a daughter-in-law. They produced Jennifer who was the delight of my life, a fairy child. At nine months she said her first word, which was "flower," pointing to one of my African violets. At three she took dancing lessons and I went with her and was allowed to watch. I started taking her to Sunday school when she was that age and then she came home to lunch with me, and after playing hide-and-seek all through the house and hopscotch on the paved terrace outside, she danced for me. When she was about eight she started improvising to the music of Josef Strauss, "Village Swallows." She had on her Sunday school dress with a flimsy white skirt. The dance remained more or less the same, around a small cushion, up on to the arm chair, down and around, and up to the windowsill and then a leap into the room, pirouettes, and arabesques, ending with a somersault.

JENNIFER

Stay forever child
contemplating music,
how to move your thoughts
In dance,
whether wing, cartwheel or horse,
whether girl you soon will be
Curve of waltz,
insouciance
into
somersault.

She once said, "I have a wish but it is impossible. I want a cloud, that one up there, to lie on." She was a child of mine. I told her that if we both looked long and carefully at the cloud we could keep it in our minds forever, so we looked and remained silent. Years later the Post Office came out with cloud stamps and I sent them to her. She found they also did cloud post cards and sent them to me, so I guess she remembered.

John and Nancy had two more daughters, Ryan and Daron Allison (she chose to be called Allison). Soon after the birth of the latter I received the greatest shock. John had been offered a job with the Federal Government in Mobile, more than three hours away. Three years later he was offered the position of Safety Director of Lee County in Fort Myers, eight hours away. Our visits perforce grew less but I did get down to see Jennifer perform in several musicals at her High School, in which she had a star dancing and singing part. I recall "Sweet charity" and 42nd Street." We always managed to pick up the threads when we met and I recalled what the Jesuits said: Give me a child until he is five years old and he is mine for life.

I grew attached to the other children too. Ryan was a mathematician which I discovered when I gave her a puzzle that involved putting rings of various sizes in correct order on three poles. She might have been seven. She said, "I must have a pattern." Allison was about four when I visited their new house in Fort Myers, which had very modern faucets that I could not understand so I asked her help. "I didn't know an Oma (German for grandmother) couldn't use faucets." When I swam in the pool next day, she said "I didn't know an Oma could swim." She made me laugh and she was also an acrobat. I missed them all very much.

Throughout High School Andrew lived for baseball, and in his senior year his team, with him as pitcher, won the State championship for a school his size. All his friends were on the team, and his schooldays were happy ones in spite of missing his father. He was twice offered a summer scholarship at the Baptist-run baseball camp in Black Mountain, N.C. He had always been very religious, and was an acolyte at St. John's Episcopal church throughout high school. He was offered a Baseball Scholarship at a small liberal Arts College, Birmingham Southern, run by Methodists. I hoped FSU would offer him one but none was forthcoming and his coach advised him to take the opportunity. He was young to leave home, only seventeen, having skipped Second Grade. At the time I was only a teaching assistant with very little money and the scholarship was a godsend. Andrew also took three other jobs; he did the stats for the school games, became "grandfather" of his dorm which involved several duties, and worked in a department store from whence he bought us all lovely clothes for Christmas. He did not cost me one penny for his college degree. He must have been one of the few Phys. Ed majors who obtained Phi Beta Kappa; he studied Greek in order to read the New Testament in that language. He obtained another scholarship for his graduate degree at the University of Tennessee, and was afterwards offered the position of Assistant Baseball Coach at his Alma Mater, Birmingham Southern. Later, when the Head Coach left, at a very early age, he was given the opportunity of taking this position. He told me he had become tired of the win-win-win syndrome and more interested in religion and had joined the Fellowship of Christian Athletes. He had met Susan, who had a graduate degree in Nursing, and when they married decided to take a position with the FCA. Unfortunately it became more and more difficult to hold religious meetings on college campuses, so he and Susan went to Pensacola where she had a fine nursing position, and he became certified to teach Math and Science as well as Physical Education in Middle School which he did for some years and coached baseball. Then he taught in a school for dropouts for he was always a ministering type and wanted to help people. When it closed he returned to public school. They had two sons, AJ and Aaron, and they were the most devoted parents. AJ was a track star and Aaron brilliant academically, President of his Senior Class. John and Andrew are very private people and they would not want me to include more of their lives.

With Keith it is rather different. From the time Andrew left home at seventeen, and John went to live in at Sigma Nu and then married young, Keith became the man of the house at twelve. One of his first suggestions was that we make a garden and by this he meant it in the English sense, a flower garden. I suggested roses, not realizing how difficult they were to grow here. He rented a tiller and ploughed up insidious ardesia, a very hard task. He then enriched the soil. We studied catalogs, and experimented with many different roses, some of which I knew from England. They needed a great deal of care and sprays of various kinds. He had to get up early to water them, but he did produce wonderful roses. I painted water colors of some of them. I discovered new flowers, particularly Impatience which did well here and various kinds of begonias. Annuals did better than perennials or so it seemed to me at first. We both worked hard in the garden.

We found Calloway Gardens in North Georgia, about four hours away, and visited there in spring and fall for a few days each year. Keith remembered gardens he had seen in England and I determined to get him back there and show him Manor Farm, if only from the road. He loved to hear of England, its history, and about my family and childhood. I realized my walk round the lake at Manor Farm when I was pregnant with him had born fruit. I had prayed "This child shall have something of England." Indeed he has He remembered Kings College Chapel at Cambridge and the boys singing at Evensong. We saw Kings one Christmas eve on television and had tapes of the carols. All the boys liked them. We always started Christmas morning with them.

Keith was not a reader but he had a photographic memory and he liked a good phrase. I was watching *Macbeth* on TV one day and he came in and heard "Stars, hold your fires, lest you see my deep and dark desires." He never forgot that. I was worried that he never read a book but somehow managed to get A's on book reports. One day I brought him Hemingway's *The Old Man and the Sea*, a short book, and said he was to stay in his room till he had finished it. He was there hours and came out with tears streaming down his face. "Look what you have done to me, Mum," he said, "you've ruined me!" I never saw him read a book again except *The Wit and Wisdom of Winston Churchill* which he discovered for himself. He heard some Churchill speeches on TV and was a Churchill fan from then on. I told him I remembered hearing the speeches over the radio in WWII and he wanted to know all I could tell.

When Andrew was at Birmingham Southern he invited his brother up for a football game. It was the first time Keith had flown alone and I advised him of the dangers at airports. Apparently he was accosted by a neo-Nazi group who asked him to join. "No thanks," he said, "I'm on the way to Temple, Shalom!" Not bad for fifteen!

He was voted the wittiest in his class. I could believe that. He had an ear for repartee and dialogue. He liked English humor and remembered Ken's remark when I once made the tea too weak. Ken said, "*It* can hardly crawl out of the pot" and Keith never forgot that. I called him "Yorick" because he could set the table on a roar at the drop of a hat. Erwin thought he should go on the stage but he was never interested in taking part in anything like that at school. He was just funny when he was with friends and he has always liked making people laugh with something of my father's humor, but he is kinder. He is an individual, like my sister, and she appreciated him.

Chapter 77

Teaching and next trip to Europe.

I loved teaching and was pleased when James was again in my Honors class but was disturbed to find he was on probation for Honors. During the last term he had Bs and even a C in a class not with me. I asked him the reason and he said he had been lobbying with the Legislature to pass a Landlord/Student Rent Act which would force the landlord to spray annually for cockroaches. He said students' apartments were overrun with cockroaches and he was the student member of a committee to try and remedy this. He had been forced to miss some classes and other people's notes had not helped him much.

I told him that Law School insisted on highest grades and he was putting his future at stake for he might not be accepted if he continued with this outside work and his grades dropped. He was so earnest. "This is something that I have to do now to help the students; no one else is interested, it is my duty." He promised once it was through (and he felt it would go through this term if he continued lobbying) he would not do anymore outside work He was so dedicated I could not persuade him, so I made a bargain with him. I knew he lived in student quarters near me for I often saw him bicycling home. I offered him a choice. If he promised to start no more lobbying once this bill was through, I would ask him to my house and go over in the evening the lecture I had given that day. He was grateful and he came regularly if he missed a class, and I learned something of teaching from it—the difficulties a student had if he had not studied world history in High School. I realized I would have to throw in a little more history. We became good friends and when I gave a paper in Orlando I stayed with his mother and father, a Presbyterian minister.

From them I learned an interesting fact. The father had a church in rural North Carolina for many years, and his parishioners were mostly descendants of Scottish highlanders who had emigrated when the clans had been disbanded after the Battle of Culloden in 1746. At a funeral it was a tradition with them to try and leap into the grave and the clergyman had to hold them back, which recalled the situation when Hamlet tries to leap into Ophelia's grave. I had never thought of this as a tradition.

My sister in England was anxious I come over the next summer and see the plot she had bought in North Wales and how her cottage was being built. She found a site looking over the bay to Harlec, the mountains all around and the ruins of a twelfth-century castle crowning the village of Criccieth. Mummy was content; she had been very happy in Wales during the war, and she had had enough of trailing up to London for the theatres. Television brought her much satisfaction. After selling the flat to the woman Erwin said would buy it they had moved to what Bettina called a "shack" in Criccieth while the cottage was being built. There was just room enough for me. I hesitated leaving Keith but he was happy to board with Betty for a few weeks. Her son was his age, born the same year, and they were very close.

Erwin was going to Vienna again and he asked me to join him, and we would take the trip to Traunstein. I would only be gone a month. The dollar was high at that time and the Atlantic ticket much cheaper than it later was. I arrived in London and was not feeling at all well, and not sure if I could make the trip to Vienna, but Ray took me to her doctor and he gave me something which made me feel better. He came from Vienna himself and told me to have an *Einspanner* for him, black coffee with whipped cream. Erwin met me at the airport and I expected we would go that evening to Grinzing. He said that he had gone to the Capuchin church to pray to the *heilige* Rita that I would get better and come and as he left the church he saw a placard advertising that the Mozart choir boys would be singing in *Schönbrunn* for one occasion, the night I arrived, so he had bought tickets. I had been disappointed the year before not to have heard them.

I had an *Einspanner* in the *Schönbrunn* café for the doctor. The white salon in which the boys sang was a long room filled with mirrors and white pillars decorated with fine golden ornamentation. It was the most beautiful filigree rococo, and when the boys entered in their eighteenth century costumes with their wigs and youthful faces it was a time warp. I remember one boy with an exquisite line of jaw and his mirror image. Someone announced a change of program; they were going to sing Mozart's "*Exultate Jubilate*" which I had loved since I was twelve. It was a high moment which is still etched in memory. When we came out the air was chill from the mountains around and after the heavy heat of a Florida summer was magical.

We took a bus trip to Semmering, the nearest high mountain to Vienna and walked in fields filled with Alpine flowers. It was forbidden to pick any. Erwin said the soil was so scarce up there they were more flowers of the sun than the soil and very fragile. He named the various mountains around and I was interested to learn that the mountain on which the summer solstice fire was lit was not the highest. He explained that there were solstice fires lit on mountain peaks all through the Austrian Alps and it depended how far a mountain could be seen through gaps, not necessarily the highest. From one solstice fire you could see another all through the Alps. The mountain that seemed highest from down below where we were might be blocked by another. I had not known that fires were lit on mountain peaks for the summer solstice; it seemed very pagan for such a Catholic country. He said he would take me to an inn on the Danube built in Roman times where a fourth-century Bacchus statue still upheld the mantel.

On a walk we took round the walls of old Vienna, we saw that most had been torn down for the Ringstrasse. We heard a grandfather instructing his small granddaughter. "The Romans were here," he said, "and we threw them out. Napoleon was here and we threw him out. The Nazis were here and we threw them out." Hardly accurate historical information, but the child murmured "*Freilich*" after each ejection, which could be translated "Of course."

We had one terrifying experience. Erwin was anxious we take a funicular up to a glacier so that I could see a crevice in the ice which would be green/blue. I was not so keen on this but he said I had a good eye for heights as I always stood in the front of a funicular. That was to see the view better, but I was not enthusiastic about walking on ice with just a rope staked at various places to hold. He said I would enjoy it; I did not. I have never been so frightened in my life, not even in the London Blitz. There were three other men who came up in the funicular and I watched them venture out on the ice. There was a foothold path across the top of a precipice, not more than a foot wide and miles of ice down on each side. They swayed from side to side with the rope. "I can't do it," I told Erwin, "I'm not a mountaineer." "I will go ahead," he said, "and hold the rope taut for you, and you will look down a crevice in the glacier and see the blue green ice that the children saw in Stifter's *Bergkristal.*

I would willingly have foregone the experience but did not want to disappoint Erwin, who was looking forward to showing it to me. He went ahead when it was our turn and got to the first stake and then twisted the rope around it somehow so it did not sag to one side so much. I realized the men were heavier than I was and would swing out further.

Perhaps as Erwin held the rope taut I would not sway out so much and am sure he made it better, but I seemed to hang over miles of precipice on either side as I put my foot down on the narrow path. It was about sixteen feet staked every four feet. I reached the crevice at last and indeed it was an explosion of blue and green down deep in it. The return seemed even worse and I was shaking when I at last arrived back at the funicular.

I had never tasted Schnapps before but when one of the men offered me his flask, I took it. It tasted like cherry brandy that Daddy had let us sip after riding, and I immediately felt better. Erwin took some too. The men congratulated me particularly when they learned I had never been on a glacier before. I did not intend ever to go on one again.

That experience must have been after we went to the Traunstein. There were no glaciers around Vienna. Traunstein was just as beautiful as ever and we had two unforgettable experiences there. We went somehow on many little trains, to Kremsmünster where Stifter had been educated. It was one of the special places Erwin wished to show me. It had a mathematical cloister.

KREMSMÜNSTER

To you was given the key
of the door in the wall
into fantasy,
a white arcaded cloister,
full of geometry.

Four square pools
with fountains,
white arches in between
reflecting liquid dancing
and scattering parabolas,
a glittering perspective
to another fairy tale.

Chapter 78

The fairy tale. "The New Paris."

Back in Florida when Erwin had been reading Goethe's *Poetry and Truth* to me, he omitted a fairy tale Goethe had written when he was thirteen, saying he would tell it to me somewhere in Austria. I reminded him of this and he said I should choose the place I liked best around the Traunsee. I chose Traunkirchen which was built on a small promontory between the two lakes of Traunsee and Ebensee. As we went by on the boat which ran every hour from Gmunden, I noticed there was a seat at the end with a willow and a poplar. Nobody ever seemed to be sitting there. Erwin agreed it would be a good place, and we could take a return boat when the tale was finished. We went there one afternoon. Traunsee lay before us with little white sailboats skimming all over, and white dignified swans taking their slower way; they seemed the spirits of the place.

Traunstein and the Sleeping Greek mountain lay before us. I could conjure up the Sleeping Greek in my mind's eye, the sloping forehead and nose never seemed to change, but the Traunstein was always changing. Crags of light gold leapt out from the darker gold but at different angles. I remembered Bill Donovan telling me marble was built from limestone and it had iron in it which made the stone appear lit from within. So it was with the Traunstein, but its shape was different when seen from Traunkirchen or Gmunden. I tried to fix it in my mind's eye, but the light and shadows seemed to move all the time.

Goethe was a precocious child and a brilliant scholar of Latin and Greek at twelve, so Erwin believed he really had written the story of "The New Paris" at thirteen; he was also aware of the Arabian Nights which were coming into fashion in the eighteenth century.

It starts with Goethe being fitted for his new Easter costume and being very pleased with what he saw in the mirror, a satin flared coat and knee breeches and a flowing cravat at the neck such as the Mozart choirboys wore. Suddenly there was a cosmic swoosh and a young man stood before him with wings on his ankles. He bowed to Goethe and said: "do you know who I am?" "You are Mercury," answered Goethe, bowing. "I have a task for you, take up one of the three apples that are in the bowl on the table," said Mercury. Goethe took up a red apple. "Hold it to the light." Goethe obeyed. It turned transparent in his hand, it turned to glass and then to a ruby in the middle of which was a beautiful young woman dressed in red, playing an instrument, and faint music was heard.

"Put that down and take up another," commanded Mercury. Goethe took up a golden apple. The same thing happened, he held it to the light, it became transparent, turned to glass and then topaz and in the centre was a lovely laughing girl with a harp, and the music sounded sweeter than before. "Take up the last apple," ordered Mercury and Goethe obeyed. It was green, and when held to the light was first transparent, then glass and then an emerald, and in the centre was a girl playing music on a lyre, and she was the most entrancing of all to Goethe. "Your task," said Mercury, "is to find husbands for these girls" and vanished while Goethe fell to the ground.

It was sometime before he regained consciousness but he remembered all that had happened and could not wait to tell his friends, but first there was the long dinner with his grandfather to get through, and although he had been looking forward to showing off his Easter costume, he could not wait for dinner to be over so he could find his friends.

The nearest friend was not home, he had gone to play in the park. His two other closest friends were with him. Goethe was a little disquieted. Frankfurt was still a walled city but in certain parts the forest outside had crept in and to get to the park he would have to pass this place alone, but he would have his friends with him when they returned in the evening when it was sometimes rather spooky there. When he reached this place he was surprised to see a beech tree growing amid the pines, which was unusual. He slowed down and opposite the beech tree he saw a plaque in the wall he had not noticed before and under it a little spring. He stopped and to his amazement saw a gate in the wall, a gate of wrought iron intricately twisted with what looked like letters but were not.

He stared at it, the wrought iron was new and magical. He peered closer to see if he could decipher it but decided it must be in some unknown language, perhaps runes.

The door opened and a man in grey stood there. Goethe bowed, "I was admiring your gate." "It is even more beautiful on the other side, please come in." Goethe hesitated, he had been told not to speak to strangers but through the gate he could now see a glimpse of lawns and flowers. He followed the man and saw velvet green lawns shining like glass reflecting blue flowers. He gasped "Is it possible to go nearer?" "It is" was the reply, "on certain conditions. You would have to remove your new costume with your sword, and dress in a robe and turban as we do here." Gone was Goethe's pride in his brave new clothes, he willingly followed the man across the shining lawns to a little green pavilion where he was given a robe and turban to wear. Around the walls were hanging whips and there was a green one among them. Goethe remembered a tale from the Arabian Nights where a green whip meant death. "Why are these things here?" he asked. "They are for those who do not obey our rules."

"Well, I'm not going to disobey any rules" he thought. The man in grey then led him through the gardens down to a bridge across a river which seemed to be made of slats for one could see the green water running beneath.

Across the river was a larger pavilion from whence came sweet music. They entered and to his amazement Goethe saw the three beautiful women he had seen in the transparent apples turned to jewels. There was also a little girl there, about

Goethe's age, who was playing the music. The woman in red greeted him: "You have come to hear us play," she said; "I will begin," and she played what seemed to be a stirring march which was thrilling to hear. Then the girl in gold played and Goethe felt she was the most beautiful girl he had ever seen, and he could not take his eyes off her. Then it was the turn of the girl in green and her music pleased him even more, he felt it was calling to him and leading him where he wished to go. When she ended the woman in red said "Alerta, take our guest for some refreshment."

The little girl arose and led Goethe to another room where a table was set with the most delicious food, but he knew not to eat strange food so he only took a grape. "Do you like toys?" the little girl asked him. Goethe denied this; he was thirteen, beyond toys. "A pity," she said as she led him through another room filled with forts and castles with moats around them and he was rather sorry as he would have liked to examine these. "We will play at soldiers," she then said and took him to a table on which were arrayed the armies of the world, the Greeks, the Trojans, the Romans, even the Amazons.

He chose Hektor and the Trojans and she chose the Amazons. "We will go and play on the bridge, the slats will give us direction," she said, so they picked up their soldiers on trays, together with cannons, and went outside. She explained the rules; the cannons were to be kept at the back and not moved beyond a certain point. They were then to shoot at each other's soldiers and try and knock them down. It soon became apparent that Goethe was better than she at shooting and she became agitated and moved her cannons forward. He protested but she took no notice and began shooting off the arms and legs of his soldiers. He saw they soon reassembled themselves and so he moved his cannons forward and shot her queen. She said "You have spoilt everything" and started to move away, crying. Goethe was very sorry and called her to return and she would not but went away, still crying. The man in grey appeared and said "You have disobeyed our rules."

There was a commotion but Goethe pulled himself up and said, "You have no control over me. It depends on me whether those women obtain husbands or if they stay forever just playing music in this beautiful garden." "Who told you that?" "Mercury." "Then come with me and take off those clothes and don your own and leave." As the man in grey led him to the gate Goethe said, "shall I ever be able to come back here again?" "Look well what you see," was the reply. "See the gate opposite the beech tree, with a plaque beside it and a spring beneath. If ever you can find the gate opposite the beech tree with a plaque beside and a spring beneath, you will be able to return" said the man and shut the gate.

Goethe ran as fast as he could to the park to find his friends and tell them this amazing tale. They all returned at once but it was already dark and they could find nothing. They returned the next day and the next and for many days and weeks and they could never find the gate opposite the beech tree with the plaque and the spring beneath. Once when Goethe was alone he thought he saw the plaque, but no gate beside it. Another boy saw the beech tree, he said, and this amazed Goethe for it was his story. He was never able to return to the enchanted garden.

The sun had almost gone down when Erwin finished this tale. "Now you must tell it soon to someone else so you don't forget it. Tell it to your sister on your Welsh mountains next week; you have a good memory, you will remember it. Don't try and look it up in *Poetry and Truth* for you will find it is different there. I have added things and you will when you tell it; that is how fairy tales are made." I was silent, felt under a spell as the light changed on the Traunstein turning from gold to rose, and then to silver, and the sailing ships were towed home, followed by swans.

I did tell it to my sister on the Welsh mountains and she was enchanted. "I hope I remember it," she said. "I could write it out for you," I replied. "Oh no," was her emphatic response, "such tales should not be read, they must be told," which was just what Erwin had said.

We made an excursion to Ischl where the Kaiser used to vacation. It was a short train ride. The river Traun was a deep green from the ice and on either side were beautiful houses built by aristocrats and rich men who also spent their vacations there. The composer Lehar had a house, and Richard Tauber. They were of different colors and their reflections were seen in the river. There was a bridge over the Traun with a mountain behind it. I liked to stop there to see the dark green of the river with its reflections and to enjoy the swooping flights of the swallows. I realized how I had missed the swallows in Florida. There was an elegant café, "Esplanade," where the Kaiser used to dine and his photo was still in the restaurant.

RIVER HOUSES

Engulfed below the restless stream
rectangular reflections
are gold stability,
the only permanence.
The drowning houses hold
against the water's pull
through diving arcs of swallow wings
and stay.

———————————

There are inns so old on the Danube
that the Roman god of wine
is carved in stone on the lintel
upholding the centuries

———————————

In the cloister of Heiligenkreuz
a tree and fountain are centered
easing the treadmill mind.
In the chancel the saints meditate
with brows and bones of tender wood
surrounding eyes at peace.
Cistercian monks of silence
whose voices only sing

release Gregorian chant.
Through Guiliano's cloister
where Christ the servant kneels
to wash St. Peter's feet
the monks retire
with faces carved in dignity,
their white robed silence
changing
into stone.

Our last excursion was to Aussee where there were some of the oldest salt mines in the world. I did not want to go down through them because I did not like caves but we saw a very interesting museum with Celtic remains thousands of years old, some of the earliest artifacts of Western civilization. It was from there that Erwin suggested we take a funicular to above the tree line and walk a little way up to the Talschluss (the end of the valley). From there we could see the great Dachstein mountain which he had once climbed. "No glaciers?" I asked anxiously. He said we would be far from the ice, we would just see the snow on the top of the distant mountain. It would be no further to walk than we had already walked up the Grunewald. We set off from where the funicular ended and soon came to the end of the tree line, the mountain proper, a little further and we would see the Dachstein.

It was not so easy walking as in the woods for it was already on the rock and little stones, scree, ran down at each step. Erwin showed me how to put my feet in sideways so as not to slip and he said that next year we should get real mountain boots and sticks; my ankles became tired and I hoped it was not too far before we saw the Dachstein. We had to round a corner of one slope and then we saw it, a tremendous mountain. I could not understand how it could be climbed. Erwin said he had climbed higher in another part of the Alps but this was the *Dach* (the roof) of this part of the world. I stood in awe and shuddered a little. "Which do you like best, the mountains or the woods?" I asked. "Oh the woods," he said, "they are more friendly to man, the mountains can be cruel."

I found it harder going down than climbing up, scree kept slipping beneath my feet. I remembered that long ago on the Dolomites, climbing with my cousins, I had run down the mountain, the slipping stones lending wings to my feet. I tried it and found it much easier. Erwin said he had never heard of anyone running down a mountain and I could easily slip. I felt if I side-stepped as he wanted I would soon sprain an ankle and said I must, it was the only way I could get down. I ran ahead a little and then waited for him, enjoying the view. He looked much more tired than I did when we eventually reached the funicular but he recovered and that night we heard the echo blowing and went to a Lieder recital at Johannort.

Next day we returned to Vienna and spent our last evening in Grinzing. The next day he put me on the plane for London and then took a flight back to the States. He would phone me in Tallahassee as soon as I returned from England, in about two weeks.

It rained nearly all the time I was in Wales, and I hoped Bettina had done the right thing. How would she see Ronnie? Mummy would go to the hotel in Criccieth for a few days and she and Ronnie would meet at Bettgellert where they had often spent time together.

Andrew and Keith met me at Tallahassee airport and they seemed glad to see me. Erwin phoned that night, he did not sound well and he said he had back pains and a pain at his side. I asked why he had not gone to the doctor. His doctor was his oldest friend in America; I had met him when on a trip to New York to study the Metropolitan Museum and the MOMA. He said his doctor had just gone on holiday when he returned and he did not like the partner. He would see his doctor tomorrow and phone me in the evening. Next day the doctor phoned and told me Erwin had died of a heart attack in his office.

Chapter 79

Afterwards.

"He died while life was still sweet on his lips; he told me you had seen the Dachstein," the doctor said. He also was from Austria and had climbed with Erwin in their youth. I could say nothing but remembered the stone memorial we had seen the year before in Heiligenblut. It had a Latin inscription honoring those who had died climbing the mountains. Erwin had said that was how he would like to die instead of in a hospital in a foreign land. In a way that was how he did because I think the ascent from or the descent back to Aussee had brought about his heart attack.

I had found no words to write about Howard's death. It is as if words have to do with life, not death. I froze as I did at Howard's death. I told Keith and we both went to Erwin's church with the windows of Chartres blue, and lit candles. Erwin had said that candles were the souls of prayers and helped the dead; he was very catholic in many ways. I do remember crossing the road with Keith and tears suddenly streamed down my face. Keith was horrified: "Don't cry

Mum, can't bear to see you cry." His face was aghast and I realized I had to pull myself together for him and choked back tears. He was only twelve and had suffered two violent deaths. Erwin had become a sort of father figure to him; for the last year he had coached him in Math on Sunday afternoons. Erwin was appalled at how little the boy knew and how little he seemed to care. I had said I thought American education at the time believed in the child going at his own pace, and Keith's pace in Seventh Grade was being funny and spitballs. He told me later he had learned quite a bit from Dr. Biel. I could never cry again; sometimes I wanted to, but the tears would not come. I had choked them back so severely.

The next day I had an urgent call from Dr. Goodman, the chairman of Undergraduate Humanities. Dr. Andrews had left to take a better job at the Folger Shakespeare Museum. Could I teach the Junior and Senior Seminars for Humanities majors? There would be an increase in salary. I asked about a line item, but he said the only line item for Humanities was for him. I would still be an adjunct but with better pay. I said I could, I had a week to prepare before classes began. I asked if I could teach the Seminar twice a week for one and a half hours, instead of a three-hour period once a week. Dr. Goodman agreed; he thought three hours was too long for undergraduates.

I was thankful I had sat in while Dr. Andrews taught *Mimesis*. I had verbatim notes, too many, and had to divide each lecture in half and simplify. I was thankful to have so much work to do. Erwin's funeral was held at Rutgers and Seymour Hess from the Meteorology Dept. went up as representative from FSU.

I had a great success teaching the Junior Seminar to the Humanities majors. James was among them. He had kept his word and done no further lobbying although he told me there was much that needed to be done. I told him it was crucial he get good grades this year so as to get into Law School. I had simplified the material for the Seminar and opened it up to discussion by asking leading questions. Ingrid had taught me how. Erwin had said it was crucial to learn the lecture by heart so as to be able to attain eye contact with students and to learn their names and call upon them by name. It was hard to learn the lecture by heart beforehand but I knew from my student days how much more alive it sounded if not read from notes, so persevered. Lively discussions ensued and I realized how intelligent these young minds were, just waiting to be given some live ideas and how much could be learned by tossing them around.

The seminar went well and so did my other two courses. Teaching was a lifeline; I had to concentrate on next day's class. In the middle of the term, I had another blow. We had a new president whom no one liked and he fired Robert Lawton, Dean of Arts and Sciences, who had helped and tried to get me a Line while my major professor would not help by having me teach one course in English. Dr. Goldman, my chairman, informed me that I would not be funded for next term; adjuncts appointed by Dean Lawton were fired. He had gone to the Acting Dean and said that I was urgently needed to teach the Senior Seminar on Existentialism next term, but it was no good. I was already busy preparing it. "Who will teach it?" I asked Dr. Goodman; "you've said you could never teach Existentialism." "I don't know," he snapped, "but I've done all I could for you. Now don't you go trying yourself."

Seven years hard work, eight and a half now counting the teaching as an adjunct, and I was to be fired. It was as if the world had come crashing down around me. I was in need of money too, as I no longer received anything from Social Security or Veterans for the older boys. What was I to do? I went to Erwin's church and prayed.

The next day I received a packet in the mail from Vienna. It was a poster of Grinzing, no note in it. Erwin must have had it sent the last night we were in Austria and it just now arrived. Through a gate in a wine garden it showed the little winding street at twilight, lamp lit, with doors opening on to other gardens and at the end of the street the floodlit church with the clock at 8 p.m. I could even make out a green wreath hanging on the first door. I felt it was a *Gruss*, a greeting from Erwin telling me not to despair, another synchronicity.

The same week James asked me in the seminar what we were going to study next term. The students knew the Junior Seminar would be followed by the Senior. I had to tell them that I would not be teaching it as I had not been funded for next term. There was a gasp of horror all around and the students wanted to know why. I told them that I was an adjunct hired by the Dean of Arts and Sciences who had also been fired and that the Humanities Chairman had gone to the new Acting Dean on my behalf, but in vain. I was gratified they seemed so dismayed.

A few days later James came to me with a typed statement signed by sixty students asking that I be reinstated as I was a very good teacher. Some had also appended their own appreciation of me and it did warm my heart. "How did you get sixty signatures?" I asked James, there were only twenty in the class. "I found out when your other classes were held and arrived early and asked the students if any wanted to sign, and they all did." I was very touched. If I could still have cried I would have, but no tears came. "I do not know to whom to give it, "James said. "I thought you would know best." I was in a quandary. Dr. Goodman had told me expressly not to go the Acting Dean; what was I to do? As I stood there in the corridor the Chaplain of the University came by, Dr. Robert Spivey. I knew him and asked his advice, telling him Dr. Goodman had told me not to do anything. "Give the signatures and statement to me," said Dr. Spivey, "I will see to it." A few days later Dr. Goodman glared at me when I entered the office. "I don't know what you have done," he said, "but you have been re-funded." I told him I had not gone to the Acting Dean, but a student had given me a statement signed by sixty students, all my students in fact, asking that I be reinstated as I was an excellent teacher, and I had asked Dr. Spivey for advice and he had taken it to the Acting Dean. "If I didn't need you so badly, I'd fling you back in his face" was Dr. Goodman's response. "At least I won't have to teach Existentialism." He was a difficult man, but he taught Romantic poetry very well, and I never forgot that.

I did not feel secure, as I had to be re-funded every term; it was like living on a tightrope. I lived for teaching and for Keith, who did his best to cheer me up. He would leave me little notes: "Darn good meal last night, love, Me" or "Peppers were great, love, Me" or "Enjoy our beautiful garden, love, Me". We took to going out to dinner once a week and he would ask me to tell him about England and the family. I thought I would take him to Europe with me next time and maybe we could make a pilgrimage to Zwettl which was a special place Erwin and I had not had time to see as it was near the Czech border and too far away from the mountains. There was a monastery there he had loved. Ray had written me I could have a Requiem said there for Erwin. Sim had died and she wanted to go to Vienna to try and see about the pension she should receive on his behalf. Austria was trying to repay refugees or their dependents who had had to leave Austria.

I thought about Erwin a lot. He was strange in many ways. He believed in messages from birds. At first I had told him he was nothing but an old Roman augurer, but he said I should not laugh at him. He grew up in the mountains where it was easy to speak to God as I knew from my youth in the woods and hills; then he was transported to New Jersey, where there were no mountains or woods; he only had the birds. "How did they speak to you?" I asked. "Well, if I needed to make a decision I would focus on a tree if I could find one or else on a roof top and if a flock flew in from the right the decision would be in the affirmative, if from the left, the negative, and if no birds came then I was on my own." I remembered Jung and his synchronicities. Erwin thought highly of Jung, who had also been a mountain man. Erwin too was very much in favor of noting synchronicities, symbols. If he saw the colors *rot-weiss-rot* (red-white-red) on a laundry van or poster he was pleased; it was a reference to Austria. He knew Kübler—Ross and liked the story she told of a child she loved who had died, who had liked ladybirds. When she went to put a wreath on his grave, she saw a ladybird there and was happy about it.

He also had a habit of saying "it has been told to me" and by this he meant he had heard in his head a voice saying something to which he should listen, as for instance, when he had seen the *heilige* Rita in the Capuchin church and then a poster outside announcing the Mozartknaben Chor singing the night I arrived in Vienna and he had been told to get tickets.

The Christmas after he died I was given Mahler's Ninth symphony on record. Keith had suggested someone give it to me as he knew I had the others. It was still on vinyl and it came in a cover with Aussee on it, where we went on our last trip. I did not think too much about that. I knew Mahler had written the Ninth there and it was concerned with death. I was given many red poinsettias for Christmas that year and had planted them in the garden and for once they flourished. I remembered Patricia had said red was the color of resurrection in the Greek Orthodox church, and I was pleased with their flaming red spikes. Next I kept hearing a voice telling me to read "The Four Quartets." I knew them well, had studied them, and had a new course to prepare for the next term so thought I would wait, but I kept getting nudges, even an article in the local paper saying it was the most profound work of the 20th century and everyone should read it once a year.

Then I got the flu and was in bed, very weak, when I got the voice again, so I took it from the shelf and started to read. It was not till the last quartet, "Little Gidding," that I came across "the communication of the dead is tongued with fire beyond the language of the living" and out of my window I could see the red flames of the poinsettias. At the same time I was listening to Mahler's Ninth and thought I recognized themes from the Fourth (the first present Erwin had given me) but spiritualized in a way, and then saw the cover with Aussee on my bed. I felt a shiver and then it was told to me that I should get up and pick three camellias. I was weak from flu and didn't in the least want to, but it was an insistent voice, so I took a tray, for camellias are hard to hold because of their short stems, and went to pick the red, the Mathotiana Rubra, which I like the best. But when I reached the bush I could find only two perfect ones so I turned to the next tree, the Frizle white, and picked one of them, and tottered down the drive to the outside table and chairs where Erwin and I used to study and rolled them off the tray on to the table, where they fell, red-white-red, the colors of Austria. I knew it was a *Gruss*, a message, a synchronicity.

I had many such messages and wrote down about sixteen somewhere but the only one I can remember is the last, and that was about four years later when I was in Antwerp with my cousin Rita on a Rubens Quatrocentennial group from

Cambridge. I did not care for Rubens but we were also going to visit Bruges and Ghent, so I went along. I soon wearied of the endless corpulent nudes at the Museum in Antwerp and wandered off from the group to see if I could find some modern paintings. Erwin had taught me a lot about art, especially the Abstract Expressionists and other Modernists, and we shared a love of Klee. One painter he admired but I did not was Magritte. I disliked the huge apple bursting through the ceiling or the bomb about to descend on defenseless bathers. Erwin said he did wonderful things with light which I should have remembered from the MOMA but I did not.

I was wandering through empty rooms when suddenly I saw by a window a painting that arrested me. It was of twilight, so difficult to convey, but this was of a wood at dusk with a single tree standing before it and the only surrealism was that a sickle moon shone across the trunk of the tree, in front of the tree. That touch of surrealism filled the whole wood with twilight. It was "the Sixteenth of September" by Magritte. I was entranced and stood there a long time, and suddenly said to myself, looking up at the window, "If there is any way of communicating that you know I at last appreciate your Magritte, send your birds," and beyond the empty window flocks and flocks of birds flew suddenly across and then disappeared and the window was again empty. It was not evening, the time when birds retired to roost; it was very strange. To me it was a *Gruss*.

It was about a year after Erwin died when a new Dean reorganized the Program of Humanities; it was no longer to be divided between Graduates and Undergraduates and Dr.

Golden of Classics was to be in charge of both. I had had a course on the *Iliad* and the *Aeneid* with him and knew he was a fine classicist. The first thing he did was to put me on a Line Item, with insurance and full benefits and a raise in pay, and he put me in charge of Undergraduate Humanities. I was to organize and write syllabi for all the Undergraduate courses, teach two of them each term and the Junior and Senior Seminars. I suggested we teach four courses of undergraduate Humanities instead of three. Up till then we had taught Greek and Roman literature and art together with aspects of the Old and New Testament in one course; the second course was on Early Christianity, Romanesque architecture and manuscripts, Dante and the early Renaissance. The third course raced through the Renaissance, *Hamlet*, the 18th and 19th centuries, and landed exhausted with little time left for the 20th century. I suggested the fourth course should start with the 18th century and neoclassicism and give more time to 19th and 20th century art and literature. I also suggested that music be added for I found the students most open to music. They did not like to read as much as I thought they should, but they enjoyed art and learning something of music. We were given extra money so I suggested we start buying tapes of Gregorian chant, early polyphony, Palestrina, Monteverdi, introduction to opera, and classical music at least as far as Impressionism.

Dr. Golden wished that one of the Seminars for Humanities majors be devoted to the history of Criticism, and did I think I could teach that. I suggested starting with Plato, Aristotle, Horace, and then on to Sydney, Johnson, Shelley before coming to the modern schools of Historical, Realist, Psychological, Formalist, and Existentialist criticism. He was happy to learn that I thought I could do it. I would have a whole summer to prepare. I then asked if the second seminar could not be devoted to Art and Music as I felt we had not given sufficient attention to music. I had found a simple book on how to teach Music to non-Music majors, and I thought I could teach that with sufficient tapes as examples. The little music I had already been able to introduce had met with great success. He was delighted and said he would be glad to learn more of music himself! I found him easier to work with than my previous chairman, although I never forgot that Dr. Goodman had taught me much of Romanticism. He went back to teaching Romantic Poetry.

As I was now secure in my position at Florida State University and earning more money than before (although still less than a man), I decided to take Keith with me to Europe next summer. We would first visit Mummy and Bettina in Wales, and then go with Ray to Vienna. She had a friend with an apartment there who could offer us free accommodation if in return we could bring some heavy posters to Vienna. Neither Ray nor I would have been able to stagger under them but fortunately Keith was now fourteen and able to cope. I was scared about Customs but Ray's friend would cope with that. I was dubious about going to Vienna without Erwin, but I would be able to show it to Keith, and afterwards we would make a trip to the monastery at Zwettl which Erwin had wanted to show me, and where I could have a requiem mass said for him.

Chapter 80

Wales and Austria.

It was the first time Keith had been to Wales and he was thrilled by the mountains and anxious to climb Snowden as soon as possible. There was no room for him to sleep at Bettina's cottage so he stayed in a bed and breakfast in the village and walked up the hill to "Malory," which had a fantastic view over Cardigan Bay to Harlech, to spend the day. We both helped Bettina set up the garden.

Below the cottage was a steep road over which we looked to the golf course and then out to sea. It was a putt-putt course and Keith was anxious to play. Bettina had binoculars from which we could watch him from the front window. There was a line of people waiting to play so he just lay down on the grass in the sunshine and went to sleep; we could see him stretched out there. Bettina was very tickled; "Bless him," she said. She was an eccentric and she liked those who did not do the correct thing but the most comfortable.

Keith's first attempt to climb Snowden was not a success. The Welsh were not always kind to strangers and someone told him the wrong way. Bettina then found the son of a friend of hers, about Keith's age, with whom he became great friends and did much climbing. Donald had climbed Snowden on leave during the war and asked me to go with him but I was content with Moel-y-gest which was at Bettina's back door, had wonderful views, and was not so strenuous a climb.

Bettina took Keith and me down on Saturday night to the beach by the lifeboat where the men gathered to sing, and we were very impressed. The lifeboat was often called out during the summer and the alarm sounded loud and clear so we could hear it half way up the mountain. Bettina was very interested in the lifeboat and their crew and horrified that they had no lights; they were often called out at night, so she donated a pair of lights. She told us that when they came past Malory, her cottage, they dipped the lights. We hoped very much we would see such an occasion and we did. It was impressive and I was proud of my sister.

Keith was fascinated that nearly everyone in the village had the same surnames, Williams or Pugh, and that the fishmonger was called Pugh!

I wondered how Mummy would settle at Criccieth remembering how she had found Sussex "truly rural." She seemed content with her balcony and lovely view, and there were neighbours, mostly from England, with whom she made friends. Mummy became addicted to television and introduced us to a serial "Dad's Army" which dealt with amusing incidents in the Home Guard during the war. Keith had seen it in England before and was delighted to watch it again. Bettina and I had always enjoyed doing crossword puzzles together with Mummy giving us suggestions, called "Huh-huhs" when we got stuck. She also sang to us, which intrigued Keith greatly. We had a fine time.

We spent a few days with Ray in London and I was pleased to see how many paintings Keith remembered in the National Gallery; he preferred the Northern to the Italian Renaissance. He also asked to go to Kenwood House again to see one of Rembrandt's last paintings which he had not forgotten, and there he discovered a Memling portrait. We also went to the Tate Gallery and Keith surprised me by picking out Seurat, a favorite of mine. Nadine, Mrs. Raymond's daughter who lived in New York and was a docent at the Met and the MOMA, had often asked us to spend some time at Christmas with her. She had a son Keith's age and was also a widow. I was pleased to discover Keith had a visual eye for he took no interest in reading which worried me, but he had a photographic memory. I decided we would go to New York and spend a week with Nadine immediately after Christmas when the boys had holidays. Keith had a camera in London this time and took many photos of his hero, Nelson, high on his column, looking out to sea.

I was uneasy about going to Vienna without Erwin but it was the only way to get to Zwettl. Ray managed to get the heavy posters through customs and Keith was able to carry them. She had the key to her friend's flat where we left them, and where we were to stay. We went to Grinzing where Ray was very popular as she could sing all the songs and we took Keith to Schönbrunn where the white mirrored salon was still a delight, although the Mozart boys were not singing.

Keith liked Charlemagne's crown in the Kunsthistorisches Museum and also Breughel's *Return of the Hunters.*

We only stayed two or three days and then took an old fashioned steam train to Zwettl, a small village near the Czech border. It was not mountainous country but woods. The train had a little platform in front where one could stand but smuts flew in my eyes from the stack and I let Ray and Keith enjoy it. The village was indeed small, by a river. We were traveling light having most of our luggage in Vienna for we knew we would have to walk to find the right place to stay. We found "The Golden Cockerel" right on the dark green river and were given a hearty welcome; apparently foreigners did not often come there and we were asked how we had found the place!. I said we had come to see the monastery and we were told to do that tomorrow, for this afternoon there was a band concert in the village square which we would enjoy. This was indeed old Austria. The band was in uniform and the villagers gathered around. After the playing stopped, girls in dirndl dresses came round with trays and I assumed they would be asking for coins but no, they were handing out little glasses of Schnapps and we were told it was a free concert!

We made our way back without difficulty to "The Golden Cockerel" and saw that it adjoined what seemed to be hospital grounds. The invalids came down to the street where they were greeted at the gate by friends who seemed to be bringing them something to drink, which intrigued us.

We thought we would take a walk before supper and were led by the river into thick woods. The river widened and there was an island in the middle on which stood a little pavilion, for all the world like "*die Pavillion aus Jad*"(the Pavillion of Jade) in Mahler's *Song of the Earth*. A few people were strolling along and lights came on and we realized that this must be the evening promenade. It was as beautiful as in an old fairytale.

Along the road to the monastery there were many shrines; it was a very Catholic part of the world. We had some difficulty getting in, but when I explained I wanted to see the Abbot to request a Requiem Mass for a friend who had often visited this monastery, we were admitted. I hoped we could hear the mass but it was not to be. There was quite a list and the earliest we could get was three weeks away when we would be back in America. I do not remember much of the monastery except a painting of the Schutz Maria, in which Mary was portrayed with her cloak around a crowd of people. We heard the monks afar singing Gregorian chant but we did not see them.

The people at The Golden Cockerel were intrigued by us and wanted to know how we had found the place. In the end I had to tell them I came to have a requiem sung for a friend who often used to visit the monastery and Zwettl. "What was his name?" I was asked. "He must have been one of us." I told them he came from Vienna, from the university, and they were most impressed.

They noticed we did not care very much for sauerkraut and asked if we would like a cucumber salad instead and produced the most delicious cucumber salad I have ever had and the method of producing it, which they called a "guillotine," presenting us with one to take home. It shaved the cucumber very thin; a little vinegar and mayonnaise with salt and pepper was added, and I have never forgotten how good it tasted.

I asked about the gathering at the hospital gates at 4 pm when villagers arrived with food and drink and patients came to receive it. They were convalescent patients from nearby and naturally their friends wanted to give them a little something to while away the afternoon; it seemed a charming custom. We heard an evening concert by the village band, which was even more festive than the afternoon concert. When they found out Ray could sing some folk songs they were delighted. It was a visit back in time.

It was only an hour from Vienna by car and when Ray's friend returned from business in Yugoslavia he came to fetch us. He had lived all his life in Vienna and had never visited Zwettl.

Chapter 81

Life goes on.

As a teacher of undergraduates I was aware that at the end of the school year the best students would ask for recommendations for graduate school; this was generally no problem for I knew all the Humanities majors well, having taught them two or more classes. With James it was different. What I had feared came to pass. Those two terms when he was lobbying for the Student/Landlord Act and his grades went down told against him. He applied to twelve Law Schools and was turned down. Each time I had written a letter of recommendation explaining the situation but it was of no avail. Law schools demanded consistent high grades. He was desperate when he came to me with the thirteenth possibility: a small law school in North Carolina run by the Presbyterian church. His father was a Presbyterian minister: this was a last chance. After writing twelve recommendations I knew it so I determined to take a risk. I would write no ordinary recommendation. I took a stiff drink before I started. I explained again that for those two terms when his grades went down James had spent all his time and energy lobbying the Legislature to pass a bill insisting that landlords spray student housing every year for cockroaches. The rental properties for students were overrun with cockroaches, and owing to his efforts such a bill was eventually passed to the benefit of all future students. I was sure that they were aware that most students entered Law School with the desire to earn money. James was one student who wished to study law in order to help poor people. I believed that a Presbyterian Law School would honor such an aim. Otherwise I could not believe in American Law and Justice. James was admitted and eventually practiced Bankruptcy Law. We kept in touch for several years.

On another occasion a Humanities major who had several courses with me wished to take her M.A. in Humanities which involved interning a course with me and teaching one class. After that she wished to continue for her Ph.D. and to write her dissertation on Women and Science. Somehow or other she had got hold of a German book written by a friend of Einstein's wife, Mileva, which maintained that Mileva had helped considerably in Einstein's Theory of Relativity, including doing most of the mathematics. This student knew no German, but a professor who had read the book told her that if she could get it translated she had the basis for a dissertation. She had no money and translation was expensive. She asked me to do it. Friends advised me not to, that it would involve a great deal of time. Also, it was written by a Serb and therefore the German was anything but *hoch Deutsch*, and very hard to translate. I hesitated but had been given considerable help in my teaching career, and also was interested in the subject. I decided to give it a shot. She took me out to dinner once a week and introduced me to a very good Chardonnay.

I regretted my decision many a time because the work was difficult but I was interested and felt that Mileva had not been sufficiently recognized. I discovered a letter that Einstein wrote to Mileva in which he referred to the Theory of Relativity as "our work" and also a reference by a Russian professor whose name I have now forgotten that her name was on the first draft. My student wrote her dissertation, after which she received her Ph.D. and landed a good job.

An English friend of mine had been deserted by her husband and left with two small girls. She managed to get her MA in Art History at the FSU Center at Florence and I suggested she then apply for a PhD in Humanities at FSU. She had a flair for art history and had discovered something about crystals and how they were used to light the Paschal candle, and she needed to do research in France and Germany. Her father in England would lend us his car if I could help with the gas and the research in French and German. I was interested and had a German musicologist friend in Aachen whom I knew would be of great help. He introduced us to the Archbishop of Aachen who concentrated on me as my English friend knew no German. He showed us Charlemagne's Bible, which was usually kept under glass; he took it out and told me to turn the pages. "Such beautiful paintings," he said "and nobody ever sees them. Turn the pages and look." I have never felt so overwhelmed by history, and felt the centuries pour down on me as I turned the pages of Charlemagne's Bible. Time really stood still at that moment and I can recall the sensation. My friend found quite a lot of the information she needed on our trip and the British Museum was interested in her dissertation.

I had taught a student German, and he had found himself a job in Ischl for the summer. While he was there, knowing he was so good with railroad timetables, I asked him to find out for me the easiest way to get from Paris to Gmunden. When Keith graduated from high school I wanted to take him to Paris because he had been so impressed with the art in the National Gallery in London. I did not want to go to Vienna again but did want Keith to see Traunstein and Gmunden, the most beautiful place I had seen.

The student went to the stationmaster in Gmunden and found out that the TGV from Paris (the train at *grand vitesse*, great speed) actually stopped for four minutes in Attnang-Buchheim where a local train went to Gmunden. I remembered stopping there and changing from the Vienna train; it was where I had first seen the mountains. The stationmaster told E. that I would have to make a special point when booking of asking the conductor to let us down at Attnang-Buchheim, for the train did not stop at the platform end of the station; however I could request help at Paris and again from the conductor of the train. I felt a little nervous but E. was sure it could be done; he had watched the train come in from Paris. Keith would have to jump down, I would then hand down the bags and, kneeling down, could hang from the train and just jump down five feet and Keith would catch me It seemed a bit iffy but it was far the quickest and cheapest way to get from Paris to Gmunden, and I was younger then.

Chapter 82

Keith and I in Europe, 1974.

After visiting my family in Wales, Keith and I took off for Paris. Unfortunately several of the museums were on strike and we could not see the Impressionists and Post-Impressionists at the converted railroad station. This was a great disappointment but Keith discovered the Rodin museum and spent a great deal of time there. Mrs. Corbould had taken him as a child across the Channel to see the Burghers of Calais and he was already a Rodin devotee. The Louvre was open but Keith was horrified there were so many safety guards around the Mona Lisa, which he did not like very much, and none around the Rembrandt. I had tried before to find the van Eyck "Chancellor Rolin," but had been unable to. The guards were not nearly as helpful as in England but Keith eventually found it tucked away above a door. It was a smaller painting than I had thought, a mistake which comes from seeing so many slides. I was very happy to see it for van Eyck was one of my favorites. Outside the Louvre I introduced Keith to French crepes sold from a barrel, suggesting chestnut for him; I took a crepe suzette and he said when he saw my rapt expression he intended to choose that next time. He loved the *bateau mouche* at night when the buildings along the Seine were all alight.

The chestnut trees were in bloom all over Paris, but they were especially beautiful clustered around Notre Dame. Keith was as entranced by the rose windows as I was, the blue and the rose. He drew my attention to some wooden carvings in the nave. They were fourteenth-century and painted. He had never seen wooden carving before and noticed a man by a tree with a spade and asked who he was. I told him that in the Gospel of John, when Mary Magdalene goes to the tomb and finds it empty, she turns around and sees someone she thinks is the gardener and asks him where they have taken the body of Jesus. He calls her "Mary" and she realizes it is not a gardener but Christ himself. "So He was a gardener too, as well as a carpenter; I will remember that gardener," said Keith. The organ was playing a Schubert Mass, and we listened to it. It was a moment when I realized how fortunate I was to have a child who was bone of my bone.

We went by the metro out to la Bagatelle, Malmaison, the rose gardens planted by Josephine, the wife of Napoleon. It was not so easy to follow the metro as the London tube and I was relieved that we eventually arrived at the last station, Malmaison. The gardens were only a short walk away and very beautiful. I loved reading the names of the roses in French. I told Keith that Napoleon had abandoned

Josephine for an Austrian princess. "She still had these roses," Keith said.

We also went to the Jardins des Plantes and were amazed to find that Rilke's Caroussel was still there.

Rilke

Dead poet who loved Paris,
your faded caroussel
of panthers, bears, giraffes
still rearing up
and circling round
the music grinding on.

no elephant is there,
not even now and then
so magical for you,
a century ago,
the music grinding on.

no children riding now,
but did they just dismount
or was it years long since
they disappeared from view,
the music grinding on.

At the ticket office in Paris they were not very helpful about leaving the *train de grand vitesse* at Attnang-Buchheim. A superior had to be consulted who confirmed it had been done but I should speak to the conductor on the train who would know more about it. The conductor seemed horrified at the idea and said the train did not stop at the platform and only waited four minutes. He advised me to get a seat next to the luggage van and try and exit from there, as it was a bit lower to the ground. I had an anxious journey. When the train stopped at Attnang-Buchheim we were already in the luggage van and it was ten feet from the ground. Keith jumped down and I passed down the bags on wheels. I knelt down on the floor of the van, then turned around and hung from the edge and let go. Keith caught me round the waist. At the same moment a huge steam train let out an enormous belch. Keith said afterwards he felt he was in a Nazi film and at any moment the Gestapo were coming. It was tricky to get the bags on wheels over railroad tracks to the Gmunden train and Keith had to heave me up on to the platform, but we made it with a moment to spare, and as I looked out of the train window I saw the purple gauze outline of the Traunstein. "Travels with Mother," said Keith, "can be a bit unusual."

At Gmunden I went to Information for places to stay. I did not want the expensive hotel in the town itself, but a house by the lake that rented rooms. We were given an address and took a taxi there. A man and woman were waiting at the door. She was a very attractive middle-aged Marschallin, he was smaller. We introduced ourselves and I said I wanted a room with a view and two beds for myself and son for a few days. He nodded and we were invited in and showed the most glorious room with a cherry tree in bloom outside and a view over the lake and mountains. We were speechless; we had never seen anything so beautiful. Frau Staffelmayer explained there was a small problem. They were leaving early next morning for the Wachau to get their annual supply of wine. They were renting a truck with friends and would return with the barrels late tomorrow evening. She invited us to dinner the following night to sample the new wine, but she would not be able to supply us with breakfast tomorrow morning. However, her daughter would come in and fix it for us if we could wait till 9 am. After our journey we had no desire for an early rising, and we thanked her. I was not even sure we would get breakfast.

"What is the name of the son?" asked Herr Staffelmayer. "Keith," I replied, "unfortunately he does not speak German." "Keet" spat out Herr S. "I cannot say such a name, I will call him Johann." Keith, who had followed this, grinned and said "Johann" and they became fast friends. Frau S. told me her husband always wished to see would-be guests and if he did not like them she had to say there was no vacancy. I was glad he liked us. Their house was about a mile from the centre of Gmunden, a lovely walk along the lake. I thought we would go there to eat but Frau S. suggested a café run by her friends a little nearer, with a magnificent view. She would phone them we were coming and what would we like to eat. I suggested Wiener Schnitzel with spinach. "No sauerkraut," said Keith who was following this, "*Gurkel salat.*" I was surprised he recalled the name of the cucumber salad he liked so much in Zwettl. This tickled Herr S. no end. "*Er spricht*" (he speaks), "he said. We had a wonderful meal and watched the mountains turn from gold to rose and then silver, and then stay alight when the lake grew dark, and the while sail ships, followed by a gracious line of swans, came to shore.

I wanted Keith to see Kremsmünster but as Herr Staffelmayer said, "It was a world journey." I knew it was possible because Erwin and I had done it from Gmunden, but it was quite a trip. We lost one train on the way home and had to wait for the next but it was worth it to see that beautiful abbey and the geometric pools under the white arcades where the monks had kept their fish. Keith took many excellent photos which I was glad to have. Erwin would never take photos, "only tourists do that." Things had changed in five years. The little cellar where the monks made brandy was now a fully fledged liquor store with Johnny Walker and Seagram's, but they still made the brandy.

Back in Gmunden I enjoyed the ascent to the Grunewald mountain by cable car. There was no track, just a little open platform with two chairs opposite each other where one could sit and hold on with ropes, while the platform swung out over the lake. It was a fantastic view but rather alarming if one had not traveled in such a way before. Keith grew quite pale when I stood up to see better. When we reached the top I was glad to see that the polished wooden plaque under the huge tree announcing "When this tree was a sapling, Maria Therese reigned" was there. All the other wooden plaques telling the story of the giant Erlaf who fell in love with a nixie from the lake had gone. They were now in the village museum and had been replaced by metal plaques. I was glad to have seen the legend in the old polished wood. We walked up to the guest house and had a meal with a good view. On the way back we met a man leading an array of ducks to a pond and calling out "*wulli, wulli*." Keith asked what that meant and I said did not know and would ask Herr S. for him. "It is how you call ducks," explained Herr S., "little ducks." "Do you mean," asked Keith, "that there is another way to call grown-up ducks.?" "When they are grown up," was the reply, "they know how to get to the water by themselves."

We had a great time at Gmunden although I was sorry it was not the season for the echo blowing from the lake at night, but we enjoyed the evening walk along the darkened promenade, watching the sunset over the lake and mountains and hearing music from the village band. Frau S. dressed up in her Steuermarkt costume for us and even yodeled one night, which was unforgettable.

I had booked the return flight to London from Salzburg rather than Paris so we did not have to face Attnang-Buchheim again, and we saw Salzburg. Keith never forgot the Mirabellengarten and a building nearby which I told him was built after the style of Michelangelo, having long rows of windows with alternate alcoves of triangles and semi-circles. Years later we saw Salzburg on the TV and Keith remembered the building influenced by Michelangelo. I told him he was the best of my Humanities students for few would have remembered after so long.

Keith was interested in architecture but he did not wish to attend college for he did not enjoy reading; he never read a book, and although I felt later perhaps he could have got through with his photographic memory and bluff, he did not wish to go. He joined a construction company on leaving school and built many beautiful houses, which would have pleased his father. I remembered how often Howard and I with the older boys had visited houses under construction on Sunday afternoons.

Chapter 83

Florence.

I was given a chance to teach at the FSU Center in Florence, Italy, for six months in 1980. Keith had left school, had a job with a construction firm, and wanted to take an apartment with a friend and I felt he was old enough; also I needed the rent from the house to pay for a flat in Florence. A friend had already found me a visiting professor as a tenant, so it worked out quite well. I asked Ray to join me in Florence; she had given my family and friends hospitality for years in London and although I always tried to bring enough Scotch I was still deeply in her debt. She could rent her house in Hampstead to an FSU family coming to teach at the London Center. Everything seemed to dovetail very well. Ray knew some musical Italian and I had taken one Italian course at FSU and we both could take more in Florence.

A friend saw an advertisement in *The Yale Journal* for an apartment on the Arno which was no more expensive than those offered by FSU, and I took that. I flew to England a few days after Christmas and spent a few days in Wales and then Ray and I flew to Florence.

I taught two Humanities courses each term; in winter Classics and Medieval; in spring Renaissance and Baroque, and each term I taught Shakespeare, the Italian plays. I was looking forward to teaching more Shakespeare; I had already taught *Hamlet* in Renaissance Humanities. I had to include quite a bit more Old and New Testament than I taught in Tallahassee in order to explain to the students the sculpture and painting; they seemed to enjoy it. Every street in Florence seemed to require a knowledge of the Bible.

What I loved best in Florence was Brunelleschi's Duomo, like a huge soaring tulip above the dark narrow streets. It seemed to catch all the sun and glow like a lamp above the city. I told the students the story of how Brunelleschi won the competition to build the Dome. Many architects submitted plans. Brunelleschi said he could do it for he could balance an egg on its tip so it did not fall over. The others tried but none could. Brunelleschi just tapped the bottom of the egg so it cracked and he could then stand it up straight. Apparently this was why he won the competition, but he succeeded where other architects had failed, by building an inner dome inside the outer, which took off some of the weight. Michelangelo asked to be buried in the church of Santa Croce so that through the church door the first thing he would see on Judgement Day would be Brunelleschi's Duomo. "I built a bigger," he is supposed to have said referring to St. Peter's in Rome, "but no more beautiful."

Signor Giachi met us at the apartment and he spoke a little English. We were to call on him for any help we needed. We called that same night. No water in the bathroom. We were in a small flat not facing the Arno, which was a blow. He came immediately and said we were to move into the front flat facing the river, much bigger and with a heavenly view. He would summon a plumber next day, not to worry. Meanwhile we gloried in the view. The plumber next day had disastrous news. Apparently the small flat had not been rented for years and water had dripped down to the flat below which was filled nearly to the ceiling with water!

Signor Giacchi said he would have to phone Mrs. Lesser in America and she would have to send money or would I phone her on his phone for he could not explain too well. "Just tell her she must send the check to my bank and not to hers," he said. Apparently great repairs were needed. The house was fifteenth century marble, walls two feet thick, and there was a one inch pipe somewhere in the marble dripping water down below. Mrs. Lesser was horrified and apologetic. We were to move to the front flat with the heavenly view of the Arno. "Once they start drilling, "she told me, "marble dust will be all over the place, even in the front flat. You better gets something to wrap around your heads." It was like being in an English drizzle, not rain but marble dust. However, we were out all day at the FSU Center and when we returned in the evening the men were gone and we sat in the little balcony with our drinks and drank in the colors.

We were on the corner of the next bridge to the Ponte Vecchio, and on each side of the river were those splendid Renaissance houses of different colors with Venetian blinds of contrasting shades. I felt I was in my old childhood paint box— light ochre, burnt ochre, raw Siena, burnt Siena, raw umber, burnt umber, Tuscan red—all the colors originally came from the soils around here. The houses were reflected into the river in slightly different shades, and there was a diagonal silver dam cutting across them, originally built to prevent attack from Pisa. The lights sprinkled from the Ponte Vecchio outlining the intricate carving on that bridge and behind loomed Brunelleschi's dome like a tremendous red tulip. Behind were the mountains and the sunset.

Each day we had about a ten-minute walk down the river to the Ponte Vecchio where we turned left and wandered through a few streets till we came to the FSU Center in Florence. Between classes we had the most delicious cappuccino in a café nearby. In the afternoons we were conducted on tours of the city by teachers who had been there some time. Two of my favorite students, Laura and Andrew, came with me and took all my classes, and another student, Vincent, became part of our group. Dr. R was a fabulous art history teacher and I learned a lot from her, but she was very shy. She kept her head down when she lectured and the boys told me they wanted to write "Hi, Dr. R!" on their shoes but they didn't. It was fascinating walking past statues and into churches only seen before on slides or in books.

Ray was allowed to audit all my classes and she also could take Italian with me. We had an excellent teacher in Dr. E, and eventually had the pleasure of studying Dante's *Inferno* with the Italian on one side and the English on the other. While we were there Zuban Mehta conducted the entire Ring Cycle in German at the opera which was at walking distance from us. I thought the Rhine Maidens were nude but was told they were in leotards. The river Rhine was indicated by two circles of green glass slightly behind each other and the nereids danced up hidden steps between them. Down at the bottom of one of the circles was Alberich in a dark cave lit with gold. Valhalla was splendid. There was a backdrop of clouds and in front three squared mirrored pillars of glass which revolved and refracted the passing clouds. I never counted Wagner among my favorite composers but I have never seen any opera so visually compelling. I was especially impressed by the square pillars which fractured the light in Valhalla. They also did several Menotti operas, *The Consul, The Medium, La Contessa, il Poeta e la Mandragorla.* We only paid for standing room seats but each time there were several vacant seats held by Season Ticket holders, and we were always able to sit.

The plumbers and masons took a long time at their work. Understandably, it was not easy to find a pipe of one inch diameter in two stories of marble two feet thick. Eventually it was found and stopped up in some way. My Italian was not adequate to understanding how, but I was needed in the financial transfer of money from US to Florence. Mrs. Lesser had not done as requested, namely, to send the check to Signor Giacchi ; instead she sent it to her bank in Florence and for some reason I was needed to witness why it was needed, and there was a dreadful to do and lengthy delays with people raising hands and wringing them. I felt it was like an opera buffo. At length Signor Giacchi exclaimed, "Deo gratias, the son of my cousin, he will fix it!" and he did. I came to understand how business was done in Italy.

In the beautiful front flat on the Arno Ray and I had a little wine and cheese party for students and faculty. Only three people could get on the balcony at a time, but there were tall windows with great views. One student told us that he had a flat on the other side of the Arno, much cheaper, and when we lost this flat we were welcome to come every night to see the sunset, especially if we brought a bottle of wine. We accepted gratefully and often made the steep climb. The view was quite different, no more reflections but slices of the green river appeared over the jagged roofs and the Duomo was floodlit and even more tremendous. We also found cheaper places to eat on that side of the Arno, lots of cafes with enormous black pizza ovens into which huge pizzas were shoved into roaring flames and came out crisp and delicious.

When the plumbers left we had to move back into the smaller side flat and Mrs. Lesser asked if we could find anybody to rent the front one. Ray was much more ethical than I. I was prepared to let things take their course and, although sleeping in the smaller, continue to have our drinks on the balcony of the empty flat. She however put up a notice advertising it in some newsagent and an American couple appeared the next day and rented it. Immediately after many friends from England and America decided to visit us, including my cousin Rita, my old schoolfriend Kay, Nadine (Mrs. Raymond's daughter from New York), Lida and Hanni from England, and Ray's daughter, son-in-law, and two-year-old baby, not all at once. Most took rooms nearby and just spent the days with us, but Ray's family stayed in the flat. There was a water shortage while they were there and Gillis bathed in the public baths. I have a wonderful photo of the baby picking daisies on the lawn at the Pitti Palace and we had a lovely time singing in the evenings.

I did take off for one weekend while they were there to visit Verona with the history professor, not for Romeo and Juliet, but because Erwin had called it "a silver Latin city" and indeed it was, even including a coliseum where they held opera in the summer. We heard a concert with a Met star, Bruson, and he must have been a home town boy for they gave him six encores. I thought they would never stop.

My visitors were always invited to attend my classes and all did except my cousin. She said she would be embarrassed. She spent the mornings in the English Library. They were also invited to take trips with us and Nadine came with us to Venice in February where a melancholy rain misted everything and the houses seemed to crumble away. We did have one fine day and lo, Venice shone again.

Each faculty member had to give a lecture on a town other than Florence. Several trips were made which for the students were free; faculty paid for their own fares. I would have liked to lecture on Siena, an hour's train trip away but the two teachers resident in Florence knew it so much better than I. I opted for Ravenna, for if one lectured the train fare was free and this was the furthest away. I went several times to Siena with the students. It was a city of rose-colored brick and the Campo Santo, the hill facing the cathedral, was paved with white ribs of ditches for the rainfall which was led down to cisterns under the cathedral. It looked a bit like the Florentine Duomo turned inside out.

Pisa was also very near and Florence's rival. I liked best the pulpits by the Pisanos, father and son, both pre-Renaissance. Nicola's *Annunciation and Nativity,* 1259-60, was influenced by the classical art of Rome where he had studied. Mary looks like a serene Roman matron. Giovanni *Pisana's Nativity and Annunciation to the Shepherds,* 1302-10, moved away from his father's classicism to the International Gothic style. His figures are smaller and more animated, the sheep are quite realistic, and the whole pulpit gives a great feeling of life and warmth. I preferred it and spent a lot of time studying both and remember them quite well. I was glad we had seen the pulpits first for the students wanted to climb the Leaning Tower and had to have a faculty member with them. I was not keen. There was a winding ledge around it with no balcony. It looked very dangerous. I was the only teacher there and the students were insistent so we started. The higher we climbed the more dangerous it felt, especially on the downside as the students rushed to the edge, Andrew foremost among them. I felt I was going to throw up and screamed "Andrew!" He must have seen I looked white and shaky for he shooed them off the edge and was instrumental in getting them down. I was staggering and had not been so afraid since the glacier. He hurried me to a café and put a glass of grappa before me. "Drink it," he said. I didn't think I could but he put it to my lips and I felt better. I always respond to alcohol. A lot of the students were scared and there was no question of going up again. A year or so later railings were placed around the ramp and when Keith climbed it in the 9Os they were there.

Ravenna was almost a thousand years back in history, at the end of the Roman Empire. The tomb of the Empress Galla Placida was one of the oldest churches, AD 425-5O, and was decorated by a mosaic of *Christ as the Good Shepherd.* Christ was portrayed like the youthful Apollo, beardless, surrounded by sheep, rocks and plants portrayed in classical mosaic by glittering bits of stone. The students were fascinated by a new art form, other than painting or sculpture, and there were many mosaics to be seen in Ravenna. In the basilica of St. Apollinaire Nuove there was a long line of martyrs in shining white as well as another youthful Christ as *Good Shepherd separating the sheep from the goats.* The students liked the procession of the *Emperor Justinian and Courtiers,* where each courtier stepped on the foot of the one beside him symbolizing that he was the greater. This was in the central church of San Vitale modeled like Justinian's great church of Hagia Sophia in Constantinople. I had to teach a great deal of Roman and early Christian history before we went to Ravenna.

In February there was snow on the mountains behind Fiesole where we often used to take the bus in the afternoon for a cappuccino and then return at sunset with the glory of Florence spread before us. It even snowed in Florence and we were told that above Fiesole there was a place to ski. Skis could be rented and the bus went there. Judy, in charge of the FSU Center, said it would be a good trip for all of us to make, as there were fantastic views from there. Several students could ski and wanted to go, Andrew and Vincent among them. When they found out that I had skied they tried to persuade me. You have more energy than most of us to climb the Boboli Gardens or to San Miniato to see the sunset every night; you are in fine shape." It was a gentle slope, and I wavered. Ray who was with us slipped on the ice and came down with a mighty crash. She had been a nurse and knew she had broken her arm. I quickly grabbed the flask of whisky that I always carried in my bag and someone else produced aspirins. Luckily Judy knew someone who could drive us down to her doctor in Florence. There were no phones, but she knew he would be home on Sunday afternoon. I felt Ray had probably saved me from a like situation.

The doctor was home and although he gave Ray something for the pain, he had to wait to set it in the hospital the following day. I was willing to cancel classes to go with her but she knew there was no one else to teach them and said she would take a taxi there and back, and I was not to think of it. With the lack of phones it was hard to cancel class and she insisted. I felt very bad about it and rushed home at lunchtime to find her in bed exhausted. The doctor had not used anaesthetic to set it. I was so horrified, I hate to think of it even now. However, she was tough and recovered quickly and was determined to come with us to Rome in three weeks.

Judy found us a room quite near the Pantheon which meant that it would be quite easy to see classical Rome, but whether Ray would be up to a bus to St. Peter's and Renaissance Rome was doubtful. But Ray was absolutely determined to see St. Peter's and to hear the Pope on Sunday speak from his little window to the huge crowd in the Piazza. Her two brothers were Catholics although she was not. Andrew and Vincent were very good to her in Rome. One carried her bags and the other stood by in case she needed his arm. I shall never forget her climbing to the top of St. Peter's. It was enormous; there was an elevator half way up but still many stairs to climb. It felt higher than a New York skyscraper, simply surrounded by space, and then a magnificent view of Bernini's Piazza, the Tiber, and Roma Aeterna. It was more emotional than expected.

Soon after Rome came Spring Break and the students were going to Pompeii and Capri but we could not afford to do so. I thought we might just stay in Florence, but Erasmo Gerato, the Italian teacher, told us it would be very crowded over Easter and he suggested we go a short trip to see what he said was the most beautiful area of Italy, the Cinque Terra. It would be by the Mediterranean but not crowded at that time of year. There were five small towns and one could get off at any train stop and then go on to the next with the same ticket. Ray longed to see the sea and so we went and it was incredibly lovely. She had completely recovered, and we stayed at Vernazza and walked along the cliffs to the other villages through fields of spring flowers. By this time we knew enough Italian to get around and it was interesting to see another Italy, the countryside by the sea, the glory of the Mediterranean.

Unfortunately, as we were walking through the meadows back to Vernazza on the last day, a sudden storm swept in from the sea and drenched us. We both came down with colds, which in Ray's case turned to bronchitis, but she said in spite of losing her voice and breaking her arm it was the best holiday she ever had. It was not exactly a holiday for me for I worked hard preparing students for what they were about to see, but it was a great time of my life. I felt so brimful of art that I would need years to digest it.

After Easter, Florence became very crowded and the last weeks were tiring. We made one more trip to Assisi where the great church did not seem appropriate for St. Francis except for frescoes of Giotto, which brought a new realism and humanity to art, very different from the glittering mosaics of Ravenna. May was glorious for the flowers. Along the Arno were gardens where the civic flower of Florence flourished, yellow, bronze and purple iris, and up in Fiesole there were daffodils. We left at the beginning of June, the students for the States and Ray and I for England, where I spent a week in Wales.

Keith met me at the Tallahassee Airport; he had a bottle of champagne iced at the house; in those days we celebrated with bubbly. He had enjoyed his independence in an apartment with friends, but Sterling was leaving for the Air Force and Keith was ready to return home. He suggested Japanese maples instead of roses for the garden and made circles of oak leaves around them to protect their shallow roots, which I called "corollas"; they set off the elegant trees. In the end he had quite an arboretum, nine different Japanese maples, which we named after our dear ones.

Chapter 84

The Arrival of D.

When I went back to teach in the fall at FSU the secretary told me we had a new teaching assistant who was taking his PhD in Classics. He came to speak to me. He said he had been told I made up the syllabi for the undergraduate Humanities, and he was glad there was so much music in it. Was I a musician? I said I had been married to a pianist and loved music and had studied a little theory. He said that as he had come past my class he heard I was teaching music. I explained I taught the Junior and Senior Seminars for Humanities majors and in those classes I tried to teach non-music majors something of music for I found they responded to classical music when exposed to it. I showed him what book I was using and asked him if he were a musician. He said he was an organist and a singer. I had understood he was in Classics. "My father doesn't want me to be a musician," he said, "and I have been to Greece and loved everything about it." I agreed and told him I had been there too.

We chatted a while and then he said "I see there is an FSU opera performance on Saturday, *The Merry Widow*; would you like to go? Then he added, "I am gay." I said I would like to see it. The last time I had was at *der Theater an der Wien* in Vienna. "There is bound to be a difference," he said and I agreed. "I'll get the tickets and could pick you up in my car," he added. I said I would pay for my ticket and would he like to come and have a bite to eat beforehand. He said he would bring a bottle of wine so we started a companionship which made a great difference to life.

The Merry Widow was atrocious. This was before the days of Lincoln Clark who transformed the opera program at FSU. They did not even waltz; they linked hands and swayed. We raised our eyebrows and in the interval he said: "Would you like to leave?" This did impress me. I had wanted to leave concerts before but never had the nerve. We went home and had another glass of wine and I asked him what he sang. "I've just sung the baritone solo in the *Messiah*." I do not know how I had the nerve but said, "I don't suppose you would sing it a capella." He was quite willing and assumed a Victorian baritone pose and sang "Comfort ye, my people." He was good. "What else do you like in the *Messiah*?," he asked. I admitted that I liked the alto "He will feed his flock." "I sing that, too," he said, and did. I was completely entranced and speechless. He could sing anything and he did not mind adjusting soprano arias such as "*Dove sono*." We developed the pleasant custom of his coming to dinner once or twice a week and either he sang or we listened to records.

The following spring the Met went on tour and came to Atlanta. D asked me if I would like to go for two performances during spring break. I was thrilled; I had never heard the Met and nor had he. We were able to obtain tickets for *The Magic Flute* and *Il Trovatore*. D drove us up in his car. I was surprised he went further north in Atlanta than was necessary for the opera, which we passed, and asked him why. "Well," he said, "I thought rather than see Underground Atlanta you would like to see the mountains. The Appalachian Trail starts just north of Atlanta." I was thrilled—the Met and the mountains too. We started early next morning and soon reached them. It was spring and the wild azaleas were golden fish in seas of green in the valleys. D strode ahead singing Mozart arias, bass, alto and even soprano; it was enchanting. We enjoyed ourselves so much we walked too far on the Appalachian Trail and were late in returning for the opera. "We shall have to skip dinner till afterwards." I felt rather hollow hearing this but we were just too late.

It was *The Magic Flute* with décor by Chagall. I did not think his trailing angels were suitable for the Masonic Egyptian scenes, *Isis und Osiris* and *In diesen heiligen Hallen,* but they lent a supernatural flavor to the fairyland scenes. The queen of the Night was good which gave magic to the performance. I had seen Ingmar Bergmann's black and white film of the opera shortly before, and had to admit I preferred it Maybe my empty stomach had something to do with it.

When we came out we found all restaurants were shut which was a blow. D was sure we would find a pancake house, but he did not know Atlanta and we passed the golden dome three times and no pancakes. We eventually we found a Macdonalds and determined to be sure and eat before the performance tomorrow. We had neither of us seen *Il Trovatore* and thought it was set in Italy. The backdrop was of grey and green crags. In the second act the colors changed to bronze and beige and brown, and I recognized Zurburan and realized that the first act was El Greco so it must be set in Spain. It was a wonderful performance.

We had a shorter trip to the mountains the second day. The whole weekend was a visual glory with the goldfish azaleas and seas of emerald leaves as well as the operas. Unfortunately the Met did not give another tour after their usual season in New York so we did not see them again until several years later when we went with Keith at Christmas to stay with Nadine in New York and saw *Die Fledermaus.*

Chapter 85

The Arrival of M.

I am thankful for M's arrival for it means there is a possibility of finishing these memoirs before I sputter out.

[Aside]

I had to drop (Asides) long ago for I realized when I came to the ten-year—old child I once was, I had to "be" that child, unencumbered by any knowledge that I learned afterwards, so I had to drop that communication so valuable to my later life.)

We evolved into a foursome including D and Keith, sometime a threesome of M, K and I, as for instance, when we went to Calloway Gardens which Keith and I had enjoyed for more springs and falls than we can remember. I recall M found the evil looking pink and green flowers under the waterfall fascinating and I remember his beautiful whistling of the Blessed Spirits. D, M, and I made a memorable trip to North Carolina in a car filled with Pavarotti tapes and bottles. It was M who introduced us into paddling in the streams which added to the pleasure. I believe "The Trout" was appropriately whistled at the time.

M's arrival, however, needs mention for it was inauspicious. The student to whom I had rented the room left, and I felt it would be good to have someone from Humanities. I learned there were three new graduate teaching assistants arriving so went into the office to inspect them. I was seated in the outer officer when M came in and announced his name. When I heard it I knew he was the right one, for it was Austrian, and popped out asking "Would you like to rent a room?" He looked surprised so I said, "I rent rooms to graduate students, I have a car and could take you to see it." At the mention of a car his expression, which was lugubrious, lifted somewhat. "Could you possibly drive me to my car which is at the Collegiate Motel? I phoned to ask how far this office was and Dr. Golden told me it was five minutes. I thought he meant by foot and left my collection of classical records in my car under a tree. That was over an hour ago." I was horrified; it was 90 degrees outside. "Of course I'll take you, my home is only five minutes from there." I drove him and he said afterwards I was the worst driver he had ever seen, but I was distressed about the records. The car was still in the shade, thank goodness. M leapt out saying he would follow me.

When we arrived home he started taking records out. "Don't you want to see the room?" I asked. "I'll take it no matter what, I'll never forgive Dr. Golden," and I don't think he did. I said there was a separate entrance but it was quicker through the house. He stopped, entranced by the magnificent stereo D had just installed for me; it included a turntable flush with the wall. Alas, it was already out of date for tapes were coming in. He also stared at the pen and ink drawing of Agamemnon and Iphigenia over the fireplace which Erwin had given me, one of the few to recognize it.

I showed the apartment which included bedroom, bathroom and small room. "The last student had a hot plate and small fridge in there," I said. "I won't do that, only need coffee" he said. I told him I could spare a space for milk, bread and cheese in my refrigerator. He asked the rent and said it was very reasonable; hopefully no work was involved as he was not good at yard work. I said I knew how hard it was for grad students, had been one lately, only wanted to cover utilities and help with the mortgage. It was important to have someone quiet He said then he was just over an expensive divorce and would be quiet except for playing classical music. I did ask him if he were a teetotaler and it was the first time he smiled when he told me he wasn't, that he made a mean Bloody Mary. I said I was glad to hear it; peaches were in and D had just introduced us to the Southern splendour of peach daiquiris which he would sample soon.

I realized Keith's clothes were still in the closet and drawers, and said I would remove them and change the bed. I then realized that D and I were leaving that night for New Orleans for two days to see an exhibition of Alexandra's Gold, staying with Ingrid and Heinz. M told me later he thought I was quite mad to leave him with all that expensive equipment. "What is your son going to think when he finds me here?" he asked. I told him Keith knew I was going to rent the room. There were no cell phones in those days; there is indeed a use for them. I would have to leave a note on the back door, through which K always entered, that he should return to his old room in our part of the house. I could see M felt it strange and Keith did too. Keith told me later "He might have been Jack the Ripper." "Nonsense," I replied, "he was a Humanities teaching assistant". "They come in all types," he replied, so I gathered there was a wary meeting between the two of them. I just hoped M and D would get on well, and D won M over by asking at their first meeting "Are you an Aries?" which was correct. I asked D why he didn't ask for Keith or me for my birth sign. "I can only tell an Aries," he said.

I had asked Ingrid to put us up for two nights. She had a bedroom for me and if D brought a mattress he could sleep under the dining room table. D said he would prefer to drive all night in the heat and I could sleep on the mattress at the back of his truck and we would get to the beach just outside Destin at dawn and could take a swim and he would sleep a couple of hours. "You better take an umbrella to shield you from the sun," he said.

I was not a beach person, had never seen the white sands near Destin, with the peacock blue green sea, like the Mediterranean. I was pleased and the swim at dawn was delicious; we spent quite a few hours there and D slept, and we arrived at Ingrid's that evening. We had invited them out but they never went out. Instead they provided us with something and said we should sample New Orleans food the next day. We brought wine. They greeted us at the front door, holding back an enormous dog, a Doberman, called Butch. He had a savage snarl but Ingrid tried to tell us it was a smile. D was very good with animals and in later years even patted a wolf, but he did not take to Butch. They talked to him in German telling him he could not eat with them that night, as Audrey did not like dogs at the table. Ingrid tentatively put his dish on the table but at the sight of my face removed it. Butch glared at me. "Where is he going to sleep tonight?" I asked. "He is going to have a great treat," we were told, "he is sleeping with us. You have his room so be sure and use the latch, which locks it. Should he get out in the night he would bound into your room and frighten you." Indeed he would. "What about D under the table?" I asked. "He is safe in the living room," they assured us," it will be locked." We decided in the morning that instead of another night under the threat of Butch we would drive through the night to Destin and I would sleep again in the truck and we would have another glorious swim.

I cannot remember much about the exhibition of Alexandra's gold. I confuse it with the Mycenean gold at Athens, but shall never forget that shining white beach.

Dr. Andrews, who taught the Humanities Junior and Senior Seminars before I did, and left to work at the Folger Shakespeare Museum in Washington D.C. told me that because I had taught Shakespeare I could stay at the Folger with friends for $2O a night, so great years of trips to D.C. followed. The four of us went up visiting Monticello and other places on the way. During the first year with M we had spent a great deal of time transferring records to tapes, his, mine, and D's; M and D had tape players in their cars so we barreled along with Pavarotti and Beverley Sills. Keith enjoyed that very much but he could not stand Richard Tauber whom he called Dicky. At Monticello, D asked the rather prim guide if there were any truth in the rumors that Jefferson had fathered a child with one of his slaves. I remember her horror. She drew herself up and said sternly. "We do not countenance such talk of Mr. Jefferson here." I was interested in the architectural features in the house, such as his bed in an open niche between bedroom and study.

Keith and I had visited the MOMA in New York when we had stayed with Nadine for Christmas and he had developed a love for Seurat and van Gogh. He was delighted to find more and was really the last to wish to leave. I think we visited Mount Vernon the first time and we all liked that even better than Monticello, but the most unforgettable sights we saw that first time were the Lincoln and Jefferson Memorials at night, floodlit. Their speeches seemed even more remarkable, cut in stone.

We went many times to D.C., staying at the Folger, and one of the most unforgettable events we saw was Nureyev dancing in *Manfred*. I saw him dance with Margot Fonteyn years before and he was already rather old but he was the best. I forget most of the ballet; it ended with him dancing over the waves of scrim to drown. D was very wrapt up in ballet and insisted on going to thank him afterwards. I was reluctant as I did not like crowds but was glad we did go. He came out in a leather jacket and his face looked like a paler leather. Keith said, "there is a thousand years of Russian history in his face." D rushed up to thank him and I heard Nureyev say "And zey vont to poosh me off the stage!"

At another time we saw a special van Gogh exhibition at the National Gallery where paintings had been brought from all over the world. After seeing so many slides of van Gogh it was incredible to see the actual paint and the thickness of it and how it contributed to the tragic realism of his face. We could not get Keith away and I was so thankful he had this opportunity even though he did not go to the university. He did not want to go, he did not like to read, but I felt guilty; I should have pushed him.

The first spring M was there we made many trips to see the flowers around the Big Bend, Torreya Park, Three Rivers, and Marianna caves, where for the first time in America I saw growing the columbine that the Northern Renaissance painters loved. It was still cool and pleasant to walk. M taught me how to compose Haiku, the seventeen-syllable Japanese poem of three lines, 5-7-5. They were supposed to contain a hint of the season and often a surprise at the end. The red rain lilies were flowering so I mentioned them, ending "O smoke go away." M liked to smoke in those days but never did in the house.

Of all the flowers we saw I remember most the oranges in bloom with fruit and flowers on the same branch and the magical scent. Flowers seemed to have no scent in Florida but the orange blossom made up for all I missed in roses, wisteria, and honeysuckle. We had the windows closed when we approached the groves for it was getting warm and we needed air conditioning. The surprise of the scent when we opened the door and stepped out was unforgettable.

We discovered that we both played the recorder, he the alto and I the descant, and playing together became a great pleasure. M was a true musician and had the most beautiful whistle and could recall the theme of any movement of any symphony or concerto. It was a shame that he did not learn the piano when he was young but he said his father thought he was sparing him and taught him chess instead, and so successfully that he became the Junior Champion of Milwaukee. He enjoyed chess but wished he had spent the time on music. He brought his recorder back after Christmas with some music and I had music too, brought from England. We started with "Flow gently, sweet Avon" to which M appended *Mit Gefühl*" which tickled me very much. I had all the music Dr. Bergmann had given me years ago including the little book Bach had written for his wife arranged for two recorders. We grew to enjoy that very much. For both of us it was a joy to be able to play music with someone else. I had joined a recorder group earlier in Tallahassee but they were more advanced and it was a bit of a strain. M and I were at about the same level and we developed the habit of coming home from school and after a glass of wine and maybe a walk round the lake just outside we would play recorders for a while, not when D or Keith was there. They did not care for the recorders.

D continued to come round about twice a week when he was not working at the Tallahassee Motel and we would play records or transfer them to tapes and he would sing. Keith enjoyed that and he also enjoyed the discussions we had on our classes and teaching. He said he was getting a university education to himself. He and I continued to spend Christmas with Nadine in New York, and we always visited the MOMA and the Frick. We saw quite a few plays. Keith loved the theatre and was very impressed with Shaw's *The Devil's Disciple* and *Othello* with Christopher Plummer as Iago. We also enjoyed Jackie Mason with his incredible humor. One year D joined us and we went to hear "Die Fledermaus" at the Met. It was an incredible sensation when the chandeliers went up beforehand.

Chapter 86

Keith.

Keith was very good about driving me to Fort Myers for he knew I missed the family. He was always a great comfort and good for a laugh. I called him Yorick "whose jibes were wont to set the table on a roar." Keith could do this too with any company.

Keith was insistent he did not want to go to college. During the summer he had worked for Riley, a contractor who built beautiful houses, and he had offered to train Keith to be Master Carpenter and then a Superintendent. That is what he wanted to do. He did not like reading and I did not know how anybody could get through college without. I think now that with his photographic memory he could have done it. He remembered everything he had ever seen or heard. It was not long before he was beating me at Jeopardy. I regret now that I did not force him but am not sure if I could have done. Mummy's father was a carpenter, and Howard's father was a carpenter and draughtsman, so he had the love of wood in his veins. In England it was not so damning not to go to college and at the time I did not realize this. Many times I had to recall what Auntie Dora said: "You can only do what seems right to you at the time, and if it turns out wrong, there is no use crying over spilt milk."

Keith said he obtained a University education by listening to M, D, and I talk, and with his memory he did learn a lot. They said he was far more intelligent than any of their students. I taught him about Plato's cave and the shadows, and he liked that; also Paul Tillich, a Christian existentialist, who wrote of "the courage to be in spite of" which he illustrated by saying that if one acted with courage in the face of all misery, guilt, and fears, one was helped by God whether one believed in Him or not, for that was what God was, constant affirmation in the face of negation. That became Keith's credo, and he named one of his Japanese maples, the one that had to face the fiercest sun, Tillich.

One of my regrets was that he never came into contact with girls. He was happy with his fellow workers, many of whom were black, and he enjoyed their humor. At graduation he had been voted "the wittiest in the class."

In a brochure put out by the company Keith was featured. It was written by the architect: "Ask any of his subcontractors or coworkers why they love to work with Keith, and they'll likely answer it's because of his quick wit and intelligent conversation, but they also have the utmost respect for his demands for high quality and outstanding performance. He has been called 'micrometer' Keith due to his exacting standards, always checking to ensure that the dimensions are correct, the right prep work done, the next step ready, the right materials in place and protected from damage. His main job is quality control, and there are few better than Keith."

His father would have been proud of him. It was from Howard he got his meticulousness. Keith loved hearing about England, unlike the other sons who were not at all interested. He liked to listen to family stories especially about my father from whom he inherited a certain rather sardonic sense of humor.

He was fascinated by words and phrases. When he was in kindergarten I had a carpool of five children in a VW bug, and one day said "I hate turning into the oncoming stream of traffic" and he was delighted by this sentence and repeated it for days, just saying "I like it . . . . the oncoming stream of traffic . . . ." I thought he would be a reader, but guess it was just the sounds of words that fascinated him, French like *coup l'oeil, coup d'état*, and he was intrigued by the umlauts in my German book. "I want an umlaut" he said; from now on I'll sign 'me' and put two umlauts over the e."

Through the years he left many notes for me in the kitchen; he started work much earlier. When my father took us riding on the downs, when we reached the five-mile gallop there was a water tower at the end and my father would always say "that tower dominates the landscape." It got on my nerves as I told Keith once. Years later I received a note "the flowers are lovely but what 'dominates our landscape' is the Temple vase on an Edo scarf."

He fell in love with Japanese maples and decided to grow an arboretum. Over the years he planted nine Japanese maples, giving each a name of family or friends; one was dedicated to Mozart's Requiem "*Rex tremendae*"; there was one to M. A flowering cherry had been named after D but ornamental trees last only fifteen years. He planted one where I used to study, while lying on the grass, listening to the opera from the stereo in the open window. He called it "Opera Afternoons" after a poem I had written there. Keith was a severe critic of my poems but he liked that one and it was one of the first published in the U.S.

OPERA AFTERNOONS

For years the snake and I
lay on the ground but separate
divided by the leaves;
the sun was his attraction
while I preferred the shade.
The boughs swayed to the music,
perhaps he heard it too.

Erratic squirrels launched
their flights above us both,
disturbing patterned shade
but only for a while
until the time of day.
The garden was not theirs
and it did not belong
to the dividers of the air,
that bringing sharp delight

remained among the leaves.

Possession is of the ground,
it was the snake's and mine.
He died on Easter Saturday,
I thought it was his skin
and he would be renewed,
but at *The Meistersingers* end
I saw it was his death.

Chapter 87

The Late 1980s.

After D and M left, I made two new friends, Martha and her husband, Dr. John Lincoln. Martha audited all my classes. She was a piano teacher and insisted that she could teach me the piano. It was always a great regret to me that I had not learned the piano. I said I would only hope to play Mozart Adagios, perhaps Andantes, and she promised I would be able to do. I practiced an hour a day for five years, and she gave me a lesson once a week and I enjoyed it very much.

Her husband was as fascinated with physics as I was. He read up the latest science journals and explained to me the space-time dimension and the latest string theory which postulated that there were more than three dimensions, in fact, eleven. I had learned of the possibility of more than three by considering a skipping rope which we know as length and breadth, but when swung included several other dimensions. Dr. Lincoln told me of a rope which included five thick strands which to us would be only length and breadth but to an ant which had to climb over each strand would include several more dimensions. We had many such discussions, and I introduced them to peach daiquiris which D had taught me to make, and this added to the occasions.

I had a surprise one day in Tallahassee. There was an English voice on the phone who said she was my oldest friend. I had to ask school or WRNS or where and then she laughed, and I knew her before she said she was Honor. She had married again after the war. Apparently she was going out to see someone in Australia, perhaps to marry him, when she met someone on the boat she liked better, and she married him. He had died and left her a nice little flat in Dorset where she now lived, but her sister—in law had brought her for a visit to America and she asked could they visit me. I had Keith and a student at home and said she could share my bed but I had only a couch for the sister-in—law who evidently did not think much of the idea and instead took Honor to Disney World. Honor said she would much rather have seen me and I was to visit her when I next came to England, so I did. It was many years since we had met accidentally in Kensington during the war, but I had sent her Christmas cards. We laughed just as much as ever. Honor had a catering business, making wedding cakes (she had trained at the Cordon Bleu) and a new boyfriend who took us both on delightful pub crawls round Dorset.

After that I visited her regularly when in England but her situation changed. She still kept the flat but she had moved in with her boyfriend who was an estate agent to a Lady Jane somebody who had a beautiful old house nearby where I was to stay. Lady Jane was interested to meet me as I taught at a university. I gave up wondering where Honor was to land next. Lady Jane had some copies of the Cluny Tapestries in her study so I told her what Rilke had written about them and she was very intrigued and insisted I come back next summer. I stayed at least a couple of summers and remember swans on the river, a lovely old house and garden. Eventually she died and Honor moved back to her flat and broke up with the boyfriend as he had put on too much weight. She became ill herself and her daughter Jane whom I had just seen as a baby at the beginning of the war and who had married in Ireland, came and insisted she live with her in a Granny flat in the garden of her house in Dublin. Jane invited me over but I realized she had so much to do to look after Honor, who became quite ill, that I could not see my way to landing on her, although I would have loved to have seen the Book of Kells and laughed with Honor once more.

Chapter 88

1985.

The first trip I made to Europe with M and D was in 1985.

M was in Vienna, having been awarded a Fulbright Scholarship there in order to finish his dissertation on Freud and Schnitzler. D had his Ph.D. and obtained a position teaching at the American School of Switzerland at Leysin, and it was decided we should meet in Munich and drive through Austria to Leysin, where I would help in finding D an apartment as I knew French.

We drove through Styria, a part of Austria I did not know. It was beautiful and I remember an evening when the grass had been cut and the scent was delicious. We also saw a Narcissus Festival where people brought bunches of those flowers on to little boats and sailed on a lake where the festival was held. D had been in Switzerland before and insisted there was no need to pay high toll to take the Brenner Pass; the farmers did not and we could follow their roads. We were lost in a snowstorm, then overwhelmed by sheep, but eventually found our way. We passed Lac Leman with mountains all around and the lovely cities on its bank, end eventually found our way up seventeen zigzags on the vine—covered mountain to Leysin.

We found the college and were given addresses for apartments and I suppose I was of some help. The next day, after visiting the College, D suggested we should drive down to Evian, which was in France, and where the food was better and cheaper. There we had the sunset, the Alpenglühen, the light gold and crushed rose petals on the snow of the mountains. I remembered how Nero had smothered his guests with rose petals and felt as if I were being crushed with the splendor. I was looking at the round tin of my childhood, Castle Chillon with the mountains beyond, but the round tin had vanished, overwhelmed. We were alone on the terrace watching, with a silent Englishman, when a window opened and a voice said: "Is it over yet?" and the man replied "Not quite," which tickled M's sense of humor with its inadequacy.

At Luzern we heard an Alpenhorn, about seven feet long, blown in a restaurant and yodeling with hearty singers. Most of all I remember the meadows full of forget-me-nots with their scent and walking through them up to the waist but not crushing them.

My mother died in the late fall, 1985. Bettina stressed she did not want me to come over for the funeral; she wanted it to be as quiet as possible. Bettina had had such a dreadful time I wanted to make it as easy as possible for her, and I had always done what she told me. I know people thought it strange but my concern was to do what my sister wanted.

She said it was a good thing Mummy went, she would have had awful suffering if she had lived, and Bettina had asked Daddy to make it easier for her to go. She told me over the phone that he answered, and she spoke in his voice, "What do you think I am doing, kid?"

I had a strange experience. In Tallahassee after Thanksgiving it was the custom in all the stores to play Christmas carols and I was used to it. Just after Mummy died, I was startled to hear "Toyland, Joyland," which she had sung to us, which I had never heard before in America. It happened that M phoned that night from Vienna and I told him of my mother's death and of hearing that tune. He rang the next day to say he had gone to the opera after speaking to me, and he could not get "Toyland, Joyland" out of his head. He had to keep whistling it. He was twice reprimanded by opera officials; it was never allowed to hum or whistle in the Vienna State Opera, especially not non-classical music.

Several summers later I stood four and a half hours in the Vienna State Opera to hear Mozart's *Die Entführung aus dem Serail*. I did not know how I could stand that long but was so entranced by the music which I knew well and the visual performance, never before so beautiful, that I managed it. There is a long overture usually played before the opera starts. In Vienna, however, the curtain rose at the first note, and Pedrillo limped in, gazing up at the huge wall of the seraglio (harem) where Osmin was seen watering a little potted plant. Pedrillo took off his boots and emptied the sand out which told the audience he had come a long way. Usually Osmin is seen in an ordinary garden after the curtain rises. It was much more dramatic to see him behind the tremendous wall of the harem. It was a great moment, and at the same time I recalled that M, against all rules, had whistled my mother's melody in that opera after he heard of her death, and it now seemed like a little message from her to me. I thought that was one of the synchronicities of which Jung spoke and which are often overlooked.

Chapter 89

First trip with students.

After finishing his dissertation, which was published, M found an excellent job at the University of Arizona where he taught and took student groups to Europe in the summer. He managed to get me on several of those trips to teach Art History.

The first time I joined him on a student tour I met them in Paris. I was to meet them at the Gare du Nord on the platform for Chartres, but the travel director had given Mark the wrong platform, and in order to make the Chartres train on time we had to clamber over a ten-foot metal fence which divided us from the main platform. The students did it fairly easily and Mark gave me a leg up and I made it with a prayer. Immediately afterward we had to crawl under a turnstile and when I got through I said "I need a drink," which was hardly the way to meet new students, but we got on all right. As I had been to Chartres many times I was to lecture there and always enjoyed doing that. At the last lecture I asked them what had impressed them most. The students mentioned a window or a statue but one girl said back at home she had seen a poster of the cathedral with a little bridge beneath, and her greatest moment was when she realized she was standing on the bridge she had seen in the poster. I rather enjoyed that.

After we had visited Chartres and Paris we took the train to Switzerland where we were to meet up with D and stay at the American College at Leysin. It was spring and the fields were again full of forget-me-nots and I realized it was the scents of Europe I remembered most, the scents of flowers and the flowering trees. D had a new apartment and a grand piano in it under which I slept on a mattress, and woke up to miles of mountains with the Dents du Midi snow lit in the distance. We stayed a few days and then D accompanied us to Italy where he taught in Venice and led us over the bewildering array of canals and bridges. I remember his lecture on Titian, the "Assumption of Mary" and had never really appreciated Titian before. It was my third time in Venice and the first time I had seen it in sunlight.

We came back to Leysin and cornflowers were in the fields with a different scent, and a girl called Marie sang a French song about a poet who had died and all the fields wept for him.

Chapter 90

Trip to Europe with Keith, M, and D.

There was an unforgettable trip when K and I were supposed to meet in Paris D and M who would drive a car from Leysin in Switzerland. At the last moment D decided to take the train as he only had a weekend to scout out a future student trip he was taking to Paris, while we were going on further to the Blois valley wine district. K and I waited hours in the Gare du Nord for M who did not arrive. Somehow or other bombs were exploding in luggage. We were told not to leave luggage unattended or it would be blown up. I left K with luggage to go to the Information desk to ask if there had been a message for Wilson and the grumpy clerk said there was none. A kind person waiting pointed out that the name Wilson was written on the board under Messages. It was only thanks to him I got M's message which was frantic. He had rented a lead-free car in Switzerland as it was cheaper to rent there than in France, but he did not know there was no lead-free gas in France and the car hire place did not have the grace to inform him although they knew he was going there. When he was running out of gas in France he found it impossible to get any lead free gas and the car would only take that, so he had to go miles out of his way to find some and would be hours late arriving in Paris. Nothing to do but wait and have another little drink.

K wanted to go to the rest room so I stayed with the luggage and there was another announcement. "Keep luggage moving or it will be blown up." With all my strength I pushed the very heavy wagon towards the rest rooms. K came out and only saw the luggage moving; I was hidden behind it. He took over and shortly there was another announcement that passengers could now be seated beside luggage, thank goodness. Nobody seemed very perturbed.

At last M arrived, worn out, and we had some champagne. We always celebrated reunions with that in those days. He had enough lead—free gas to get us to Chartres where we were to stay and to return to Paris to change the car for a non-lead-free automobile. He had arranged to meet D's train and we rushed to the platform just in time to see D taking a train to Chartres as we were not on the platform to meet him. Only I knew where were staying in Chartres! It was a chapter of accidents! Only D had driven from Paris to Chartres before and knew the way off the periphery, a sort of detour round Paris which we were unable to get off. We saw the road to Chartres beneath but could not reach it.

It was a dreadful predicament and M suggested we drive off into a little park where we might find someone to give us directions, and we did. M was about to give him the Ragusa chocolate he had brought from Switzerland for our delectation but I managed to substitute some Snickers from the USA instead. K suggested we get some wine but we were anxious to get to Chartres to meet D's train as otherwise he would not know where to go. As we drove into Chartres about 2 am who should we see crossing the square but D. His first question was "Have you any wine? I've had a terrible time!" K suggested we listen to him in future.

The next day Keith left for Le Mans for the 24-hour race to which my sister had given him a ticket for his birthday. She had arranged everything for him with a friend, including where he was to stay and how he was to get to the race, where everyone would speak English. Le Mans was a few stations from Chartres but I was afraid he would be so tired after the 24—hour race he would sleep past the station, and I told him to say "Chartres, Chartres, *s'il vous plait*, Chartres" when he got in the carriage. D wanted to go into Paris the next day to scout out for his next student trip but I decided to stay for a whole day at Chartres. I thought M was going with him but to my delight he decided to stay at Chartres, and we had a wonderful morning with sunlight lighting up the windows and a guide lighting them up with words. It was bitter cold and we turned into a bistro for a cognac when I remembered my sister telling me Daddy always drank Armagnac not Cognac and I should try it. We ordered Armagnac not knowing what we were getting, and it came into the room ahead of itself in balloon glasses with the most heavenly aroma, which turned the dark room into gold before we even sipped it.

Keith arrived back safely with wonderful stories about being doled out toilet paper by a French woman which annoyed a British blimp colonel type who had attached himself to Keith. He seized more than he was given and said to Keith "Haven't we taught them anything?"

Next day D went back to Switzerland to await us several days hence, and we three traveled back to Paris, to the Gare du Nord, to try and exchange the lead-free car for a car that would drive on leaded gas, all that was available in France. M had all the documents and hoped I was capable of explaining that he had been misled in Switzerland by renting a lead-free car when they knew he was going to France, which only had leaded gas.

The station was full of people and somehow we were separated from Keith who needed the toilet and mercifully found someone who understood his needs and pointed the way, but there was a turnstile in between. He had not understood he had to put in money and leapt over it and was berated by an attendant. He threw money at her and ran to a stall only to find she was standing by him in the stall handing him his change. "Did you tip her?" asked M. "I gave her all I had," said Keith, "but do not care for the French toilet system." This was before we had pointed out to him the *pissoires* in Paris where men stood covered only from knees to shoulder to fulfill their needs.

Eventually we got the car changed to lead-free and started for a wine trip through the Blois Valley where we saw the fourteenth-century castles and took part in the wine tasting, degustations. The castles were beautiful but very much the same. Keith could not see enough of the buildings and the latrines while we were waiting for the four o'clock wine. I remember the nasturtiums in the gardens and Blois, a fairy tale city. Poitiers, one of the oldest Romanesque cathedrals, was disappointing and crumbling away and looked better in the slides we had shown to students. We had a fantastic French meal there with an unforgettable raspberry mousse and arrived at Annecy where we were to meet D. There was a lake there which was all a lake should be, but I was worried about meeting D in the parking place behind the biggest hotel which he said was the Esplanade, but there was no Esplanade. M and Keith were sanguine that we would wait by the road from Switzerland and look for a Swiss CH license, and lo and behold they found him.

We then set off on the *Route du vin* through *Alsace* and Lorraine, through beautiful villages interspersed with vineyards and graveyards which showed how these wine lands had been contested over the centuries. I remember Riqueville and Kaisersberg where Schweitzer was born, and was surprised to see how many scythes or scimitars were in the French cemeteries until I remembered France ruled Algeria for a long time. It was a drive through history. Everybody seemed to speak both French and German and on signs at the various inns were the names of owners with French first names and German surnames. It was a beautiful drive but melancholy with the sense of history.

I think it was on this trip we went on to Reims where we went through the caves of champagne and learned how Dom Pérignon had first discovered how to give it bubbles by infusing fertilized grapes into already fertilized wine. Mark took a photo of Keith embracing the statue of Dom Pérignon who had announced, "Brothers, I have bottled the stars."

From there we went on to Switzerland where we were all to ascend Mont Blanc. Keith was out of his mind with delight; this was a higher mountain than Traunstein and covered with snow. We went up on lifts but at the third stop I could breathe no more. All I wanted was to descend and have a cappuccino. M was so kind as to accompany me down and set me at a table where I could see the mountain and the hang gliders, blue, red, and violet, which were so incredibly beautiful against the snow. But I was thankful to be drinking coffee at ground level. Keith ascended Mont Blanc, and I knew that was an experience he would never forget.

Chapter 91

Student trip to Vienna, Budapest, and Prague.

I remember one student trip when M and I were in Vienna with students, and I wandered off and found the Kapuzinekirche where *die heilige Rita* had saved me from the urns containing the hearts of the Hapsburgs which Erwin had wanted me to see. There was a notice up that today was her *Festtag* and there would be a mass in her honor that evening. I felt that was too much of a synchronicity to miss and asked M if I were needed that evening. He said he had given the students carte blanche to eat where they wanted, which was generally Pizza Hut, and he would come with me. I had told him about *die heilige Rita* and he was interested that she was the saint for the most hopeless cases.

A small crowd gathered in the church that night and after the Mass a monk was handing out red roses which were her symbol. I went up to get one and left M in his seat but the monk came down especially to him and handed him a rose. It was a strange occasion; afterwards we went to a café Auden had patronized and there was plaque there in his honor. I quoted his lines

> Who in his own backyard
> has not felt the secret his heart cannot quote
> which goes to show that the bard
> was sober when he wrote
> that this world of fact we love
> is insubstantial stuff
> and all the rest is silence
> on the other side of the wall
> and the silence ripens,
> and the silence all.

In Vienna I went to the State Opera for the first time and had the strange experience of remembering how M had whistled my mother's tune "Toyland, Joyland" when I had told him over the phone of her death. I heard it again in my mind after the incredible experience of Mozart's *Abduction from the Seraglio*.

We went on to Budapest, which I did not think as beautiful as Vienna, although there was a fine view over the river to Pest. We took a river trip to see an old Hungarian village where everything had stayed the same since the 18th century. On the way back I sat down opposite a seat with four little schoolgirls who obviously wanted to talk but we did not know how. I tried German, French, English; it seemed hopeless but I suddenly remembered what I thought was "sing" in Latin and it did the trick and they burst into song, lovely folk tunes. M had been hanging over the side of the boat looking at the water but came to the table to hear them and really it was a high point of the trip. We were arrested in Budapest for not stamping our bus tickets twice. I was sure we had and it was just a ruse to get money out of Americans. M had a contingency fund but it threw a damper over the occasion.

We arrived in Prague after a very long train journey, tired and dusty, and were told at our hotel there was nothing to eat there. The concierge, who did speak German, told us there was a bistro which might have food around the corner. I asked what food was in Czech, and was told something. He took all our passports which terrified the students but we tried to reassure them that often happened in Europe. I learned quickly that corner meant something different in Prague; there were always seven different streets stemming from one corner. I did not see how anybody who was not native could find their way around. I felt that might have contributed to Kafka's state of mind. We found the bistro where no one spoke German, but I said what I was told was the Czech for food and was greeted with a shake of the head. "Drink, not eat." The place was full of waiters and waitresses hanging round the walls; I was sure one of them knew German, and although I understood their reluctance to speak it, our situation was desperate. It was evening and the students had had nothing since breakfast. Erwin had said in a difficult situation study the faces and approach the most sympathetic. I concentrated on one young girl and said in German "One of you must speak German. These students are starving, please give them food." The girl smiled and said in German, "I will ask the cook." She came out and said "Beefsteak." Two students protested that they were vegetarians. I cursed inwardly but asked for cheese, and they eventually brought thin pork schnitzels with a piece of celery on each and a little cheese.

It was not a good welcome to Prague but it was the most beautiful city since Florence. So many churches, Romanesque, Gothic, and Baroque; so many magnificent tombs and the Castle Hradschin on high. I thought of Rilke growing up there; it was no wonder he was fascinated by death; it was celebrated everywhere, perhaps most significantly on the Charles Bridge, where statues of saints loomed down on passersby, sometimes wreathed in river mist.

I was most impressed by the art in the Hradschin. This was before the Berlin Wall came down so we had no catalogs available, but I recognized the paintings beloved by the Hapsburgs: Rubens, Titian, Velasquez, Rembrandt, seen also in Budapest and Vienna. What I did not expect were five Picassos of the Blue Period. The Art Director before the war must have been very astute to realize their worth. I had never seen that many early Picassos together and they were so beautiful. I realized what a blow to civilisation World War I had been and how it had shattered the artists and that they had realized its implication in their art. The beauty and melancholy of those Blue Period Picassos has never left me; I felt their loss.

I brought my water colors with me and did some painting there and could not get over the subtlety of the colors. Each building seemed to have been aware of how well it went with its neighbors. I remember some steps down to the river, with a café alongside, and how even more beautifully it was reflected in the water. The streets were mostly cobbled and I sprained my ankle but did not wish to stop wandering around and was afraid to lose the others. I was walking with M one day and it started to rain so went under a colonnade but realized soon the colonnade had swerved and in panic started back thinking I had lost M, but he had realized the swerve and followed me. Once we both were lost and a kind Czech who spoke German said "I will have to take you there; one cannot give directions in Prague."

Chapter 92

The Nineties.

In 1990 Keith made a disastrous marriage, which did not last long, and he returned to the home where he had been born and lived in the adjoining flat that I had previously rented to students. He found solace in his Japanese maples, and in listening to Beethoven concertos and symphonies. He joined the community chorus, directed by André Thomas, and sung in Beethoven's Ninth and in the Mozart Requiem.

Bettina invited us for a summer visit to England but she did not want us to come to Wales and found a place for us to stay in West Sussex and I was delighted to see how unchanged it was from our childhood. Manor Farm and Ticehurst were in East Sussex which had been much more built up. As we drove over the downs I asked my sister if she did not regret going so far away to Wales. Ronnie had developed a bad leg and could no longer drive so they could not meet as they had done for years, and although they telephoned each other they had not met for some time. Bettina said she did not regret going to Wales, she loved its wildness, and Ronnie would not have been able to meet in Sussex either. He was being looked after by his brother and sister-in-law. I felt sad about this.

I was happy to see that Bettina and Keith still got on so well together. They were both so close to me it was a delight that they felt akin. Both were a little unusual, especially Bettina who had always "dreed her own weird" and Keith with his love of gardens and art was not the run of the mill. Bettina took us to see the Old Man of Wilmington which we had known as children. This was a gigantic man outlined in the chalk of the Downs. No one knew how long it had been there; some said it was prehistoric but I could never understand why the grass did not grow back over the chalk outlines. It was close by the Roman road which Chaucer's pilgrims had taken to Canterbury and Keith was thrilled with all this history. It was a lovely summer day as we climbed the stiles and ascended the downs and there looked over the Weald with its colored fields that I had always loved. Bettina asked me if I remembered lying on the downs together as children with buttercups and poppies nearby, when I told her to remember that afternoon always as it was, and she had. I felt abashed that I had forgotten that moment till then.

We finished the trip by a visit to my cousin in Cambridge where we went everyday to Evensong at King's College Chapel. In the music I heard there under the fan-vaulted roof I found the solace that I used to find in the garden at Manor Farm.

My uncle had left me some money so I could afford a trip to England in the summer vacation; sometimes I took Keith and occasionally left him at home with friends. I always visited Ray and took her for a long weekend to Oxford which we both loved. We went in May when the chestnuts were out along the river and the college gardens were filled with wallflowers and tulips. We strolled along Addison's Walk, enjoyed the river, and heard Evensong at one or other of the colleges.

I also visited Nan and Ken in Devon which was even more deeply in the country. I had grown to know their son Richard, who had been a very bright child. He'd asked his mother once why he could not walk on the water as he had so much faith. Nan was rather nonplussed but said perhaps he did not have enough. "I shall never have more," she told me he said, and that was true for he lost it completely when he went to Oxford.

Ken did very well with his Ford Tractor franchise. He was the only one in Devon to sell and repair Ford tractors, and they soon left their thatched cottage with the well and bought a beautiful Georgian house in which the last bishop of Crediton had lived, so it was "the Old Palace" because bishops were always supposed to live in palaces. It was however just a simple Georgian house, very beautiful and, once they had put in central heating, comfortable. Nan had lots of visitors and was a very good cook. They ate the main meal in the middle of the day which was the country custom, strange to me but it meant that Nan could relax with Ken in the evening over a drink. They had a beautiful old walled garden which made such a perfect background for lupins and delphiniums. Ken became Mayor of Crediton and the first thing he did was to abolish pay toilets for women.

He thought it unfair that women had to pay. It made the headlines and I do not know whether it was for that or just because he was Mayor but he and Nan were invited to the Queen's Garden Party more than once. After the war Royalty abolished the debutante parties and had Garden Parties in the summer for all sorts of people.

In the end when the teaching load grew heavy my correspondence with England lapsed and I was sorry about this. I loved their letters. Cyril and Frances, the friends made with Howard, were excellent correspondents. Cyril would always write me in the spring that the daffodil buds had started to droop, a sign they would bloom very soon, and it brought me something of the spring in England. They also told of our godson, John Howard, who was a very bright child and I always visited them when in England.

One summer, and I forget when, Keith and I went to England to see Bettina, but she did not want us to come to Wales and found a place for us to stay in West Sussex and I was delighted to see how unchanged it was from our childhood. Manor Farm and Ticehurst were in East Sussex which had been much more built up. As we drove over the downs I asked my sister if she did not regret going so far away to Wales; Ronnie had developed a bad leg and could no longer drive so they could not meet as they had done for years, and although they telephoned each other they had not met for some time. Bettina said she did not regret going to Wales, she loved its wildness, and Ronnie would not have been able to meet in Sussex either. He was being looked after by his brother and sister-in –law. I felt sad about this.

Chapter 93

My sister's death.

I did not think my sister looked well, and indeed in the next year we found out that she had stomach cancer. She had two dreadful operations that were not successful. I offered to come over but she was adamant that I should not. "I want you to remember me climbing the downs as we used to do." She had to go to hospital and managed to get a phone in her room and I phoned her every night. She did not care for cut flowers but she loved cyclamens and that Christmas I phoned World Flowers to send her a white cyclamen which were in season at that time. I insisted on that and nothing else and they promised. I wondered whether to tell Bettina it was coming or let it be a surprise, but am glad I told her for they sent cut flowers. Although she had not long to live she had lost nothing of her spirit and refused to take them. They insisted and she said her sister from America was phoning that night and she would tell her to cancel her check to World Flowers for they had promised a white cyclamen. After some to do, they went away and returned with a white cyclamen, the most beautiful and largest she had seen. She had it put on top of a cupboard so all the ward could see it, and even in the night lights it showed its gracious shadow. That was the last thing I could do for my sister.

We knew she did not have long to live. She made me promise not to come for the funeral. Kenneth, our cousin, had said he would take care of all arrangements and she wanted me to remember her as she was on the downs, and not dying or dead. She knew that Keith's disastrous marriage had come to an end and he had come home for solace in his garden and Japanese maples, and she wanted us both to remember her as she was. She said if she could she would get through.

I was working in the garden one day, for once not thinking specially of her but of the weeds, when I heard her voice clearly. She called me by the childish name that only she used and said she was all right. I heard from Kenneth that day that she had died the day before, and checked EST with Greenwich Mean Time carefully to find out that she had died when I heard her. Somehow this seemed important, to know whether it was her last living thought or after death. It was definitely after her death.

Chapter 94

Klee.

M had been given a grant in 1993 to do research in the Klee Archives at Bern for his forthcoming book on Klee, *Of Angels, Things and Death,* and he asked me to come with him to translate the French criticism and to explore the possible connection between Rilke and Klee. My dissertation had been on *Rilke's developing concept of Death*, and it was known that the two artists had met in Munich during WWI, and that Rilke had written Klee a letter from Soglio.

It was the best trip we had together, no students to worry about and a very interesting subject. We decided not to stay in Bern but to find a *Gasthaus* in a village in the mountains around. We had our evening snack at a wonderful salad bar in Bern, and then with a bottle of wine took off for the strange little place we had found. It had a blossoming cherry tree outside which had drawn me to it, and an imposing landing on the first floor, lined with heavy cowbells, and a beautiful old chest at the end. We arrived back before sunset and climbed the hill behind up to a stand of beeches.

I knew they were beeches from afar because of the light color of their leaves. It was strange. As soon as we reached the beeches and not a minute before, we heard cowbells and saw a vast panorama of snow mountains, at one and the same moment. It was the same every night. We never heard the cowbells till we reached the hilltop and saw the snow.

Only Mark had permission to work down in the archives; he brought up to me the relevant material, so I sat and worked by a window or wandered through the light halls which held Klee's enchanting paintings. I had always loved Klee since I had seen his exhibition in London during the war. I found a letter which Rilke had written Klee from Soglio, a village high up in the Alps, where he had been given hospitality by de Salis, who owned a fine house there. Rilke had sent Klee a strange poem, "*Ur-gerausch*" (Primitive Sound) in which he described the new invention of the phonograph where a needle went round a wax cylinder and produced music. He imagined what sound a needle would make going around the coronal suture. There was indication that Klee had received the letter for when he was working at the Bauhaus he painted a picture which showed its influence. There was some French criticism to translate, but we both were impressed by the influence Buber had had on Klee, and I learned a great deal of Buber that summer. I was astounded by the acknowledgment Mark gave me in the Introduction; I had never been so touched, for I had done very little and enjoyed myself so much.

We decided to explore the surroundings at the weekends and were wondering where to go. As we strolled around Bern we saw an old ragged poster on one of the advertisement columns, "Soglio." We decided to go there although it was quite a way, into the Italian Alps. Mark found it on the map and we started in a mountain mist which was quite scary because there was often a precipice at one side of the road. Mark was an excellent driver and did not seem to worry over the possibility of meeting sheep, so I kept quiet but was very relieved to see the mist clear eventually and a delightful Gasthaus where we had the best and largest cappuccino ever. From then on the sun shone as we drove over snow topped mountains to Soglio which was the most fascinating village. On the hill up to it were many little wooden houses, larger than beehives but smaller than pig styes. What were they? We were told they were used to dry the chestnuts which were used to make bath oil, rather as the oast houses in Sussex dried the hops to make beer.

We went to have lunch at the de Salis house, now a hotel, and had the most delicious tomato bisque. We knew we could not stay there for it looked very expensive but we saw the library where Rilke worked, and that gave me a frisson. There was a garden adjoining which he would have liked, looking out on to the mountains. We were told that Soglio was the birthplace of Giacometti, but he had left early and there was none of his work there. We wandered round the village which had cobbled streets, many wrought iron grilles over the lower windows, and shutters on the higher ones which would have reminded Rilke of Prague. We saw very few people. I bought a little vial of chestnut oil which smelt delicious and then it started to rain.

We saw something astounding which stopped us in our tracks, five tall thin poles of different heights with what looked like jagged metal crowns atop. Every door was shut, there was no one to ask. I put up the umbrella and Mark took a photo of me staring at them bemused in the rain. We concluded that perhaps they were some sort of memorial to Giacometti; they were not his thin men but they were of metal and thin. We never found out.

SOGLIO

They used to call it Badedas
but now it's Vita bath Spring Green,
a bubble path of chestnut woods.
In Soglio in snow
the huts of chestnuts climb
the mountain woods
for men have known for centuries
that chestnut oil was balm for bones.
A count once owned the land
and built a splendid house and left
but others climbed the winding ways
and made the chestnut oil.
For months the chestnuts dry on boards
beneath the roofs against the snow,
sun, rain and moon
until the time is ripe for oil,
a patient trade.

The poet Rilke stayed a while,
the narrow steps and wrought iron grilles
reminded him of childhood Prague.
While there he wrote "Primeval Sound"
and sent it to the artist Klee
who recreated it in paint
through winding ways.

The next weekend we went to Lauterbrunnen and
Iseltwald and *la grande Suisse* with its three great Alps of
the Virgin, the Monk, and the Ogre across a lake which
reflected them and floating clouds. We went to Wengen
where I had skied with Donald as a girl. The next week we
found the best place of all to stay, Murten, a 12th-century
village with just three streets which crossed each other and
were surrounded by the old wall where we could walk on
top. Just beyond was a lake with grass around it and a seat
which seemed always empty at sunset so we sat there each
evening and watched. Blackbirds would start singing. I had
not heard them since England and could not express the
joy their liquid notes gave me. We sat still and saw the light
gradually change across the lake; it was the nearest I ever
came to contemplation.

blackbird evening spills
liquid bars of bronze and dark
from recumbent hills

While at Murten I wrote another Haiku remembering the first place we stayed with the cherry tree and the high hill we had to climb. beech in leaf above last year's rust cowbells announce distant fields of snow

I originally wrote "melting." M also wrote Haiku but he would not give them to me but would only say them. I remember they were good and wish I had them.

There was a special evening at Murten when it was raining and from the shelter of the wall we looked at the village lights on the cobbled streets. I noticed the cobbles were copied from the circles a stone made when thrown into water, and determined to have a cobbled drive at home, fashioned in the medieval manner. The only snag about Murten was that parking had to be paid, and it seemed as though M was always putting coins in the meter.

We saw so many beautiful and interesting things it is hard to recall them all. In Bern there was in the town square a huge chessboard with life size pieces, and it was seldom not in use. While working at the Klee archives we bought our lunch daily; *Speckbrot* (ham roll) but not like any seen before, a large homemade biscuit with bits of ham cooked in it; it was very good and only cost a schilling. For the same price we bought a little bottle of red wine each and went to the car to enjoy it and often a little nap. On the flight home I asked M what he had enjoyed most. He was as pleased as I was at finding Edelweiss and gentians. There was one place we stayed so high and close to the mountains that it looked as though they were falling through the windows. Another time night fell suddenly and the huge mountain in front was suddenly dark and from each side splashed stars, such huge and watery stars. Erwin said it was no wonder that Rilke moved to ever drier climates for there the stars are larger. M made me laugh; he pondered my question a while and then said, "perhaps the *Speckbrot, Rotwein* and sits in the car." I laughed more with Mark than with anybody except Keith or Nan.

Chapter 95

Nan.

Nan died early. Her mother and sister both had diabetes and it did not seem to bother them very much but when Nan came down with it she became very ill. She wrote me she could no longer work in her flower garden. Then she seemed to get better and Richard took his parents for a summer vacation to the Isle of Wight where they had first met. I was happy about that until I received a cable from Richard: "Mother dying wants to hear from you. Write and cable." I cabled and wrote a long letter the same day recalling the many times we had laughed together for I knew that would mean most to her. I started with our first meeting when I had brought her breakfast in bed and arrived with one cornflake in a cereal bowl for the rest had blown away. I reminded her how she had once told me she ate other people's skins while looking at the baked potato skins I had left, how we collected strange headlines such as "Patton takes bite out of Nazi bulge." I included a story which she had always liked. When young I often quoted Shakespeare and the lines from Othello before he strangles Desdemona: "Yet I'll not shed her blood/ nor scar that whiter skin of hers than snow, and smooth as monumental alabaster/ yet she must die or she'll betray more men./ Put out the light and then, put out the light." I had gone to the opera with another friend to hear Verdi's *Otello* who, during one of the intervals, said to me, "Has he sung yet those lines you are always quoting, 'switch off the light, switch off the light'?" Nan had always enjoyed that.

In those days airmails took four days from U.S. to England. It was over a week before I heard from Richard that she had received the letter. She smiled when he read it to her and told him to tell me she had wanted to write me but was too weak. She had her foot amputated and died soon after. It was terrible. I wrote Ken of course but it was Richard who replied saying he hoped if I came to England again (he knew my mother and sister had died) that I would visit his father who did not want to see anybody but would like to see me as I was so close to Nan, and Keith too. We decided we would go to England in the summer vacation next year.

Then my granddaughter, Jennifer, wrote me. She knew I had always wanted to take her to Europe with me, but her mother, Nancy, hated flying and refused to let Jennifer fly till she was 21. I understood this. Jennifer said she was now over 21 and had graduated and wanted so much to go to Europe. I told her perhaps the best thing now was to send the money for her and her boyfriend to go. She replied she would rather go with me as I could show her more. This touched me and at the same time I heard of a faculty member who was teaching at the Florence Center for a year who was coming home for Christmas and wanted to rent his apartment very cheaply for three weeks at Christmas. The apartment was on the other side of the Arno, at the foot of the Michelangelo steps to San Miniato, with a fantastic view over Florence. It seemed a synchronicity. It had been a dreadful year. Keith's disastrous marriage had ended, Bettina had died, and Keith had suffered with me over this. In some ways he was closer to his English relations, certainly to Bettina. He loved art and where better to study it than in Florence? Jennifer did too, and they got on well together. Also I had three frequent flyer tickets that expired that year. We decided we were meant to go to Florence for Christmas and also to England next summer to see Ken and Richard. Bettina had left me the proceeds of the sale of her cottage in Wales, and I felt she had made possible this extravagance.

Chapter 96

Florence again.

Keith, Jennifer, and I left for Florence the week before Christmas. It was the first time Jennifer had flown. We met her in Atlanta and flew from there to Milan, and then took a train to Florence and a taxi to the apartment where we were met by someone from the Florence Center who had the keys. The apartment was in a 15th-century building but had been completely modernized. It was in the first street where the 12th-century wall ended but the gate in the wall was opened and closed night and morning as it had been for centuries, although one could get through on our street. Customs died hard in Italy. This fascinated Keith. It was dark when we arrived, we were very tired and Jennifer said she would go to bed; we had had something to eat on the train. I said I would like to walk a few steps up and see Florence floodlit and Keith came with me. Only a few steps up Michelangelo's steep climb and we saw the Duomo lit up, like a tulip as I had always thought. Many other churches were lit and the green river. We could not resist going down to the river and then we saw the oldest bridge, the Ponte Vecchio alight, with lanterns in its little shops. We had to go further and could not stop. We went up to the David statue in the Piazza Vecchio and he loomed enormous in the night. It was a fantastic first impression of Florence for Keith, and on the way back we saw a taverna with a door open, a fire inside, and a table with a bottle of wine. We went in and had the most delicious crepes with red wine; it was a marvelous meal and I felt sorry Jennifer had missed it.

Next morning we got out the map and made plans. I thought the Bargello first where one sees the beginning of Renaissance art; Donatello's and della Robbia's laughing boys which are so full of the joy of life. The competing designs by Brunelleschi and Ghiberti for the Baptistery doors were also there. The latter showed more of the classic influence which was doubtless why they were chosen. It must have been a hard choice to make; Brunelleschi's designs showed more Gothic intensity. He never sculpted again but left with Donatello for Rome, determined to be an architect. We then went to see the Baptistery where Ghiberti had spent so many years of his life designing those incredible doors, which introduced perspective and the human body in motion. I showed them all the doors, including the latest which were not bronze but gilded, and which Michelangelo had called "the gates of Paradise."

Keith felt sorry for Brunelleschi but I said he returned to build the Duomo, the dome for Florence Cathedral which had been left without a roof for years until he came along able to build one big enough. I told them what I had taught the students: there was a competition for that too, which he won by saying he could make an egg stand on one end. He challenged others to try and no one could until he tapped the bottom of his egg and it then stood up. Others protested that they could have done that too; "but you didn't think of it," he is supposed to have said. He had seen the Pantheon and other domes in Rome and he designed a plan which had an inner as well as an outer dome which divided the weight. Keith and Jennifer climbed to the top to see how he had done it. I showed them then Michelangelo's grave in the church of Santa Croce. He had asked to be buried near the door so that on Judgement Day the first thing he would see would be Brunelleschi's dome. "I built a bigger," he said, "but no more beautiful."

We none of us liked the interior of the Baptistery very much with its medieval frescoes of horrible demons dragging people to hell. I was glad to see that Donatello's wooden statue of Mary Magdalene was safely in her place again. During the terrible floods of the 1970s in Florence the water in the Baptistery had risen to the top of her dais and even touched her feet by the time an art historian paddled through the water and took her on his shoulders and carried her out and thus saved a priceless Renaissance treasure, and an unusual one. There was no Platonic influence here; she was an old woman, haggard and worn from her years in the desert after the death of Christ, which was believed to have been her history in medieval times.

I told Jennifer and Keith that Michelangelo had been brought up in the Medici Academy where Plato was taught, and that this influence was seen in his statue of "David." Plato had taught that Ideal Forms were only seen in the mind. We do not see Goliath, we have to imagine him. This is also seen in his "Prisoners" where forms are seen, writhing in the stone, waiting to be born from the sculptor's mind. Ideal Beauty is in another world and this was an influence on Botticelli in his "Birth of Venus." She is portrayed as Ideal Beauty, the goddess rising from the sea and sailing to shore on a shell. Botticelli was condemned by the monk Savonarola for idealizing a heathen goddess and under his influence Botticelli destroyed some of his classic paintings, but Savonarola came to grief himself in this new age of the Renaissance which glorified the classics, and he was burnt at the stake in the Palazzo Vecchio.

My children did not care for the Uffizi Gallery as much as I did. Keith said he grew tired of the endless Annunciations; both preferred the statues. I repeated what I had told the students in 1980. I made them appreciate the influence of the Northern Renaissance in the painting by Hugo van der Goes "the Adoration of the Shepherds," which showed a realism that astonished the Florentines: the shepherds were dirty and unshaven. The Florentines under the Platonic influence were used to portraying everyone in religious paintings as beautiful; Raphael's apostles were always aristocratic and well dressed. Florence was impressed by the Northern realism, by the artists' use of landscape that was shown in detail, becoming more than just a background, and by their symbolism in flowers and in handmade objects. The artists of the Northern Renaissance did not focus on the beauty of the human body as did the Florentines but rather on the beautiful things men had made, jars and lamps which they used as symbols of the divine, and above all, in flowers as symbols.

I had told Jennifer to bring good walking shoes for we would be walking all through Florence. On every street were statues. At first she was surprised we had to go as far as the Ponte Vecchio to buy a croissant or pastry for breakfast and then on to a café for cappuccino, but she soon became used to it and took charge of the map. Keith loved Fra Angelico and the cells he painted individually for every monk, and he also liked Masaccio's frescoes which showed human movement and dignity He particularly liked the shadow of St. Peter healing a sick man.

We did not do any cooking in the apartment except for one day, but bought very good cheese and bread for lunches, with olives. These were sold in little holes in the old town wall; a man stood with a barrel, green olives in one hole and black in another. We usually bought olives on our evening walk to the Boboli Gardens to see the sunset. It was a long steep climb, and Jennifer and Keith tried to teach me how to flick the olive pits off my thumb but I never seemed to reach the distance they did. Often the pit just fell off in an embarrassing way which made them laugh. Sometimes we took the alternate route up the Michelangelo steps to San Minato. It was even steeper but not so long. I preferred the longer walk for we would gradually see the olive trees appear in their grey green skirts and then the tremendous dark magnificence of the cypresses. From the top of the

Boboli gardens we saw the green river with its evening reflections, colored houses with different shades of shutters, like the paints in old paint boxes, light sienna, burnt sienna, raw umber. I told them the paints had all come from the soils of Tuscany and Umbria, and how fascinated I had been years ago when I first learned that in Florence.

We watched till all the buildings were floodlit: the churches, Giotto's campanile, the pointed chalice of the Duomo and the bridges, especially the lantern-lit Ponte Vecchio down below. This was Keith's especial favorite and he bought two little replicas of it and gave one to Jennifer. Ours is still on the top of the 18th century desk Howard once sanded and refurnished.

Keith wanted to go to Pisa to see the Leaning Tower and wanted Jennifer to go with him. I was coming down with a cold and felt exhausted and longed for a day in bed. Jennifer felt the same so we both stayed in bed next day and let Keith go off by himself. He had a flexi pass and I told him he might have to fight for it as it seemed to me that M and I always had trouble with flexi passes. I think European conductors knew we were foreigners and tried to scare us that we had not paid for them. He did have trouble but made it. He promised he would not climb the Leaning Tower unless it had railings around it. He had seen in a photo in the National Geographic that they now had railings, but I still shuddered remembering how the students had crowded to the edge years ago. I told him to pay special attention to the pulpits in the Pisa cathedral by the father and son, Pisano. They ranked with Donatello as my favorites. I was sorry not to go but too tired. We had already been to Siena, built of rose-colored bricks, with the hill rising up from the cathedral covered in bricks with white channels to let the rain run down into the cisterns under the cathedral. It seemed a little like the Duomo turned inside out. I always thought of Siena as "the rose-red city half as old as time" although that line belonged somewhere else.

Keith came back raving about Pisa. There were railings, he had climbed the tower, and even found a builder who spoke English. They had a glass of wine together and he had learned a great deal about the problems with the tower. He liked Pisa better than Siena for it had the green Arno River like Florence, and the reflections. He saw the Pisano pulpits and liked the son's more than the father's. It was strange; the father had more classical influence in his pulpit; Mary looked rather like a Roman matron, while the son had reverted to the International Gothic intensity, and it was more emotional. Both Jennifer and Keith had good eyes for art. When Jennifer saw the *Rondanini Pieta*, the last statue by Michelangelo, she said that the woman holding Christ's feet had been done by another artist, Keith agreed. Years later Jennifer sent me a Bonsai olive tree in a little pot to remind me of the olive trees we had seen in Florence.

Chapter 97

Last trips to Europe.

In the summer of 1998 Keith and I came to England again. We were going to visit Ken, but on the way, arriving at Gatwick, we rented a car and went to visit Manor Farm again. When he was twenty Bettina had driven us through the right-of-way to the lake, which I had tramped three times when pregnant with him, saying "this child shall have something of England," and we had gone round it together. I knew we could do that again, but when we passed the wrought iron gates leading to Manor Farm I somehow felt we should enter and ask if we could see the garden that I had loved as a child. The Landaus, who then owned Manor Farm, were incredibly welcoming. They were delighted to see us, they let us walk through the garden, through the cherry orchard, up through the bluebell path to the woods, down to the lake the way I had gone when I was young, not using the right-of-way open to cars. The bluebells were out, Keith saw them. I hoped for nightingales, but there were so many thrushes and blackbirds I could not be sure I heard them. The Landaus asked us to come again.

We then went on to London to pick up Ray who was to join us in this drive round southern England. We first visited Dolf Polak and his wife Thalia at Havant in their lovely old house. Thalia had developed cancer early and Dolf had retired from medicine to look after her. He taught the violin. locally. He had once been the second violin in the Amadeus Quartet which I had often heard rehearse at Oaklands, the Polak's house, during the war. I had met the Amadeus Quartet again when teaching in Florence, and Norbert Brainin, the first violin, remembered me, which touched me very much.

While staying in Havant, we visited Portsmouth and saw the H.M.S. Victory, Nelson's ship, which was a great thrill for Keith who had admired Nelson since he had seen him on his column at Trafalgar Square when he was eight years old.

It was rather a sad journey we were making. Most of my friends seemed to have lost their spouses early. Sim had died a year after Howard, and Stefan a few years later, both of a heart attack. Hanni was left a widow young but all her children had obtained scholarships to Oxford or Cambridge, and she herself got a B.A. on the University of the Air, so she was all right. She had a job; she went round interviewing people about various products. She was successful at this which did not surprise me as she was always good at getting on with all sorts of people; I remembered her in the shelter. I would miss laughing and talking Wienerisch with Stefan but the one I missed the most after Nan was Cyril. He died of the flu the preceding winter. It was he who had kept me in touch with England through his wonderful letters. He wrote me when the first crocuses came up, when the daffodil buds drooped about to bloom, when the almond trees came out against the green skies of March and then the pear and the cherry trees. I missed his letters dreadfully and then he and Howard had been such close friends. Frances and I agreed that both our husbands had not made friends easily; no one ever took the place of Howard for Cyril, and it was the same for Howard. They both loved gardening so much. I remembered how Mr. Piggott had asked me when I told him I was engaged to an American: "Is he a gardening sort of man?" Howard certainly was, and his son, Keith, followed him.

From Portsmouth we took the ferry to the Isle of Wight which Ray and I had done often in the WRNS. We visited the Saxon church at Niton, but the house where we had lived in Ventnor had now returned to being a hotel. I showed Keith the steep hill where Ray had taught me to ride a bike without holding the handles. The best place we saw was on the other side of the island we had known, Tennyson's Walk. This was rather like Beachy Head, a steep gash of white cliffs into the sea and a long climb up the downs. It was very beautiful.

Then we visited Hanni in Salisbury. Keith had been there as a boy more than once and he loved the Cathedral, but Hanni introduced us to Old Sarum, which had some of the Roman ruins and there were wonderful views from there. She also took us to Stonehenge which we could get near in those days. She told us her birthday was on June 2l, the summer solstice, when the sun's first rays were supposed to shine at a special place among the stones. For ten years they had arisen before dawn to try and see this but each time it rained, so in the end they gave up. We then dropped Ray with her sister in Dorset, and we were shown the model village that Prince Charles had instigated. I had always admired the Prince; he was the only Royal who liked classical music and cared for old architecture. He had got into trouble for criticizing the American style skyscrapers which had been erected on the WWII ruins of the docks, and along the Thames.

I remembered parts of Dorset I had driven through, first with Humphrey and then with Honor. It was a lovely county, very unspoilt, and then we came to Devon which was quite different with its red soil and its high hedges, which you could not see over unless there were a five-barred gate.

It was strange driving up to the Old Palace in Crediton with Keith. Nan and Ken had always met us at Exeter, but Ken seemed so pleased to see us and soon made us laugh. He asked me to make the tea. It was a long time since I had been through the English ritual of warming the pot, putting in teaspoons of tea and then letting it brew. Even my sister had found tea bags in beakers much easier. I made the tea so weak Ken said "it could hardly crawl out of the pot." Keith had always liked Ken's sense of humor. Nan had told me a story of how she once said to Richard as a child, when he had hurt himself, the age old nursery comforter:

"Poor little fing, not a fever on his wing, to fy, fy," and Ken had chimed in with "Let's wring his bloody neck!"

Ken did not talk about Nan's illness, for which I was grateful. We discussed the Isle of Wight which we had all seen lately and agreed that it had not changed much since the war. Ken said he did not have many visitors but he did not want them; he was writing a book on St. Boniface who had been born in Crediton in the 9th century, and then went on to Holland and Germany to convert the people there to Christianity. I remembered that some years ago Ken, in his capacity as mayor of Crediton, had been invited by a Dutch mayor to come and celebrate the thousandth anniversary of where Boniface had landed in Europe. Nan had gone with him and they had had a wonderful time, and afterwards received another invitation to the Queen's Garden Party. Boniface had some connection to the church in Crediton to which the Old Palace adjoined.

Ken took us driving round parts of Devon Keith had not seen, and we enjoyed our time with him. We then picked Ray up at her sister's and went on to the Cotswolds where Howard and I had had our last vacation together. I liked Chipping Norton and the other villages of honey-colored stone with their little rivers. I told Keith Bettina had asked me when Tunbridge Wells grew too crowded if she should move to the Cotswolds or Wales. I had advised Wales for we both loved the mountains, but felt now she might have had an easier life further south. She loved to garden and the winter salt storms were death to flowers, and she could not keep a donkey there which she had had wanted to do.

Also she and Ronnie might have kept closer, but Keith said he felt the Cotswolds would have been too touristy and crowded for Bettina, and the wildness of Wales suited her. I wished we had known West Sussex was still so unspoilt and had advised her to move there. Keith said he was glad to have known Wales and to have climbed Snowdon.

We left Ray in London and went on to visit my cousin Rita in Cambridge. She was another who had lost her husband early. Brian died of a heart attack after visiting us in Tallahassee. He had been prisoner of the Japs in WWII and had taken part in the dreadful march to Bataan. I asked him once how he thought he had been able to survive; was it his faith (his father was Canon of Ely and he had had a religious upbringing). He said he thought it was because he was more of a vegetable than others; he did not take things so deeply. He was a crack shot, and shot for the Crown and had been awarded a medal by the Queen. Rita had sold their big house and garden and was in a top floor apartment building in a lovely part of Cambridge. She could not understand how Keith and I wanted to go to Evensong at King's every day we were there; Keith was as keen as I was to go and I think his love of music increased from hearing over the years the music under that beautiful fan-vaulted ceiling and the 15th-century Northern Renaissance windows.

Chapter 98

2001, Last Trip to Europe.

This time Keith and I flew to London and then took the Chunnel to Paris. It was amazing how quickly we reached our destination, but Keith said he did not enjoy it so much as the Hovercraft on which Mrs. Corbould had taken him as a child across the Channel to Calais to see Rodin's *Burghers of Calais*. It was fourteen years since he had seen Paris and he was disgusted that many museums were on strike again. He could not see Monet's "Nympheas" or the Impressionists or Post-Impressionists. He spent a long time again at the Rodin Museum. We met up with M and his students at a hotel near the Lachaise Cemetery where so many famous people were buried, including Heloise and Abelard. M was convinced it was more worthwhile to see Chartres than Versailles so we went there again. I was not a lecturer on this trip but M got us special rates, and I was called upon once. M had to take a girl to hospital and missed the train to Chartres. The students were quite willing to collapse on the grass but I made them rise and led them to the North Porch which has some of the most peaceful and devout sculptures, all prefigurations of Christ, David asking, Solomon as Judge, John the Baptist as Savior. The same figures are repeated in the stained glass windows. I told the students Chartres was built in the 12th century, an age of faith when even lords and ladies had dragged the stones to the cathedral. It was the one and only time Keith heard me lecture.

We returned to London where Keith and I stayed with Ray but met M and his students at the newly opened Globe Theatre on the South Bank, built as it was in Shakespeare's day. Ray did not come; she had already been and said the seats were very hard. Mark obtained two seats under cover but said he wanted to experience "King Lear" as a groundling. However, it soon started to rain and Keith said his English blood would enable him to stand it better than M, who looked perfectly miserable, so he took his place. I had only seen *Lear* once with John Gielgud and his voice was still in my ears. We could not help being amused in the storm scene when Lear stripped to the waist and exposed his British pink and white. After years in Florida we were used to tans.

We also went with M's group on a bus to Stratford for *Hamlet*. Again I heard echoes. I remember most the ride back after the matinee. It was a May evening with long shadows beginning to creep over the colored fields, but this time the hawthorn hedges were in bloom, great mounds of snow with glints of gold within that Miss Risdon had told me were the long gold stamens. I had not seen them bloom since a child. They only last a week or so until rain dashes the frail flowers. I suddenly had the feeling, this was my farewell to England. There was no reason to think that, but I knew it was the last time I would see the dark gold of barley, light gold of wheat, silver green of oats with a splash of mustard here and there ; this time they were crowned in their glory with snow boundaries. "Lie long, high snowdrifts in the hedge/ that will not shower on me," wrote A.E. Housman in his song of exile. I looked at M, asleep against the window; he was so tired, it is tiring carting students around, I would not wake him. I looked "my last on all things lovely" and saw that Keith, sitting with Ray a few seats back, was also looking out.

After 9/11 I took no more trips to Europe. Keith and I flew to Phoenix to see M the Christmas after and it was so dreadful I never wanted to fly again. We were held up hours outside the airport in Atlanta, due to a false "orange scare," could get no message through to M, and after waiting six hours he left. We arrived at 3 am and I was so tired I put my winter coat down on the carpeted airport floor and went to sleep. Keith said he had to prevent someone kicking me to see if I were dead.

M actually flew back from Europe on 9/11 and was unable to land in New York and landed up somewhere in Newfoundland, not at an airport, because people came out and gave them food and invited them to their homes. It was a frightening time and the world seemed a different place afterwards.

Chapter 99

Teaching 28 years.

I realize that in writing about all the trips made to Europe together, I left out the everyday round of teaching, making new courses, grading endless papers (the only time I allowed myself a Snickers Bar), attending committees, advising students, and bringing up three boys without a dryer, but of course this went on all the time.

As well as teaching, I joined the German club of which I was chairman for a while, until Ursel, who had been a Humanities major before getting an MA in German, took it over. She could manage the Internet and could handle E mails. She and her husband and I became great friends. She had one of the best minds; she reminded me of my German teacher, Ingrid. Her husband was an ornithologist and ringed birds and lent me a tape of the nightingale singing, which was a great delight. I also met Michelle and Horst who had lived in Lausanne for many years where Michelle played oboe in the Lausanne Orchestra. Horst was from Vienna, a physicist who helped in discovering the last Quark, and I took a course he taught for laymen which was very interesting. I also joined the French club, where I made a French friend, Irene, with whom I used to walk in the woods and talk French. Later I joined the FSU Book Discussion group, and took part in giving programmes for all these groups. For some years I participated in the Comparative Literature and Film Club which had a conference every year, at which M sometimes gave papers. I kept busy.

Keith and I were fortunate in having Marlene and her daughter Toni, and Dwight and family as friends who always invited us for festive occasions. His school friends, Mark Ice and his wife Diane, Sterling and Carey, Bill and Janet, did the same. Keith's friends became mine, as D and M had become his. I think this is rather rare.

It was Keith who introduced us to a new milieu. He joined the Community Chorus in order to sing in the Mozart Requiem and later in Beethoven's Ninth and after much persuasion he joined the church choir at St. John's which made a great difference in our lives

I loved teaching and, according to my student evaluations, was successful in getting ideas over. After Dr. Golden put me in charge of Undergraduate Humanities in 1975, I suggested changing the basic courses from three to four, as we ran out of time by the 20th century, and also in order to include more music. I found students were interested in music. They were used to listening on their earphones and I found no difficulty introducing them to the chestnuts of the classics, starting with Gregorian chant, polyphony, the beginnings of opera, and the development of the concerto and symphony. I gave them 20 chestnuts which they would have to identify on the final and they usually did extremely well. They were interested too in art and how it reflected the times. The trouble was with reading. Each year it grew increasingly difficult to get them to read what I considered the bare minimum for an educated person. Reading was definitely on a downtrend. I thought of how the printing press had changed the world of the image to the world of the word, and now it was changing back again to the image.

I taught the Humanities majors a Junior Seminar on Criticism starting with Plato, and ending up with existentialism and eventually deconstruction. This was difficult; some of the students seemed to take to it easier than I did. I found it hard to agree with Derrida that once an author was dead, a critic's view of his work had as much validity as the original. Writing just cloaked the ideas and needed revising. I had considered an author's text was sacred but learned in the end something from Deconstruction. For instance, I had never agreed with the standard view of the *Aeneid* as extolling Aeneas, a pious Stoic, filled with the glory of Rome. I asked every classicist I met why, if so, did he go out the gate for false dreams? I never was given a satisfactory answer. I found Virgil most profound in his poetry of Dido, and her lament when Aeneas leaves her is unforgettable. She says that if only she had his child and if "a little Aeneas were playing around by her in the hall she would not feel so utterly bereft." I found it incredible that a Roman stoic should have been so sympathetic to a woman's point of view. And then there was his melancholy *Lachrimae rerum, qui mortalia tangunt* (the tears of things which touch the heart of man.

I gave a paper on Dido. I had given many papers at conferences on Rilke which were well received and I tried to get them published, but there was always the difficulty of getting through both American and German editors. The latter wanted many footnotes and the former as few as possible and I was not successful. This was depressing. If I had started my academic career earlier I might have found more time to devote to getting published, but there were always new courses which I had to devise and revise, the incessant grading and counseling, and then three boys to bring up. I did try and get published a paper on *The Deconstruction of the Aeneid* and the Editor liked it, but it fell through. I consoled myself with the fact that I had several poems published.

I also felt very strongly, long before Michael Wood gave a broadcast series on it, that Shakespeare was Catholic in his imagery, especially in *Hamlet* with purgatory, and Claudius at his prayers, but I found it in several places, and taught it. Shakespeare's parents were married under Queen Mary and his first years were under a Catholic regime. I remembered that Erwin had said he had read hundreds of books and forgotten the contents of most, but he remembered odd remarks his professors had said; I hoped this was true. I recall teaching Shakespeare's Sonnet no. 73:

That time of year thou mayst in me behold

When yellow leaves, or none, or few, do hang
Upon those boughs which shake against the cold,
Bare ruined choirs where late the sweet birds sang.

I told the students that perhaps the last line referred
not only to winter branches but to the ruined choirs of
churches which Henry VIII had destroyed, and they agreed.
I also made them see that the commas in line 2 referred to
individual falling leaves.

My chairman, Dr. Golden, was impressed with my view
of the *Aeneid* and said he would get together a Symposium
to discuss it and he did. He got some of the best classicists
to FSU and I remember in particular Dr. Wendell Clausen
of Yale, who had the same point of view as I did and much
more ammunition to back it up. There were many brilliant
minds at the symposium and I learned that an Italian critic,
Sforza, had put forward in the thirties that Virgil was not a
Roman, that his father's lands had been confiscated, and that
his best friend Gallus had been exiled, and that he was forced
by the Emperor Augustus to write an epic which would do
for Rome what Homer had done for Greece, and that in the
end he wanted to destroy it, but his friends saved it.

I had been successful in recruiting many new students
to Humanities majors, which pleased my Chairman and
Dean. After the grueling stretch of Criticism in the Junior
Seminar I gave them the pleasure of watching and learning
from Kenneth Clark's *Civilisation* film which linked art and
music. Knowing that watching a film was not conducive
to making notes I gave them before each class a series of

twenty questions, ten of which would be on the final. I also gave brief lectures on the history of music. I did not have any trouble with absenteeism. They really enjoyed learning in this class, but also I had a stipulation in all my classes that more than three unexcused absences made a half drop in grade! I introduced something new. Students had a to write a Senior Thesis on any subject provided it included more than one art form, e.g. Impressionism in Art and Literature or in Literature and Music. I received many interesting papers including "the '*Commedia dell' Arte*' in Art "(Watteau and Picasso), the Harlem Renaissance, several papers on witchcraft in the various arts, and many other unexpected subjects. There were only ten *Civilisation* films so that left five weeks over in the term and during that time each student was required to give a ten-to-fifteen minute oral presentation on the Senior Thesis chosen. Music could be played, art shown, but each student was to give a lucid presentation in educated English, without any "like" or "you know." I was horrified at the uneducated use of the English language even by seniors, and this certainly helped improve their language skills, which they would need in graduate school or if they went on immediately to any kind of job in the outside world. This proved very popular and the number of Humanities majors continued to increase. I had a little Schadenfreude when they fell off when I left.

I also had the majors to a party at my house at the end of term when we discussed a given subject such as "What is Art?" or "What did you enjoy most studying this term?" For many years I continued it at my house but then the

Episcopal Student Center opened a room for such events, and that was just opposite the building where I taught, and it proved much easier for students to get there (for not all had cars), so I moved it there. One student told me it was the first time in her four years of university that she had ever been in a teacher's house or together in a social gathering. Howard had told me how much it had meant to him to be invited to his professor's house at Yale.

I looked forward every fall term to seeing the new lot of fresh young faces, all Honors, so willing to learn. There was always one who looked like Andrew did at eighteen, a Candide type, but all wore shining morning faces. Boys had not yet started to leave fringes of Spanish moss around their chins, and although I did not really like baseball caps on backwards, put up with it perforce. The girls of course were all in jeans but some still sported colored shirts. The mode of tattered and torn denim had not yet arrived. As I saw their young faces each year, I remember recalling Wallace Stephens's lines, "Beauty is momentary in the mind—the fitful tracing of a portal/ but in the flesh it is immortal." I used to wonder how many I would touch and awaken to ideas. It seemed to me that the bond between teacher and student is one of the most profound there is. What I had learned from my teachers and books, ideas learned and discussed with M and D, how many of these would I be able to teach and pass on not only to students, but to Keith, my most attentive Humanities student, as he often told me. He called his Japanese maple that had to stand the fiercest sun, Tillich, after the Courage-to-be-in—spite—of.

In the last four years I had the pleasure of teaching the most brilliant Honors student, Sarah. She was a musician, a double major and she also knew Latin and German. She knew much more in Latin than I, but was easily convinced of my view of Aeneas. She did an Honors thesis with me on Rilke, so I was able to teach her something of the poet who had meant so much to me. I sometimes thought that the times I had received or given a new idea was the same as James Joyce called "stasis," a moment of standstill when one experienced grace. The only other thing like it was when Jennifer, my granddaughter, told me she was going to name her first child after me. I was struck dumb.

I was happy teaching and felt in the right place but the technological age was hard for me. Computers were now marching to their success and I was very untechnological. My good friend, Pat, who died early of cancer, managed to teach me to use a word processor which was a great help, but I was not drawn to incessant E mails, and preferred to write and receive a few letters. M tried to persuade me to write my memoirs, but it was many years before I agreed to do so. We had corresponded by then for over twenty years with mutual enjoyment. He felt life had changed so much since I was a child that it would be of interest to others to hear of childhood in England, when lavender was still sold in the streets with the centuries old refrain, when there were no such things as toasters and one had to hold bread on a fork before a fire. Also, of course, I had been through the Blitz in London, and later the V2 rockets and the W.R.N.S.

I was reluctant to retire but was getting on in years, and I remembered my mother's dictum: Go when you are sparkling. I had a great Retirement party with wine and many friends, students, and faculty, several of whom gave speeches. I was given a plaque of appreciation by the Honors Society as well as by the Humanities Program. I was glad that Dr. Golden had written on the latter, "Gladly wolde (s) he lerne and gladly teche" from Chaucer. I had asked James Monroe to the party as he was instrumental in my being kept as a teacher, and we had kept in touch, but he was a busy lawyer and could not come. His parents did. It was a great occasion for me and for Keith who attended.

Chapter 100

The Smile of the Acrobat and Tai Chi.

The first thing I intended to do after retirement was to try and get my poems published in a book I had written about a hundred poems during my life and had had many published in England and the States, especially by the Sparrow Grass Poetry Forum, and knew they sometimes published small books of poetry. It was a tremendous job to get them in order, and my good friend, Debby, who was also a poet and editor, helped me. I knew from the beginning that the title would be *The Smile of the Acrobat* from Rilke's *Fifth Elegy* which was on Picasso's blue period painting, *Les Saltimbanques (The Acrobats)*. I had a copy of the painting which I wanted as a cover, but the Editor told me it would be far too expensive. I had to make do with a stick sketch of my own of a boy on a tight rope smiling at his mother down below who was turning aside, and as Epigraph, Rilke's lines, translated by J.E. Leishman and Stephen Spender in *The Duino Elegies,* London: Hogarth Press, 1948. Rilke had described in detail the various acrobats standing around waiting for their show, and in particular the small boy gazing at his mother with the suggestion of a smile which she did not see. "That smile/Angel! Oh, take it, pluck it,/ that small –flowered herb of healing!/Shape a vase to preserve it . . . /Praise it, with florally soaring inscription,/ "*Subrisio Saltat*".

In the Commentary on the Fifth Elegy, l27, it is suggested 'that the Angel is to place the smile in a vase or urn . . . with an inscription in abbreviated Latin, like those on the bottles and jars in a chemist's shop. Written in full, the inscription would read: *Subrisio Saltatoris*, Acrobat's Smile."

It seemed to me that Rilke's lines stood for those happenings in life that are full of meaning and yet so often go unnoticed. When I tried to arrange my poems in some sort of order I saw that they fell into those written early in England, then those in Tallahassee, poems written after returning to England after fifteen years absence, then those written in Europe, and the last poems in Tallahassee. One could see a life flung between different places had something acrobatic about it, but that was merely incidental, not the reason for the title in which I tried to indicate my debt to Rilke.

I have included a few poems in these memoirs and thought I would add two short poems.

OLYMPIC GYMNASTS

Like kites of shredded paper
or seeds of sycamore
but not of weight and bone,

the girls thrust up in air
as if on wings
like butterflies
flung out by cruel winds,
the years of discipline
that gave them grace
but robbed their youth.
A phantom child forgot routine,
a callous voice announced
"Her life is over now"
at seventeen for China.

BY CHANCE

By chance
the random light
will snatch a certain branch
and fling it forward
all in gold
against the coming night.
until a sudden cloud
subdues the flame
like laughter
as quickly as it came.

After my poems were published, I joined a class of Tai
Chi, exercises founded centuries ago by Buddhist monks
to be done in a confined place, such as a monastery. There
were 108 movements which were supposed to help and

strengthen all muscles and joints. They had odd names, like "Ward off monkey" or "Flying like clouds." I enjoyed them very much and made new friends. Harriet was the first; she had sung with OSS during WW2 and was happy that I recalled some of Noel Coward's lyrics. Nancye was next; she reminded me a little of my sister in that she loved horses and cars and could recount wonderful stories. When she was fifteen she was staying with her parents in Sarasota and just obtained her learner's driving license. A friend persuaded her to drive them both to see the circus there one evening, without asking permission. When they returned to the car, a VW bug, they found an elephant had sat on it! Just imagine the explanations! Then came Jan, a neighbor, who became a dear friend. She had taught kindergarten for thirty years and still volunteered. I saw her teach and was very impressed. She was also the most practical person I had ever met; there was nothing she could not fix. We had lunch together after class, joined sometimes by Brenda, a brilliant photographer of butterflies and flowers. Carmen was also a neighbor and followed Tai Chi but took different classes so she seldom lunched with us, but she became a good friend. It was like being at school again; I did not think I would make new friends after retirement but I was mistaken.

Chapter 101

After the accident.

I was in an accident as passenger in 2007, and broke some ribs, and everything seemed to go wrong after that. Some months later, I had a TIA for thirty minutes and could not remember my prayers or any Shakespeare. I had to go to the hospital and had a small procedure, but from then on had problems with circulation. I sprained a toe which did not heal and I could not walk without a cane. For some while I could take Dial-a-Ride but when I could no longer walk up my steep drive, Dial-a-Ride refused to come down. I was completely dependent on my friends and they were wonderful. Jan, Carmen, and Nancye took it in turns to take me to the doctor and for a whole fall Nancye made me homemade chicken soup every week. Marlene, although she lived the other side of town, helped too. Keith took me to church and to choir practice in a wheelchair when it was too painful to walk and often took time off from work to take me to the doctor. A new friend, Lisa, did too and brought wonderful meals. My son Andrew, who had always kept in close touch, phoned me regularly every Wednesday, and sent me encouragement in letters and texts. Nancy, my daughter-in-law, drove up all the way from Fort Myers to spell Keith occasionally for a long weekend. I was most fortunate.

I realized I could have been far worse off. I could still read and friends brought me books and for a long while Kathy at the library sent me books free through the mail under the handicapped service, until that was stopped except for large print books.

For years M had been trying to persuade me to write my memoirs and I resisted as I did not think my life was that interesting, but he insisted that growing up in England before the war and living through WWII would be interesting to people and so I started. I was amazed how much I remembered of my childhood; in many ways it was clearer than the recent past and I enjoyed reliving those days. Strangely, I did not feel very different from the child who gate-crashed the Hampstead Public Library with a card with my father's name forged by my sister. I still remember very vividly that young librarian who helped me and showed me what to read. I remember the first garden at Finchley, the wonderful Elizabethan garden at my uncle's farm, and the last garden, started by Howard and carried on by me and then Keith. I relived the pleasure I had in study and all I learned, digested, and later taught. I realize I was very lucky to have been able to study as I did at Florida State University, get three degrees there, and then be enabled to teach at that university.

I was also very thankful for the friendship of D and M with whom I could discuss topics in which I had always been interested, and through them get to Europe, learn more, and teach a bit of European art history there. I could never have organized a student trip myself; it was a lot of detailed work of which they themselves grew very tired. After five years teaching at the American School in Switzerland, D returned to the States and took a Post Doctorate Degree in Opera Direction with Lincoln Clark at FSU, so I had the pleasure of another year of his company and he eventually obtained a fine position as Opera Director at the University of James Madison.

Keith and I both enjoyed the years M spent at the University of Arizona at Tucson where we visited him often at Christmas and saw the fantastic sunsets under the mountains of the moon. M published his dissertation and the book on Klee, *Of Angels, Things and Death,* and then became Honors Dean at the University of Tennessee and later head of the English Department. He developed a great interest in Iris Murdoch and became the definitive American critic on her work and edited a book of essays on her. When I no longer wished to fly, Keith would drive me to meet D and M for Christmas, sometimes in New Orleans, where we visited Ingrid and Heinz; sometimes to Savannah where we fell in love with the sea oats at Tidee Island, and sometimes they used to come here for a Christmas dinner and on to St. George's Island. When I could no longer cook, M found a wonderful condo at Destin right on the beach and we settled there for Christmas.

Keith has never lost his love for unusual phrases. Once I told him I had been to a slide lecture by a professor who had visited Pompeii and he showed frescoes which I felt sure were Etruscan but had never seen in my art books. "Aren't those Etruscan?" I asked him. "Well," he replied, "there were lectures in the evening if one wanted to go heavy, but I was always too exhausted," so from then on we both adopted this use of the word "heavy." Keith would give me a book on physics with the note "feel one of us should go heavy, love, me" with umlaut.

He's always enjoyed seeing plays, especially Shakespeare, and would remember lines even in his teens. I received a note once "Screw your courage to the sticking place, My courage is in those swelling buds of "H" (the Japanese maple at the back whom he had christened after his father). After seeing a TV production of Macbeth he'd repeat to me the lines: "Stars, hold your fires, lest I see your deep and dark desires."

When daffodils were first introduced to Tallahassee he knew I loved them from England and found out that to grow them here they should be planted nine inches deep with an electric drill to keep them cool in the hot summers. He planted a hundred which was a quite a chore and we waited anxiously for spring when they more than delighted us. He brought the first ones in with a note, "This is the trumpet call, my defining moment in my belief in spring." And after a long awaited rain, "Drink, daffodils, drink!" Each year he put in about a hundred more so we soon had drifts of them from December to April. One note received was "Daffodils and an Egg McMuffin, you truly have 'Peace in our time'.

love, me," with umlaut. Another note was "I will believe in daffodils, I will believe in spring. love, me," with umlaut.

Keith left for work long before I got up so I would find notes to cheer me. After my accident I had a weakness in my wrists, as well as my feet. and found it hard to open things, so would find "I cut you up some of the "chest" (my father's joke) with gravy, so marked in fridge. Love me, umlaut." Another time I found "Corbett Canyon top pre—loosened in fridge, and Cabernet de-corked with easy rubber stopper. Also released your yogurt out of box. love anon with umlaut." I was amused once by his piling apples on to a dish and to get a note the next morning, "Hard to figure out which apple to take. Don't want to upset my 'Cezanne balance.'" After a painful night it was cheering to find "Flowers in dining room and porch are lovely. Please find comfort in them. Love me with umlaut."

One Christmas he presented me with *The Wit and Wisdom of Winston Churchill* with the attached note, "You had said that some characters in Tolstoy were more real and alive than some people you have actually known. I am reminded of this and present to you, One Word, One Man, Churchill!"

Chapter 102

Music at the Close.

It is now time to make an end. I am over ninety and feel part of history. When the movie *The King's Speech* came out, telling of how George VI was cured of his stammer, people were amazed that I remembered hearing the speech, the Declaration of War against Germany in 1939. Someone said it gave her goose pimples to think I had heard it and I realized I had become history. I remember so well the bombers coming over London, every night at 6 p.m., the low drumming they made, the sirens, the relief of the All Clear. I did not think I should live through the Blitz; so many did not. My cousin Donald who died at Caen, aged twenty-four, on D-Day plus six, is as clear to me as people I see daily. My sister and Aunt Dora are very clear too, especially lately. My first garden at Finchley where I fell in love with the bluebells, and the garden at Manor Farm, the orchard with the nightingales, and the lake around which I walked when pregnant with Keith, are as clear to me as the garden where now I live, started by Howard, and carried on by Keith.

Sometimes I think I remember landscape, trees, and flowers, better than people. Most haunting perhaps is music.

I was blessed with three sons, and fortunate that they turned out well. John and Andrew, with their beautiful wives, produced delightful children and it was interesting to see the DNA of my parents, my in-laws, and myself in children and grandchildren. It was one of the greatest moments of my life when Jennifer, told me she wanted to call her daughter after me. Audrey grew up as I did loving fairies and books. John, although fair while my father was dark, had much of my father in him; Andrew was the product of Howard's DNA and Puritan ancestors, and he looked like his father, and had his same grin. In Keith I saw myself, my love for England and its countryside, my father's wit and ready repartee, and I was fortunate that after his tragic marriage ended he chose to live in the house where he was born (which is most unusual in America) and for all his life has been the most congenial companion anyone could wish. His friends became mine, and mine his—a strange mixture of generations. M and D became his close friends too, and we have had many wonderful times in Europe, Arizona, New Orleans, Savannah, and Destin.

After Keith had sung in the Community Chorus for two years, I persuaded him to join the church choir for we had a new and wonderful choir director. He was reluctant for he did not read music, but he had a good ear and had developed a love for classical music through hearing so much at home. He soon grew to care for the Liturgy, the Magnificats and Nunc Dimittis, and the précis which makes up the church service and for which so much beautiful music has been written. Dr. Calhoun liked the early English choral music, such as Byrd, Weelkes, Gibbons, Purcell, as well as the later Victorians, Stanford and Parry, and the moderns, Howells and Rutter. For two years Keith was too shy to speak to her, although he made friends in the choir. I asked him to ask her to sing the Holst version of "In the bleak midwinter" instead of the later Darke, but he refused, so I asked her, saying I thought Holst's music to the line of "snow was falling, snow on snow" was the most perfect musical rendering of the words. She was more than happy to do so and said I could come to rehearsals if I liked.

I told her I could not sing but could read music and would like to attend choir rehearsal. She put me in the back among the basses which was a great delight to me. I had always followed the soprano line but it gave me infinite pleasure to hear the basses and tenors. They made me an Honorary Member of the Choir, and presented me with pomp and ceremony a certificate in beautiful calligraphy, which I cherished as much as my PhD.

I sat next to the most wonderful bass and told him I looked forward to hearing him as Sarastro. He said his teacher wanted him to sing opera but he had learned from his choir director, Betsy Calhoun, that the best thing was to teach others to love music as she did, and that is what he wanted to do. ""In opera," he said, "it would all be directed on myself, for my glory, would rather give it to others." He was a devout young Menonite; I told him I thought opera singers gave delight to many, but he said that way was not for him. For my birthday Keith, who by this time had overcome his shyness, asked Betsy if the choir could sing William Blake's "Jerusalem," set to music by Parry, which I had loved since schooldays. Keith's friend, Lisa, who became a great friend also, obtained the music from the Internet and the choir sang it, with this bass, Jeremy, as soloist, which was a most wonderful surprise. The pianist was then the organist at St. John's, Roger Ponder, who was an old student of Howard's, who returned to Tallahassee after many years away. We became good friends, he lent me interesting books, and we went to concerts together, until I became too lame. Then he kept me supplied with books and with pound cake.

For my next birthday, Keith in conjunction with Lisa who again supplied the music from the Internet, and Betsy who organized the birthday bash, had the leading tenor sing a song from World War II, "There'll always be an England." I had not heard it since VE Day; it was sung during the war on the radio, in pubs or at dances, so it brought back a throng of memories that nearly choked me. It was sung especially during and after the Invasion, and I remember standing, on the white cliffs near Dover, seeing those Mulberry contraptions with all the men on them, sailing away to Normandy, and waving.

I spent many happy hours in choir rehearsals, and it seemed to me that all I had ever learned was distilled in the music that Betsy Calhoun chose, directed, and shaped. It was as though the music, architecture, love, and happiness I had learned from Howard, the Shakespeare from Mel

Faber, the philosophy from Jack Ice, the German literature from Ingrid and Erwin, the Modern Physics from Steve Edwards, Hans Plendl and Horst Wahl, the ideas I had learned and exchanged with Mark and Don and Keith, and what I had learned myself from Rilke and other books, all knowledge became one and diffused in music. Perhaps all true knowledge came from one source, from the Good. I remembered that Dohnanyi had said he believed there were two forces in the world, good and evil. I was thankful I had learned at St. Johns (and from Rabbi Kuschner) that God's rule was not almighty on earth, that the Church had not always been in the right, but the good came from God, and was received in many ways, and perhaps one of the clearest was in the music I heard week after week directed by Betsy. I realized that Jeremy, the bass I admired so much, was right in choosing to learn to teach music as she did, rather than in the glory of an operatic career. It came to me that I was truly blessed in receiving the music ministry she gave. I learned a lot and felt that was perhaps why we were on earth, to learn and that we would go on learning after death.

Keith's friend from school, Sterling, persuaded Keith to get me a satellite radio which played only classical music—opera, orchestral music, piano sonatas, and etudes. Lieder were sometimes sung, so I was supplied with music. A woman came to see me, saw windows all round the living room, filled with leaves, and said "You have a beautiful prison." I agreed, but I also had a son who took me in the wheel chair to concerts, Verdi's *Requiem* in which he sung, and to choir and church services, so I had music at the close.

ST. JOHN' S CHOIR REHEARSAL

The end of day, and tired
the choir awaits,
all eyes on her,
the antelope
who leaps across the room
releasing music from the air
while adding depth
and easing care.
The basses, tenors, clouds
upon soprano hills,
the altos, streams of light,
above it all her descant sounds
ascending lark
unearthly clear.
The patient piano always there.

CPSIA information can be obtained at www.ICGtesting.com
Printed in the USA
LVOW100749020212

266615LV00002B/1/P